Regency 06/14

REFLECTIONS IN A SERPENT'S EYE

Reflections in a Serpent's Eye

Thebes in Ovid's Metamorphoses

MICAELA JANAN

OXFORD
UNIVERSITY PRESS

OXFORD
UNIVERSITY PRESS

Great Clarendon Street, Oxford OX2 6DP

Oxford University Press is a department of the University of Oxford.
It furthers the University's objective of excellence in research, scholarship,
and education by publishing worldwide in

Oxford New York

Auckland Cape Town Dar es Salaam Hong Kong Karachi
Kuala Lumpur Madrid Melbourne Mexico City Nairobi
New Delhi Shanghai Taipei Toronto

With offices in

Argentina Austria Brazil Chile Czech Republic France Greece
Guatemala Hungary Italy Japan Poland Portugal Singapore
South Korea Switzerland Thailand Turkey Ukraine Vietnam

Oxford is a registered trade mark of Oxford University Press
in the UK and in certain other countries

Published in the United States
by Oxford University Press Inc., New York

British Library Cataloguing in Publication Data

Data available

Library of Congress Cataloging in Publication Data

Data available

Typeset by SPI Publisher Services, Pondicherry, India
Printed in Great Britain
on acid-free paper by the
MPG Books Group, Bodmin and King's Lynn

ISBN 978–0–19–955692–2

*For Timothy Dominic Dalton and Terence Damien Dalton
the best band of brothers*

Acknowledgements

GIVEN the generosity this book's gestation encountered, it has in truth entailed more debts than I could adequately acknowledge. But I can try. The book originated in an offhand remark from Joseph Farrell, who visited Duke in February 1998 to lecture on '*Ovidius auctor* and the Tropes of Classicism'. Chatting informally about the *Metamorphoses* afterwards, he noted antiquity's most famous myth gone missing from antiquity's most famous compendium of myth: 'Why *won't* Ovid talk about Oedipus?' Pregnant silences have always intrigued me. This one inspired me to revisit Ovid's Theban cycle, the logical setting for a *Metamorphean* Oedipus. There I discovered how many more mysteries Ovid's hapless city posed. Both Joe's canny, timely question and his willingness to share his own 'Theban thoughts' greatly fostered the project's germination.

A *cohors optimorum* richly blessed the book's passage from germ to fruit. Paul Allen Miller has been a constant source of erudition, inspiration, and friendship; he read many versions of the manuscript and discussed various points with Socratic patience. Sharon James responded sagaciously to my arguments at assorted North Carolina coffee shops, helping me slice through scholarly knots of Gordias. Once, to clarify the book's potential thematic connections, she diagrammed them on a cocktail napkin (I still have that precious napkin!). David Konstan trained his usual probing questions and insights upon all my chapters, which immeasurably sharpened their focus. Alison Keith sifted Chapter 7 judiciously, and also shared her own work on Silver Latin epic in advance of publication. At a crucial stage, James O'Hara read Chapters 1, 4, and 5, bringing to bear upon them his Vergilian *auctoritas* and gift for clarity. Terry Aladjem also perused Chapters 1 and 2, sprinkling editorial Lourdes-water over my stylistic defects. The exacting and detailed criticisms of Oxford University Press's two anonymous readers greatly strengthened the entire book.

My colleagues at Duke's department of Classical Studies, present and former, all embody the soigné company for which Ovid languished on the borders of Romania. Generous with their expertise and time, they prevented me from many foolish errors. In particular, Francis Newton and Diskin Clay commented meticulously on several chapters of the book—as did Michael Gillespie and Andrew Janiak, sharing their profound knowledge of Hegel and Kant respectively. Carla Antonaccio, Mary T. Boatwright, Peter Burian, Kent Rigsby, Joshua Sosin, and Jennifer Clare Woods lent me their erudition in areas far from my own specialty.

Hilary O'Shea has been a wonderfully supportive editor; over the years, her patient and punctual inquiries about this project long-aborning encouraged my efforts to finish it, just as her advice and guidance have seen it to press. Also at OUP, Jenny Wagstaffe, Kathleen Fearn, and Dorothy McCarthy sagely answered my many questions regarding the arcana of publication. Heather Watson's keen-eyed copy-editing made many a crooked way straight. On this side of the Atlantic, Kevin Smith's expertise in copyright law and Holly Ackerman's in Latin-American poetry helped guide me through the *oscura selva* of copyright permissions. Willis Goth Regier, *magister sententiarum*, patiently and gallantly hunted through five volumes of Emil Cioran's *Cahiers* to find the original form and source of Cioran's Delphic maxim. The canny Chris Wilson-Simpkins discovered the true author of 'Go Loudly, Pentheus' (a poem misattributed in its most widely circulated reprinting).

My thanks are due to audiences at the University of Wisconsin-Madison, University of Toronto, Oxford University, University of London, Stanford University, University of California-Santa Cruz, and University of California-Santa Barbara, who kindly listened to the results of my ongoing research and refined its direction with their questions and observations. A sabbatical leave combined with a year as Fellow at the Franklin Humanities Institute in 2005–6 allowed me to complete my first draft of the whole manuscript. Two grants from the Duke's Arts and Sciences Committee on Faculty Research enabled me to enlist research assistance during 1999–2000 and 2002–3.

Of course, any misuses of such beneficence as remain in the following pages are entirely my own cross-grained responsibility.

M.J.

Contents

A Note on Citation

In my text, I have cited both ancient and modern works according to the conventions of classical philology (and provided my own translations, except where noted). The abbreviations for ancient texts are taken from *The Oxford Classical Dictionary*; those for journals, from *L'Année Philologique*. My text for Ovid (unless stated otherwise) is that of R. J. Tarrant (*P. Ovidi Nasonis Metamorphoses*, Oxford 2004); for Freud, *The Standard Edition of the Complete Psychological Works of Sigmund Freud*, ed. and trans. James Strachey. Citations from the *Standard Edition* of Freud appear as '*SE*', then the volume number, followed by a colon, then page numbers: thus, '*SE* 23: 209' = 'Standard Edition, volume 23, page 209'.

Jacques Lacan's work has been steadily, though not yet completely, translated into English over the years. Where possible and desirable, I have cited both the French text and the most commonly used English translation, so that 'Lacan 1973, 127–128/1981*b*, 138–140' means 'pages 127–8 in *Le séminaire de Jacques Lacan, livre XI: les quatres concepts fondamentaux de la psychanalyse, 1964*, which appear as pages 138–40 in Alan Sheridan's translation, *The Four Fundamental Concepts of Psychoanalysis*'.

Other Abbreviations:

OLD P. G. W. Glare, ed., *Oxford Latin Dictionary* (Oxford, 1982).

KrV Immanuel Kant, *Kritik der reinen Vernunft* (1781/1787). A/B pagination conforms to the convention of referring to the first edition as 'A' and the second edition as 'B'.

PhG G. W. F. Hegel, *Phänomenologie des Geistes* (1807).

1

Introduction

'Happy Birthday, Romulus'

As for the day they began to build the city, it is universally agreed to have been the twenty-first of April, and that day the Romans annually keep holy, calling it their country's birthday. At first, they say, they sacrificed no living creature on this day, thinking it fit to preserve the feast of their country's birthday pure and without stain of blood. Yet before ever the city was built, there was a feast of herdsmen and shepherds kept on this day, which went by the name of Palilia. The Roman and Greek months have now little or no agreement; they say, however, the day on which Romulus began to build was quite certainly the thirtieth of the month, at which time there was an eclipse of the sun which they conceived to be that seen by Antimachus, the Teian poet, in the third year of the sixth Olympiad. In the times of Varro the philosopher, a man deeply read in Roman history, lived one Tarrutius, his familiar acquaintance, a good philosopher and mathematician, and one, too, that out of curiosity had studied the way of drawing schemes and tables, and was thought to be a proficient in the art; to him Varro propounded to cast Romulus' nativity, even to the first day and hour, making his deductions from the several events of the man's life which he should be informed of, exactly as in working back a geometrical problem; for it belonged, he said, to the same science both to foretell a man's life by knowing the time of his birth, and also to find out his birth by the knowledge of his life. This task Tarrutius undertook, and first looking into the actions and casualties of the man, together with the time of his life and manner of his death, and then comparing all these remarks together, he very confidently and positively pronounced that Romulus was conceived in his mother's womb the first year of the second Olympiad, the twenty-third day of the month the Aegyptians call Choeac, and the third hour after sunset, at which time there was a total eclipse of the sun; that he was born the twenty-first day of the month Thoth, about sunrising; and that the first stone of Rome was laid by him the ninth day of the month Pharmuthi, between the second and third hour. For the fortunes of cities as well of men, they think, have their certain periods of time prefixed, which may be collected and foreknown from the position of the stars at their first foundation.

(Plutarch, *Romulus* 12.2–6, Smallwood–Clough translation)

Plutarch was probably living under one of the best loved of the Roman emperors, having survived several of the most hated, when he reflected thus upon the germ of fate contained in the birth of kings and of nations.[1] The contrasts among regimes from Nero (ruled 50–68 CE) to Domitian (81–96 CE)[2] and Trajan (98–117 CE)[3] would have made the question of Rome's fate momentous to any contemporary imperial denizen. Plutarch depicts the answer to be derived from Tarutius' cosmology as ruling humans and cities by the same principle: their lives unfold according to a rationale crystallized at the moment of their conception. This vision of the cosmos makes the related questions, What is the city? and What shall the city be? functions of the question, How did it begin? Nonetheless, however vital to Plutarch's generation the emperors' chequered history had made these queries or the aetiological assumptions behind Tarutius'

---

[1] Plutarch [1932], pp. 31–2. The chronology of Plutarch's works is a notorious mare's nest, but *Romulus* 15.7 refers to *Quaest. Rom.* 285c (Question 87). The *Roman Questions* in turn mention that Domitian once allowed a flamen to divorce his wife (276e); Plutarch so clearly expresses his strong disapproval of the emperor's rescission that the passage probably was written after Domitian's death. If that is true, then *Romulus* must also postdate Domitian. That would mean Plutarch had lived through the reigns of Nero and Domitian, and was probably composing his life of Romulus under Trajan. See Jones 1966, 69.

[2] Nero was the last emperor of the Julio-Claudian house, Domitian the last of the Flavians.

[3] Trajan became the first Antonine emperor.

responses, neither the questions nor the answers could have been more pressing than a century prior, when the very changes took place that made Roman emperors possible. In the immediate aftermath of the Roman republic's demise, while Augustus was constructing his constitutional position as *princeps*, Vergil wrote the poem that very quickly became Rome's national epic. By no coincidence, his *Aeneid* probes Rome's redefinition indirectly, by concentrating on the founding of the polity the principate is seen as refounding.[4]

To be sure, the fate of cities regularly organizes ancient epic, its narrative spun largely from defending or taking the polity from the enemy.[5] The *Iliad* records the defence of Troy, while the *Odyssey* recapitulates the fate of the principalities that attacked it (none escape unscathed).[6] Ennius' *Annales* traces what of Troy becomes Rome, from the former's defeat to the latter's wars against Macedonia and Istria.[7] The fragments of Antimachus' *Thebais*, Choerilus of Samos' *Persica*, and Naevius' *Bellum Poenicum* narrate war against

---

[4] Suetonius records the view of Augustus as 'refounder' of Rome:

cum quibusdam censentibus Romulum appellari oportere quasi et ipsum conditorem urbis, praeualuisset, ut Augustus potius uocaretur, non tantum nouo sed etiam ampliore cognomine, quod loca quoque religiosa et in quibus augurato quid consecratur augusta dicantur, ab auctu uel ab auium gestu gustuue, sicut etiam Ennius docet scribens: 'Augusto augurio postquam incluta condita Roma est.' (Suet. *Aug.* 7)

For when some deemed it proper to confer upon him the name of Romulus, as being a second founder of the city, it was instead resolved that he would better be called Augustus, a surname not only new, but of more dignity, because places devoted to religion, and those in which anything is consecrated by augury, are called 'august', either from the word *auctus*, meaning 'increase', or *ab auium gestu gustuue*, 'from the flight and feeding of birds'; as appears from this verse of Ennius: 'When glorious Rome by august augury was built.'

See also Gary Miles's analysis of how Livy's first pentad constructs Augustus as the latest in a series of 'refounders' of Rome that includes Romulus and Camillus (Miles 1995, 75–136).

[5] As John Henderson notes (Henderson 1998, 165).

[6] Argos loses King Agamemnon to treachery, Pylos and Sparta are caught up in sterile war nostalgia, and Ithaka witnesses the Trojan War restaged in miniature, as the 108 suitors, and then their grieving parents, lay siege unsuccessfully to King Odysseus' household.

[7] I refer to the second edition of the *Annales*, expanded by three books detailing the accomplishments of junior officers in the Istrian and Third Macedonian wars (189–171 BCE); the first edition would have ended around 189 BCE, covering events from the war with Seleucid King Antiochus (Dominik 1993, 37–8). However, see James Zetzel's interesting deconstruction of this *communis opinio*, arguing the

Thebes, between the independent Greek city-states and Persia, and between Carthage and Rome respectively. Even the *Argonautica* takes shape around fear for the governances of Iolcus and Colchis: Pelias implicitly and Aeëtes explicitly dread Jason's threat to their thrones.[8] However, before the *Aeneid*, nowhere in this civic-centred genre do we see an epic focused exclusively on a city's founding. To be sure, both Naevius' and Ennius' epics anticipate Vergil insofar as they link national history to mythical origins. The Trojan prelude to Rome's founding appears to have figured in at least three of the seven books into which Naevius' posthumous editor Lampadius divided Naevius' poem, while Ennius' first book traces Rome's path from Troy's fall to the death of Romulus.[9] Yet Naevius' chief subject matter remains the

evidence does not unambiguously point to three books added to Ennius' initial fifteen (Zetzel 2007, 13–14).

[8] Pelias sends Jason on an almost certainly fatal quest for the Golden Fleece, because a prophecy has told the King of Iolcus that a 'hateful doom' awaits him from the machinations of the half-barefoot man he will see coming from town (*AR* 1.5–7). As the son of Pelias' half-brother Aeson, Jason is in the indirect line of succession to the throne. Jason's shipmate Argus implies to King Aeëtes that Pelias feared a coup. Argus states that the Iolcian king got rid of Jason because the latter was 'the most distinguished member of the Aeolids' (*AR* 3.335), the noble family to which Pelias, Aeson, and Jason all belong. Some versions of the myth give Jason an even stronger claim, insofar as they record Pelias as having usurped the throne from Aeson. When Jason reaches Colchis, King Aeëtes states openly what Pelias' actions only implied: he accuses all the Argonauts of plotting to steal his throne (*AR* 3.375–6).

[9] For the fragments of Naevius' epic, see *Fragmenta Poetarum Latinorum* (a volume to which many scholars have turned their hands: Emil Baehrens first in the series, Jürgen Blänsdorf most recent). Speculation abounds on the original order and content of Naevius' epic. Henry Rowell offers a useful overview of the history of the question from the 16th to the mid-20th centuries. Rowell's own schema proceeds from Wladyslaw Strzelecki's suggestion that the *Bellum Punicum* did not begin with Rome's aetiology, but revisited the mythohistory in a 'flashback', much as the *Odyssey*'s plot accommodates Odysseus' fabulous adventures between books 9 and 12 (Strzelecki 1935, Rowell 1947). Strzelecki's hypothesis has generally met with favour, especially as it offers a way logically to reconcile the ancient book numbers preserved in our MSS with the contents of the fragments assigned to these books (see e.g. Mariotti 1955). In assessing Vergil's debt to Naevius, Michael Wigodsky unfolds the major problems in reconstructing the *Bellum Punicum* (Wigodsky 1972).

Time has treated Ennius' epic more kindly, allowing more of the *Annales* to survive, and thus more certainty regarding its content and structure. Otto Skutsch has produced an authoritative edition of the fragments that lets us see the poem's broad plan (Skutsch 1985). Denis Feeney's chapter on both fragmentary epics offers a useful introduction (Feeney 1991, 99–128).

First Punic War. Ennius even more comprehensively tracks Rome from Troy through events of the Third Macedonian War (189–171 BCE); Rome's foundation is a stepping-stone—albeit an important one—to the nearly six centuries of subsequent history the *Annales* comprises. By contrast, Vergil focuses on a tightly circumscribed period—one that, strictly speaking, does not even include the foundation of Rome proper, only the 'necessary and sufficient conditions' for its germination in prophecy and internecine bloodshed.[10] A few years bound the *Aeneid*'s whole dramatic action; larger perspectives on Rome's future are confined to ekphrases such as the survey of unborn Roman heroes (*Aen.* 6.756–886) and the scenes of Roman conquests on Aeneas' Shield (*Aen.* 8.626–728).

Vergil responds to the years of chaotic transition between Rome as republic and Rome as principate by concentrating his narrative intensely upon her origins, as if their re-vision were indispensable to shaping a new end, a new *telos*, for the Eternal City. The *Aeneid*'s foundation story bears the burden of (re)defining Rome as world-city and nation-state at a moment in history when the touchstones of her identity were being radically reconfigured (most notably her long history of democratic government). As David Quint has observed, the *Aeneid* decisively transformed epic for posterity into a genre that was overtly political: 'Vergil's epic is tied to a specific national history, to the idea of world domination, to a monarchical system, even to a particular dynasty.'[11] The post-Augustan epicists carry forward the gravamen of Vergil's rethinking of the genre; they regularly use the mythohistories of various towns (including Rome) as theatres for restaging and pondering recent Roman politics, directly or allegorically. Rome, Carthage, Thebes, Iolcus and Colchis offer Lucan, Silius Italicus, Statius, and Valerius

---

[10] Rome is to be the last in a series of precursor cities. Aeneas' founding of Lavinium is predicted, but will take place only after the cessation of hostilities—i.e. after the poem ends (*Aen.* 1.258–9, 12.193–4). The *Aeneid* also prophesies, rather than witnesses, the establishments of Alba Longa and Rome (e.g. *Aen.* 1.261–77). The only 'city' Aeneas might be said to establish is the garrison he sets up at the mouth of the Tiber. Perhaps its name is Troia, if the white sow truly puns on a (poorly attested) ancient word meaning 'sow'. But its status is deeply ambiguous: as Hardie points out, Vergil describes the place both as city and garrison. Its boundaries are marked out with a plough, the ritual appropriate for a city, but it is called a *castra*, 'military camp' (Hardie 1994, 10, citing *Aen.* 7.157–9).

[11] Quint 1993, 8.

Flaccus the imaginative venues within which to trace the political causes and consequences of one man's domination. These poets take their essential organizing questions from Vergil: What is Rome? How did we get here? Where are we going?

However, they do not also borrow Vergil's specific narrative form: post-Vergilian Latin epic concerns itself with metropolises, but does not concentrate on their origins per se. The exception is Ovid's *Metamorphoses*, which in its third and fourth books narrates the inception and early history of Thebes. Like Vergil, Ovid confines himself to the years closest to the foundation: his Cadmus has not even died yet when the story of the city he founded concludes. That urban aetiology is all the more surprising in that Ovid's epic is otherwise anomalous to a polis-centred genre. As Philip Hardie has observed, the *Metamorphoses'* cities appear chiefly as incidental back-drops,[12] reduced to mere names or isolated features (e.g. 'altam l coctilibus muris...urbem'—'lofty Babylon's baked-brick walls', 4.57–8). Much of the poem's dramatic action takes place in sinister untamed wilderness, an affront to the imposition of order and control over nature central to how the Romans imagined their power in the world.[13] Founding a city quintessentially expresses this power by imposing culture upon nature,[14] as Vergil indicates when the mandate of Heaven smooths Italian rivers for Aeneas and marks with fecund animals auspicious grounds for the Trojan's foundations (*Aen.* 8.81–9). By contrast, Ovid's one extended foundation tale within his aggressively pastoral epic depicts a porous and vulnerable Thebes, menaced by wild places that regularly lure its citizens outside the city walls to their doom.[15] Impossible for any god to say of this Thebes—as Vergil has

---

[12] On the eclipse of the city in favour of the countryside in the *Metamorphoses*, see Hardie 1990, 224.

[13] As evidenced in the ruthlessly orthogonal groundplans of Roman coloniae, the refusal of Roman roads to swerve though it meant ploughing through rock, the placing of milestones along those roads so as to make open space refer to the cities between which it intervened (Rykwert 1976, Purcell 1996, Zanker 2000).

[14] Hardie 1990, 225.

[15] From 13.623 onwards, the *Metamorphoses* does nominally contain the story of Rome's founding. However, Ovid divides the story of Aeneas' journey from Troy to Rome, the founding of Alba Longa, and the reigns of the early Alban and Roman kings into hasty summaries bracketed between leisurely divagations into extraneous narratives. Anius' magical daughters (13.632–74), Polyphemus' love for Galatea and

Jupiter declare for Rome—'imperium sine fine dedi' ('I have granted them limitless dominion', *Aen.* 1.279).

Hardie has thoughtfully analysed Ovid's Theban cycle by sifting the thematic and structural inversions Ovid worked upon Vergil's epic. Taking his cue from Froma Zeitlin's analysis of Thebes' role as an 'anti-Athens' in Athenian drama—the place where everything goes wrong, and whose example Athens must avoid at all costs[16]— he has persuasively demonstrated that Ovid's Thebes functions similarly—as an anti-Rome, or even more specifically, 'the first anti-*Aeneid*'. But it is also the last Latin epic to engage Vergil on his own topical ground. Although Vergil's successors in Latin epic can all be seen to respond to the *Aeneid* thoughtfully and vigorously,[17] none but Ovid accepts the formal challenge and essays ktistic epic by choosing a city's origins as his topic.[18] The post-Augustans shape

revenge on her lover Acis (13.740–897), Circe's passion for Glaucis and retaliation against his beloved, Scylla (13.898–14.74)—all these stories and more interrupt the narrative line of Rome's history, swallowing most of the narrative space in the poem's last books (cf. Hardie 2002a, 192). What of Roman history does appear in the poem Ovid gives short shrift, as exemplified in the fact that he devotes five words to raising the walls of Rome ('festisque Palilibus urbis | moenia conduntur', *Met.* 14.774–5). Moreover, the lines' very structure denies these five words the status of a satisfactory consummation to the tale of Rome's birth. Ovid carefully breaks the phrase between two lines with enjambement, so that the words themselves do not coincide with any structural endpoint, and he places the key verb with which Vergil memorably ends his epic, *condere*, in an unmarked position at the middle of a line. By contrast to this almost erased Roman foundation-tale, Ovid's Theban cycle follows the city through an intricately interwoven set of tales from inception through three generations until Cadmus and Harmonia leave the city in despair (Hardie 1990, 224). There are only two interruptions to the Ovidian mythohistory of Thebes, and these are more apparent than real. The first is the tale of Echo and Narcissus, the second an excursus into Orchomenos (about forty miles north-east of Thebes) that ends with Bacchus' punishment of the Minyeides (4.1–415). Yet Narcissus' story is intimately tied to the Theban cycle by details that mark him as a substitute for Thebes' most famous mortal son, Oedipus (Loewenstein 1984, 41–5; Hardie 1988, 86; Gildenhard–Zissos 2000; I examine this connection more fully in Ch. 5). And since Orchomenos' trials involve Thebes' most powerful son establishing his worship in a nearby Greek city, they, too, thematically cohere with the Theban cycle.

[16]   Zeitlin 1986, 103, 117.
[17]   See e.g. Hardie 1993, both as a succinct and thoughtful overview of the *Aeneid*'s most immediate *Nachleben*, and a helpful source of bibliography on this vast topic.
[18]   Although—as one of my anonymous readers points out to me—Lucan's *Bellum Civile*, the first Latin epic to be called an 'anti-*Aeneid*', might be said to narrate Rome's 'unfoundation' by civil war.

their epics around Vergil's political questions, and construct their answers from the vantage Ovid's Theban cycle offers upon the *Aeneid*. As I shall argue more fully in the concluding chapter to this book, Ovid taught the post-Augustans how to read the *Aeneid*. Nonetheless, only Vergil and Ovid share a specific focus upon the incunabula of the world-city as the key to its nature—a commonality that makes the *Aeneid* and the Theban cycle singularly affinitive. Both unfold from the implicit assumption that what defines a phenomenal field is its (often elusive) cause.[19] The phenomenal field here is not *a* city, Rome, but *The* City—the Platonic ideal of the organized human community, and of the nature of its travails. That vantage on Augustan epic expands the scope of inquiry beyond asking how Ovid's Thebes is an anti-Rome to why it should be so. What are the general principles that allow Thebes to stand for Rome, rather than miring each city in the data peculiar to its own mythohistory? What abstract logic of the commonweal is at work here—of its cohesion, its identity, and its governance? These queries in turn press us to examine just how Ovid asks, and answers, the specific questions the *Aeneid* poses to human beings as political animals. What is the relation between city and citizenship? (Does the polity require the sacrifice of all individual desires in favour of collective state interests, a pattern seen in Aeneas' gradual divestiture of all individual will?) How does ideology work to form this relation? (In what ways do Aeneas' perceptions of the temple paintings at Carthage, the parade of heroes in the Underworld, and the images on Vulcan's marvellous Shield shape him into Rome's proto-citizen?) Where, and how well, does the polity's law police the border with crime? (When Aeneas kills Turnus at the *Aeneid*'s

---

[19] Not an assumption peculiar to the Augustans, but one to which they and their immediate predecessors may have been better attuned by their study of the poetic aetiologies of Callimachus' *Aetia* (O'Hara 1996, 21–111). Callimachus' poetic narrative focuses on the origins of various Hellenistic cultural observances as a guide to their present-day forms and significance. Tracing the roots of today into distant yesterdays promises reassuringly to bridge the gulf between the revered Greek past and the present of Ptolemies' courtiers removed to Alexandria, Egypt (Zanker 1987, 121–3; Bing 1988, 70–1). Wendell Clausen has argued that the appearance of the Greek poet and scholar Parthenius in Rome sometime during the Third Mithridatic War (75–65 BCE) better enabled late Republican Latin poets to absorb Callimachus' influence (Clausen 1964). Parthenius would have helped poets such as Helvius Cinna, Gallus, and Vergil to negotiate Callimachus' difficult Greek and recondite allusions.

conclusion, does he commit murder, or visit condign punishment on a would-be usurper?)

The answers to these questions unfolded in the following pages focus on the patterns and details of the *Aeneid* Ovid found most meaningful, most suited to appropriating the authority of Vergil's inquiry into the problematic of The City. What Ovid wrested and reshaped from Vergil amounts to a shrewd, but often tendentious, reading of the *Aeneid*. Stephen Hinds's recent contemplation of allusion and intertext shows how poets commonly flatten the complexities of their source texts. Ovid in particular often frames the *Aeneid* as a hesitant and unsystematic precursor to his own *Metamorphoses*, the older epic timidly sketching as dispersed hints what Ovid gathers into a bold economy of insight. Needless for Hinds to say (or anyone else), that is less than fair to Vergil. But acknowledging such tendentious distortion as a working principle between the *Metamorphoses* and the *Aeneid* reveals much that is new about both poems.[20] My discussion of the Ovidian Thebes' address to the *Aeneid* may appear at times to scant the true complexity of Vergil's daedal epic—the ways in which the murmur of its polyphony complicates any reading of its politics, ethics, sympathies, and ideological commitments. Yet I strive to follow where Ovid's reading of Vergil leads, and to show the value of that pursuit, insofar as it reveals Ovid's Theban cycle as more than a cautionary negative of the *Aeneid* organized about a desperately disintegrating anti-Rome. Rather, Ovid's response to the problematic of The City Vergil had framed reveals a deeper bond between the two cities than the dyad 'Rome' and 'anti-Rome' initially suggests. As the *Metamorphoses'* Theban cycle portrays the two cities, they do not contradict one another, as though they could not occupy the same conceptual space. Like Romulus and Remus, they are mutually implicated twins; each logically defines and supports the other. Thebes may be the anti-Rome, but from the vantage of city-as-abstraction, it is also Rome's ineluctable obverse, the illusory 'other side' of the Möbius strip that turns out to be part of the same single surface after all.[21]

---

[20] Hinds 1998, 104–22.

[21] Responding to Zeitlin's thesis of Thebes as a negative Athens on the Greek tragic stage, David Konstan has argued that tragedy instead dramatizes in Thebes the

THE SUBJECT OF INTERTEXTUALITY

I have sketched a Latin epic genealogy that makes the meaning of each poet's address to Rome a function of his epic's relation to its generic counterparts—clearly an intertextual model of exegesis. Intertextuality has in the last few decades become the dominant mode for analysing epic. It crucially shapes such important studies as: Quint on the thematic and ideological dialectic between history's epic 'winners' and 'losers',[22] Hardie on the Silver-Latin epicists' self-conscious tropes of Vergilian paternity and inheritance,[23] Hinds on the *Annales* and *Aeneid* as organizing antipodes for poets' 'do-it-yourself' literary histories,[24] Gian Biagio Conte on the *Aeneid*'s reinvention of the 'epic code',[25] and Alessandro Barchiesi upon the figures that mark epic's 'literary self-consciousness'.[26] Examples could be multiplied of the important contributions these and other intertextualist scholars have made to the interpretation of ancient literature.[27]

These discussions of epic are among the many studies of Latin genres conducted under the explicit or implicit methodological aegis

Athenians' own deeply problematic inclinations toward vengeance, violence, and injustice (Konstan 2006*b*).

[22] Quint 1993.

[23] Hardie 1993.

[24] Hinds 1998, 52–98.

[25] Conte 1986, 141–95.

[26] Barchiesi 2001, 49–78, 129–40. This study was preceded by a book-length intertextual study of the *Aeneid* in relation to Homeric epic (Barchiesi 1984); Barchiesi shows how Vergil's echoes of Homer illustrate two ideologies at war in the *Aeneid*: archaic, Greek-style heroism vs. Roman 'civilization'.

[27] Among which some of the most interesting examples would be Conte's mapping of the complex textual relations surrounding *De Rerum Natura*, including Empedocles, the *Georgics*, and Ovid's *Amores* (Conte 1994*b*, 1–34); R. O. A. M. Lyne on how the *Aeneid*'s resonances with Catullus 66 destabilize the epic's heroic ethos (Lyne 1994); Stephen Hinds on the self-annotating 'Alexandrian footnote' (Hinds 1995); the essays of Don Fowler, Stephen J. Harrison, Debra Hershkowitz, Stephen Hinds, Patricia Rosenmeyer, and Alessandro Schiesaro in the special issue of *Materiali e Discussioni* devoted to intertextuality (Hinds–Fowler 1997; Fowler's introductory essay also includes a helpful guide to previous bibliography on intertextuality and classics). Versions of Hinds's *Hermathena* and *MD* essays later appeared in Hinds 1998.

of intertextuality. In the last few decades, such studies have greatly increased, with good reason. As Don Fowler notes, examining parallels between texts has long been a focus for classics, a discipline in which the commentary plays an almost uniquely central role in the interpretative community.[28] Yet until recently, the object of these studies was labelled 'allusion', a word that implies conscious intention and relatively narrow focus, as if we could say things like 'Vergil wanted lines *abc* in the *Aeneid* to remind his reader of lines *xyz* in Ennius' *Annales*'. In fact, we cannot know the author's mind with such certainty. Neither do we read or write texts in ideal isolation—say, a page each from the *Aeneid* and the *Annales* before us, and all other literature magically, if temporarily, expunged from our minds. Intertextuality better accounts for the real complexity of interpretation by treating literary texts as special cases of the general rules governing linguistic significance. Words attain meaning by virtue of their relationship to the semantic code obtaining within a particular language community; any utterance or grapheme signifies only in relation to the history of usage within that community.[29] Literary language raises to the second power this production of significance: a poetic text assumes meaning in relation to the myriad other instances of enunciation that are the literary tradition. The corollary inference is that such a text will richly repay intensified inquiry into the wider penumbra of passages it can be seen to reread.

But it also means that context is theoretically limitless, not circumscribed either by 'what the author meant' or 'what the contemporary audience could have understood'. The influence of intertextuality on the study of Latin poetry generally can be seen in a broader scholarly perspective on the way poems talk to one another. Intertextual studies cast their nets wide, and trace the various volleys in the literary conversation through multiple relays and ever-more elaborated layers of significance. They are also more willing to acknowledge how the intertextual relation can support diametrically opposed interpretations of the same passage. When texts converse unbounded by the interpretative limits of the author's intention or

---

[28] Fowler 1997, 14.
[29] Cf. Bakhtin–Volosinov 1986, 95; Bakhtin 1986, 93–4.

the contemporary reader's understanding, the effects of their interaction cannot be contained within univocal limits.

However, what has largely gone missing from this generous embrace of meaning is a full accounting for all three of its transactional
anchoring points: author, reader, and text.[30] The scholars named
above do try to account to varying degrees for the subjectivity
these points of reference imply. Yet they tacitly posit an ideal Carte-
sian subject as master of meaning (whether as author, reader, or text).
Hence the punctual mention of 'hidden authors',[31] 'actual authorial
initiative',[32] and 'literary self-consciousness';[33] of 'model readers',[34]
'intended addressees',[35] and 'successful readings';[36] of the need to stay
'bound to the text'.[37] Such analyses are circumscribed by a model of
the subject without desire, without an unconscious, and thus fully
present to her/himself.[38] That model will illuminate very well some
kinds of data to be derived from the intertextual study of ancient
epic. But it will miss others generated by the internal contradictions
imperial Latin epic has frequently dramatized. Vergil set the pattern
for these inconsistencies, both personal and collective, with an
Aeneas so often opaque to himself,[39] founder of a nation who

[30] See especially in this respect Hinds 1998 and Edmunds 2001.
[31] The title of the book published from Conte's 1995 Sather Classical Lectures on
Petronius' *Satyricon* (Conte 1996).
[32] Hinds 1998, 50.
[33] Which entails 'a glance toward the production of the text and the figure of the
author' (Barchiesi 2001, 142).
[34] A term coined by Umberto Eco (Eco 1979, 7) and used by Conte (Conte
1986, 30).
[35] e.g. Conte 1994*a*, 3. Cf. Giorgio Pasquali: 'Le allusioni non producono l'effetto
voluto se non su un lettore che si ricordi chiaramente del testo cui si riferiscono'
(Pasquali 1968, 275).
[36] Edmunds 2001, 62.
[37] Conte–Barchiesi 1989, 90 n. 12.
[38] An essentially phenomenological model that suspends questions of the perceiving subject's—or for that matter, the perceived object's—ontology or epistemology.
Edmunds in particular allies himself with such a phenomenological framework
when he adopts Hans Robert Jauss's reader-orientated hermeneutic methodology
(Edmunds 2001, xiii); Jauss was greatly influenced by the German phenomenologist
Moritz Geiger (see e.g. Jauss 1974, esp. 316 and n. 76). On the hermeneutic limitations imposed by such a conceptual framework, see Paul Allen Miller's learned review
of Edmunds's *Intertextuality and the Reading of Roman Poetry* (Miller 2003).
[39] For example: does Aeneas recognize the irony of describing himself as 'pius
Aeneas' when he addresses the dead Lausus, whom Aeneas killed in an act of *pietas*

never himself achieves a final nationality.[40] As for the rest of Vergil's stateless Trojans and hostile Latins, at the end of the *Aeneid* they have yet to struggle together into Romanness. Similar divided loyalties split Lucan's and Statius' ruling houses, while paranoia and self-delusion internally fracture their leaders Caesar, Pompey, Eteocles, and Polyneices. As self-interest and insanity strain family, civic, and psychic ties, private hostilities spill into public civil war for the citizenries of Rome and Thebes.[41] Even Silius' 'good' war against an external enemy shows Rome's dashing military paragon, Scipio Africanus, and his troops defeating Carthage only by aping Carthaginian vices. To illuminate fully such problematic negotiations of individual and collective selfhood, we need another construct of the subject. Studies have skilfully elucidated the many conflicting voices in these Latin epics, both within and between the *dramatis personae*—but what exactly is the nature of the subjectivities to whom these voices belong, whom they address, who note and who (over)hear the conversations? A better understanding of the fundamentals of intertextuality can answer those questions.

The tradition of the autonomous, whole, fully 'self-present' subject I have sketched above is ultimately foreign to the conceptual origins of intertextuality. Inspired by the work both of Jacques Lacan and Mikhail Bakhtin, Julia Kristeva had decisively broken with that modelling of the subject when she formulated the concept of inter-textuality in her 1969 publication *Semeiotike: recherches pour une sémanalyse*. She later expanded upon the idea of intertextuality in her 1974 doctoral dissertation, *La révolution du langage poétique*. *Semeiotike* prefaced its discussion by introducing and developing

---

(the boy was defending his father)? Or an even stickier puzzle of self-knowledge: was Aeneas planning to leave Dido and Carthage in secret or not? His instructions to Sergestus and Mnestheus to prepare the Trojan fleet for departure clandestinely point one way, his explicit denial to her another. In between is his stated intention to wait until the right time to tell her. But is this true, or a prevarication designed to soothe his comrades' consciences—or his own?

[40] On the general subject of inconsistency in Latin epic, see now O'Hara 2007 and its bibliography. On the problem of Aeneas' national identity, see Reed 2007, 173–202.

[41] On the theme of madness as a thematic element in Latin epic depictions of civil war, see Hershkowitz 1998*a*, esp. 68–124, 206–99.

Mikhail Bahktin's dialogism,[42] a view of language specifically moored to the positions of speaker and addressee.[43] Intertextuality reflects Bakhtin's idea that language acquires meaning through the exchange of enunciations in actual speech acts. The fundamental unit of language is thus not the sentence, but the utterance. Sentences are repeatable; utterances occur in specific situations, and in dialogic exchange. Utterances elicit responses and are shaped in anticipation of a response; they belong to both speaker and listener. Because utterances are tied to specific situations, they carry the markers of experience. Every social group or generation has its own character-istic vocabulary and mode of expression that reflects its experience and apprehension of the world. Bakhtin calls this multiplicity of languages within language 'heteroglossia'. Literary works develop the potentials of the interaction between heteroglossia and dialogism, by orchestrating an intense dialogue among language's different tongues. The result is to make each tongue and the assumptions about the world twined into its warp and woof 'contested, contest-able, and contesting'.[44]

At the same time Kristeva's incipient notion of intertextuality laid Bakhtin under contribution, it also drew heavily upon the psycho-analytic work of Jacques Lacan. Kristeva moved in the same intellec-tual circles as Lacan, met him personally after emigrating from Bulgaria to Paris in 1965, and studied his *Écrits*, first published in 1966. She coined the term 'intertextuality' to describe writing not only as communication, but as subjectivity. Her model of the subject as emerging from, and constructed in, language reveals the concept's debt to Lacanian psychoanalysis. Kristeva's model of intertextuality involves two axes. One is the vertical axis between the text under examination, and its orientation toward the anterior or synchronic literary corpus. This is the relation upon which intertextual readings of Latin epic have lavished their attention. But the less often analysed horizontal axis stretches between the speaking subject and the ad-

---

[42] In the chapter entitled 'Le mot, le dialogue et le roman' (Kristeva 1969, 143–73).

[43] In *Revolution*, Kristeva exchanges the term 'intertextuality' for 'transposition', in order to emphasize its operation as based upon the transposing of one signifying practice into another, a passage from one sign system into another.

[44] 'Discourse in the Novel', 332 (in Bakhtin 1981, 259–422).

dressee, indicating that the word always belongs both to the writer and to the reader.[45] Kristeva's speaking subject is not the writer as a psychological individual; rather, the writer is only a blank space, a zero function that marks the condition of possibility of a subject of narration and an addressee. The reader seeks the author in the narrative text by heeding the content of the narration, especially the pronouns and proper names that designate characters. The author thus functions as a floating signifier to which the reader may reference the multiple subjectivities operating within the multivalent text. The reader transforms the narrative text into an author construed as an organizing point of orientation. Reciprocally, the reader is always presupposed in what the writer writes. In Kristeva's schema, textuality does not express an entity that pre-exists it. Rather, writer and reader are produced by the text; all three are open and interpenetrating systems whose separation cannot be cleanly defined.

Even more unsettling, the subjective positions within this triad severally escape closure and unity. No clear, monadical notion of a psychological self can govern either the writer or the reader; after all, they are strictly effects of language, like the text that constitutes and is constituted by both. Kristeva's subject of narration ultimately splits in two—into the subject of the enunciation (*le sujet de l'énoncé*) and the subject of the utterance (*le sujet de l'énonciation*).[46] Kristeva adopts from Lacan this notion of the subject as divided by entry into language. In his eleventh *Séminaire*, Lacan illustrated the difference between the speaking subject ('le *je* qui énonce') and the spoken subject ('le *je* de l'énonciation') by glossing the Liar's Paradox. As he explains, the pronouncement, 'I am lying' is a paradox only to whoever fails to realize that the statement involves two subjects. Between the subject who speaks, and the subject, the *je*, of the statement itself, only one dissembles.[47]

It is Lacan's divided, decentred, unstable subject-in-language that ultimately anchors Kristeva's notion of intertextuality. His speaking subject is the subject of desire, subtended by the wish to overcome

---

[45] Kristeva 1969, 145.
[46] Kristeva 1969, 156.
[47] Lacan 1973, 127–128/1981*b*, 138–140.

her/his own fractured state and to coalesce as a whole, a clearly defined self.[48] Lacan has articulated with precision and nuance how this desire both motivates and vitiates the formation of the organized human community, the group from which the self can derive its identity. Refocusing through Lacan's inherently split model of subjectivity how Ovid's Thebes engages Vergil's *Aeneid* sharpens the contours of these two intertexts' common subject matter: the beleaguered birth of a new citizenry. Both the Theban cycle and the *Aeneid* depict political identities shattered by exile and driven to find new individual and collective selves. Where hostile Greeks compel the Aeneadae blindly to seek an alien homeland, a furious king of Tyre drives his son Cadmus and his retainers to strike root overseas. In their new land, Boeotia, a monstrous snake immediately strips Cadmus of his emigrant Tyrians; he and Thebes must find citizens in the contradictory extremes of divine marriage (Cadmus and Harmonia) and bestial spontaneous generation (the fratricidal Spartoi, sprung from the teeth of the murderous snake). In introducing to the intertextual probing of these epics Lacan's speaker and listener who yearn for wholeness, I seek to plumb fully the colloquy between Vergil and Ovid's commonalties desperately adrift. I focus specifically on incoherence in all its senses—on what the subject as master of meaning can*not* compass in Ovid's Theban cycle, and what therefore tears city and citizens apart. Where his Thebes egregiously does not make sense, Ovid foregrounds the kinds of subjective contradictions implicit in the *Aeneid*'s vision of Rome. By so doing, Ovid not only rethinks the conceptual premises of Vergil's foundation tale, but crucially shapes how Vergil's epic successors will in their turn respond to the *Aeneid* (as I shall argue more fully in my last chapter). It will therefore be important not to 'explain away' Thebes' aporiae, but to seek a systematic methodological framework capable of relating one impasse to another. My goal is to elucidate from these conundra

---

[48] The idea of a primordial lack in human beings as the motive force behind desire can be traced back to the ancient world; its most magisterial articulation is Plato's *Symposium*. In this dialogue, Aristophanes' tale speaks of an aboriginally divided being that perpetually seeks its lost other half (*Symp.* 189c–193d). On a more rarefied plane, Diotima's speech outlines the principles of substitution and displacement that palliate original need; with philosophy's guidance, these principles can lead the desiring subject to the ideal Good (*Symp.* 201d–212a).

additional layers of meaning and better relate them to their historical context. Lacan offers an appropriate perspective from which to engage the quintessential questions round which both the *Aeneid*'s paradoxes and Ovid's response to them, are organized: Is there a nation to be had from this unpromising history, a people from these contingent persons? If so, how and what kind?

In answering these questions, we must also take account of the historical specifics shaping the intertextual transaction between writer and reader, including Vergil's and Ovid's contemporary Roman readers. In the pages that follow, I examine the ways in which the Theban and Roman myths of foundation, both based on fratricide, speak to the divided subjectivity Lacan maps as a universal and transhistorical human condition. Yet it is also true that actual, protracted civil war wracked Rome from roughly the mid-second century BCE up to Augustus' defeat of Mark Antony (31–30 BCE).[49] Augustus' victory in turn enabled the concentration of patriarchal power in his hands, via the institution of the principate as Rome's form of government. Clearly neither of these is the experience of Everyman, or Everycity. How, then, can a psychoanalytic perspective do them justice?

The transhistorical perspective of psychoanalysis is essential to assess these facts precisely because they *are* less than quotidian in human history. We cannot compare different historical eras without the background assumption of continuity. Were every phenomenon absolutely particular, it would be impossible to talk about it, much less understand it. Only the existence of transhistorical categories—the universal—allows us to conceptualize the particular.[50] Fredric Jameson's *The Political Unconscious* demonstrates this point, showing how Lacan's thought can specifically illuminate literature while 'preserving the phenomena' bequeathed by the text's historical context.

---

[49] Appian's book on Rome's civil wars dates the beginning of the repetitive cycle of internal strife from the land-reform activities of Tiberius and Gaius Gracchus in 133 BCE (*Bella Civilia* 1.1).

[50] An idea that stretches back to Hegel, whose thought thus grounds seeming antipodes in methodologies for analysing human culture. Both psychoanalysis and Marxism sink their conceptual roots into Hegel—which means that psychoanalysis shares conceptual roots with contemporary historicism, indebted as the latter is to Marx.

As a committed Marxist, it is no surprise that Jameson begins his book with the words 'Always historicize!' Yet Jameson argues cogently that Lacan's category of the Real corresponds to the Marxist category of History. I shall elaborate upon the Real presently, but suffice it to say here the Real represents that for which cultural symbolization systems cannot account. These systems include literature, but also ideology, propaganda, ritual—the various ways in which symbolization continually attempts, and ultimately fails, perfectly to resolve social contradiction. The Real marks the necessary limitations of symbolization systems, and thus their ultimate collapse, a principle of generation and succession that drives History. The Real generates change precisely by its capacity to persist, and insist, within human affairs.[51]

Jameson articulates the Real's relation to History as a literary critic who finds Lacan's ideas compelling. But even thinkers with no ready sympathy for Lacan recognize the particular and the universal as necessarily coupled in the study of human culture. For example, Jacques Derrida in *Le facteur de la vérité* aims to refute Lacan by reassessing his *Seminar on Poe's 'Purloined Letter'*,[52] which Lacan himself had implicitly opposed to Marie Bonaparte's classically Freudian reading of the same tale. Bonaparte exemplifies a semanticist form of psychoanalytic criticism, which views the text's particulars as so many signs of the author's unconscious wishes and fears; the goal of such analysis is to trace within the author's text the private, individual traumata transformed into fiction. By contrast, Lacan's reading of Poe's tale shifts the focus away from personalities either outside or inside the text, and onto the way the narrative itself functions as a formal system. His interest is to map how language as a social system constitutes the (authorial or narrative) subject,

---

[51] The ideas in this paragraph owe much to Paul Allen Miller, particularly to his masterful accounting from the vantage of a Lacanian historicism for Roman erotic elegy's brief irruption into history (Miller 2004, 1–30, but esp. 10–12).

[52] Lacan's analysis of Poe's tale was originally delivered orally in 1955 as part of his second Seminar entitled 'Le Moi dans la théorie de Freud et dans la technique de la psychanalyse'. It was published separately as 'Le Séminaire de la lettre volée' in the journal *La Psychanalyse* (Lacan 1957) and again in *Écrits* (Lacan 1966, 11–61). The most recent translation into English from the text in *Écrits* is by Bruce Fink (Lacan 2006a, 11–48).

rather than seeking the encrypted 'true nature' of the subject as the 'real meaning' behind the text's language. He analyses the intersubjective relations in Poe's tale as determined, not by the *dramatis personae* involved, but by the chain of signifiers that traverses them.[53] For Lacan, the way language—most specifically the purloined letter—structures these interchanges generates the principal interest of the tale.

Derrida's deeply sceptical reading of the *Seminar* finds fault with its emphasis on universalized structures within the tale. In Derrida's eyes, Lacan scants what is specific to Poe's story and so undervalues the attention to peculiarity a reading such as Bonaparte's offers.[54] Yet however committed to recuperating the singular Derrida may be, however much this disposes him to look more kindly than Lacan upon Bonaparte's methodology, Derrida also shows that her semantic, particularist reading of Poe depends on concepts and frames of reference only a more formalist, universalizing reading such as Lacan's can truly employ. And the reverse is also true: Lacan relies upon semanticist features to construct his formal, Oedipally triangular relationships among the tale's protagonists.[55] These two

---

[53] Specifically, by the way a certain incriminating epistle containing indiscreet declarations circulates among a series of persons each grasping for advantage. The triangular pattern of relationships among the characters remains constant in Poe's tale. King, Queen, Minister, Prefect of Police, and amateur detective C. Auguste Dupin all occupy in turn three positions: the one blind to the letter's significance; the one blind to how the letter may be taken with impunity; the one who, seeing both blindnesses, exploits them by stealing the letter. Yet the repetition of this trigon is only perceptible through difference—through the letter's own restless migration always to another place, and through the various characters' sequential occupation of these places as defined by their grasp of the letter (in all senses of that phrase). Ultimately, the letter escapes all of them—and us as its would-be readers: its scandalous contents are never disclosed within the tale.

[54] For example, Derrida contends that by leaving out of his account the role of the unnamed narrator who records the adventures of Dupin—the quirky details clustering about Dupin's friend and room-mate, bizarre double to the amateur detective in his bibliophilia and melancholy—Lacan effectively treats Poe's text as a mere purveyor of the 'truth' of repetition disclosed by Freud, which is also the truth of the signifier more generally (Derrida 1987, 484–96).

[55] An example of such semanticism would be the details of the Minister's apartment Lacan cites as evoking the female body as frame of reference. The Minister has devised a feminine disguise for the incriminating letter by turning it over and addressing it to himself in a delicate female hand, so that it might pass unremarked. Lacan describes the letter, hiding in plain sight, as sprawling 'like an immense female

forms of reading (semanticist/particular vs. structuralist/universal) are implicated in each other and are logically inextricable, Derrida observes.[56]

Jameson's and Derrida's postmodern perspectives on the universal and the particular in literary studies pertain beyond latter-day *belles-lettres*. Both find a mirror in territory more familiar to classicists— Charles Martindale's *Redeeming the Text*, a trenchant meditation on Latin poetry and the hermeneutics of reception. Martindale confronts the sense of estrangement necessarily involved in reading poems written millennia ago in a language we can never truly make our own. The discipline of Classics trains its intellectual resources upon bridging the temporal abyss between modernity and antiquity, upon making the ancients' unvarnished particularity clearly visible to us. Yet Martindale insists upon the importance of that abyss as constituting an ineluctable interpretative continuum: other readings across time (e.g. Vergil's of Homer, Dante's of Vergil, T. S. Eliot's of all three) have not simply shaped our interpretations of the past, they have constructed the readability of the texts we interpret. Meaning is both commons and commodity, produced and exchanged socially and discursively, thus implicating reader and text inextricably in the *longue durée* of exegetical tradition. Martindale thus views with scepticism the foundationalist goal of radically historicist literary analysis: to regain the reified text-in-itself and a meaning placed beyond contingency.

We all approach the reading of texts with the baggage of our values and our experience, with certain categories, assumptions, prejudices and 'fore-understandings'. To have such baggage is what it is to be human; *without it we could not read at all* . . . the here and now is always the locus of discourse stretching back into a largely lost past and forwards to an unknown future.   (Martindale 1993, 5, 6; emphasis in original text)

---

body . . . across the space of the Minister's office when Dupin enters it'. Lacan has some fun at Marie Bonaparte's expense in parsing the exact anatomical significance of the letter's hiding place, a rack dangling between the jambs of the Minister's mantelpiece (Lacan 2006*a*, 25–26).

[56] 'Formalism and hermeneutic semanticism always support one another: question of the frame.' See also Derrida's more detailed analysis of the necessary mutual implication of abstract ideality and tangible materiality in interpreting the purloined letter's significance (Derrida 1987, 432, 463–4).

Martindale's brusque dismissal of hermeneutic nostalgia leads to this paradox: 'any text has to be treated *both as transhistorical and as contingent upon a particular moment of history* if it is to be interpreted'.[57] His conceptual premisses for the principled interpretation of antiquity thus coincide with Jameson's and Derrida's in their address to more modern artefacts of culture. The principled attention of such widely divergent thinkers to the interplay between universal and particular underlines the importance of this dialectic to interpretation. Hence my conviction that the transhistorical conceptual framework of Lacanian psychoanalysis will enable us to uncover hidden historical structures in Ovid, the 'semantic conditions of possibility'[58] that have made the poem both writable and readable.

My examination of the *Aeneid* and of Ovid's Theban cycle as intertexts concentrates specifically on the shared problematic of identity both foundation tales pose (rather than a line-by-line or motif-by-motif comparison). Conditioning that problematic is a systemic crisis in Rome's self-understanding both as nation and as state, after more than a century of civil war in a republic resolves itself (uneasily, if lastingly) in one-man rule. Both epics seek in the beginnings of a city's and a nation's mythohistory what accounts for the essential features of the polity's present-day configuration. More broadly, the two examine the principles upon which the nation-state is founded, asking (in essence), What constitutes a community and a member of that community? What does it mean to be Rome/Thebes or Roman/Theban? Ovid unfolds fully the darker side of these questions, a side the *Aeneid* had implied but circumscribed within a millenarian discourse of Rome's ascendancy. Ovid's troubling story-cycle probes deeply into how and why the Fabled City becomes the Doomed City—how a polity's organizing principles go awry, what vitiates and problematizes political identity.

---

[57] Martindale 1993, 104.
[58] The phrase is Jameson's (Jameson 1981, 57).

THEBES' TWO FATHERS

Lacan's conceptualization of the Father is essential to bridging the gap between the divided psychoanalytic subject taken in isolation, and the collective of such subjects that is the polity.[59] For Lacan, the Father is an abstract principle of legislative and punitive power the paternal role exemplifies, rather than a biological function.[60] The Father not only informs the law—the basis of the regulated society, like Thebes—but more abstractly 'polices' the conceptual boundaries that are the essence of the Symbolic (Lacan's term for the cultural symbolization systems whose categories underlie the linguistic and social order, and upon which the possibility of signification depends).[61] It is in relation to the Father that one achieves identity as an individual, as a citizen, as a collective—even as Man or Woman. Each identity depends upon an implied binary (self/other; Theban/non-Theban; Man/Woman); the stability of that defining boundary rests in the paternal metaphor.

---

[59] The Father is not one of Kristeva's particular interests, though she does devote some attention to the Father as associated with law and prohibition in *Histoires d'amour* (Kristeva 1983). She has rather marshalled her intellectual energies toward elaborating her concepts of the maternal, and all the subordinate ideas that this subsumes: the chora, the semeiotic, 'herethics'—and to brilliant effect. Only in Lacan does one find a relentless pursuit of the Father in all his manifestations, including His senseless, licentious, violent side, and the implications of that side for any human community. For this reason, in order to analyse the political side of the Theban cycle, my methodology reaches behind Kristeva to the psychoanalytic roots upon which her notion of intertextuality rests.

[60] Especially in so patriarchal a society as ancient Rome, where governmental authority is modelled on the authority of the *paterfamilias*. As W. K. Lacey points out (Lacey 1986), the chief positions of authority in Rome (e.g. the consulship) sketch a conceptualization of state dominion different from any Greek society's. Rome's offices were few in number, but conferred on the magistrates who occupied them broad discretionary powers over a wide sphere of responsibility. The occupants of these offices were thus more like parents to the governed—able to act and to improvise within broad limits—than like functionaries merely enforcing the detailed and specific demands of a legal code. Not by accident were senators called *patres conscripti*, nor Augustus eventually honoured as *pater patriae* (2 BCE).

[61] 'C'est dans le *nom du père* qu'il nous faut reconnaître le support de la fonction symbolique qui, depuis l'orée des temps historiques, identifie sa personne à la figure de la loi' (Lacan 1966, 278).

Yet the separations and distinctions set in place by the paternal metaphor do not take place without remainder. Their pathological by-product is a figure of violence, licentiousness, and terror whom Lacan christened *Le Père Jouissant*, or the Father of Enjoyment. This side of the Father figures the sadism, tyranny, and irrationality that also accrue to the law, but that must be occluded in order for the law to function. It is this side that pertains most closely to Ovid's Thebes. Whereas the *Aeneid*'s vision of Rome offers the (bare) possibility of integrating and justifying the nation's more violent and chaotic side within the divine historical plan devised by Jupiter, *pater omnipotens*,[62] no such fortune exists for Ovid's Thebes. Both immortal and mortal paternity for the Thebans only eases their slide toward Hell.

Thebes takes its origin from two apparently quite different Father figures, Jupiter the rapist of Europa, and King Agenor. Homer calls the king of the gods 'father of men and gods' (e.g. *Il.* 20.56, *Od.* 1.28; echoed in, e.g., Livy 1.12.5), though no source tells us unambiguously that Jupiter created human beings, and he fathers relatively few of the gods. Nonetheless, he functions paternally by broadly controlling events in heaven and earth. He regularly mediates conflicts between mortals and gods, and surpasses all other gods in power.[63] Zeus-as-patriarch is the stern imposer of order and justice who strives to give Achilles the honour that is his due, warn Aegisthus not to kill Agamemnon, and save Odysseus from languishing on Calypso's island. But that figure contrasts starkly with the other, more carnal sense in which Zeus-Jupiter fathers gods and men. As sexual terrorist, he perpetrates a series of rapes on lesser divinities and mortals that produce multitudes of offspring. That aspect of Jove, the licentious egoist who imposes his will solely for his own gratification, sets in train the events that introduce Ovid's Theban cycle. Desiring Europa, Jupiter arranges to abduct her by duplicity. Assuming the shape of a particularly comely bull, he lures the princess to mount his back and then carries her off to Crete (*Met.*

[62] For this as one of the titles Vergil regularly bestows on Jupiter, cf. e.g. *Aen.* 4.25, 6.592, 7.770, 12.178.

[63] As he sternly warns the Olympians when he commands them to remain neutral during the Trojan War, if they all together took hold of one end of a golden chain, and he single-handedly pulled against them, yet he could pull them all up, and the earth and sea after them, and dangle the whole lot from the top of Olympus (*Il.* 3.18–27).

2.846–75). Europa's mortal father Agenor reacts by assuming the contrasting paternal-sovereign role, demanding proper familial and social order. Rousing himself on behalf of his daughter and subject, he commands his son and subject Cadmus to find his sister. Cadmus is presumably to restore her to her family, or else regularize her situation through marriage, thus restoring proper relations between Man and Woman either by bringing Europa under her father's tutelage, or her new husband's. But if Cadmus fails to find her, Agenor forbids him to return (*Met*. 3.3–5).

These two Ovidian father-figures could not differ more strongly at first glance: Jove the wanton divine transgressor, Agenor the stern mortal enforcer of propriety. Yet any reader of the *Metamorphoses* will also recall the rather different depiction of Jove in the epic's first pages. Ovid describes Jupiter as *pater* for the very first time when Jove, like Agenor, sets himself the task of compelling due order. Indeed, Jupiter reassumes his Vergilian title of 'almighty father' when he deploys his lightning against the rebellious Giants (*Met*. 1.154). However, not ten lines later, Jupiter is again *pater* and police under more dubious circumstances (*Met*. 1.163). His rage kindling at the perceived degeneracy of the human race, he calls a council of the gods, and persuades them that all mortals must be destroyed. He alleges the necessity of keeping the world safe for terrestrial divinities like the nymphs (*Met*. 1.192–5)—the very demigods who will number frequently among his rape-victims. Notwithstanding, Jove offers evidence for the impiety of only one man (Lycaon), reporting with apparent indifference the fact that everyone else had humbly worshipped him when he made his presence known (*Met*. 1.164–243). The lack of proportion between offence and response transforms Jupiter's alleged attempt to extirpate crime into yet another instance of crime. Similarly, Agenor's implacable command to Cadmus, 'find your sister or do not return', is an instance of criminal virtue, in Ovid's assessment: his injunction makes the king 'dutiful and criminal by virtue of the same deed' ('facto pius et sceleratus eodem', *Met*. 3.5).[64] Tension between paternal discipline and tyranny, fatherly care

---

[64] Throughout this book, I have taken my Latin text of the *Metamorphoses* from R. J. Tarrant's Oxford Classical Text edition (Tarrant 2004). All translations are my own, and aim for faithfulness to the Latin text rather than eloquence.

and sadism, regular and irregular sexual unions, informs Ovid's portraits of Jove and Agenor, and draws the two closer together, as each father-figure wavers undecidably between benevolence and cruelty, discipline and licentiousness.

Jove and Agenor at once embrace antipodes of virtue and vice, but converge upon one another insofar as the extremes of their two paternal characterizations show good and evil, crime and law as obverse and reverse of the same coin. Together, they father Thebes, in the sense of being the city's collectively necessary, but singly insufficient causal conditions.[65] The idea of the city emerges on the horizon from the moment that Agenor responds to Jupiter's abduction of Europa with his injunction to 'find Europa or don't come back'. No mortal can match wits with Jove (*Met.* 3.6–7), so Cadmus' exile and his need to establish a new home are inevitable. But unlike his father, or his sister's rapist, Cadmus is very far from an autocrat; ironically, the only command we ever see him give is to instruct his followers to fetch water for a ritual sacrifice to his unsuspected nemesis, Jupiter (*Met.* 3.26–7). Cadmus' chief characteristic is his readiness to sacrifice himself for his subjects: when the men seeking water lose their lives to the dragon haunting the pool, Cadmus risks his own life to avenge their deaths with the beast's extinction (3.58–9). He later offers himself to the gods on behalf of the city, asking them to change him into a snake if that will appease the wrath they have

---

[65] Jove may seem far removed from Theban 'paternity', given that, unlike Agenor, he has no direct contact with Cadmus. But Ovid makes the god's rape of Europa and Agenor's reaction to it the first and second links in the chain of causality leading to Thebes' founding, and in that sense, both are the city's progenitors. It is certainly all one to Juno: she rejoices in Actaeon's violent death because it afflicts the family of her rival Europa, however distant in geography and consanguinity ('a Tyria conlectum paelice transfert I in generis socios odium'—'she transfers the hatred drawn from her Tyrian rival [Europa] to the other members of the family', *Met.* 3.258–9). For all the difference it makes to his wife, Jove might as well have been progenitor to the royal house of Thebes, as he was to the royal house of Crete. Moreover, Jove, unlike Agenor, returns in person to the city he sparked. There he fathers (quite literally) the one divine force Ovid shows as shaping the city's mythohistory well beyond the royal house: Bacchus, Jove's child by the Theban princess Semele. The new god rallies the general population of Thebes to his rites, thus setting the stage for the Cadmeans' and the city's further disasters (such as the violent death of Bacchus' cousin, King Pentheus, at the hands of his mother and aunt; Ch. 6 below addresses this story in more detail).

regularly visited upon Thebes (4.574–5). Jupiter and Agenor as two menacing extremes-that-touch paradoxically create the circumstances under which an entirely good man becomes king.

Yet good King Cadmus establishes and presides over a Thebes punctually visited by disaster. Thebes' first citizens are the Spartoi: 'the Sown Men' spring from the serpent's teeth Athena commanded Cadmus to plant. Far from cohering as a community, the dragon-brothers' first act is to engage in inexplicable and spontaneous civil war. Only Athena's intervention eventually halts the slaughter (3.102–30). Thebes' subsequent history unfolds as a series of bizarre metamorphoses and violent deaths visited upon various members of the royal household, often at the hands of their own kin. The mystery inheres in how everything can be so right with the King, and so wrong with his city. It is as if the two baleful fathers of Thebes, Jupiter and Agenor, managed to infect the city even at a distance of time and space. How is that possible? And what exactly do these two fathers have to say to Ovid's contemporary Rome?

These questions require both a transhistorical and transcultural perspective, if we are to account rigorously for why the mythology of a Greek backwater town pertains to the lived experience of an Italian world-city.[66] In this regard, too, Lacanian psychoanalysis offers a useful intellectual framework. As noted in the previous section, the broad structures organizing Lacan's subject and the world that transects and shapes her are universal and transhistorical (as I shall detail below)—yet exactly this fundamental continuity throws into sharper relief disjunctions across time, space, and cultures. While the psychoanalytic concept of 'trauma' names the persistent kernel of unintelligibility and illegibility within the subject and her world, historically specific narratives enfold that unassimilable kernel. They mark the rifts and discontinuities in ideology, in discourse—in what counts for reason at a specific historical and cultural moment—while simulta-

---

[66] And not only in Ovid's eyes: Varro also construes Rome and Thebes as twin cities. Thebes he names as the oldest of all cities, having been founded by King Ogygus some 2,100 years ago; though only 700-some years old, Rome is Thebes' corollary as the most ancient city on Roman territory (*Rust.* 3.1.2–7). Varro indicates that Ovid did not invent the 'mirroring relationship' between the two cities, but rather drew upon a connection already established for the Romans, a connection whose principles the *Metamorphoses* imaginatively elaborates. (My thanks to the anonymous reader who drew my attention to this passage in *De Re Rustica*.)

neously attempting to 'explain away' such ruptures. The narrative of the Roman family and of the father's role within it is one such paradoxical narrative crucially germane to Ovid's own times. I address it first, so as to make historical specifics the framework within which to essay the broader embrace of Lacan's thought.

Composing in the generation after Vergil, Ovid wrote the *Metamorphoses* when Augustus had all but fully entrenched his new regime. The political system Augustus crystallized entirely redefined the *res publica*, such that the social and political institutions of a republic now appeared to support the idea of one-man rule.[67] His promulgation of the family as nucleus and ideal model for the state was critical to this transformation. Although the idea of the family as the commonweal's basic unit was not new—Cicero and Aristotle had asserted as much (Cic. *Off.* 1.54; Ar. *EN* 1160^a–1161^a)—it conceptually fits a *de facto* monarchy far better than a republic. A Roman family had only one, male head, the father. It was thus at some fundamental level unsuited to model 'the public thing',[68] wherein elite Roman male citizens more or less equally competed for state offices and the dominion that accrued to them. Yet the family's embodiment of an inegalitarian, hierarchical order of power and authority aptly mirrored Augustus' consolidation of rule. The regulation of relations between Man and Woman signally marked his paternalistic sway (just as we noted in Agenor's and Jupiter's cases). Augustus introduced legislation that criminalized adultery, promoted marital fecundity while penalizing the childless, and dictated who could freely wed whom.[69] He read to the Senate, and recommended to the people, the entirety of Quintus Metellus' speech 'On the Need for Larger Families'[70] (Suetonius, *Divus Augustus* 89). He promoted his own family—their marriages, children, and public conduct—as models of morality and citizenship. The monuments of his regime centred the state's ideal functioning upon marriage and

---

[67] The following discussion of the relation between family and state as an Augustan ideologeme is heavily indebted to Beth Severy's and Kristina Milnor's shrewd and learned expositions of the topic (Severy 2003, Milnor 2005).

[68] The literal meaning of the Latin phrase *res publica*.

[69] The *Lex Iulia de adulteriis* and *Lex Iulia de maritandis ordinibus*, passed in 18–17 BCE.

[70] Delivered when Metellus was censor in 131 BCE (Livy, *Ep.* 59).

progeny, as exemplified by the images on the Ara Pacis Augustae ('the Altar of August Peace'). The sculpted faces of Augustus' family exemplify the productive peace he has brought to Rome, as the royal household's husbands, wives, and children gather to offer sacrifice to the goddess Pax. Drawing from ancient myth rather than contemporary personalities, Augustus' restoration of the Basilica Aemilia showed the rape of the Sabine women, the founding act of Roman marriage. When these women later interpose their bodies to bring peace between their warring husbands and fathers, their selflessness exemplifies virtuous wifely and daughterly conduct.

By contrast, those women who simultaneously threatened marriage and the state appear as cautionary effigies. Matching the Basilica's virtuous Sabines is Tarpeia, the perfidious Roman Vestal who necessitated their risky intervention. She admitted Sabine soldiers to Rome's fortress, and was killed at their king's command. Whether a traitor for love of Sabine king or Sabine gold,[71] she represents female desire and agency out of control—the very antipode to the Sabine brides' subordination of self to family loyalty.[72] A similar instance of disaster wrought by female self-involvement decorated the ivory doors to the Temple of Apollo Augustus built within his Palatine complex. One panel depicted Queen Niobe's punishment when she had boasted that her marital fertility surpassed Leto's; she drew upon her offspring the deadly wrath of Leto's child, Apollo. Lest we miss the point that wifely hubris has undermined both Niobe's family and her nation, the matching panel shows national hubris effecting the same end: Apollo drives the terrified Gauls from their disastrous assault on Delphi.[73] All these public animadversions to marriage,

---

[71] For greed: Livy 1.11.6–9; Ovid, *Fasti* 1.261–2; for love: Propertius 4.4.

[72] Natalie Kampen has cogently argued for dating the Basilica's frieze to the years just after restoration began in 14 BCE and for its subject matter as designedly reflecting the emperor's own interests; my discussion of its images summarizes her work. The Basilica's frieze mirrors the concerns of Augustus' moral legislation of the same period, which regulates sexuality and procreation; he also paid for the Basilica's restoration, which strongly suggests that it served his advantage to do so. I believe Kampen has demonstrated just exactly how the frieze's images advanced the emperor's agenda (Kampen 1991).

[73] In 279 BCE Pausanias records the details of the Gauls' generally ill-fated expedition against Greece; according to him, Delphi was the occasion of their definitive rout and subsequent attempt to retreat (Pausanias 10.19–24).

children, community and to what threatens all three align family and state as correlative objects of the emperor's concern. Not by accident does the Senate name Augustus *pater patriae* in 2 BCE.

Of course, in that same year, the emperor exiled his only daughter Julia for the crime of adultery to a primitively accommodated island. A decade later (8 CE), his granddaughter Julia repeated her mother's crime and suffered the same fate. Augustus may not have been completely surprised; well before the crisis of the elder Julia's banishment, he regularly expressed dubiety regarding the general modesty of her conduct (Macrobius, *Saturnalia* 2.5.3–7). But when in palmier days Augustus joked about that conduct, he tellingly mapped family onto state. He quipped to his friends that he had two gadabout daughters, Julia and Rome, who both gave him trouble.[74] His friends could have responded that whatever accounted for Rome's misconduct, the two Julias came by their profligacy honestly; Augustus had the name of a womanizer. His wife Livia was herself reputed to procure virgins for his delectation (Suetonius, *Div. Aug.* 69, 71). Ovid's licentious Jupiter may allude to the scandalous side of Augustus' reputation. But given that the poet yoked the god's cruelty and randiness to Agenor's harsh austerity, Thebes' two fathers more particularly exemplify Ovid's gift for exposing the soft underbelly of any ideology, including paternal authority. After all, Augustus found that ideology ready to hand when he began constructing himself as father of his country. The contradictions of paternity that manifest themselves in Thebes' history are fundamental rather than merely contingent. Lacan can help explicate with rigour Ovid's delineation of these contradictions by unfolding exactly how and why the conceptualization of the Father necessarily comes to grief.

Lacan's meditations on the Father as both the ordering centre of the human community, and the menace that must be excluded in order for that community to come into being, help us trace a precise logical connection between both of Thebes' contrasting proto-parents and its eventual doom. Lacan recurs to Freud's two

---

[74] 'Itaque inter amicos dixit duas habere se filias delicatas, quas necesse haberet ferre, rem publicam et Iuliam'—'in fact, among friends, he said that he had two gadabout daughters that he had to put up with, the Republic and Julia' (Macrobius, *Sat.* 2.5.4).

most significant formulations of the father-figure, the Oedipus complex[75] and *Totem and Taboo*, rethinking their significance for the
individual subject and for the formation and regulation of society.
Lacan's 'return to Freud'[76] read Freud's work in a structured and
logical way (including its gaps and silences) so as to reveal certain
implicit patterns of thought. In order to develop the full implications
of these patterns, he deployed post-Freudian developments in various humanist disciplines. Structuralist linguistics heavily influenced
his initial formulations of the father's function, which he linked with
the institution of language. He punningly glosses the role of father
as the 'Non/Nom-du-Père' (also known as the 'paternal metaphor').
The Father's prohibitive force (his 'No') is reducible to a substance-
less though potent signifier (his name). But the insubstantiality of
paternity also points to the son's ability to inherit that name and to
occupy the place of the father. The Father thus figures the promise of
upward mobility—the promise that in a system based on intersubjective exchange, including the exchange of signifiers, everyone's
desire can ultimately find its place. The chain of signifiers that links
subjects in discourse both moulds and situates these subjects within a
social network, making of their desire the foundation for a community, most especially their desire for identity.

   This description of the Father's function illustrates Lacan elaborating chiefly upon Freud's formulation of the Oedipus complex. But
as Charles Shepherdson notes, another side to the Father emerged
within Lacan's meditations around 1960, when he began to doubt the
paternal metaphor could be established so cleanly or unequivocally.[77]
At that point, Lacan sketched what Jacques-Alain Miller has called

---

[75] The term 'Oedipus complex' does not appear until 1910, but the outlines of the
theory are already evident in the letters to Fliess (e.g. letter of 15 Oct. 1897) and begin
to be fleshed out in the 'Three Essays on Sexuality' (*SE* 7: 130–243). Freud refined his
ideas about the Oedipus complex throughout his lifetime, returning to it even in
'Female Sexuality' (*SE* 21: 225–43) and the *New Introductory Lectures on Psychoanalysis* (*SE* 22: 5–182), published respectively eight and six years before his death in
1939.
   [76] Self-styled, as in the title to his lecture to the Neuro-Psychiatric Clinic of
Vienna, 7 Nov. 1955: 'La chose freudienne, *ou* Sens du retour à Freud en psychanalyse' (Lacan 1966, 401).
   [77] Shepherdson 2000, 117–18. The cited pages are to be found in Shepherdson's
essay entitled 'From Oedipus Rex to *Totem and Taboo*'. In the discussion that follows,

'the formula of the second paternal metaphor', which 'corresponds point-by-point to the formula of the Name-of-the-Father', but that nonetheless forces us to operate with the 'inexistence' and 'inconsistency' of the Symbolic.[78] This second formulation turns to Freud's second meditation on the Father, which reaches beyond the conscience-stricken king of Greek tragedy to an obscene, baleful figure lost to the obscurity of prehistory. This is the primal father of *Totem and Taboo*.

The four essays collected in Freud's 1913 publication render in psychoanalytic terms the logic of, and the relation between, two phenomena of tribal society. These are

1. the totem, defined as the animal held sacred by the clan as a subdivision of the tribe. All the clan members identify with the totem, which thus brokers their identity as a unified group;[79]
2. the taboo, which is at its base a ban on touching a designated object, exemplified in the near-universal prohibition on incest.

Incest fuses the concept and consequences of both phenomena by forbidding intercourse between any two members of the same totem, so that avoiding incest by exogamy delineates clan membership.[80] Freud's explanation for these intimately linked concepts posits as their cause an aboriginal monster, a tyrannical father based on Darwin's idea of the 'primal horde' as the *Ur* social unit.[81] Within the primal horde, this all-powerful father kept the women of the family for himself, while driving away his sons as potential pretenders to his place. But one day (Freud speculates), the excluded sons rose up in resentment against their father, killed him, and ate him in a cannibalistic feast aimed at incorporating some of his power in each of his murderers. However, beset by guilt at their own deed, they all agreed to forswear the very object for which they had shed blood: the women of the horde. Women had now to be exchanged exogamously

---

I have relied heavily upon that essay's thoughtful and lucid exposition of how Lacan's thought on paternity evolved.

[78] Miller 1994, 85.

[79] Freud, *SE* 13: 2–3.

[80] Freud, *SE* 13: 4, 27.

[81] Darwin 1986–9, 22: 614–15 (from *The Descent of Man*, originally published 1871).

with other groups; hence the inception of the incest taboo. In addition, the sons designated the totem animal as the representative of the father. To 'undo' their cannibalistic patricide, they forbade the eating or exploitation of this animal in any fashion, except as part of a ritual slaughter and feast in which the whole clan participated and bore the symbolic guilt collectively.[82]

Though overtly framed as an inquiry into 'the origin of religion and morality',[83] *Totem and Taboo* scrutinizes the way these overlapping sets of prohibitions create an ordered society. Freud essentially poses the question, How does the clan—an ordered association of members with more or less equal rights governed by law—spring from the disorganized, tyrannical primal horde? More simply, How do the abstract, egalitarian, rule-bound ties of a society emerge from the blood ties of a hierarchical family for whom the father and law are one? The question implicitly posed by Ovid's Thebes as the bastard child of Agenor and Jupiter's egoism mirrors but reverses Freud's: Given the regulated community's occluded genesis in tyranny and exploitation, how, why, and in what form does the primal Father return to perturb the commonweal? Freud's answer to the question of origins may well give us pause as dubious anthropological history; Freud himself wavered over whether his story of aboriginal murder should be taken as historical fact, or as a fantasy that nonetheless had the status of a psychical reality, able to inspire symptoms across succeeding generations.[84] Yet the principles it sketches illuminate the seamy underside of the polity's genesis, and so illuminate the grim history of Thebes as paradigmatic Doomed City.

From Freud's speculations on human prehistory Lacan gleaned the idea of a punishing and perverse underside to the Symbolic law, exemplified in the guilt the sons feel at the death of their father. Their continued adherence to the laws they have imposed upon themselves in the wake of their father's death, and even upon their descendants, indicates that compunction still haunts them. As Shepherdson points out, this flatly contradicts the order of justice articulated in the myth of Oedipus, wherein self-reproach accrues only to the transgressor of the

[82] Freud, *SE* 13: 141–5.
[83] Freud, *SE* 13: xv.
[84] Freud, *SE*: 157–61.

law.[85] In theory, the same ought to be true of the Symbolic Father's function: only those who violate his prohibitions should feel guilty. But experience does not confirm this; a blameless life and a racked conscience are not uncommon yoke-fellows. The repentant clan-brothers' self-imposed penitential restrictions come closer to this irrational concomitance: guilt attaches to those who *follow* the law. To explain these phenomena, Lacan postulates the existence of a perverse feature within paternity, an element of transgression not opposed to law, but belonging to law itself. This element marks the Symbolic order as incomplete or excessive (insufficiency and superfluity amounting to the same thing, since what is missing and what is in excess both lack a proper place within an organizing structure). The Symbolic contains (in every sense of that word) a pathological remainder.[86]

RSI

A precise assessment of the ontological status of that remainder requires positioning the Symbolic in relation to its corollaries, the Imaginary and the Real; it is to this last category that the pathological excess within the Symbolic belongs. The Real, the Symbolic, and the Imaginary divide human experience among them and form an interlocking system (often abbreviated 'RSI'). Lacan referred to these three elements of his schema as 'registers'; they are intertwined, simultaneous worlds of experience, analogous to registers in music. Briefly, the Real is the realm of pure being without relation or determination, comprising that which is forbidden entry into representation. Nothing is either present or lacking in the Real, since the ideas of absence or presence require the prior concepts of division and distinction—concepts native to the Imaginary and especially to the Symbolic, but not to the seamless Real. The Imaginary is so named as the realm of images, not of the imagination—our own

---

[85] It is true all of Thebes suffers from the plague that Oedipus' transgressions call down upon the city, but only Oedipus ever reproaches himself (cf. *OT* 1287–9, 1381–5, 1433, 1440–1)—logically enough, since he is the only Theban to have offended, albeit unwittingly.

[86] Shepherdson 2000, 119, 144.

shadows cast upon the world. It is a narcissistic and aggressive realm wherein projections of self onto phenomena conjure both affirming reflections of ourselves and doppelgänger rivals threatening to supplant us. The Symbolic is the realm of exchange and sociality, comprising semiotics (paradigmatically language), institutions and protocols. The Real is not reality per se, but rather the 'beyond' of both realms that can only be conceived as amorphous nullity—and yet is not exterior to the Symbolic and the Imaginary, but rather marks their point of internal limitation.[87] In the Symbolic specifically, the Real is perceptible at any point where a supposedly sovereign rationale confronts an incompatible but not inherently refutable element,[88] and where it thus 'visibly *fails* to disambiguate itself'.[89] For example, the Real intrudes upon the Symbolic in the fantastical shapes of hallucinations and neurotic symptoms, which despite having no material basis exert powerful influence on human lives. Such delusion eliminates Spartoi blood from the Theban royal house: King Pentheus, child of Agave and the Spartos Echion, appears to his mother, aunts, and their fellow Bacchae to be a wild boar to be hunted down and killed (*Met.* 3.710–31). That the Theban women's madness overtakes them in worship also underlines the Realness of the divine. The gods are of the Real, because they, too, lack nothing and so both contradict and transcend whatever rules govern limited mortality. Where immortals intervene in the Symbolic with portents or oracles, the irreducible ambiguity of these signs reveals their provenance in the Real. Divine prophecy predicts the future by virtue of being misunderstood: clear-sighted, fully knowledgeable interpretation would prevent what is augured from arriving punctually. In the Theban cycle, prophecy is freely dispensed: Cadmus is told he will end his life as a snake (3.97–8), Narcissus that he must not know himself (348), Pentheus that he will stain his kinswomen with his blood (521–5). Prophecy is just as uniformly and necessarily misinterpreted. A Cadmus who grasped the difference between metamorphosis and guilt would not sacrifice his humanness to redeem Thebes (4.571–5). A Narcissus who fathomed what it meant to know

---

[87] Miller 2004, 5, 10.
[88] Žižek 1992, 72.
[89] Copjec 1994: 176–7.

himself would avoid reflection (3.415–17). A Pentheus who understood just how his kin could be bloodied would better estimate Bacchus' 'unmartial' crowd (3.531–42, 553–6). But such perspicacity would short-circuit predicted events and make game of the gods. The three aspects of the RSI triad—self-projection, social and linguistic codes, and the unintelligible limits of both—all work together in the examples listed above to sweep greater Thebes toward disaster. Mapping the complex detail of their interaction in subsequent chapters will illustrate the triad's usefulness for analysing Ovid's Thebans and his Thebes as exemplars of political subjects and the polity. As Paul Allen Miller notes, RSI's conceptual scaffolding allows us to theorize the relation of self to community without simply opposing one to the other, nor making either the other's shadow. Neither is this an essentialist troika of eternal verities: each term relativizes and recontextualizes the others. No one Imaginary, no one Symbolic obtains, only specific examples that relate to one another in different ways—nor is there any one Real. Because the Real marks the limits of any self-projection and any communal system of norms and codes, it also marks the varied ways in which any given ideological system or personal projection comes up against its own finitude.[90]

But where is the Father in all this? His place within the triad can best be mapped against the emergence of the human subject from the living being. The Real delimits this emergence within the Imaginary and the Symbolic, an intervention that can be summarized as two separate, hypothetical moments. (These moments mark logical priority rather than temporal succession, punctuating the subject's always-simultaneous participation in all three RSI registers.) By constituting a point beyond the subject, the Father first intervenes as the cut that separates the Real from the Imaginary and the Symbolic. He is the other who returns to the subject an image of her own unity and control of the physical world, like a reflection in a mirror.[91] Any other of either biological sex can perform this function; the Father

---

[90] Miller 2004, 5.

[91] 'L'assomption jubilatoire de son image spéculaire par l'être encore plongé dans l'impuissance motrice et la dépendance du nourrissage qu'est le petit homme à ce stade *infans*, nous paraîtra dès lors manifester en une situation exemplaire la matrice symbolique où le *je* se précipite en une forme primordiale' ('Le Stade de Miroir', *Écrits*, p. 94).

is simply a convenient label for this office. Yet the image of unity He grants paradoxically splits the subject between 'here', and 'over there' where her reflection is, organizing her identity around a gap or lack. The perceived image is both the basis for jubilant identification, as confirmation of the subject's majesty, and for aggressive jealousy, as a rivalrous other who threatens to usurp the subject's proper place.

This model of the subject split between the Real and the (as-yet undifferentiated) Imaginary/Symbolic excavates the roots of psycho-analysis's deep pessimism regarding the human subject's potential for sociality.[92] These roots strike deep into Hegelianism, as Lacan's mirror image underlines: the subject and her equivocal image reproduce Hegel's Master/Slave dialectic, in which two mutually dependent, mutually defining antagonists 'struggle to the death' for 'recognition' (*Anerkennung*). Each antagonist strives to be recognized as an independent subject (rather than a dependent object) by the other as independent subject, purely and without condition. The internal contradictions of that goal utterly thwart its fulfilment: a subject who relies upon another's recognition to found her subjectivity is by definition not independent. Moreover, the wish that this recognition take place 'purely and without condition' means it must be rendered freely, without compulsion or ulterior motive on the other's part. Any suspicion that fear of offence, a wish to curry favour, irony, or any other *arrière-pensée* tinges the other's recognition will reduce the subject to an object, regarded as a means to an end rather than an end in herself. Like the mirror-image, the other is to self both a source of self-affirmation and a source of anxiety.[93] The Father thus precipitates the subject into a self-concept founded on misrecognition and rivalry. Ovid's Thebes regularly witnesses the grim consequences of a self defined in conflict, as subjects seek to establish a self inviolate by eliminating the mirroring other. Diana, Juno, and Bacchus all meet their mortal counterparts respectively in the hunter Actaeon, Jove's

---

[92] A pessimism manifest in progressively greater degrees in Freud's social and cultural studies, such as *Beyond the Pleasure Principle* (1920), *Group Psychology and the Analysis of the Ego* (1921), *The Future of an Illusion* (1927), *Civilization and its Discontents* (1929), and *Moses and Monotheism* (1939). All these read the proverbial state of nature as interminable conflict.

[93] The core of my summary comes from §180–§183 in the *Phenomenology of Spirit* (Hegel 1977).

consort Semele, and the would-be coryphaeus of Theban hearts and minds, King Pentheus. All these gods see all these human reflections as threats to their essential majesty, and so destroy them.

But however fraught with tension, the subject's perception of the mirror-other conceptually enables the Father's next incision, between the Imaginary and the Symbolic. The subject who identifies herself with a discrete, fixed, and stable image can also imagine objects of constancy and identity in the world. From this flows the idea of equivalence between objects, grounded in their recognizable, if putative, permanence.[94] The void round which the subject's identity is organized motivates the pursuit of such objects, in a (doomed) attempt to 'fullfill' that lack. Equivalence makes her pursuit possible by laying the ground for exchange and interchange, the basis of the Symbolic. The subjective void that gapes in the Imaginary will be reduplicated in the Symbolic: not just language, but the whole mesh of Symbolic relations that constitute her social being reflect the subject back to herself.[95] Hence Lacan's alternative name for the Symbolic: 'the (Big) Other'. The Symbolic network of social and linguistic relations functions as does the antagonist in the Master/Slave dialectic. Like Hegel's opposing duellist, it offers the point of reference from which the subject's existence depends. Once distinguished from the Imaginary, the Symbolic conjures the Father as the Name-of-the-Father. No longer a rival to be overcome, but an irrevocable law, the Name-of-the-Father references a principle of mediation, difference, and intersubjectivity wherein every subject's desire will find its place.[96]

Yet all these humanizing separations have their disruptive residua. The line drawn between the Real on the one hand, and the Symbolic and Imaginary on the other, gives rise to four phenomena, four conceptually related aspects of the unrepresentable inferable within the realms of representation. All four phenomena particularize the baleful, mesmerizing power of the Real Father (the Father of Enjoyment), the perverse counterpart to the Symbolic Father (the Name-of-the-Father).

---

[94] Rose 1986, 173.
[95] Salecl 2000, 3.
[96] Shepherdson 2000, 128.

1. The first corollary of the Real's division from the Symbolic and Imaginary is what Lacan calls the Thing. Because this separation is logically prior to symbolization, this loss cannot be represented, but simply persists as the 'black hole' round which desire, and the subject's being, is organized. Calling this void 'the Thing' draws on Kant and on Freud, insofar as transcendental idealism and psychoanalysis both designate as *das Ding* an entity that is radically unknowable. The Thing has the status of a noumenon, in the strictly Kantian sense: it is not a possible object of experience, only to be posited in the mind as a conceptual placeholder, measuring the limits of sensible knowledge and of pure understanding.[97]

[97] Cf. Kant, *KrV* A256/B311, A289/B345. Lacan signals that he has borrowed the term *das Ding* from both Kant and Freud in his seventh seminar, *L'ethique de la psychanalyse* (Lacan 1986/1992, esp. 68/55; 71–102/71–84). However, he appropriates the term from Kant *per viam negativam*: Lacan fastens upon a use of *das Ding* that Kant repudiates as absurd. In Kant's 'Versuch den Begriff der negativen Größen', for example, the philosopher remarks that it would be ridiculous to take the negative pole of a contradiction as something positive and 'to think of a particular sort of object and to call it a negative thing' ('so würde es ungereimt sein darum eine besondere Art von Dingen sich zu gedenken und sie negative Dinge zu nennen', Kant 1902–, 2: 174–5). But this is precisely what Lacan does when he defines *das Ding* as that which structures all human reality and yet can only be found as missed (Lacan 1986, 65/1992, 52).

This side of the conceptualization of *das Ding* Lacan derives from Freud, particularly from the very early and never published *Project for a Scientific Psychology*. In that essay, Freud speaks repeatedly of 'the thing'; around this term cluster the ideas of constancy and of unknowability—of something per se excluded from thought processes, but nonetheless persistently organizing cognitions and/or symptoms that point to itself (cf. *SE* 1: 328, 331, 349).

Lacan offers a definition of *das Ding* in Seminar VII that alludes to this Freudian perspective: 'The world of our experience, the Freudian world, assumes that it is this object, *das Ding*, as the absolute Other of the subject, that one is supposed to find again. It is to be found at the most as something missed. One doesn't find it, but only its pleasurable associations. It is in this state of wishing for it and waiting for it that, in the name of the pleasure principle, the optimum tension will be sought; below that there is neither perception nor effort.

'In the end, in the absence of something which hallucinates it in the form of a system of references, a world of perception cannot be organized in a valid way, cannot be constituted in a human way. The world of perception is represented by Freud as dependent on that fundamental hallucination without which there would be no attention available' (Lacan 1992, 52–53; the French text can be found in Lacan 1986, 65–66). For further exposition of *das Ding* and its role in structuring human experience, see Žižek 1991b, 160–9, and Žižek 2001, 141–89. I have relied greatly upon Žižek's illuminating discussions.

2. The second result is the subject's retrospective, unconscious construction of a paradisal plenitude supposedly once enjoyed, a fantasy in which desire and lack have no place. This fantasy combines the blissful and the fatal, insofar as the subject exists only by virtue of her division from the homogeneous and undifferentiated realm of the Real. To regain that imagined primal Eden would therefore unravel the subject. Lacan organized the intrusions of this deadly bliss into the Symbolic under the term *jouissance*, or 'enjoyment'. Stripped to its essentials, *jouissance* can be defined as the point of breakdown in a logical system, one of the points where the Real becomes visible within the Symbolic as deadlock. But the gap in the system that is *jouissance* also exerts a powerful, potentially destructive fascination—the power to overthrow the order of the subject, for good or ill.

3. The third outcome of the cut is *objet a*. The particular object-causes of desire that Lacan calls *objets a* are not defined as a discrete set of particular things: anything can, in theory, become an *objet a*. Rather, they pivot upon a relation to loss. Fundamentally, *objet a* is the primordially lost object, emblematic of the paradise from which the subject was putatively expelled upon emerging from the Real.[98] As such, *objet a* simultaneously marks, and covers over, a gap or lack in the Symbolic, as a memorandum of the Real within the Symbolic. Fantasy rather than the objectively specifiable properties of the object conditions the subject's relation to *objet a*, which in turn both covers over and points obliquely to the unrepresentable Thing. The paths described by the desiring subject in pursuing various *objets a* make the contours of the Thing emerge by bending around it, just as gravity— the universal force of physical attraction between objects—bends space in the Einsteinian universe. From time to time a particular *objet a* will be elevated to the status of the Thing; then it will no longer be seen as exchangeable, but command unswerving allegiance. Yet, as with *jouissance*, there can be no direct encounter with the Thing without negating the path whereby the subject became a subject, which would undo her. Our innermost desires must remain hidden in the Unconscious; where and when they emerge—where the

---

[98] Rose 1986, 182–3; Borch-Jacobsen, 1991, 229–30.

Thing sends us ciphered messages in the form of disturbing symptoms, of radically unacceptable *objets a*—they beckon toward psychosis.

4. The fourth outcome is the superego, a direct heir to the primal Father, and incarnating His commands. This Father is entirely bent on His own pleasure, which is conceived by the subject as unlimited, so that His interest lies in prohibiting anyone else from such pleasure. The captious superego legitimizes nothing, it simply imposes rules. Because the superego deprives the law of its normative meaning—the sense that 'to do such-and-so is enough, it satisfies conscience'—its senseless law actually undermines the law as a self-consistent, just system.

All four phenomena manifest themselves in the inflections of doom specific to Ovid's Thebes, as I shall detail fully in the chapters that follow. Let just one storyline sketch in brief how these tokens of the Real impinge upon Boeotia. Juno and Jupiter's internecine Sex Wars culminate ruinously in the Theban cycle; while the *Metamorphoses* contains many tales of desire that go fatally awry, only the Theban cycle so clearly links desire to radical loss and to the limits of knowledge. When god and goddess quarrel over which sex gets more pleasure from intercourse, each avows that the other is thus privileged at her/his expense (3.316–22).[99] Their disagreement conceptualizes desire as an irremediable relation, not just to lack, but to loss: 'The other sex has possession of an enjoyment that is rightly mine.' They see relations between the sexes as bliss stolen by the other; that resentful yearning reproduces the Lacanian subject's relation to *jouissance*, to *objet a*, and ultimately to the Thing behind both. Juno and Jupiter's mutually invidious conclusion glosses their intensifying sexual strife as a crescendo wherein Jupiter embodies the Real Father's licentiousness and Juno His sadistic superego: he seeks a growing number of sex objects whom she finds increasingly horrible ways to punish. But their core *disputanda*, (non)knowledge and

---

[99] In theory, Juno could disagree on the basis of the belief that pleasure is equally allotted to men and to women, but antiquity never seems to imagine that egalitarian arrangement between the sexes' relative pleasure (Gantz 1993, 529). By common agreement, women are the lustier of the two sexes: cf. e.g. Prop. 3.19, Ovid, *Ars* 1.275–342.

desire, only spill into the human sphere when they choose transsexual Tiresias to adjudicate their wrangle over sex; the outcome closely connects desire to the inconceivable. Tiresias sides with Jupiter, whereupon Juno blinds the man for purporting thus to fathom Woman. Jupiter compensates him with second sight, an incomprehensible wisdom insofar as it claims truth value but cannot account for itself rationally (3.322–38). But the effects of the dispute eventually penetrate even more deeply and destructively among mortals: the new prophet is the one who warns the *Metamorphoses*' first human lover against self-knowledge. When asked by Narcissus' mother, Liriope, whether her son would enjoy longevity, Tiresias replies that the boy will have long life only 'if he does not know himself' (3.346–8).[100] The logical corollary of the soothsayer's pronouncement is that if Narcissus *does* come to know himself, the subject of that knowledge will not see old age. Narcissus qua knowing subject of himself will cease to be, either because he dies or—always the other possibility in the *Metamorphoses*—because he changes into someone/something else. Tiresias thus articulates the boy's nemesis as a noumenon, an object impossible of experience for Narcissus qua knowing subject. Narcissus eventually proves the truth of the warning when he knows himself to be his own object of desire: that revelation promptly unravels Narcissus' self, driving him into madness.[101] What Narcissus cannot know—cannot know and still be an integrated subject—and what he truly desires prove to be the two interdependent sides of his self-destruction.[102] This and the other

---

[100]
> de quo consultus, an esset
> tempora maturae uisurus longa senectae,
> fatidicus uates 'si se non nouerit' inquit.
>
> (*Met.* 3.346–8)

When consulted about whether [Narcissus] would see the extended hours of a ripe old age, the doomsaying prophet replied, 'if he does not know himself'.

[101] The measure of Narcissus' madness is that after learning he has fallen passionately in love with his own image, he reverts to addressing that image as though it were another independent person, begging his reflection not to desert him (*Met.* 3. 477–9).

[102] Shadi Bartsch reaches a similar conclusion in her examination of the Narcissus tale as a meditation on the connection between vision and philosophy, sight and insight: 'In Ovid's hands, and *because of the uniquely Ovidian insertion of a prophecy about self-knowledge*, the story becomes one that is not only about love, vision, and

stories that interlock about Juno and Jupiter's polemic mould Boeotian perdition around the relation of desire to the Real.

Not by accident do the residua of the Real manifest themselves
within a narrative of city-founding. The Thing, *jouissance, objet a,*
and the superego organize subjectivity in a way that constitutes both
the chief impetus and the chief stumbling block to intersubjectivity;
they shape the weal and woe of individuals and of the ordered
community. *Totem and Taboo* best illustrates how all four concepts
fit together in a political context. To begin with, the taboo object is a
species of *objet a,* marking a certain Real excess generated by the
Symbolic itself. Once blood-ties are supplanted by the more abstract
relations that define the clan, the taboo is a function of the clan's self-
constitution within the Symbolic. That constitution depends on the
redeployment of signs and the common observance of social protocols. In Freud's account, the Father during His ascendancy *is* power:
power inheres in His person, and law exists only as an extension of
His will. By participating in the cannibalistic devouring of the
Father's body, the patricidal sons erase that sign of power. At the
same time, each incorporates in himself a share of the Father's power,
and a share of the crime in killing Him. The observances that emerge
after the murder are still forms of the Father's will: the incest taboo
continues to veto the sons' access to the women of the clan, and the
sacred status of the totem animal in its exceptionalism reflects the
Father's superiority. Yet these prohibitions also abstract and detach
power from the Father's person, redistributing it elsewhere within
the body politic. The totem animal represents the Father, but also
localizes and limits His power. And insofar as the clan supposes a
mystical connection between each of its members and the totem, the
animal becomes a signifier in which they root their collective identity,
rather than in the Father's material body. The totem's corollary
proscription, the incest taboo, also grounds an egalitarian common-

---

the self, but also about philosophy: if the story is erotic because the act of seeing leads
to love, it is also philosophical because the gaze mirrored upon the self leads to what
Ovid has chosen to call self-knowledge. And it functions as well as a warning, because
*when looking and loving meet up with knowing—that is, when Narcissus realizes that
his specular double is himself—he dies there, by the side of the pond'* (Bartsch 2006, 85;
my emphases).

alty insofar as the exogamous exchange of women establishes a principle of reciprocity. Both the totem sanctified and incest repudiated conjure law as an abstract set of prohibitions separate from the will of any one member of the clan.[103] Yet however reasonable the proscriptions that flow from the totem's sacred status, the animal's objectively specifiable properties cannot account for that status. The totem founds a rule-based system unable to explain the totem itself. The opacity of the totem's fascination marks it as *objet a*, and as logically correlative with the primal Father's occlusion. The paradox of *objet a* is to be both the foundation of Symbolic law, and illegible within that law—just as the elimination of the primal Father in a bloody furore mysteriously allows an abstract, regulated order of cohesion to emerge among the brothers.

The concomitant of the totem, the incest taboo, draws *jouissance* into relation with *objet a* and with the Father of Enjoyment, the tyrannical, licentious underside of the law that upholds the brothers' society.[104] The women of the clan, forbidden to clansmen by the interdiction on incest, exemplify the way that a fantasy of the stolen plenum underpins the object of praeternatural desire. Once upon a time, Freud's tale imagines, the primordial Father enjoyed fully, he controlled and kept to himself all the women of the horde. But once the Father was overthrown, no one of the brothers could assume His place, could attain that *jouissance*. To do so would fundamentally destroy the equivalence among clan members, and the clan's exogamous relations of exchange with outsiders. In sum, it would demolish the Symbolic codes that define the clan. The tabooed women both mark, and cover over, an imagined loss of fascinating and dangerous enjoyment. They mark it insofar as no clansman can enjoy them as the Father did; they cover it over, inasmuch as being willingly renounced, they commemorate the clan's triumph over the Father.

In this tense play between dispossession and renunciation, the superego becomes visible. As mentioned, the guilt accruing

---

[103] I am much indebted for these observations to Mark Blackell's lucid discussion of *Totem and Taboo* (Blackell 2001).

[104] Cf. e.g. the discussion of the connection between *jouissance* and the primal Father in Lacan's 1971 Seminar, 'D'un discours qui ne serait pas du semblant' (Lacan 2006*b*, 177–178).

to the brothers after the death of the primal Father paradoxically accompanies their adherence to the law His death establishes, rather than its violation. This guilt implies the existence of a perspective from which the subject is always judged to come up short. Though the Father must be killed or excluded for the group to come into existence, He can never be entirely expunged. Perversely, He keeps returning in the form of the superego, a hypercritical, persistent semblance of the primal Father's omnipotence and cruelty. *Jouissance*, *objet a*, and the superego are all interdependent; all emerge when the law of the Symbolic is imposed upon the living being, so as to yield the subject. They are the three by-products of this imposition that can appear in the Symbolic (the Thing being excluded by definition). They all betoken a plenitude of being imagined as gone, a plenitude associated with the Real and the Real Father. Yet they are not the remainders of some primitive bliss, but fundamentally different phenomena generated by the Symbolic itself. Their pathological side is evident in the mesmerizing but destructive power of *jouissance* and *objet a*, and the bitter, haranguing voice of the superego.[105]

The Theban cycle repeatedly dramatizes the return of the Real Father as a power trailing the attributes of his corollaries the superego, *jouissance*, and *objet a*—a force malevolent and despotic, but also alluring, to menace Thebes and her citizens. The middle section of the cycle exemplifies this seductive violence in interlocking exercises of *force majeure*. When Bacchus and his rites burst upon Thebes, a devotee describes him as a fascinatingly pretty little boy who takes sadistic delight in playing cat-and-mouse with unbelievers (*Met*. 3.605–14, 629–86). When King Pentheus opposes Bacchus' worship, he threatens imprisonment, torture, and death, rejecting any extenuation (3.577–81, 692–5); yet Bacchus' devotee Acoetes fascinates him such that he listens to the man's long tale of miracles with patience and the wish—quite out of character—to calm his own rage (3.582–707).[106] And when Pentheus' perfervid Thebans

---

[105] Shepherdson 2000, 120–1, 146.

[106] Ovid's version of Pentheus' story is 218 lines long (*Met*. 3.513–731) and Acoetes' narrative of his conversion to Bacchus' worship occupies fully half of it (*Met*. 3.582–691 = 109 lines). Yet Pentheus—elsewhere always ungovernable and scornful of reverence toward Bacchus, always impatient and barking orders (e.g. *Met*. 3.514–15, 526, 564–73)—listens to Acoetes' every word without interruption,

witness his spying upon their Bacchic rituals, they trump both god and king in cruelty and incivism. They tear Pentheus limb from limb as he pleads for mercy, delusively exulting in victory over this 'wild boar' (3.717–18, 728). Always, before this side of the Father, the subject is proleptically guilty, the polity reduced to mob spirit.[107]

SEX AND THE CITY

One unexpected guise in which the Father of Enjoyment returns to haunt subject and community is *La Femme*, or 'Woman'. The logic of Woman's particularly tight integration of lure and threat merits detailed attention, because it can parse to a nicety what Thebes suffers from its many bewitching female persecutors (as I shall show presently). Lacan conceptually opposes 'Woman' to 'a woman', or 'women'. Shepherdson neatly illustrates the difference with set-theory: whereas 'women' in the plurality is an open set (this one and that one and that other one, without totality or essence), Woman is a fantasy that appears to incarnate the totality, to close the set of all

ostensively to calm himself (a motivation Pentheus never offers or implies before or after this moment). The anomaly makes the king's alleged intent seem like an embarrassed cover for momentary captivation by the god's power, even at second hand. (My reading of this passage assumes that the majority of scholars rightly accept 'uires *absumere*' ['diminish strength'] as the correct reading, rather than the 'uires *assumere*' ['augment strength'] that appears in some manuscripts.)

[107] It might seem incongruous to associate Bacchus with the Father, especially since the Greek mythological tradition underlines Dionysus' status as son. Not only his boyish prettiness, but the extraordinary circumstances of his gestation and birth from Zeus' thigh, mark him as his father's child. Yet the Romans eventually assimilated Dionysus to the Italian god of fertility and wine worshipped as *Liber Pater* (Bruhl 1953; Simon 1990, 126–34); perhaps for that reason, the poets regularly address Bacchus as 'pater' (for exhaustive references on this practice, see Bömer's commentary on *Met.* 13.669, 'Bacche pater, fer opem!' (Bömer 1969–86, 6.379)). In the *Fasti* specifically, Ovid speculates on why boys put on the toga of manhood at Liber's religious festival, the Liberalia. Among other reasons, the poet wonders whether Bacchus, being eternally poised between boyhood and youth, most appropriately oversees such a transition, or whether his status as father fits him to do so. Ovid does not appear to see a contradiction between the god's two roles.

women by representing Woman as such.[108] It is from this perspective that Lacan calls Woman 'one of the names of the Father',[109] meaning that both Woman and the Father of Enjoyment are imagined as totalities without lack or exception. *Totem and Taboo* shadows forth that correlation, insofar as the primal Father is conceived as a point of full enjoyment: in enjoying all the women, He enjoys 'the whole of women'—a totality equal to Woman. Neither He nor Woman are marked by the lack the subject suffers upon emerging within the Symbolic, which means that neither is 'castrated', in the Lacanian sense of that term. As entities without deficiency, both the primal Father and Woman belong to the Real; they are antithetical to the ideas of lack, desire, and exchange that organize the Symbolic.

Yet Lacan regularly cancelled Her definite article: 'La Femme' indicates Woman's status as an impossible fantasy—an idea he also expressed as 'Il n'y a pas *La* Femme' ('*The* Woman does not exist').[110] Non-existence does not weaken the power of Her mirage, anymore than the impossibility of the primal Father's position checks His force either as envied phantasm or punishing superego. The conceptual permutations of Woman and *Père Jouissant* correspond precisely: the further the paternal metaphor drifts toward the obscene, cruel Father of Enjoyment, the further Woman glides from mere object of fantasy (an *objet a*) toward the status of the Thing. She is as sinister as the Father in that guise: the Thing destroys by eliminating desire as the subject's condition of possibility. Woman as traumatic Thing takes such shapes as the Fatal Lady of courtly love, supreme object of the lover's desire and paragon of all women, yet devoid of specific properties. Reduced to her essence, the *femme fatale* comprises nothing more than a series of endless, impossible demands—the various tests of love so dear to the heroines of Roman erotic elegy, medieval romance, opera, and *film noir*.[111] Diana and Juno embody this aspect of Woman in Thebes, being two different shapes of implacable exigence brought to bear on relations between

---

[108] Shepherdson 2000, 108; cf. Lacan's remarks in his twentieth seminar on The Woman as an 'open set' (Lacan 1975, 14–15/1998, 9–10).

[109] Lacan 1976, 5.

[110] Lacan 1975, 13, 68/1998, 7, 72–73.

[111] Lacan 1986, 167–184/1992, 139–154.

the sexes. As noted, Juno enacts the Real Father's draconian censure by harrying every female her husband ever touched. By contrast, Diana focuses her anger on only one offender, Actaeon, seen as a threat to her *severa virginitas* (3.254–5). Yet both goddesses punish transgression against a law of modesty their victims were helpless to preserve: Jupiter's partners were forced into sex, and Actaeon blundered by accident upon Diana unclothed. The purity of the avengers' justice, exacted without regard to mitigating circumstances, makes it indistinguishable from malevolence. It thus reproduces the Real Father's relation to law as nothing more than the arbitrary exercise of His will.

Juno and Diana's vengeances offer particularly harrowing visions of male–female relations. Their reprisals collapse the difference not just between justice and crime, Woman and the Real Father, but also between the Real and Symbolic Fathers. The Symbolic Father's authority is supposed to guarantee conceptual boundaries; the notional waters muddied by the goddesses' savage sexual justice makes male–female interactions an impasse wherein contraries collapse. Juno and Diana's actions take the contradictions described by the subject's essential conflict with itself—a relation to the other that blurs affirmation and rivalry, narcissism and aggression—and write them large over intersexual relations. But this subjective conflict refuses to be reduced to order in intersubjectivity, least of all by social arrangements designed to produce complementarity between the sexes. Neither marriage, as represented by connubial Juno, nor sacred celibacy, as figured by militantly chaste Diana, resolves the battle of the sexes into harmonious rationality. These divine sexual failures correspond to the core of Lacan's ideas on sex. His twentieth seminar, *Encore*, maps out sexual difference as the name for a certain deadlock inherent in the Symbolic order; what he calls 'the absence of the sexual relationship' is a point of logical breakdown that resists every attempt at symbolization.[112] Sexual difference thus constitutes yet another intrusion of the Real into the Symbolic, one that marks the latter's inconsistency and insufficiency. Near the centre of *Encore*, Lacan tabulates in four graphic formulae of sexuation the non-relation between Man and ~~The~~ Woman, essentially retelling the story of

<hr/>

[112] Lacan 1975, 65/1998, 69.

the primal horde from *Totem and Taboo*. He transposes Freud's dramatic narrative of pre-history into an atemporal relation between signifiers, a logical matrix within which the consequences of sex-as-deadlock unfold. The shift from historical aetiology to formal logic highlights sexual 'taxation without representation' by tracking those formless, traumatic Real elements that nonetheless haunt the systematic organization of intersubjectivity.

The four formulae are as follows:

$$\exists x\bar{\Phi}x \qquad \bar{\exists}x\Phi x$$
$$\forall x\Phi x \qquad \bar{\forall}x\Phi x$$

$\forall$ and $\exists$ are quantifiers, standing respectively for 'all' and 'at least one'. The subject's defining lack Lacan designated with the symbol Φ. Cancellation of any of these symbols indicates its negation ($\bar{\forall}$, $\bar{\exists}$, or $\bar{\Phi}$). Φ stands for 'the phallic function', which is yet another way of designating the paternal metaphor and its twin avatars, the Real and Symbolic Fathers. The phallus is purely a signifier;[113] it designates *the* object of desire, the unattainable, unspecific-because-universal Platonic Ideal of all objects. As such, the phallus is an empty set: it corresponds to the position of the primal Father as an excluded, unattainable fantasy of complete enjoyment and mastery. But like the arithmetical cipher, the phallus as a thing of naught confers value through notional contiguity. Underwriting other objects of desire, it inspires the relations of exchange and equivalence in which the Symbolic is rooted. To that degree, it corresponds to the other (side of the) Father, the neutral, aloof figure who anchors the Symbolic and guarantees the law that subtends it. Taken together, the left- and right-hand formulae respectively map out what it means to align oneself with the signifier 'Man' or 'The Woman'—terms defined neither by biology or anatomy, but by different positions assumed toward lack and desire, the Janus-headed hinge of subjectivity.

The four formulae can be rendered as four statements. Two pertain to the position of Man:

There is one x that is not subject to the phallic function (= $\exists x\bar{\Phi}x$).

Every x is subject to the phallic function (= $\forall x\Phi x$).

---

[113] And should most certainly not be confused with the penis.

The first statement summarizes the logical positions of the primal Father and Woman: both are imagined as full and complete, therefore not subject to the phallic function, the void that constitutes the subject. The second statement summarizes the position of all us mere wanting mortals. These two formulae express in symbolic logic the relation Freud sketched in *Totem and Taboo* between the murdered primal Father and His remorseful, patricidal sons: only by virtue of an excluded exception—the dead, licentious Father—is the totality of 'all' constructed. The clan's totality comprises all those subject to castration by the incest taboo; the taboo balks each clan-member's desire, but also installs the principles of equality, reciprocity, and exchange that govern and unite the clan.

The two corresponding statements on the side of ~~The~~ Woman are these:

There is no x who is not subject to the phallic function ($= \exists x \overline{\Phi} x$).

Not-all of an x is subject to the phallic function ($= \overline{\forall} x \Phi x$).

The first sentence corresponds to the fact that 'The Woman does not exist', i.e. there is no point of exception that constitutes the totality of women as a set in the way that the primal Father constitutes all men/all human beings as a set. The second sentence expresses the idea that something of a woman escapes the phallic function. 'Not-all' of a woman (which we may write as ~~The~~ Woman) submits to the phallic function that is the very basis of the Symbolic—meaning, not all of Her can be inscribed within communal norms and protocols. There is a long historical tradition of female figures who view with scepticism the institutions and rules that constitute the Symbolic. Women such as Aristophanes' sexual saboteuse Lysistrata, Plautus' sardonic slaves Syra and Astaphium, Propertius' and Ovid's cynical procuresses Acanthis and Dipsas discern the particular interests behind claims of universal benefit to the community from following the rules.[114] The deceptively mild-mannered Echo is one of these, an inconvenient

---

[114] Lysistrata organizes a 'sex strike' to end what she characterizes as virtually a civil war (*Lys.* 1128–35) after cynically but accurately gauging men's investment in martial values against their interest in sex; Syra exclaims in disgust over the double standard of sexual behaviour for men and women (*Mercator* 817–29); Astaphium explains a courtesan's 'exploitation' of men as a function of her need to provide for her future when she is barred from marriage (*Truculentus* 224–47); this last essentially summarizes the views of Acanthis and Dipsas, also.

female who refuses fully to submit to others' restrictions on her desire and her language (as I shall argue in Chapter 4). The prescripts she and her sisterhood contemn supposedly rest on complete knowledge, knowledge without any deficiency. ~~The~~ Woman rejects such universalist claims; the Symbolic rules of reason and non-contradiction cannot account for Her knowledge.

What should be readily apparent from my brief summaries of Man and ~~The~~ Woman is that the two pairs of statements are not symmetrical. Lacan states all the rules that govern the male side with reference to the universal and entire ('all are...', 'there is one who...'), whereas he frames the female side in relation to the particular and the partial (not 'all are', but 'there is none who is not'; 'not all of...').[115] *Encore* does not see Man and ~~The~~ Woman as the classically symmetrical dyad, each sex completing the identity of the other (his authority confirmed by her compliance, his reason restraining her emotion, his public responsibilities balanced by her private domesticity, etc.).[116] Rather, they are a mutual misfire, two terms that perpetually fail of coincidence. No guarantee of sexual identity or fulfilment can be wrung from the dance of these formulae

---

[115] Shepherdson 2000, 75–6.

[116] This ideal of a complementary-but-unequal relationship is enshrined in Roman law and institutions. Throughout her life, a woman is required to be under a man's guardianship. If she becomes independent through the death of her father or spouse, she is still required to have a tutor, chosen from the male agnates, or (if she had been married) from her husband's family. She cannot take any legal action that might diminish the family property (e.g. the sale of land, slaves, or livestock), nor can she make a will, without the tutor's consent. Marriage effectively makes the wife the adopted daughter of the *paterfamilias*, whether that be her husband, or her husband's father (on women's status in law, see Gardner 1986).

These restrictions speak to a woman's putative disabilities. The contrasting texts that praise a woman do so because she concerns herself with the affairs of the house, not of the public sphere from which she was largely excluded. An example is the 1st-cent. BCE inscription lauding Amymone: 'hic sita est Amymone Marci optima et pulcherrima | lanifica pia pudica frugi casta domiseda'—'here lies Amymone, the wife of Marcus, the best and most beautiful woman; she made wool, was dutiful, modest, thrifty, chaste, a stayer-at-home' (*ILS* 8402). Inscriptions extol similar virtues in 2nd-cent. BCE Claudia and 1st-cent. BCE Murdia (*ILS* 8403 and 8394 respectively). The criteria remain largely unchanged over the centuries. In the early principate, Livy marks Lucretia's exemplary virtue by having her husband and his fellow officers find her at home with her maidservants spinning wool well into the night, whereas the other men's wives had been carousing with their friends (Livy 1.57.8–10). Even in the 4th cent. CE, Ausonius still praises his mother for her 'fama

around the radically empty signifier of the phallus; hence the absence of the sexual relationship. This miscarriage underwrites the power of Woman: if She really did exist, She would confer symmetry and fixity upon a complementary relation between the sexes. Man's relation to Her as the essence of women, a totality neatly organized by a single logical principle, would ground His identity.[117]

The four graphic formulae analysed above occupy the top portion of the graph Lacan deploys in *Encore*. I have reviewed them in detail because the patterns of tyranny, destruction, arrogance, and antagonism woven through the Theban cycle regularly assume the contours of sexual conflict—Juno against Jupiter, Diana against Actaeon, Echo against Narcissus. Yet the way these skirmishes evolve transcends mere anatomical sex: the fundamental antagonism stretches between the ideological blind faith summarized in Man and Woman, and their sceptical antithesis, ~~The~~ Woman. When Juno, Diana, Pentheus, and Bacchus all unquestioningly credit their own justice, they tear away at Thebes and its citizens by aligning themselves with the serene self-complacency of Man. On the other hand, when Narcissus and Echo together enact the irreducible ambiguity at the heart of identity and language, they align themselves with ~~The~~ Woman's dubiety, marking the limits of faith in the Symbolic as the world's flawless mirror.

~~The~~ Woman's miscreance bears upon one grapheme from the bottom portion of the sexuation table that must be discussed here. (Since the rest of the graphemes pertain only severally to individual tales within the Theban cycle, I reserve their discussion to the appropriate chapters.) '~~Woman~~ → S(Θ)' links the non-existence of Woman to the Symbolic (the Other) as 'barred', unable to form a discrete, flawless whole. Evidence of this incompletion emerges in the conceptual deadlocks we have tabulated above as the Real's intrusions upon the Symbolic: *objet a* as desired object whose objectively specifiable properties

pudicitiae lanificaeque manus'—'reputation for modesty and hands busy making wool' (*Parentalia* 2.4).

When the women of Augustus' household began to take on more public functions in the middle principate, this was exceptional, not a privilege extended to Roman women in general. Moreover, these communal offices were constructed as extensions of the traditional female duty to support the politically active men of the family (see Severy 2003, 7–32, 140–57).

[117] See Janan 1994, 28–31, 66–8, for a discussion of the Lacanian texts relevant to the idea of the sexual non-relation.

cannot explain its desirability, *jouissance* as bliss whose whole substance is its absence, and the superego as implacable law that undermines law. These phenomena are all instances of Symbolic non-sense, to which the non-existence of Woman as a totality without exception corresponds logically. They all warrant the scepticism of ~~The~~ Woman. Man and ~~The~~ Woman are in essence asymmetrical but interdependent vantages on the world: Man makes a logical whole of identity, community, Law—of the entire farrago of being—by excluding the unconformable. ~~The~~ Woman is balked of such universalities by Her refusal to dismiss anomaly. Exactly that conceptual faultline falls between the paired but asymmetrical idea(l)s embodied in Vergil's Rome and Ovid's Thebes. Both narratives organize themselves around the query Plutarch trained upon Romulus and Rome alike: What fortune (*tuchē*) did the beginning bequeath to the founder and his city? The *Aeneid* seeks an answer as Plutarch's Tarutius did in his 'future-perfect' calculation of Romulus' horoscope: Vergil's epic constructs origins for Rome onto which a history both hopeful and fearful is projected retrospectively. But in the next generation, Ovid recollects Remus' foundation manqué, and so changes the question he asks of the origins: What had to go missing so that time might begin for the actual founder and his city? Thebes evidences what Cadmus tries in vain to leave behind; her bizarre mythohistory at first glance makes her Rome's irrational and phantasmagoric antitype. Yet her giant snakes and gender-switching prophets have less to say to Rome than her homelier, and thus more sinister, examples of teratism: men born to instant fratricide, parents divinely inspired to rend their children, beauties cursed with self-love. To whatever degree these instances of radical violence, internecine strife, and solipsism are fantastical, they are objectively so: they constitute Rome's unthinkable genesis, the 'enjoyment' that must be sacrificed, expelled, or renounced for the field of desire and Symbolic exchange to emerge. Rome takes shape as ordered, cohesive social entity—an entity constituted by a field of social relations based on exchange and nominal equality, governed by law—only in virtue of the violence, tyranny, fratricide, and monstrosity breathing on *ein andere Schauplatz*.[118] For Rome to exist, Thebes must be.

---

[118] Freud's resonant pharse for the Unconscious (*SE* 4: 48/*GW* 2–3: 51), where the Real work of dreams—and nightmares—is staged.

2

'In Nomine Patris'

Ovid's Theban Law

Soy la virgen
la mujer
la prostituta
soy la sal
el mercurio
y el sulfuro
soy el cielo
el infierno
soy la terra
me ves iluminada
maternal
no confíes en mí
te puedo condenar
a las tinieblas.

Claribel Alegria[1]

STRANGER IN A STRANGE LAND

Seeming signs and wonders are the special province—and providence—of ktistic literature. Divine direction being a regular feature of foundation legends, the god[2] often indicates where the colony

---

[1] 'Hecate' (Alegría 1993).

[2] Most often Apollo, since consulting the Delphic oracle typically features in foundation legends (Dougherty 1993, 15–16, 18–21).

should be founded in a riddling oracle—for example, where 'a goat loves the sea' (Diod. 8.21.3) or 'two whelps lap at salt water' (Hesych. *FGrH* 390 F1.3). The first oracle plays on the word *tragos*, which means 'goat', but also designates a wild fig tree; Phalanthus establishes Tarentum where he finds such a fig tree dipping its branches into the sea. The second oracle indicates a site marked by two rivers named Cydarus and Barbyses, whose names suggest small dogs; there the Megarians founded Byzantium. It is that tradition of an impossibility more apparent than real upon which Vergil's prophetic harpy Celaeno draws when she predicts that before the Trojans can ring with walls their promised city, they will be 'forced to eat their tables' (*Aen.* 3.255–7). The Aeneadae fulfil her dire prediction harmlessly upon landing in Italy by eating the wheaten cakes on which they have piled food (*Aen.* 7.112–17).

The key to these oracular impossibilities is that they turn out not to be impossible: although appearing to require natural anarchy, their fulfilment auspiciously restores proper order to the natural world.[3] By contrast, it is Thebes' especial fate to be born from real freakishness. The forefathers of autochthonous Thebes are the Spartoi, magically sprung from the teeth of the dragon slain by Cadmus. Reflecting their savage paternity, they immediately engage in general fratricide, like an army of Romuluses and Remuses.[4] Thebes' second-generation colonizers boast a heritage only slightly less odd, and no less marked by bellicosity. The émigré Cadmus marries Harmonia, the daughter of the love goddess Venus and the war god Mars. Venus and Mars are each separately parents to Rome's two most illustrious founding-fathers, Aeneas and Romulus respectively, both mortals who become gods. Yet in the case of Thebes, the combined efforts of both Olympians produce a child who nonetheless puzzlingly suffers all the same mortal vicissitudes as her husband, including being transformed into a snake at the end of her life. Cadmus and Harmonia's children and their children's offspring (who in at least one instance, the marriage of Agave and Echion, intermarry with the authochthonoi) are ominously *proles Mavortia*, 'offspring of Mars'

---

[3] On colonization oracles that depend on seeming *adunata*, see Dougherty 1993, 45–60.

[4] As Hardie notes (Hardie 1990, 224–5).

(*Met.* 3.531). This is the bloodline that yields Agave and Autonoë, the mother and aunt respectively who rip apart their son and nephew Pentheus with their bare hands. Thebes' orgins are thus stained with mortality and bellicosity both for its émigré and authochthonous population.

Savage nature, manifest *ab origine* in Thebes, spills over from the city's human history into its natural history. A fantastic and dream-like countryside besieges Ovid's *urbs Thebana*—a countryside (as we shall see) of monstrous expanding and contracting serpents, and weirdly perfect springs multiplying uncannily across the Theban landscape. What does it mean that the first and only city to assume substantial shape within the *Metamorphoses* looks physically less like civic pride than a psychotic's nightmare? Where exactly does the city's environmental misery come from? And what does all this say about that *other* city populated by the 'offspring of Mars', and burdened with a haunted past, Rome?[5] It is to these questions that this chapter addresses itself.[6]

A strange surrealism colours the harrowing circumstances of Thebes' founding. Despairing of finding his sister and returning to Tyre, Cadmus determines to establish a new city for himself and his followers in Boeotia under the guidance of Apollo's oracle. Searching for water for sacrifice, his followers encounter a lonely spring—and next to it, a cave marked by a vine-arch wherein hides the monstrous snake that takes their lives. The snake must pay with its own life once Cadmus discovers the slaughter (*Met.* 3.6–94).

---

[5] The connection between the two cities' genealogy is remarked by W. S. Anderson (Anderson 1997, 391).

[6] Stephen Hinds has analysed the *Metamorphoses*' preoccupation with landscape; among other shrewd reflections, he develops the by-now standard observation that Ovid's *loci amoeni* regularly frame violence when he elucidates the metapoetic significance of this pattern. Ovid simply throws into relief what was already implicit in the literary tradition: 'Even in the classic Virgilian form of pastoral itself the idyll is often out of the reach of the bucolic protagonists, lost, deferred, or called into question; arguably the sense of a threat to harmony immanent in a harmonious setting is a constitutive feature of the landscape tradition at large' (Hinds 2002, 131). Hinds's observation elucidates the conceptual parallel between star-crossed Thebes and its deceptively idyllic environs: city and countryside meet as 'paradises lost', insofar as each takes shape around a point of exception that prevents their organic unity and harmony.

The bizarre details of the snake's two hostile encounters with the Tyrians exceed even the generous parameters of mythic logic, defying all rationality as the narrative unfolds. For example, the serpent changes eerily in magnitude and force. Its size when it attacks the men is greater than that of the constellation Draco (3.43–5),[7] but when Cadmus kills the beast and pins it to an oak tree, it has mysteriously shrunk to the height of that tree (3.90–2).[8] Moreover, this single oak stops a beast that, twelve lines and no significant wounds earlier, easily mowed down the woodlands in its path (3.80).[9]

The strangeness of the serpent-haunted landscape metastasizes across the Theban cycle. Immediately after recounting Thebes' founding, Ovid turns to the doom visited upon Actaeon, Cadmus' grandson. His misfortune is to surprise the goddess Diana bathing; angered, she transforms him into a stag whom his own hunting hounds rend. He unwittingly stumbles upon her bath because, exhausted from the hunt, he sought refreshment; like his uncle, he finds his menace in a lonely spring next to a cave marked by an arch (3.157–62). The unusual combination of features that mark the serpent's lair—cave, spring,

---

[7] Both Friedrich and Anderson (Friedrich 1953, 103; Anderson 1997, 343) observe that the snake has raised roughly half its body-length into the air in order to survey the forest, and even that much does not yield to the constellation Draco in extent:

> ac media plus parte leues erectus in auras
> despicit omne nemus tantoque est corpore quanto,
> si totum spectes, geminas qui separat Arctos.
> (*Met.* 3.43–5)

and raised up more than halfway into the light breezes, it looked down upon the entire glade and so much of its body was as great as the one that divides the twin Bears, if you could see it all.

'If you could see it all' ('si totum spectes', 45) imagines straightening out the winding thread of stars that make up the constellation and beholding its entire length at once. The idea of treating a constellation as so much snarled string matches the fantastic plasticity with which Ovid has endowed the Theban landscape (Henderson 1981, 47). Friedrich also comments on the snake's eventual diminution to the length of the oak tree.

[8] Edgar M. Glenn explains the snake's initial magnitude as expressing the fear of Cadmus' men (Glenn 1986, 30). But Cadmus is not terribly courageous, either: for example, the Spartoi terrify him and cause him to reach reflexively for his weapons, until one admonishes him that he has no part in the conflict (3.115–17). Why does he not see them or the serpent as larger than life, if terror is at the root of such a hallucination?

[9] Anderson notes the contradiction (Anderson 1997, 346).

arch—behave just as magically as the serpent itself: they reproduce themselves across time and space to reappear at Diana's bath.[10]

That elements from the site of Cadmus' first loss (his men) should recur uncannily at the site of his second (his grandson) defies probability. However, no less improbable is the appearance of Diana's retreat. Ovid insists that the site has come into being with no artifice ('arte laboratum nulla', 3.158), but that nature's efforts nonetheless look like art ('simulauerat artem | ingenio natura suo', 3.158–9). Notwithstanding his emphasis on the venue's naturalness, his elaboration on the *locus amoenus'* weird perfection impresses us rather with the site's artificiality. The water is perfectly pellucid, the grass runs clear to the edge of the water—the last two details indicating that not a pebble or speck of mud mars the environs (3.159–62)— an arch has even been spontaneously hollowed from the stone.[11]

How are we to explain these uncanny features of the Theban landscape—the miraculously expanding and contracting serpent, the precisely repeated features of the menacing *loci amoeni*, the immaculate pool? They mark Thebes as the site of a supernatural Nature, as if the very earth were instinct with a violation of the natural order. Yet we witness no theurgy here that would cause this loss of reality—not as when (nearer the middle of the Theban cycle) Bacchus horrifies the Tyrrhenian sailors by making ivy grow from oars and shipmasts, and by conjuring the images of tigers and lynxes

---

[10] Springs are fairly standard furniture for the *locus amoenus*, and caves only slightly rarer, but the arches described in both the snake's and Diana's haunts are not so common. Having sifted through Deferrari's concordance to Ovid (Deferrari 1939) for any word that could possibly refer to an arch, and then scrutinized the contexts of these words in the *Metamorphoses*, I can attest that the poem gathers together this particular trinity of features only in these two closely juxtaposed passages.

[11] These two founts anticipate Narcissus' fatal pool, also unnaturally and incredibly perfect. Its waters are completely free from mud, and surrounded by grass. Though overhung with trees, no branch ever falls upon it. Despite being in the midst of a wood accessible to living beings (Narcissus finds it, after all), neither animal nor human visits it. It never even feels the sun (3.407–12). Narcissus is Boeotian, not Theban, but the derangement in the Theban universe that began with Agenor curses greater Thebes, too. Narcissus blunders into the same unnatural, uncanny landscape as Cadmus and Actaeon and, like them, ultimately loses himself to its fatal power.

(3.664–71). Rather, something has gone amiss in Thebes that fundamentally impairs the logic of its physical world.

These strange details of the Cadmeioi's first and second encounters with their unfolding doom look like nothing so much as hallucinations. Yet they cannot be attributed to any one person's psychosis, since these strange sights appear to different people at widely various times: to Cadmus' men, then to Cadmus, then (a generation later) to Actaeon. It is as if these strange visions accrued to the whole of Thebes, or at least to the line of the Cadmeioi and their followers. Reframing our understanding of the symptoms will help parse this 'collective psychosis'. Lacan offers a reading of hallucinations that maps them onto the social, cultural, and institutional forces that move through the subject and shape the apprehension of phenomena.[12] Hallucinations represent a disturbance in the way we understand the world, in the categories of understanding subsumed by the Symbolic. Any system of categories only functions to the extent that each can be distinguished from the others. The Symbolic therefore fundamentally crystallizes the principle of alterity, the idea of distinction that prevents us from experiencing the world as a homogeneous continuum. The question we must ask is not, Why are the Thebans psychotic?, but, What has so disturbed Thebes' Symbolic that distinctions between 'astronomically huge' and 'merely large', 'here' and 'there', 'then' and 'now', 'artificial' and 'natural', have disappeared?

Surprisingly, we cannot turn for explanation to the usual culpabilities that besmirch Thebes' history in the form of category-violations. Ovid banishes from his purview the city's better-known acts of incest and kin-carnage, the deeds that confuse distinctions between 'mother' and 'wife', 'father' and 'foe', 'brother' and 'enemy'. Jocasta, Laius, Oedipus, Polyneices, and Eteocles do not appear in his narrative of the city, nor for that matter anywhere in the poem.[13]

---

[12] See Lacan's discussion of hallucination as a symptom of psychosis generally in his essay 'On a Question Preliminary to Any Possible Treatment of Psychosis' (Lacan 1966, 531–583/1977, 179–225) and his seminar on the psychoses (Lacan 1981a/1993). Malcolm Bowie lucidly discusses Lacan's conceptualization of hallucination in particular and psychosis in general (Bowie 1991, 106–10).

[13] Unless you count as an appearance Themis' throwaway half-line predicting Polyneices' and Eteocles' mutual murder: 'fientque pares in uulnere fratres', *Met.* 9.405.

Nonetheless, Ovid preserves the essence of the Labdacids' history in his record of their progenitors the Cadmeioi by extracting from their category-violations the underlying notion that makes them significant: the law.[14] The Labdacids' confusion over kinship relations and the protocols that accrue to them—killing and embracing the wrong people—sketches *in nuce* not only the misperceptions that plague the Cadmeioi, but also the way discrimination entwines with social prohibition to subtend the law. It is from the aboriginal vitiation of Thebes' law that her hallucinatory landscape arises.

ALL THE DEADLY VIRTUES

Ovid quite naturally focuses on law in recounting Thebes' foundation and early history; law is the very idea upon which the polity qua regulated community ineluctably rests and the notional frame that defines both offence and punishment. But Ovid's Thebes is an anomaly, which dramatizes law more in the breach than the observance. It takes its origins from transgression—from Jupiter's rape of Europa, and Agenor's cruel spurning of his son, Cadmus. Divine rape is fairly common in foundation stories,[15] and familial harshness is not unknown.[16] However, though Ovid presents the god in a less-than-flattering light, and will return to examine his libidinal repercussions even more stringently elsewhere in the Theban cycle (notably in the Semele episode), the poet reserves his explicit judgement for the mortal malefactor. Ovid focuses upon the way Agenor's particular

[14] By 'law', I mean the principle of prohibition that informs and subsumes all social protocols, rather than any specific, formal legal code.

[15] e.g. Poseidon's rapes of the nymph Ascra and of an unnamed nymph are responsible for the founding of the eponymous Ascra and of Chios respectively (Paus. 9.29.1, 7.4.8); Zeus' violation of the nymphs Thebes and Aegina results in the establishment of their namesake cities (Pind. *Isthm.* 8.16–23); Mars' assault upon Ilia catalyses the founding of Rome (Livy, 1.4.2; Vergil, *Aen.* 1.273–4). Carole Dougherty discusses the significance of this pattern as exemplifying the colonizers' conquest and fecundation of the colonized land (Dougherty 1993, 61–80).

[16] A parallel story can be found in Telamon's banishment of Teukros, the half-brother of Aias, in anger over Aias' death shortly after the Trojan War. Apollo then directs Teukros to found a new Salamis in Cyprus (Eur. *Hel.* 68–163).

offence exemplifies law gone awry by introducing for the first time in the *Metamorphoses* an oxymoron the poem will revisit often: the coincidence of *pietas* ('dutifulness') and villainy.[17] Agenor's command to Cadmus to find his sister or else remain in exile (3.3–5) renders the Tyrian king 'facto pius et sceleratus eodem' ('dutiful and criminal by virtue of the same act', 3.5). Franz Bömer observes

Das is offenbar nicht nur ein rhetorisch wirkungsvolles und von Ovid gern variiertes . . . und nahezu sprichwörtliches . . . Oxymoron. Diese Vorstellung gehört auch zu tieferen Bereichen des römischen Glaubens. Sie stellt eine der ursprünglichen Komponenten des später so komplexen Gebildes der römischen pietas (I 204) dar, nämlich die pietas der consanguinei.[18]

Bömer's gloss connects Agenor's command with law—with law's specific instantiation in the conflicting claims of social protocol organized but not rationalized under the rubric *pietas*; he thus indicates how this Phoenician imperative speaks to Roman precepts.

---

[17] For example: under the guise of reuniting two sisters, Tereus movingly persuades Philomela's father to entrust her to himself, all the time plotting to rape her ('ipso sceleris molimine Tereus | creditur esse *pius* laudemque a *crimine* sumit'—'Because of the effort he puts into his *crime*, Tereus is believed to be *dutiful* and earns praise for his evil intention', 6.473–4); Procne in turn determines to kill her son as vengeance for her husband's violation and mutilation of her sister Philomela ('*scelus* est *pietas* in coniuge Terei'—'For Tereus' wife, crime is *scrupulosity*', 6.635); Aeëtes' daughters, deceived by Medea, unwittingly murder their father while trying to renew his youth ('his ut quaeque *pia* est hortatibus *impia* prima est | et, *ne sit scelerata, facit scelus*'—'because of [Medea's] exhortations, according as each daughter is *filial*, she is the first to be *unfilial*, and *lest she be criminal, she commits a crime*', 7.339–40); Meleager's mother determines to avenge her son's murder of her brothers by ending his life ('*impietate pia* est'—'she is sisterly because she is unmotherly', 8.477); Amphiaraus' son Alcmaeon avenges his father by killing his duplicitous mother ('ultusque parente parentem | natus erit *facto pius et sceleratus eodem*'—'avenged upon one parent for the sake of the other, their son will be *dutiful and criminal by virtue of the same act*', 9.408–9); Myrrha's father praises her as *pia* for her wish to have a husband like him, when she knows her wish is born of her illicit love for him ('*pietatis* nomine dicto | demisit uultus *sceleris* sibi conscia virgo'—'at the word "*devotion*", the maiden, conscious of her own *wickedness*, hung her head', 10.366–7).

[18] 'This is obviously not just a rhetorical oxymoron, [though] striking, enthusiastically varied by Ovid and almost proverbial . . . This concept belongs to the deeper realms of Roman belief. It constitutes one of the original components of the later quite complex structure of Roman *pietas* (I. 204) namely, the *pietas* of blood-relatives' (Bömer 1969–86, 1.446).

But references to *pietas* are comparatively rare in the first five books of the *Metamorphoses*—odd for a section of the poem so steadily focused upon relations between the human and the divine.[19] Casting about for an interpretative context with which to construe Agenor's villainous dutifulness, Bömer has fastened upon the only other narrative before the Theban cycle to contemplate *pietas*: the story of the Flood. In cross-referencing *Metamorphoses* 1.204, Bömer points to the way in which contraries of *pietas* reflect a perverted polity—or rather, two. In the aberrancy of eternal and divine Olympus, both ancient Thebes (as embryonically present in Agenor's severity), and contemporary Rome, find their counterpart.

The verses to which Bömer specifically refers find Jove angered by Arcadian King Lycaon and calling the gods to council ('dignas Ioue concipit iras I conciliumque uocat', 1.166–7). Jove soon lashes his fellow gods into indignation over the human wrongs he allegedly witnessed and suffered when visiting earth. But Ovid soon draws into view recent events in the Roman empire by comparing the Olympians' moral outrage to the horror Augustus' people felt at a foiled attempt on the emperor's life.[20]

> Confremuere omnes studiisque ardentibus ausum
> talia deposcunt. sic, cum manus inpia saeuit
> sanguine Caesareo Romanum exstinguere nomen,
> attonitum tanto subitae terrore ruinae
> humanum genus est totusque perhorruit orbis.

---

[19] Scholars such as Brooks Otis have noticed the pattern; within his quadripartite thematic division of the poem, he labelled Books 1–2 'The Divine Comedy', Books 3–5 'The Avenging Gods' (Otis 1970, 84–5).

[20] Suetonius says that there were many such conspiracies against Augustus (*Divus Augustus* 19; cf. Dio 55.4.3), but exactly which one Ovid had in mind is impossible to tell. Some scholars assume that Ovid refers rather to Julius Caesar's assassination (e.g. Haupt-Ehwald 1915; Lafaye 1928; Lee 1953; Otis 1970, 99; von Albrecht 1999, 179). However, the point of comparison is an attempt that failed, just as Lycaon's plots against Jupiter did not succeed (Anderson 1997, 172). Also, Bömer points out that the adjective *Caesareus* (which Ovid introduced into Latin) nowhere else in his oeuvre refers to Julius Caesar. Bömer summarizes the arguments for reading *Caesareo sanguine* as Augustus' mortal peril, and cites both the ancient resources and modern scholarship pertinent to the question (Bömer 1968–86, 1.87–8).

> nec tibi grata minus pietas, Auguste, tuorum est
> quam fuit illa Ioui.

(*Met.* 1.199–205)

[The gods] all rage together [with Jove] and, with burning eagerness, they demand to know who has dared such things. Just so, when the traitorous hand[21] was rabid to destroy the Roman people with the blood of Caesar's heir, the human race and the whole world trembled, thunderstruck from their tremendous terror of sudden catastrophe. Nor was the devotion of your people, Augustus, less pleasing to you than was that [devotion of the gods] to Jove.

The context for 1.204 adduces two instances—one mythical, one historical—that match Agenor's order to Cadmus, in that the ethical claims of *pietas* cannot be made logically consistent within them. The mythical example falls into two parts, beginning with an obvious instance of *pietas* subverted. Jove proposes to destroy the entire human race (1.188) in order to punish Lycaon, the only man whose offences against *pietas* Jove specifically describes. The flaws in the god's case have been remarked often.[22] To summarize briefly: by Jove's own account, when he entered Arcadia as a manifest god, everyone began to worship. Only the Arcadian king Lycaon mocked his subjects' reverent prayers, then compounded the offence against *pietas* by attempting first to murder Jove and then to feed him human flesh (220–30). On this flimsy evidence, Jove claims that all humanity is corrupt beyond recall and must suffer for it (242–3). Most surprising of all, he saves Lycaon from the general destruction, albeit transformed into a wolf (232–9). As a wolf, Lycaon cannot speak; bestial slavering and reddened eyes now mark the maniacal nature once half-concealed in his human form. But as W. S. Anderson points out, unlike his worshipful, now-defunct subjects, Lycaon still gets to pursue his former pleasures: 'solitae cupidine caedis | uertitur in pecudes et nunc quoque sanguine *gaudet*'—'His customary lust for

---

[21] *Manus* could also mean 'band', and indicate multiple assassins; I translate it as 'hand' and construe it as metonymy for a single enemy because that matches the comparandum: Lycaon as a single foe. But whether the attempted murder Ovid had in mind was a lone effort, or a conspiracy, makes no difference to my argument.

[22] Anderson's commentary offers an excellent line-by-line analysis (Anderson 1997, 168–76), but James O'Hara has now further sifted the various logical contradictions in Jupiter's report. See O'Hara 2007, 116–17 (which also lists previous bibliography on the question of how to assess the god's speech).

slaughter he turns against cattle and even now takes pleasure in blood' (234–5).[23]

Jove's confrontation with Lycaon establishes a story-pattern repeated several times in the *Metamorphoses* ('god punishes scorner of the gods'), but only this and one other instance of it expose comparably thorny conceptual flaws in *pietas*. Non-coincidentally, that twin instance takes place in Thebes, the third point in the triangle of corrupt polities elucidated above: 'Olympus—Rome—Thebes'. Jove's reprisal against Lycaon foreshadows his son Bacchus' revenge upon Pentheus, another lone-infidel king among a sea of apparent converts (3.577–733). Although the son is more restrained than his father— Bacchus does not punish wholesale for Pentheus' fault—he maddens Pentheus' mother and aunt murderously against the king, so that they rip him apart in a Bacchic fury (710–33). Here, too, *pietas* eerily accommodates ethical antipodes: 'just punishment for a god's lèse-majesté' is also 'kin-murder'.[24] Because all three instances of *pietas*

---

[23] Anderson 1989, 98.

[24] The tension Ovid represents between divine and human notions of the Good in his Bacchus–Pentheus narrative draws upon the same tension Euripides dramatized in his *Bacchae*, a play that both supplements and contrasts with Ovid's Theban narrative (as I shall detail more fully in Ch. 6). At the play's end, Cadmus has seen both the royal family and Thebes devastated through the loss of the royal scion and king, Pentheus—and this despite the fact that only three Thebans held aloof from Dionysus' worship: Ino, Agave, and Pentheus. Although he acknowledges that the god was wronged, he also reproves Dionysus' revenge as pettiness: 'orgas prepei theous ouch homoiousthai brotois' ('it is not fitting that the gods resemble mortals in their anger', *Bacchae* 1348). To this Bacchus really has no answer; he responds without addressing the substance of Cadmus' criticism, thus underlining how fundamentally indefensible his position is: 'palai tade Zeus houmos epeneusen pater' ('long ago father Zeus ordained these things', 1349). By making the contradictions of *pietas* the mythohistorical and conceptual entrée into his Theban cycle, Ovid implicitly adopts the critique Euripides Cadmus' levels at the god: the very punishment Bacchus exacts for Ino's, Agave's, and Pentheus' threat to his status puts that status into question. And Euripides makes that point more than once in his oeuvre: near the end of *Herakles Mainomenos*, Herakles rejects the idea of gods having needs of any kind, especially such as would drive them to betrayal, violence, or arrogance (1340–6). In the play, Hera pursues her usual shrewish vendetta against Herakles as the child of her sexual rival, Alcmene, by driving him murderously insane (822–73); within the framework of the play, Hera clearly exists as effective cause, apparently belying Herakles' belief only in gods without desire. Yet her actions do not fall beyond human judgement, and the words of Zeus's illegitimate son effectively strip the goddess of her status.

are linked by comparable ethical paradoxes and similar venues, each amplifies the disturbing effect of the other two.[25] Each underlines the degree to which these ethical contradictions inform the very idea of The City.

But to return to heaven and the world's infancy: even more conceptually intricate than the thematic repercussions of Jove's outrage is its Olympian development. The gods' reaction to Jove's brief sketches an even subtler example of *pietas* subverted than either wholesale noyade, or intimate carnage; it raises more interesting questions about just how the word floats free of any dependable moorings of meaning. Why do the Olympians greet such clotted, sadistic reasoning with enthusiastic approval, and what is the logical consequence of calling that approval *pietas*? When Jove fulminates over human wickedness (*ora indignantia soluit*, 181; *frementi*, 244), his fellow gods show their *pietas* (204) by blustering right along with him (*confremuere*, 199, an Ovidian neologism). This represents divine anger as infectious—and as Denis Feeney notes, the all-too-human failings of Ovid's Olympians, most especially their anger, pointedly revisit the problem of theodicy that had preoccupied the *Aeneid* and the majority of its epic predecessors. Ovid presents us with a problem of judging the divine we simply cannot evade.[26]

---

[25] The antitheses of justice and injustice embraced by divine vengeance return in Ovid's version of the Demeter–Persephone tale—the more starkly because Ovid's redaction of the myth as contained in the *Homeric Hymn to Demeter* contrasts markedly with Callimachus' reaction to the same *Hymn*. As David Konstan has shown, Ovid prefers to reproduce the wholesale savagery of the *Homeric Hymn to Demeter*. Ovid's corn-goddess, like the hymn's deity, blames all of humanity for her daughter's rape and punishes them with famine, when the gods alone connived at the crime. By contrast, Callimachus' goddess narrows the scope of her direct revenge for Erysichthon's premeditated sacrilege to him alone, inflicting him with bottomless hunger. Erysichthon's family also suffers because of his suffering, so the divine intervention is not precisely a 'surgical strike'. However, it is considerably more modest in its scope than the Homeric or Ovidian versions, where what matters to the powerful is to respond savagely to any thwarting or slight. The proportionality of the response, and the guilt of the punished, are far secondary considerations. As Konstan remarks of the *Metamorphoses*' redaction of the Demeter–Persephone story, it 'adecuada a la visión general que Ovidio tiene de la aristocracia imperial en Roma' ('[it] accords well with Ovid's general view of the behaviour of the imperial aristocracy at Rome'; Konstan 1996, 67).

[26] Feeney 1991, 198–200 focuses specifically on the Lycaon episode, but his entire chapter on the *Metamorphoses* is enlightening on the problem of theodicy in Ovid:

But what is the appropriate conceptual frame within which to judge it? For example: can we take the ardour of Jove's godly audience purely at face value? Just after Jove has reminded the Olympians of the difference in power between himself and them ('uos . . . regoque', 197), some of the gods ratify his plan verbally, others 'play their parts by approving wordlessly' ('alii partes adsensibus implent', 245). The theatrical metaphor in *partes implere*[27] construes the council's responses as a passion play enacted for Jove's consumption—and one in which, oddly enough, both speaking and not speaking mean exactly the same thing.[28] Jove's will trumps all other considerations in determining (in all senses of that word) the will of the council. Their *pietas* cannot be construed in isolation from their position of subjugation.

Ovid reverts to recent history when he compares the gods' approval to the *pietas* Augustus' people tendered him on the occasion of his mortal danger. The comparandum both reproduces and magnifies the political complications of the Olympian council—and of Cadmus and Agenor—as citizen-subjects confront ruling authority. Once again, a would-be assassin has assaulted *pietas*—this time offending doubly. Every citizen owes both civic and filial devotion to the emperor, who embodies the state and is 'father of his country' (*pater patriae*). Punishing the assassin, the *inpia manus* (200), therefore constitutes a defence of *pietas*. Fear of world cataclysm (201–3) implies a stringent reprisal against him, just as fear of universal chaos provokes Jove's deadliest response to humanity's putative

---

'By calling such explicit attention in his first simile [likening Jove's convoking the Olympians to Augustus' summoning the Senate to his Palatine residence] to epic's procedure of analogy, Ovid appears to promise that divine action will be at least systematic and comprehensible. Yet judgements prompted by the poem persistently lead the reader towards seeing the gods as escaping beyond human categorization—*only to defeat our attempts to conceptualize that escape in any other than human terms*' (203, my emphasis).

[27] Noted by Lee 1953, 99; Bömer 1968–86, 1.99.

[28] The fulcrum on which the contrast turns might not be words, but sound—i.e. between voiced, but wordless, approval, and silence, since *adsensus* can mean approbation voiced only within the mind. But whatever the specifics of their contrasted behaviour, both groups of Olympians are assumed to have ratified Jove's plan.

wickedness.[29] However, the claims in both instances are patently hyperbolic; beneath Ovid's brief sketch of the father of gods and men and the father of his country emerges the outline of the terrifying Real Father's visage. Threats to *pietas* are adduced to authorize an exaggerated reaction and unhesitating approval of bloodlust (a reaction specified in Jove's case, implied in Augustus').

But when Ovid addresses the emperor, whose hyperbole is this? The Olympians' subservience has now been transferred to the narrator: it is Ovid's voice that extravagantly equates Augustus' demise

---

[29] Augustus did not err on the side of gentleness when responding to real or perceived threats to himself. For example, in dealing with cases of treason, Augustus broke with what had become accepted custom in the late Republic, the right of a citizen to avoid enforcement of a capital charge by voluntarily going into exile where he would. By contrast, Augustus began either to specify the place of exile (as he did when he relegated Ovid to Tomis) or to find ways to enforce the death penalty even upon those who had chosen flight. C. W. Chilton remarks that 'during the last century of the Republic citizens became immune, in practice and then in theory, from the infliction of the death penalty' (Chilton 1955, 73) But in his analysis of the treason trials of Augustus' reign, he concludes that 'Augustus by arbitrary action extended the scope of the law of treason and went beyond its penalties' (Chilton 1955, 76). The fates of Aulus Terentius Varro Murena and Fannius Caepio exemplify this extension. Both were found guilty of conspiracy in 22 or 23 BCE (presumably under the *Lex Julia de maiestate*) and condemned to death—as the traditional formula had it, to *interdictio aquae et ignis*. Voluntary exile would normally have satisfied this sentence, but both men were instead waylaid while fleeing into exile and put to death. Lawrence J. Daly argues convincingly that Augustus exceeded the legal parameters of *interdictio* in ensuring that both were executed. Not all scholars agree with his analysis (a summary of the range of views appears in Daly 1983 and 1984), but they are all of one mind in regarding the deaths of Murena and Caepio as a problematic break with tradition *de facto*, if not *de iure*.

Nor is this pattern of judicial harshness apparent only to modern scholars. Dio generally characterizes Augustus as having a vicious temper that affected his actions as a jurist. Dio relates an anecdote in which Maecenas came across Augustus holding court and about to condemn to death many of the accused. Maecenas narrowly averted this by tossing into Augustus' lap a tablet inscribed, 'Arise at last, executioner!' (Dio 55.7.1–2).

There is an exception more apparent than real in Dio's and Seneca's rhetorical fables of Augustus' clemency toward the conspirator Gn. Cornelius Cinna. Suspected of plotting against Augustus while he was in Gaul, Cinna was supposedly pardoned at Livia's behest (Dio 55.14–22; Seneca, *De Clementia* 1.9). Yet even these authors acknowledge that such clemency was unprecedented. Seneca has Livia characterize Augustus' previous pattern of responses to such attempts as *severitas* (*De Clementia* 1.9.6). Dio's Livia remarks that not only has Augustus killed 'many' (*pollous*), but that his motives for doing so are assumed to be far from impartial: he has condemned out of resentment, greed, fear of the brave, envy of the virtuous (55.18.5).

with the world's end and characterizes universal dread of this as *pietas*. The poet's obsequiousness implicitly condones any response, however severe, to the *inpia manus*. How can the same voice imply that the Olympians' *pietas* toward Jove is toadying, but then adopt their obsequiousness when describing the *pietas* of Augustus' subjects? What exactly does the word mean if it can shelter beneath its aegis both sadism and sycophancy, the exaggerated reprisals of the rulers and the self-serving approval of their subjects?

The dramatic frame within which Ovid deploys *pietas* at 1.204 makes it impossible to recover its exact meaning, because he speaks to the emperor (204–5). Addressed directly to Augustus, *pietas* cannot enjoy a purely constative status. By comparing the devotion of the Olympians to that of Augustus' subjects, Ovid implicitly praises the emperor as a man who inspires loyalty, and implies that whatever vengeance he takes against the plotter sets right a wrong, just as Jupiter says his own reprisal will (*Met.* 1.240–3). Yet aimed at the emperor, the sentence can only be flattery. As Paul Allen Miller has pointed out,

Flattery only functions to the extent that it calls attention to its own excessive, hyperbolic nature. It is the sly rhetorical wink that says, "this is a compliment," that says "I am exalting you and recognizing the power differential between us." The court poet is thus always already both flatterer and ironist . . . He cannot praise without recognizing the subordination that makes that praise possible and necessary, and in so doing, calling into question the nature of that praise.[30]

Pietas both must, and cannot, mean what it says in the address to Augustus: in order for the sentence to be flattery, the devotion of the emperor's subjects must be understood as sincere. But as flattery, we cannot ignore the rhetorical nature of the compliment and free the word of irony. The way that the Flood story (along with its address to Augustus) hopelessly problematizes the exact value of *pietas* unfolds the consequences both for language and for law of the power differentials in play. It thus sets the stage for the ethical contradictions of Agenor's command to Cadmus. Both passages revolve around

---

[30] Miller 2004, 228. Miller cites Videau-Delibe 1991 as the germ of the idea that the court poet is ineluctably caught between irony and flattery.

authority (Jupiter, Augustus, Agenor) 'laying down the law', yet each instance constitutes a disturbance in the Symbolic such as I have argued accounts for Thebes' surreal landscape. If by saying *pietas* Ovid both means what he says, and its opposite, if the same deed can make the doer both *pius* and *sceleratus*, loyal subject and sycophant, why cannot a serpent be both astronomically huge and merely large at the same time, why cannnot the same landscape montage be both here and there in space and time, be contrived and artless?

To be sure, Ovid elaborates the contradictions of *pietas* throughout the *Metamorphoses* after calling Agenor a dutiful criminal explicitly evokes them. When Procne avenges her sister Philomela by killing her own son, when Meleager's mother ends his life for ending her brothers' lives, when Alcmaeon murders his mother to punish her betrayal of his father, their acts reveal how easily bloodthirst can cohabit with duty. But those further paradoxes are all present *in nuce* in Agenor's command to his son—and nowhere else but in Thebes does the *Metamorphoses* unfold in such detail the consequences of these paradoxes for the polity's basis in law. No notion of the Good can secure the authority of King Agenor's injunction. His harshness toward his son contradicts his fatherly devotion to his daughter, so that his order can at best articulate the internal conflicts of *pietas* rather than take refuge under its authority.[31] That his command has force despite its internal logical incongruity exemplifies the law's

---

[31] In unfolding before his readers the dilemmas of a criminal *pietas*, Ovid drew upon a reserve of cultural experience both he and much of his audience shared. Seneca the Elder has preserved numerous examples of the hypothetical legal cases students were made to argue, pro and con, as part of their education in oratory. These *controversiae* are often fantastically improbable, but their complicated plot lines make simple recourse to the letter of the law impossible as a solution to the case. For example, as a problem arrayed under the legal precept, 'Children must support their parents, or be imprisoned', Seneca presents this case: 'Two brothers fall out among themselves. One had a son. The uncle fell into poverty; though his father forbade it, the nephew supported the uncle. Because of this, he was disinherited, but did not protest. The uncle received an inheritance and became rich. Now the father has become poor; though the uncle forbids it, the young man supports his father. Now the young man is being disinherited', *Contr.* 1.1. Ovid's probing of *pietas* would have enlarged upon the habits of mind shaped by rhetorical training in such thorny paradoxes. See Kaster 2001; Bloomer 2007 (with bibliography); Connolly 2009. (My thanks to the anonymous Oxford reader who drew my attention to the importance of Seneca's *controversiae*.)

absolute status: Cadmus obeys the decree of his father and sovereign because it is the law, not because it is truthful, just, or even expedient.

I do not here claim insight into Cadmus' consciousness: the text records none of his reflections on the command except his wish to avoid his father's wrath when he cannot find his sister (*Met.* 3.7). We may imagine that Cadmus finds his father's dictum unjust, ridiculous, demeaning—or, on the other hand, that he considers it completely within Agenor's *patria potestas* and kingly right. My point is that his father's decree does not depend for its effectiveness on Cadmus' subjective impression of it. Ovid articulates the command's own self-negation (*sceleratus/pius*) such that he obviates obedience based on reason; all that he leaves Cadmus is compliance on the basis of acknowledging authority.

'OLD FATHER ANTICK THE LAW'

Though the prepotent authority that exacts Cadmus' obedience is twofold—Ovid sketches in Agenor a father dictating to his son *and* a king charging his subject with a task—it is of little personal substance. We know nothing about Agenor's nature other than that his son fears his anger (3.7). Yet the king of Tyre is the proximate human cause for a storied ancient city, Thebes.[32] How do we explain this odd collocation of ideas: the advancement of civilization tied to a relentlessly abstract yet cruel agent whose commands entwine ethical antipodes?

Agenor's dictum and the absolute obedience it commands represents *en germe* the Father's law, but the wrath Cadmus fears vitiates Agenor's neutrality: having chosen his daughter over his son, Agenor forces his son to flee 'patriamque *iram*que parentis' ('his father's country and his *wrath*', *Met.* 3.7). Agenor's anger shadows forth the

---

[32] As noted in Ch. 1, the city has an ultimate divine cause in Jupiter, but the god has no contact with the city's founder, Cadmus. For that reason, I defer a more detailed discussion of Jupiter's influence upon the city until I can contextualize it by analysing his direct interventions in Thebes' history, such as his affair with Semele (Ch. 3) and his gifting of Tiresias with second sight (Chs. 4 and 5).

obverse of the law's cool austerity, the superegoic cruelty that makes him *sceleratus* and a type of the Real Father; it also sketches a conceptual basis for Thebes' woe.[33] His hostile pitilessness toward his son undermines the structural necessity that, as king and father—doubly the guarantor of the law's neutral status—he be detached and impartial.

This is hardly an idea new to the ancients: Cicero gave the ideal that the law and its human instruments be neutral magisterial articulation in *De Re Publica*. He refutes the Greek philosopher Carneades' claim that only the varying shapes of self-interest and utility peculiar to each society stand behind the law, not justice—for if there were such a thing as autonomous, neutral justice, laws would not differ between countries (*Rep.* 3.8–11). Cicero responds that laws differ from nation to nation only when and where they fall short of natural law, which is universal, unchanging, unaffected by time, place, or agents (3.22). Legislators and magistrates should be this law's neutral instruments: ideal statesmen govern the people as the mind governs the body (3.22). Cicero's mind/body metaphor implies a power whose ultimate interest mirrors the good of the governed: a sane mind cannot pursue interests at variance with those of the body housing it. He confirms this implication in a letter to Atticus that preserves a part of *De Re Publica* our manuscript did not:

---

[33] I have argued that ancient philosophy and literature—the Sceptics and Epicureans, Livy and Propertius—testify to a lively sense of the law's capacity for cruelty insofar as it is a system of cross-referenced and mutually defining rules ultimately ungrounded in any secure meaning, or 'truth'. This cruelty is inherent rather than contingent, insofar as it is most extreme not when law is ignored, but rather when law is practised in its utmost rigour (Janan 2001, 138–52). This conforms to the *Metamorphoses*' first and most striking picture of law: a source of terror. The Golden Age is Golden because the people need not fear the force of law.

> Aurea prima sata est aetas, quae uindice nullo,
> sponte sua, sine lege fidem rectumque colebat.
> poena metusque aberant, nec uerba minantia fixo
> aere ligabantur, nec supplex turba timebat
> iudicis ora sui, sed erant sine uindice tuti.
> (*Met.* 1.89–93)

Golden was the first age established, which—with no avenger, of its own accord, without law—cultivated trustworthiness and virtue; punishment and fear were absent, nor were threatening words strung together on the posted bronze tablets, nor did a fawning crowd fear the face of its judge; they were safe without a defender.

Consumo igitur omne tempus considerans, quanta uis sit illius uiri, quem nostris libris satis diligenter, ut tibi quidem uidemur, expressimus. Tenesne igitur moderatorem illum rei publicae quo referre uelimus omnia? Nam sic quinto, ut opinor, in libro loquitur Scipio: 'Ut enim gubernatori cursus secundus, medico salus, imperatori uictoria, sic huic moderatori rei publicae beata ciuium uita proposita est, ut opibus firma, copiis locuples, gloria ampla, uirtute honesta sit. Huius enim operis maximi inter homines atque optimi illum esse perfectorem uolo.' (*Ad Att.* 8.11.1)

Therefore I spend all my time considering how great must be the strength of that man whom I have with considerable energy limned in my books (as it may seem to you). Do you grasp, then, that moderator of the republic from whom we want all things? For in the fifth [book], I think, Scipio says: 'As a safe course is the aim of the pilot, health of the physician, victory of the general, thus the aim of this governor of the republic will be a blessed life for its citizens, so that [their life] may be secure in wealth, rich in resources, well endowed with glory, honourable for its virtue. I wish that man to be the accomplisher of this, the greatest and best work among human beings.'

'Scipio's' words make it clear that the best statesman administers the commonwealth so as to promote its welfare without regard for his personal interests or prejudices—just as the pilot, the physician, and the general serve others and not themselves in the ideal practice of their professions.

Cicero's unselfishly aloof statesman aligns with one end of the spectrum of the Lacanian Father's possibility—with the magisterially aloof Symbolic Father, the one whose 'No' is absolute, but unbiased. By contrast, Agenor figures the outrageous Father who embodies the sadistic, senseless underside of the law—the Father of Enjoyment. The aspect of enjoyment that bears the Lacanian sense of 'the point of breakdown in a logical system' is crucial here. The internal and occluded contradiction in law between its appearance of austere neutrality and its dark substratum of violence and cruelty produces as its symptom the obscene Father. Thebes begins here, sprung from a crisis in the law and in the function of the one who imposes law. The Father in his Symbolic capacity normally guarantees the neutral stature of the law precisely in virtue of being an empty signifier without a signified. His community coheres through his capacity to be a signifier that means everything insofar as it does not mean anything in particular and thereby enables everyone to recognize himself/herself in it. (Not by accident do the *Metamorphoses'* last three books reduce the very types of the Roman ideal king, Aeneas and Numa, to frames for other people's stories.)[34] As a corollary nullity, the law he anchors is in running order only when it is void of the speciality that is prepossession—when it is 'blind' and thus raised above particular passions.[35]

The contrast between Agenor's embodiment of ignorance and Cadmus' is instructive here. Ovid describes Agenor as *ignarus* when his daughter disappears. But the king responds to his own partial knowledge by assuming, incorrectly, that Europa can be found by human means—and thus ordering his son to find her or to exile himself, as if only a failure of Cadmus' will could prevent him from finding her. He judges Cadmus 'with extreme prejudice', assuming poor faith where none is in evidence. On the other hand, Ovid also repeatedly describes Cadmus' nescience. Cadmus 'does not know' that his daughter Ino and grandson Melicertes have been changed into sea-birds by Venus after they leapt from a high cliff ('nescit Agenorides natam paruumque nepotem | aequoris esse deos', *Met.* 4.563–4). Similarly, although his grandson Actaeon's disappearance

---

[34] Such a Father/King is Vergil's Aeneas, a self-abnegating figure who contrasts strongly with his epic predecessors, such as the wilful and passionate Achilles and Odysseus. Aeneas' kenosis is crucial to his status as the proto-Romans' organizing centre: he is the vessel of the Roman future, to whose collective promotion individual desires must be sacrificed (as David Quint argues; see Quint 1993, 83–96). Until the last books of the epic, Vergil sequesters Aeneas from the particular passions that inspired his deceased heroic peers and that laid waste their communities (e.g. Achilles' angry refusal to help the Greeks defeat Troy, and Odysseus' pitiless slaughter of the suitors, the flower of Ithaka's youth). Aeneas' belated access of perfervid wrath erodes his statesmanlike status: he kills young Lausus, obscenely overmatched in battle (*Aen.* 10.810–32), then Turnus as the Rutulian prince begs for mercy (*Aen.* 12.930–52). Precisely these acts most put into question Rome's viability, insofar as they exemplify the triumph of *furor* over the detachment necessary to the polity's governance and coherence.

Ovid borrows and exaggerates the Vergilian Aeneas' supreme self-effacement when he minimizes the narrative of their voyage, while making him and his followers little more than a plot device for eliciting other people's stories (e.g. Anius and his daughters (13.632–74), the Sybil (14.122–53), Achaemenides (14.167–222), Macareus (14.223–319), Picus and Canens (14.320–440)). Numa he reduces to the same status: the Roman king has little function in the plot of the epic other than to provide a pretext for the story of Myscelus' founding of Croton, and for Pythagoras' long harangue on metempsychosis and vegetarianism (*Met.* 15.1–478).

[35] Žižek 1992, 156.

is his 'first cause of sorrow' (*Met.* 3.138–9), Cadmus cannot know what happened to Actaeon once he changed into a nondescript deer. In fact, Cadmus is generally innocent as to how and why the gods intervene in Thebes' history. At the close of the Theban cycle, he bases his offer to be transformed into a snake in order to mollify the gods on the belief that Thebes' travails stem from divine wrath: the gods are angry because he killed the dragon at the fount. He does not know that all Thebes' troubles stem from other causes, such as Juno's resentment of her rivals. Yet in his benightedness, Cadmus acts as the type of the Symbolic Father. His offer of self-sacrifice indicates that he regards himself impartially—as if he were no less subject to the law of reprisal he believes harasses his city than its lowliest citizen, despite being the city's founder and king.

Cadmus' reaction to nescience is self-sacrifice and kenosis, whereas Agenor's reaction is wrath and cruelty. The Father's blindness is a necessary—but not by itself sufficient—condition for good kingship. And in Thebes, Agenor's self-centred ignorance as the city's distant Father trumps the on-site Father Cadmus' self-forgetting ignorance.

To the extent that Agenor figures but sketchily in Ovid's history of Thebes, he could be thought of as an 'empty' signifier, did his irrational anger not mark him with particularity and partiality, badges of the Father of Enjoyment. Thebes' subsequent history unfolds this original flaw as a series of deadlocks inscribed not only into her society, but into the realm of the divine and eventually into the physical itself (e.g. in the supernatural landscapes discussed above). The Spartoi's congenital acts of kin-murder anticipate the bloodiest acts of their successors, the Labdacids. As if proxies for Oedipus, Polyneices, and Eteocles, the Spartoi enact the internecine strife that fundamentally characterizes the myths Ovid excluded from his narrative, the strife that will ultimately destroy every Theban dynasty and Thebes itself.[36] But after the Spartoi, Ovid's Thebes suffers at the hands of gods rather than men, as if the misery had waxed too large

---

[36] The mythic history of Thebes ends with her sack by the Epigonoi, the sons of the seven heroes who enlisted in Polyneices' cause to retake the city from his brother Eteocles. The 'After-born' set out to finish what their fathers left incomplete at their deaths (*Il.* 4.405–10). Polyneices' and Eteocles' quarrel thus indirectly inspires this group's destruction of Thebes.

for mere human agents, however supernatural their origins. Only after Cadmus leaves his mortal father behind, and reaps citizens whose only father is a monster with godly patronage, does the full power of Jove's divine paternity of Thebes begin to be felt. Only the gods—the hypostases of the Father's absolute authority—can now represent the expansive, insatiable vengeance of *Père Jouissant.*

THE EMPTY LAW

Cadmus is the first to experience this malevolently augmented punitive power in his new land when castigated for slaying a monster. The huge serpent whose teeth will supply Thebes her first aborigines destroys her first immigrants by devouring Cadmus' men as they piously quest for water to make an oblation to Jove (3.26–49). After Cadmus has killed the serpent and stands contemplating its immense body, a voice admonishes him, 'quid, Agenore nate, peremptum | serpentem spectas? et tu spectabere serpens' ('why, son of Agenor, do you stare at the slain snake? You, too, will be gazed at as a snake', 3.97–8). Ovid had in passing called the serpent 'Mars' snake' ('Martius anguis', 3.32), elliptically evoking the tradition that makes the snake sacred to the war-god, and its death a source of anger to him.[37] But Ovid contradicts previous mythic tradition by juxtaposing the killing and the prophecy, insofar as their proximity insinuates a causal connection between Cadmus' augured transformation and the serpent's death.[38] Most commentators do not even attempt to articulate

[37] Scholiast on the *Iliad* (ΣA *Il.* 2.494 = 4F51); Eur. *Pho.* 931–5.

[38] Of the extant sources that precede Ovid, Euripides' *Bacchae* has Bacchus cryptically refer to Cadmus' and Harmonia's changing into snakes as 'what the oracle of Zeus says' ('chrēsmos hōs legei Dios', *Bacch.* 1333), whereas Ares appears as the saviour who will eventually convey them to the Fields of the Blessed (*Bacch.* 1338–9). However, a long lacuna precedes this prediction; it is just possible that the missing lines contained a reference to Ares' wrath. Apollodorus offers no explanation as to why Cadmus and Harmonia change into snakes, but has Zeus convey them to the Elysian Fields (*Bibl.* 3.5.4). Hyginus states that Ares destroyed Cadmus' children out of anger at his snake's death, and may imply—given that he mentions Cadmus' and Harmonia's transformation into snakes—that they also owe their transformations to

a just relation between the punishment[39] and Cadmus' actions. His intentions are praiseworthy—to avenge his men's horrible demise (3.58–9)—nor could he have known the snake's sacred status. Yet Cadmus' offence in killing the snake uncannily mirrors the paradox of Agenor's iniquity in ordering his son to find Europa or stay exiled. Once more, a man stands at the conjunction of contradictory ethical claims, Cadmus like his father caught between *pietas* and *scelus*. But this time one of the claims only becomes visible as breached: Cadmus learns too late that his vengeance for his men's death offends the snake's divine patron.

The obscure voice belatedly foretelling Cadmus' retributive metamorphosis points to a peculiarity in the structure of the law that governs Thebes. Thebes' law (an idea that includes the often mysterious unwritten set of prohibitions and injunctions that govern her citizens' fates) is a form empty of content. Though it enjoins upon its subjects an absolute duty to follow its injunctions—there is, for example, no amelioration for Cadmus merely because he had good intentions, or for his just life and just rule afterwards—these are unknowable except as already violated. This empty but implacable form of the law visits its consequences not only upon Cadmus, but also upon Actaeon, Semele, and (more gently) upon Tiresias. Actaeon offended Diana by stumbling unwittingly upon her bath (3.141–2, 175–6), Semele innocently asked for an embrace from her lover Jove that she could not survive (3.287–8); both are killed. Tiresias ignorantly struck a pair of copulating snakes and was transformed into a woman (though he regains his gender by the same act several years later, 3.323–31). All these stories describe the arc of unwitting transgression and inexorable punishment characteristic of the Theban most saliently absent from Ovid's cycle: Oedipus. Though Ovid silently banishes Oedipus from his Thebes, he yet compels Cadmus

this cause (*Fab.* 6). However, he does not say so explicitly. It must be noted that since Ovid precedes both Apollodorus and Hyginus by nearly two centuries, the mythographers' evidence as to what versions the Roman poet may have known is open to question.

[39] As far as I am aware, the single exception is Glenn (Glenn 1986), who blames Cadmus for not inferring from the snake's monstrous size and the wood's virgin nature that he was encroaching on sacred territory. Yet that bizarrely assumes Cadmus ought to have carefully studied the conventions governing the *Metamorphoses* before colonizing Boeotia.

and his fellow Thebans to act out again and again the conceptualization of law that governs Oedipus' doom.

To be sure, other characters in the *Metamorphoses* suffer, often at the hands of the gods, often arbitrarily; however, relatively few of these punishments accrue to transgressing completely unpredictable taboos, visible only as trespassed. Only two clear examples exist outside the Theban cycle: Dryope transformed into a tree after plucking a flower that hides the nymph Lotus (9.326–93), and Ocyrhoe become a horse after prophesying Achilles' future (2.635–75).[40] Yet these two are isolated instances, each singular in its book. Ovid uniquely clusters in his Theban cycle a number of tales structured on the Oedipal principle that fault can only appear in retrospect. Cadmus killing the serpent, Actaeon seeing Diana naked, Tiresias striking the copulating snakes, all fall into this category.

This diabolical law in Thebes reflects and intensifies the force of its originator. Both Thebes' empty law and Agenor as its *Père Jouissant* pose a set of self-contradictory commands. The contradiction of Agenor's order to 'find your sister or do not return' accrues to himself, the commander, as he offends against *pietas* in the very act of conforming inflexibly to its injunctions (3.5). In Thebes, the gods' implicit injunction to the artless doomed magnifies and distorts this inconsistency, so that the paradox now accrues to the command itself: 'obey a prohibition whose content you cannot know in advance'. Ovid's representation of Theban law reveals it as the ultimate instantiation of impossible demands, an arc that stretches from the internal contradictions of *pietas* to the gods' jesuitical traps. Before this side of the law, we are all always guilty.

VIRGIN AND MONSTER

Though a number of stories within the Theban cycle illustrate this empty law, Ovid was at pains to mark one as most fully mirroring the

---

[40] The flood in *Metamorphoses* 1 that destroys humanity for the fault of Lycaon alone might also qualify, because (as I have noted above) it is never entirely clear how humans so offended Jove. But again, this is an isolated incident within the text.

story of Thebes' foundation and elaborating the principles that govern its origin. I have already mentioned the repeated landscape features that figure both in Cadmus and Actaeon's fates. But the story of Actaeon's encounter with Diana also repeats the narrative sequence of transgression that Cadmus' encounter with the snake established: an intrusion upon maiden territory and a censured vision constitute trespasses of a prohibition that only becomes visible *ex post facto*.[41] Apollo directed Cadmus to follow a heifer who 'nulla passa iugum curvique inmunis aratri' ('has never suffered the yoke and is free from the curved plough'), and to found his city wherever she rested (3.10–13). This virginal beast led him to a virgin land, unsettled by human beings. There he found the spring where the serpent inhabits a wood 'untouched by the axe' (3.28–34). The snake's association with purity belies its malignity, yet killing it earns Cadmus punishment and censure for 'staring' at the snake (3.97–8).

Diana also punishes Actaeon for accidentally intruding upon chaste territory—her pool is ordinarily remote from trespass (3.157). Assuming that he has seen her naked, she contemptuously challenges him to tell of that forbidden sight, when his transformation will make it impossible: 'nunc tibi me posito uisam uelamine narres, | si poteris narrare, licet' ('now you may say that I have been seen by you naked—if you *can* say it!', *Met.* 3.192–3). As Diana reproduces for Actaeon his grandfather's first bitter taste of Boeotia, she also mirrors Cadmus' serpent-enemy.[42] The snake was an object of terror and visual fascination, beautiful and repellent at the same time: it shimmered with gold and flaunted a crest, its eyes glittered with fire, but its body swollen with poison housed triple tongues and three rows of teeth (3.32–4). So too does Diana's sinister majesty visually dominate her encounter with Actaeon; the camera's eye of the narrative focuses on her form, barely noticing Actaeon until he becomes a stag.[43] Maidenhood personified

---

[41] Barkan 1986, 42–3.

[42] Barkan infers the parallel between Diana and the serpent on the grounds that the goddess is 'placed in the center of, once again, a *locus amoenus*'. He does not elaborate the other details that point up the resemblance (Barkan 1986, 44).

[43] By the end of the Diana/Actaeon story, we readers cannot offer a single physical detail to flesh out Actaeon's portrait, where by contrast we can describe what weapons Diana doffed to bathe (javelin, quiver, arrows, 166), what clothing the goddess was wearing (a *palla*, 167), how her hair was arranged for the bath (bound up in a knot,

associated with maiden space, she bathes (like the serpent) in a secluded pool. She overawes and destroys the trespasser (as the snake does Cadmus' men, and nearly Cadmus himself).

In punishing the unwitting offence, Diana's retribution against Actaeon resembles the mysterious god's threat to Cadmus; the god's threat in turn mirrors Agenor's menace to his son. The numinous voice forecasts Cadmus' transformation, implicitly foretelling punishment for an act that *ipso facto* the divinity defines as a crime. In turn, the voice that foretells retribution both mirrors and refines the logic of Agenor's parting injunction to Cadmus, because it retains sadistic implacability while removing choice. In theory, Cadmus might have found Europa, as Agenor demanded, but he cannot *ex post facto* choose not to have killed the snake. Diana repeats this turn of the screw by also making the law's demand unknowable except as denied: Actaeon cannot know he is in danger of violating her implicit requirement—'do not look on me naked' (3.192–3)—until he has already trespassed against it (or she thinks he has; why Ovid's reader cannot be so certain I shall detail below).[44]

But more than simply repeating the significant details of Cadmus' tortured role in Thebes' early history, the Diana/Actaeon story expands the consequences of the Father's cruelty into the realm of the erotic. When Diana steps into the grove and before our eyes, the narrative's focus plays over the goddess's 'maidenly limbs' (3.164) and 'loose-flowing hair' (3.169)—both poetic erotic topoi, as Bömer

170), what her relative height was compared to her attendant nymphs (she was taller by a head, 181–2), what colour suffused her face when rage at Actaeon's intrusion possessed her (the red of a dawn or dusk, 183–5).

[44] Ovid underlines the parallel with Cadmus' conundrum posed by the empty law by insisting on evaluating Diana's execution of Actaeon within the conceptual parameters appropriate to law. He thus represents the youth's death not simply as the consequence of godly pique, but an index of the law's functioning. The Ovidian narrator carefully weighs Actaeon's intention, for example, concluding that his offence is not a 'scelus' (142) but a 'Fortunae crimen' (141). He also assesses whether the boy's punishment fits his trespass, reporting that some censure Diana's retribution as 'more violent than is just' ('uiolentior aequo', 253), while others praise it as 'worthy of her strict virginity' ('dignamque seuera I uirginitate', 254–5; I have more to say about this division of opinion below). These statements focus the reader's attention on the criteria that pertain to judging a criminal offence formally, and to judging its judgement.

notes.[45] At the same time, the poet carefully catalogues each nymph's separate service to Diana: catching her cast-off garments and weapons, binding up her hair, unfastening her sandals, dipping urns and pouring the water over her naked body (3.165–72). Borrowing from the conventions of erotic poetry, the details of Diana's elaborate toilette represent her as a desirable *puella* ('mistress'), while at the same time emphasizing her dominance over all others. Organizing all around her in a relationship of subordination and ministration to her physicality constructs Diana, not just as *an* object of desire, but as *the* object of desire. Yet she attains this status precisely by being unattainable. Just how do erotic desire and a virgin goddess meet conceptually?

They meet as another face of *Père Jouissant*—of implacable necessity wedded to fixed impossibility—but embodied in a particular shape, that of the fatal Lady of courtly love.[46] The forbidden Lady is one expression of the vicissitudes of desire, which Ovid articulated in his own *Amores, Heroides,* and much of the *Metamorphoses* (Echo's vain pursuit of Narcissus restages them just outside his Thebes, 3.370–401, as we shall see in Chapter 4). Ovid consistently dramatizes erotic desire as a study in impossibility: the lover pursues, addresses, and celebrates the beloved, but can never really be said to possess the object.[47] Such utter futility combined with universality conforms to Lacan's idea of the sexual non-relation, whereby the very condition of desire's possibility makes it unfulfillable. Desire springs from the subject's constitutive internal division that drives him or her to seek (vainly) a putatively lost wholeness. The lover is simply a special case of the general lot of humanity as discussed in Chapter 1: he ultimately longs to be recognized as a subject by another subject, unconditionally, but can only direct this longing to another divided subject, his beloved. An unconditional answer from her side, a 'yes' not haunted by doubt and unrepresented desire, is impossible.[48] The

---

[45] Bömer 1969–86, 1.494–6.

[46] As Lacan himself acknowledges when he is articulating the psychoanalytic significance of courtly love (Lacan 1986, 182–183/1992, 153).

[47] As Hardie has observed, and upon which he elaborates (Hardie 2002*b*; see esp. 30–1).

[48] See Janan 1994, 28–31, 66–8, for a discussion of the Lacanian texts relevant to the idea of the sexual non-relation.

forbidden Lady palliates this impossibility by converting it into prohibition: the sexual relation no longer appears non-existent, but forbidden instead.

But turn over this coin, and you will find the Father's 'No!' The Father's law ultimately reflects the subject's internal scission, insofar as the desire that motivates submission to prohibition also compels erotic pursuit. The wish for wholeness pursues recognition, but whether by fulfilling a lover's demands or by bowing to the protocols of cultural institutions—whether by striving to be recognized as 'beloved' or 'good citizen' or 'model child'—makes no essential difference.[49] Yet the nadir of the prohibition these various kinds of requirements embody is the empty law before whom we are all unworthy and all proleptically condemned—the law of *Père Jouissant*. The Lady's version of this unconditionality appears not merely as a simple 'no', but as arbitrary, impossible demands. Diana instantiates this particular face of Woman that mirrors the Father of Enjoyment's iron exactions and combines it with fatal fascination. Not by accident does Actaeon replay his grandfather as a Cadmus ensorcelled by the inexorable.

THE LADY VANISHES

Given that Diana appears as the quintessential object of desire (thus presumably the cynosure of all eyes) and that the offence she specifically punishes is being looked at, it is odd that no one—not we the readers, the narrator, or Actaeon—can be said unambiguously to have seen Diana's alluring form directly. The only person the text notes as 'seen', without qualification, is Actaeon himself, blundering into the grove ('uiso . . . uiro', 3.178–9). Once glimpsed, though, we abandon his viewpoint entirely, and behold nothing but nymphs wailing, beating their breasts, running to cover their mistress. We do not again focus on Diana until the nymphs have already surrounded her. At this point in the story, a passage describes the blush

---

[49] As Lacan indicates in his essay, 'The Subversion of the Subject and the Dialectic of Desire in the Freudian Unconscious' (Lacan 1966, 793–827/1977, 292–325).

that suffuses her face 'when seen without her clothes' ('uisae sine ueste Dianae', 185). Indeed, she is without clothing—but not without her nymphs as a visual barrier. Though technically naked, she is completely surrounded by her compact crowd of shorter attendants; Actaeon (and we) can still see her only from the neck up (3.178–82). Her sarcastic injunction to Actaeon to boast of having seen her naked seems to presume he did so, yet it is not clear what he saw in all the flurry. In point of fact all she challenges him to do is to *boast* of having seen her naked—a quite different offence, and something she might expect as much from a young man's bravado as his actual experience. But did he even see her face clearly? Certainly *we* do not: at the precise point where we at last focus on her visage, it disappears from view. Ovid dissolves her countenance into a picture of the sun striking clouds, describing thus the colour of Diana's angry flush.[50]

This reluctance to look at Diana directly logically concurs with her status as Woman, i.e. as the socially constructed idea of the feminine. The erotic *puella* in whose image and likeness Ovid models Diana expresses one aspect of this collective conceit. The tale's odd coyness in describing the goddess slyly suggests that she is just as much an object of fantasy as the *puella*. Ovid had already implied Diana's chimerical status in his description of her bath, insofar as its erotic power depended on the mediation of several layers of intertext, poetic conventions from his own and others' work. He pressed into service these allusions to literary hypostases of Woman in order to represent the bathing Diana's allure. Ovid's alternately conventional and elliptical descriptions of Diana indicate that Woman can never function 'in Herself', but only when approached by indirection. Looked at straight on, Her allure disappears—as it does when the text baffles our final sight of the icily angry Diana. Instead of describing a beautiful face, Ovid gives us only the inhuman: clouds and sun (3.183–5). Bömer rightly perceives that the comparison underlines Diana's inhuman terror: 'Der Zorn der Göttin ist fürchterlich; seine Gewalt darzustellen, dafür eignet sich nur der Vergleich mit den

---

[50] Ovid shows no similar qualms when representing how Daphne looks to Apollo: he goes over every part of her body, albeit not in graphic detail (1.497–501).

Elementen.'[51] Face to face with Diana, Ovid gives us, not beauty, but the elementally pitiless and the subject's destruction.

However awful Ovid's vision of Diana may be, constructing her on the model of the Fatal Lady indicates her fundamental status as a fantasy who materializes the antagonisms internal to Thebes. She does not originate the corruption that plagues Thebes, she is merely its symptom, mirroring as she does the Father of Enjoyment.[52] The antagonisms she betokens originate (ultimately) in Agenor's command to Cadmus and the aberration in the Father's function it represents. As outlined above, the (proto) Theban environment has already evidenced the Father's corruption before Diana ever appears in Ovid's narrative, in expanding and contracting snakes, and movable, anachronic, too-perfect landscapes. Thebes sprouts freaks of nature as a logical corollary to a fundamental disturbance in its Symbolic.

Diana's status as a fantasy only obliquely visible would seem to make her rendezvous with Actaeon ultimately a missed encounter. Yet whether either sees the other directly, Diana and Actaeon do mirror one another (as Leonard Barkan and John Heath note);[53] the semblance and difference they embody is crucial to Ovid's unfolding Theban narrative. Both goddess and young man are hunters, and, being tired, both seek relief in the cool wood. However, their direct encounter engenders antagonism between the two, drawing a difference between them by turning Diana into violating subject, Actaeon into violated object. Diana, whom the narrative constructs as Actaeon's double, is also his rival and deadly enemy.[54] This is not so remarkable: the two have simply played out the kind of disastrous encounter between god and mortal in a secluded place the poem

[51] 'The anger of the goddess is appalling; in order to depict its force, only comparison to Nature is suitable' (Bömer 1969–86, 1.498).

[52] 'Tout abri où puisse s'instituer une relation vivable, tempérée, d'un sexe à l'autre nécessite l'intervention—c'est l'enseignement de psychanalyse—de ce médium qui est la métaphore paternelle' (Lacan 1973, 247/1981*b*, 276). See also Slavoj Žižek's discussion of *film noir* as an exfoliation of the consequences of the paternal metaphor's failure (Žižek 1992, 149–69).

[53] Barkan 1986, 45; Heath 1991, esp. 240–1.

[54] The struggle between doubles briefly sketched between Diana and Actaeon will be fully realized in the encounter between full cousins of Cadmus' line: Bacchus and Pentheus.

often describes.[55] What is remarkable is that Diana returns Actaeon to himself by destroying him: in the first moments of his transformation, when his own dogs snap at his heels and his death is certain, he can declare unequivocally—but only silently—'Actaeon ego sum: dominum cognoscite uestrum!' ('I am Actaeon: acknowledge your master!' 3.230).[56] This savage dénouement sketches a third configuration of the logical consequences from the Father's devolution into *Père Jouissant*. In the face of the Father's 'No!' deteriorating into senseless, impossible demands (originating with Agenor, repeated and amplified in the serpent's divine patron, and culminating in Diana), the subject cannot sustain himself, his integrity. Rather, he splits in two, into himself and his double, with whom he engages in antagonistic struggle. Rather than finding his lost wholeness in addressing the other, he encounters only the most grotesque and painful recapitulation of his constitutive internal division: Actaeon-deer.

JUDGING DIANA

Ovid's summation of the judgement rendered on Diana's grisly vengeance against Actaeon weaves together the separate strands of law and the erotic, the Father and the Lady, that we have traced through Actaeon's story. We are told

> rumor in ambiguo est: aliis uiolentior aequo
> uisa dea est, alii laudant dignamque seuera
> uirginitate uocant; pars inuenit utraque causas.
>
> (*Met.* 3.253–5)

---

[55] Cf. Segal 1969.

[56] Barkan rightly points to this line as evidence of Actaeon's self-recognition, but claims that here Actaeon has 'for the first time' a sense of his own identity, that he 'discovers himself' (Barkan 1986, 45–6). I find no evidence for this primacy, nor do I believe as he does that Actaeon's 'identity has been multiplied'. To say that 'the transformation has turned Actaeon into subject and object at once, into victim and human perceiver' is merely to articulate some of the antipodes into which the subject's aboriginal internal division splits him.

opinion is divided: to some the goddess seemed more savage than was just, others praise her and call her worthy of her exacting virginity. Each group finds reasons.

The starkness of the second opinion seems inexplicable (how did poor startled Actaeon's accidental intrusion threaten Diana's virginity?), until the next line supplies the perspective from which it is articulated:

> sola Iovis coniunx non tam culpetne probetne
> eloquitur, quam clade domus ab Agenore ductae
> gaudet et a Tyria conlectum paelice transfert
> in generis socios odium.

(Met. 3.256–9)

Only Jove's wife does not disclose whether she blames or approves; she rejoices in the destruction of the house derived from Agenor and she transfers the hatred drawn from her Tyrian rival [Europa] to the other members of the family.

The sudden focus on Juno's animadversions reveals that the debate over the justice of Diana's act transpired among the gods. Not by accident does Ovid set the debate in the divine sphere, the realm of the absolute: Diana's apologists have banished the human considerations of motive and intent that might otherwise soften their judgement. But Juno's *ad hominem* evaluation of Actaeon's fate reveals the dark underside of this absolutism: her joy in his death is equally willing to banish considerations of motive, intent, or even agency in selecting objects of retribution (little difference to her that Actaeon had nothing to do either with Europa's or Semele's connections to Jove). Her revealed cruelty casts suspicion on the unarticulated motives of her punctilious peers. Juno is the unlovely truth of the *laudatores Dianae*.

She is also the uglier side of Diana's relation to the Father. Diana's numinously alluring presence—the riveting dawn of her anger that paralyses Actaeon, the fascination of her *seuera uirginitas* that banishes all other considerations from her evaluators' minds— masks the Father, in the sense that she obscures the subject's traumatic relation to the Father and to what really underpins His law. In order to centre a unified polity, the Father must remain ignorant of the dark licentiousness and cruelty that ultimately inform his judgements—the sadism behind the pious severities of the gods that Juno's vindictive ruminations throw into relief. His law must be presumed

universal and neutral in order to function; its commerce with enjoyment—with the irrational and libidinous, epitomized in *Père Jouissant*—must remain hidden. Diana, however eye-catching, merely
measures the degree to which the Father has been fatally indiscreet
in Theban history.

After the *Metamorphoses*, Ovid had bitter occasion to revisit the
Diana–Actaeon story. As an exile, he chose the figure of Actaeon to
represent himself as an unwitting offender in *Tristia* 2's long apologia
to Augustus. The logic of this allegory implicitly casts the emperor in
the role of Actaeon's punisher, Diana (*Tristia* 2. 105). Actaeon's
reappearance in the poetry of a subject banished at his emperor's
command highlights what is already implicit in the *Metamorphoses*
story: the perverse conundra of the (Theban or Roman) citizen
before *Père Jouissant*'s law, and its seductive, destructive contradictions embodied in Diana. In *Tristia* 2, Augustus (like Diana) assumes
the place of the elegiac *puella*, of the consummate object of desire.
Ovid (as *exclusus amator*) pleads with the emperor to remove the
barrier that stands between the poet and his desire—reintegration
into Rome, the one civic community in which Ovid desires membership. Augustus has, in fact, become Rome: in *Ex Ponto* 2.8, when
Ovid gazes upon the emperor's image, he 'seems to see Rome'
('videor mihi cernere Romam', *Pont* 2.8.19).[57] But far from being a
mere nullity who holds the state together by allowing its citizens to
recognize their various selves in the emperor's blank neutrality, it is
now the task of the citizen to discover and to reflect the emperor's
desire. *Tristia* 2 remarks that Augustus was merciful to Ovid because
he let the poet live and spared him a Senate trial (2.122–38). As Miller
has noted, the consequences of such a trial would likely have been
worse, because

the very fact of a public trial on charges brought by Augustus would have
required all who wished for the *princeps'* favor to demonstrate their loyalty
by demanding the harshest penalty.[58] Is the poet's thanks ironic here
or insincere? How would we know the difference: for it is the very denial

---

[57] Green 1994, 326; Miller 2004, 218.
[58] This is based on Paolo Cutolo's insight, as Miller acknowledges (Cutolo 1995,
40–1).

of the due process of law owed a Roman citizen that constitutes the emper-or's mercy.[59]

That summary judgement could be construed as clemency shows the extent to which Rome's law has revealed itself as Thebes' empty law: the accused is always already guilty, whether judged by emperor or Senate. Like the sycophant Olympic council overawed by Jove's bluster about Lycaon and corrupt humanity, 'justice' now consists of the Father's human instruments scrambling to magnify his dis-pleasure, so as to visit it mordantly upon his offender.

Ultimately, Ovid's Thebes is less a place where the paternal func-tion that founds the law and the polity has gone awry than where our ignorance of its true nature lies in tatters. In that sense, it oddly mirrors the end of Vergil's *Aeneid*, which founds Rome upon an act that seemingly resolves the internal tensions of *pietas*, at least mo-mentarily. Aeneas avenges his young comrade Pallas by killing Turnus, the boy's murderer and Aeneas' only rival for control of Italy. Vengeance and virtue join hands in the sacrifice: *furor* returns but *imperium sine fine* is vouchsafed. Ovid traces the same coherence between these antipodes of *pietas* and *furor*, to radically different ends. Ovid forces upon us the knowledge that the conflict between bloodlust and duty that characterized mythic Thebes, and both contemporary and embryonic Rome, is no conflict at all. They are only the *recto* and *verso* of our traumatic encounter with pre-Sym-bolic chaos, an encounter in which the Father—Agenor, Aeneas, Augustus—is our (illusory) shield. At the heart of civilization's severity, the rule of the law, lies chaos, cruelty, and malign enjoyment.

[59] Miller 2004, 229.

3

'Th' Unconquerable Will, and Study of Revenge'

Juno in Thebes

Still she's a heavenly creature, bountiful
And splendid even in anger; what is more,
How can I blame her, godhead being so dull?
Her immortality must prove a chore
Did not some screaming rage restore the full
—Now, why have I not thought of this before?—
The full immediacy, that zest of strife
And plural of spouse which is the spice of life.

A. D. Hope[1]

The previous chapter reviewed the causes of Thebes' troubles, and its first signs: the city's Sidonian origins in Jupiter's lust and Agenor's wrath, its Boeotian founding upon the blood of Sidonians and Spartoi, and the dawn of its divine persecution when Diana slaughters Actaeon. But the greatest source of Theban trouble appears on-stage only after Diana has culled her single victim from the city. While others debate the justice of the virgin goddess's vengeance, Juno ponders how she might emulate it (3.253–72). She will do so often, and borrow from more models than Diana's reprisal. Juno visits destruction upon the Cadmeans on more occasions, and more severely, than any other god (measuring by sheer body count). In fact,

---

[1] From 'Jupiter on Juno' (Hope 1992).

all her vengeful efforts recorded in the *Metamorphoses* culminate in Thebes—logically enough, since two of her rivals, Europa and Semele, are connected to the city's existence. And Ovid's Juno is a goddess inspired to retaliation by sexual rivalry like nothing else; in fact, nothing *but* sexual jealousy motivates her vengeance in this poem.

The *Metamorphoses*' cankered Juno bears witness to what David Konstan argues is the Augustan era's own invention: romantic jealousy.[2] Konstan critically analyses ancient literature to show that pre-Augustan exempla we have assumed to fit our modern understanding of jealousy lack various crucial features (e.g. anxiety over another's loss of affection for oneself). He credits Horace, *Ode* 1.13, with first visibly and paradigmatically integrating the elements of modern romantic jealousy. The ode coordinates anger, sadness, and fear, all inspired by the sense that the beloved's preference for another rejects the lover; an aspect of the lover's very identity is thus threatened. Konstan also notes that the early Empire's historical conditions favoured such a development: at least among the Roman elite, an ideal of reciprocal love in marriage was gaining ground.[3] Augustus' promotion of 'family values' as the centre both of a peaceful, harmonious Rome and of her model citizen's aspirations helped foster that ideal.[4]

Such an analysis helps us see how Ovid's goddess reflects broad historical developments; yet by itself, it cannot explain why his Juno contrasts so markedly with Augustan epic's other famous portrait of Junonian enmity. Horace's contemporary and Ovid's predecessor Vergil had given the *Aeneid*'s Juno a much more expansive portfolio of motivation: among her grounds for harrying the Trojans she included love for a city and fear for its eclipse (Carthage), along with fondness for a man (Turnus). Although Ovid took pains to evoke Vergil in his own portrait of Heaven's Queen, nothing remotely comparable widens his Juno's vindictive tunnel-vision. That is not to say the *Metamorphoses*' goddess focuses solely on her rivals as objects of redress; many more than they suffer her depradations. In fact, Ovid arranges Juno's reprisals in the first four books of the poem as a

---

[2] Konstan 2006*a*, 219–43.
[3] Veyne 1978.
[4] Milnor 2005, 239–84.

crescendo of payback. At first she torments only her rivals, inflicting temporary discomfiture, but she eventually expands her purview to include the rivals' kith and the kin, and to inflict the most hideous transformations and deaths upon them all. And then, sudden and ferocious as Juno's onslaught has been, she disappears from the poem forever as avenger in the flesh. Every act of Junonian vengeance subsequently narrated in the *Metamorphoses* appears only as someone's recollection of, or even mere speculation on, the goddess's intervention.

These facts raise a number of questions. Why does Ovid gesture toward the *Aeneid*'s Juno of wider vision,[5] yet pointedly make sexuality alone the engine of his goddess's revenge, when subtracting nobler motives seemingly degrades Juno's significance from Vergilian counter-fate to mere shrew?[6] Why does Ovid arrange Juno's revenge against her *paelices* in an escalating series, when there is nothing in the antecedent myths to suggest this? Why does this series climax at Thebes? And why does Juno the Avenger disappear from the poem as the present agent of her own wrath after executing her Theban devastation?

Stephen Wheeler and Philip Hardie have both scrutinized the trajectory of Juno's wrath, and the reasons behind it.[7] Wheeler traces in the various battles between Jupiter and Juno over the god's *amores* a narrative organization and rough timeline. Within Ovid's otherwise amorphous poem, these 'other-woman' episodes build upon and refer to their predecessors.[8] He attributes Juno's escalation to her frustration over the way Jupiter frequently ameliorates her punishments (I shall have more to say about this presently). That instances of her revenge fade and nearly disappear by the end of the book he

[5] Hardie painstakingly analyses Ovid's allusions to Vergil's Juno (Hardie 1990, 231–5).

[6] As Otis notes (Otis 1970, 132).

[7] Juno's savage temper in the *Metamorphoses* has garnered less scholarly attention than seems due, given that instances of it regularly punctuate the poem. In addition to Wheeler 2000 and Hardie 1990, I can find only three other scholars who have in the last few decades devoted any concentrated attention to Juno's anger in the *Metamorphoses*; these are Nagle 1984, 239, 243–6; Curran 1978, 224–6; O'Bryhim 1990. None of these addresses the questions I have raised here.

[8] Wheeler 2000, 73.

ties to Ovid's plan of clearing space for Jupiter's dialectical evolution
from mere philanderer (repeatedly inviting his wife's wrath) to lofty
arbiter of fate 'associated with apotheosis and the Caesars' in the
poem's closing books.[9] Yet Wheeler offers no explanation as to
why Juno's revenge should peak at Thebes, nor why she reappears
thereafter only in memory and ekphrasis.

For Hardie, on the other hand, the intensity of Juno's assault upon
Thebes directly measures the degree to which Ovid's foundation tale
reflects upon the *Aeneid*. After all, Vergil organized his tale of Rome's
legendary genesis around Juno's hatred of the Trojans. The Ovidian
goddess's harassment of nascent Thebes thus underlines her indebt-
edness to Vergil's Juno, whose chief function in the *Aeneid* is to
oppose Rome's founding. Like Brooks Otis before him, Hardie
sees that in Thebes, Juno imitates but greatly exaggerates the Vergilian Juno's acts of vengeance.[10] She heaps multiple ills copied from
the *Aeneid*'s many victims onto a single sufferer, or realizes in her
spiteful campaign what Vergil's Juno could only wish.[11] Though she
shares the Boeotian stage with other divine avengers (Diana, Nemesis, Bacchus), she overshadows them all by adding her Aeneidic
repertoire to their patterns of reprisal: she harries more, and more
innocent, Thebans.[12] For example, she caps the whole series of divine

---

[9] Wheeler 2000, 105.

[10] Hardie 1990, 231–5; Otis 1970, 130–3.

[11] For example, Hardie notes that in deceiving Semele, Juno borrows a name, a
guise, and two Junonian retributions from the *Aeneid*. She assumes the shape of
Beroë, Semele's nurse. But 'Beroë' was also the name (and guise) Juno's agent Iris had
assumed in *Aeneid* 5 while inspiring the Trojan women to fire their ships. In the
Metamorphoses, Juno makes sure that it is Semele who will burn—and who will also
drown in the Styx (*mersa*, 3.272), thus realizing the Vergilian Juno's attempt to sink
Aeneas' ships in *Aeneid* 1 (*Aen.* 1.40 *summergere*, 69 *submersas*). As for realizing the
Vergilian Juno's wishes: Juno wishes she could use Jupiter's weapon against her enemy
in *Aeneid* I as Pallas had (*Aen.* 1.39–49). Ovid's Juno actually manages this when she
arranges for Jupiter to destroy Semele with his own lightning (*Met.* 3.301–9). For all
these points, see Hardie 1990, 232.

[12] The sheer number of Juno's Theban victims surpasses Diana's and Nemesis',
who destroy only one apiece, Actaeon and Narcissus respectively. Moreover, Juno's
prey are all innocent, unlike Bacchus' casualties (with the possible exception of
Semele—though how a mere mortal woman is supposed to say 'no' effectively to
the resistless rapist Jupiter is anyone's guess). No object of her wrath has defied her or
scorned her divinity, as the Tyrrhenian pirates (3.614–20), Pentheus (3.513–16), and
the Minyeides (4.37–8) set Bacchus at naught.

vengeances against Cadmus' house with the Grand Guignol gesture of summoning a Fury from Hell. This had been the Vergilian Juno's resource against Amata and Turnus in *Aeneid* 7 (323–560) when she once again derailed Aeneas' plans to establish himself and his followers in Italy. Yet Ovid's Juno instructs her demon to drive Athamas and Ino to murderous madness, as her hated rival Bacchus did Pentheus' mother and aunt (*Met.* 3.710–31).[13] Moreover, Ovid offers no real conclusion to Juno's trajectory of emulative hatred for a city and its people. Where Vergil's Juno ultimately subordinates her animus against the Trojans to Jupiter's plans for founding Rome, the Ovidian Juno remains to the end unrepentantly unreconstructed, yielding her hatred of Thebes to no one and nothing.

But for what reason? Even if we assume, with Hardie and Otis, that Vergil's Juno suggested the model, what exactly compels Ovid to exaggerate it? Why resurrect the goddess with circumscribed motives and an expanded thirst for vengeance?[14] Why is a Juno even more Satanic than Vergil's useful to Ovid?

Answering these questions requires unfolding the nature and structure of the Ovidian Juno's wrath. Tracing the evolution of her outrage through the early books of the *Metamorphoses* will help us analyse its culmination in Thebes. As noted, the single source of her fury in the poem is Jupiter's sexual appetite for other females. Yet the hatred Juno harbours for the nymphs and women lucklessly involved

---

[13] Hardie 1990, 232–3.

[14] Admittedly, both Vergil and Ovid drew upon unpromising material, the Hera-Juno of mythology being a generally dour figure. Yet the goddess has kinder moments that Ovid could have included in his epic more easily than Vergil in his, simply because the *Metamorphoses* is a broad mythological compendium. For example, though Ovid tells the story of Jason and Medea in *Metamorphoses* 7, he never mentions Hera's aid to the hero. Other authors tell us: Hera pushed the *Argo* safely through the Symplegades (Apollodorus, *Bibliotheca* 1.9.22); in company with Athena, she prevailed upon Aphrodite to intercede with Eros, so that he caused Medea to fall in love with and aid Jason (Apollonius Rhodius, *Arg.* 3.83–9); Hera expressed her intention to protect him even if he should go to Hades to free her would-be rapist, Ixion (Apollonius Rhodius, *Arg.* 3.61–3).

Also, given a choice between mythical variants, one of which shows Hera in a better light, one in a worse, Ovid will choose the latter. For instance, he prefers the versions of the Callisto tale that make Hera rather than Artemis responsible for the nymph's transformation into a bear (for the different versions of Callisto tale, see Gantz 1993, 725–8).

in these infidelities is all out of proportion to its material cause, given that almost all are rape victims. Far from wishing to undermine Juno's marriage, they would reject Jupiter's advances if they physically could. The Ovidian narrator himself observes that Juno's reaction takes insufficient account of their unwillingness: had Juno seen Callisto struggling against her rapist Jove, he says, she would have been kinder to the nymph (*Met.* 2.434–6).[15]

The chief apparent exception to Jupiter's string of rape victims is Theban Semele. Juno can undo her precisely because she is Jupiter's lover, not his victim. Disguised as Semele's nurse Beroë, Juno persuades Semele to ask Jove to come to her with the same supernatural majesty with which he embraces Juno. Having foolishly sworn by Styx that he will fulfil his lover's wish even before he has heard what it is, Jove must grant Semele's request. His full sublimity incinerates the girl (3.256–312). Semele's doom turns upon her having a quasi-conjugal relation of affection with Jove. Receiving her lover regularly, she may ask him to embrace her differently next time; having a lover's relationship with him, she can count on his affection to grant her request before his reason vetoes it.

Semele's repeated and willing adultery might broadly seem to justify Juno's revenge upon her. But Juno's vindictiveness also curses the blameless, such as Semele's sister Ino and Ino's family. Ino evidences no intention to deceive Juno or desecrate her marriage; her only offence is to be proud of her husband, her two children, and her nurseling Dionysus, the child of Jove and Semele (4.420–2).[16] Yet against her Juno's vengeance blossoms into even greater virulence than in her punitive expeditions against Semele herself. Ino's ruin trains the whole history of Juno's destructive powers over mind and body upon the hapless woman's family and retainers.[17] The *Metamorphoses'* preceding books depict Juno retaliating against her

[15] Of course, Ovid draws upon a mythological tradition that generally represents the gods defending their status and prerogatives with overkill, either unable or unwilling to fine-tune their punishments. But it is exactly that normalization of what absolute power can visit upon the helpless the *Metamorphoses* subjects to ruthless scrutiny.

[16] As Bömer dryly remarks, 'Ist im allgemeinen kein strafwürdiges Vergehen' ('This is not generally a punishable crime', Bömer 1969–86, 2.141).

[17] Wheeler 2000, 73.

husband's victims and théir succourers by inventive corporal or mental manipulation. Juno's minion Argos prevents bovine Io from reassuming human form (1.624–9); her Fury goads Io to desperation (1.724–7). After Juno changes Callisto into a bear, the nymph's son nearly kills his mother (2.476–88, 2.496–504). Juno makes Echo partially mute (3.359–69), and persuades Semele unwittingly to request her own destruction (3.287–8).

But Juno amplifies the horror of Athamas and Ino's doomed household by combining mental and physical transformations with kin-strife and kin-murder (4.420–562). A Fury maddens Athamas into killing his infant son; his wife Ino, also maddened by grief or by the Fury (4.520), leaps into the sea with her other son in her arms. When Ino's sorrowing handmaidens complain of her fate, the goddess transforms some into stone statues, others into birds. Juno has arranged an end for this noble house that (as Hardie notes) recapitulates and magnifies disasters previously inflicted on other Cadmeans, such as Dionysiac possession, a son's mutilation, and animal transformation.[18]

This catalogue of outrage that shows Juno expanding her vengeance until it encompasses not only her rivals, but their family and friends, treats sexual rivalry as if it were a contagion that tainted all connected to Jupiter's paramours. As the poem progresses, Juno strikes deeper as well as wider: her persecutions grow in severity, from Io's relatively short-lived trials that have no permanent consequence to Athamas and Ino's extravagant suffering and its irreversible outcome. The more rivals Juno exterminates, the greater her efforts to obliterate more, and to crush their associates, too. It is as if the remainder touched by her husband's lust, however tangentially, became proportionally more dangerous and contaminating by the elimination of their fellows, the danger more concentrated the fewer the offenders. Juno seems to invest her husband's inamoratas

---

[18] Hardie 1990, 232. Hardie is particularly interested in the way Juno recaps her *bête noire* Bacchus' acts of vengeance, so that he emphasizes the transformation of some of Ino's companions into birds as an echo of the Minyeides' metamorphosis into bats. Yet, viewed simply as humans changed into animals, the companions also mirror Actaeon's transformation. Juno's revenge amplifies *both* Bacchus *and* Diana's malevolent acts against the Cadmeans.

and their associates with mysterious, infectious powers only she can perceive.

Why does Juno's fury over her husband's infidelities keep spiralling upwards in its virulence and scope?[19] As noted, Wheeler tries to explain by pointing to Jupiter's regular interventions to ameliorate the effects of his wife's wrath upon his paramours. Jove saves Io from the animal torments Juno visits on her by seeming to promise his wife future fidelity (1.734–7);[20] after Juno transforms Callisto, Jupiter's timely double catasterism prevents her unwitting son from matricide (2.505–7); the god lessens his thunderbolt's power when he last comes to Semele, a delicacy that fails to save her, but allows him to rescue their son Bacchus (3.302–15). Wheeler regards these ameliorations as preventing Juno from 'setting the balance straight'.[21] But that analysis begs the question. It assumes that having your husband incinerate your rival could be viewed as just either from the perspective of Ovid's audience or from that of some more absolute moral position. How otherwise would having your errant spouse cremate his paramour in the act of love *not* be 'enough vengeance' for his infidelity?

---

[19] It might be said that here Ovid simply follows Vergil's lead, insofar as Juno's second large-scale intervention against the Trojans in the *Aeneid* significantly expands upon her first. In the first instance, she has Aeolus stir up the winds in an attempt to drown the refugees at sea (*Aen.* 1.34–80); in the second, she sends Allecto to involve all the Italians in war against the Trojans (*Aen.* 7.286–322). Yet that alone would not explain Ovid's structure: his Juno's pattern of revenge is a steady crescendo, whereas in between *Aeneid* 1 and 7, Vergil's Juno has her less ambitious moments. For example, she tries to divert Aeneas' mission of foundation bloodlessly to Carthage; when that fails, she later sends Iris to drive the Trojan women docked in Sicily to set fire to their ships. If successful, either plan would strand the Trojans outside of Italy, but would not compass their deaths, as her efforts through Aeolus and Allecto do.

[20] Wheeler adduces A. G. Lee, who notes that Jupiter's promise to Juno—'numquam tibi causa doloris I haec erit', *Met.* 1.736–7—involves a clever ambiguity. 'The referent for the demonstrative *haec* is ambiguous: it may refer to *causa* or to Io. In the former case, Jupiter would abjure adultery; in the latter, he would only renounce Io' (Wheeler 2000, 74; Lee's original comment reads as follows: 'haec: there is prob. a double meaning; either "this sort of behaviour on my part will never again cause you pain", or "Io will never etc."—implying that there may be others. Jove intends Juno to take the promise in the first sense; he swears to it only in the second', Lee 1953, 142).

[21] Wheeler 2000, 72.

RETINAL RIVALRY

The very limitlessness of Juno's spiralling vengeance implies a discontent that springs from reasons structural rather than contingent. That the best efforts of a goddess who can bend both mind and matter to her will should repeatedly fail of satisfaction points to a desired object not fortuitously unavailable to her, but fundamentally impossible to attain. Juno's unanswerable sufferings in fact coincide with Freud's description of 'pathological' melancholy, as opposed to 'normal' mourning.[22] Freud divides into two types grief over the loss of a beloved person (or of an abstraction that has supplanted one, such as homeland, freedom, an ideal, or the like). There is little to choose between the observable features of mourning and melancholia; both alike absorb all available psychic energy, so that the outside world, its activities and its objects, hold no interest for the withdrawn and dejected sufferer. Where the two conditions crucially differ is in the steadfastness of the melancholic's attachment. The mourner gradually succeeds in detaching from the loss, so that sooner or later she can again turn her attention to other foci of interest and resume her normal life. By contrast, the melancholic irrationally clings to the lost object, persisting in her longing for what she cannot have.

It is inadequate, however, to rest at this superficial level. We fall into tautology if in analysing Juno's pathological violence we merely label it pathology. Freud's conceptualization of loss possesses more profound resources—and as elaborated in Lacan's thought, it can help us explicate the logical impasses of the sexual relation that shape Juno's role as divine sponsor of marriage. Ovid's ever-frustrated, ever-betrayed, but absolutely undeviating goddess of conjugal relations reflects a force that, far from being a twisted neurosis of the minority, in fact pandemically structures our lives as subjects of loss.[23]

---

[22] 'Mourning and Melancholia', *SE* 14: 238–58.

[23] The thought behind Freud's short essay on mourning and melancholia eventually founded his important analysis of the key components of identity in *The Ego and the Id* (*SE* 19: 12–59); in that essay, Freud concluded the ego was constituted by the remains of abandoned object-cathexes. The ego thus comprises the accumulated residues of loss. By no coincidence, the current epoch of loss—the twentieth and

Juno enacts on an Olympian scale the dilemmas attendant upon human desire. The loss she finds so intractable mirrors the condition of the desiring, because fundamentally lacking, human subject. Yet her inconsolability specifically suits her office as the goddess of marriage. Viewed from a Lacanian perspective, comfortless Juno discloses an integrity we had missed when comparing her to Vergil's queen of the gods. Where Freud values mourning as normal, contemning melancholia as illness, Lacan finds melancholy the richer concept. Freud attends pragmatically to the fact that mourning eventually accommodates itself again to life and to the satisfactions it offers even without the mourned. By contrast, Lacan focuses upon the ethical moment of melancholia's stubbornness. He sees the ethics of fidelity as inextricably tied to the substitutive relations that ensue from the subject's fundamental lack. Human beings can choose either mourning, or melancholy. They may seek after fulfilment in objects seen as a series whose elements are more or less interchangeable, so that attachment to one never ultimately prevents its exchange for another. Or they may construe their fulfilment as depending on one object valued as the non-pareil and thus raised above commutation. From this perspective, mourning betrays the beloved object, while melancholy remains faithful, refusing to renounce its

twenty-first centuries, beset by war, genocide, diaspora, globalization, and a general loss of faith in civilization's 'master narratives'—has produced new interest in the relation of loss to subjectivity. Such formidable thinkers as Giorgio Agamben (Agamben 1977), Julia Kristeva (Kristeva 1987), and Judith Butler (Butler 1997) have taken up and developed the implications of Freud's thought, and used it to address the question of loss as a basis for resistance. Loss can found a particular type of melancholic resistance to the 'normal', whereby the subject creatively persists and resists the regulations of culture. Though Agamben, Kristeva, and Butler each approaches the question from quite different perspectives, all see melancholia as containing the possibility of the subject's freedom. In that respect, their inquiries overlap with Lacan's ethical construction of melancholia, especially as developed in his seventh Seminar, *The Ethics of Psychoanalysis,* where he examines Sophocles' Antigone and her 'irrational' defiance of King Creon beyond any tangible gain for herself or her dead brother Polyneices (Lacan 1986). The work of Lacan, Kristeva, Butler, and Agamben has inspired and engaged other interventions on the topic of melancholia and loss. Among the most interesting are the following (a list meant to be selective rather than exhaustive): Santner 1990; Abrams 1993; Heidbrink 1994; Brown 1999; Žižek 2000*a*; Ng–Kazanjian 2003; Forter 2001 and 2003.

attachment;[24] marriage is one of the highest social formalizations of this refusal. Juno's pathology is the dark side of her office as the goddess of marriage; her malevolence springs quite logically from the marital premises of fidelity, carried to bitter extremes.[25]

This raises a further question: what exactly is Juno's melancholically lamented object, and why can she not obtain it, so that she may cease to grieve over it? We noted at the beginning of this chapter that all instances of Juno's wrath in the *Metamorphoses* ultimately stem from her husband's infidelity. Juno focuses upon the sexual relation as the root of her ills: her anger devolves upon her rivals (and by extension, their kith and kin), as if in copulating with her husband, even involuntarily, they had stolen something precious and irreplaceable from her. But what, exactly?

Nothing unique to herself, alas: Juno grieves over a sexual fulfilment unavailable to anyone, as becomes obvious from the one tiff between her and Jove not directly sparked by an infidelity. In a black-comic interlude incongruously inserted into the chain of Thebes' disasters (Semele has just combusted), the drunken Jupiter baits his wife by claiming that women get more pleasure from the sex act than men do. He frames the claim as a general proposition, and she rejects it as such:

> 'maior uestra profecto est
> quam, quae contingit maribus,' dixisse 'uoluptas.'
> illa negat.

> (*Met.* 3.320–2)

'Really, your satisfaction is greater than what falls to the lot of us males.' She denied it.

---

[24] The classical expression of this concept is Lacan's analysis of Sophocles' *Antigone*, as mentioned above (Lacan 1986, 285–373/1992, 243–324). See also Slavoj Žižek's explications of the conceptualization of mourning and melancholia (Žižek 2000*a*; 2001, 141–52).

[25] Leo Curran has also argued that Juno's vindictiveness springs from her office as goddess of marriage. He sees in her viciousness a reflection of Roman society's equally irrational and unforgiving sexual mores, but he makes clear that these mores often come all too uncomfortably close to modern sexual attitudes (Curran 1978, 225–6).

According to the logic of his assertion and her negation, the proposition is true, or untrue, for all women and for all men, not just for Juno or Jupiter in particular. As noted in Chapter 1, this means something is missing from the sexual relation per se—and, oddly enough, Jupiter and Juno each frame the problem as something missing from their sex's experience that is present in the other's. Juxtaposed, their responses mean the sexual relation is fundamentally deficient for both sexes; whence otherwise their common feeling of being swindled?

Among the *Metamorphoses'* females, it is not only the abandoned wife Juno who feels this way. The disguised Juno easily persuades Semele that her sexual relations with Jupiter lack something, that she is missing a splendour only Jove's wife enjoys. The goddess's facile victory is striking: though Jove visits his paramour faithfully, though he gives every sign of being enslaved by love (ready as he is to grant her ultimate wish before she even articulates it), yet when Juno-Beroë alleges that his embraces fail of some further sublimity, Semele instantly believes her. Of course, when Jove visits Semele for the last time to engage reluctantly in lovemaking's divine apogee, she finds the bliss she craves to be death and destruction (3.302–12). Nor can we suppose that making love to Jupiter is any happier for Juno. Her clear and firm belief that females miss what males enjoy in lovemaking argues that, *sub specie aeternitatis*, Juno is only marginally less cheated than Semele. The queen of the gods has all of time in which to savour her dispossession—world without end of burning without relief.

Juno's persistent dissatisfaction again points toward Lacan's elaboration of Freud's categories of desire as loss and as lack. For Lacan, loss veils lack: the melancholic reacts to the fundamental impossibility of a perfectly complementary relation between Man and Woman, lover and beloved, by converting what she never had into an object she no longer has and for which she mourns eternally and unsatisfiably. Juno's bottomless desire revolves around just such a fictive object, something neither she nor anyone else ever possessed: the sexual relation. Like the melancholic, the goddess's festering anger confuses fundamental lack with contingent loss. Her reading of relations between the sexes disputes the implicit assumption, 'I never was able to find my other half, my complete (sexual) complement, in

Jupiter (because that is impossible).' Rather, the logic behind her words and actions can be summarized as, 'I do not have an ideal relationship with Jupiter because of my rivalry with (Io/Callisto/ Semele); this female has supplanted me, and if only she were eliminated, everything would be perfect.' Her rivals' putative alienation of Jupiter's affection becomes the single explanation for all Juno's ills, and their fault a miasma that stains all their kith and kin. As she eliminates each rival, yet fails to attain the perfect unity she desires with her husband, she spreads her net wider, as though the fault were a sublime, indestructible substance communicated and spread from her rivals' bodies to each and every one of their near and dear. Everyone must suffer, even the innocent: Inachus, Arcas, Athamas, and Ino.[26] 'Lost or alienated sex with Jupiter' becomes Juno's equivalent of the Unified Field Theory, the single explanation that brings the heterogeneous phenomena of the world to order, giving it a structure and sense of orientation, a trajectory of desire.

An example of this monocausality emerges in Juno's explanation for the weather. When clouds appear on a sunny day, she immediately suspects that her husband is trying to conceal one of his infidelities from her. To give her credit, she is correct: Jupiter has gathered the clouds to conceal his rape of Io (*Met.* 1.597–609). However, that does not lessen the oddity of her leap of logic in its uncompromising resort to causal determinism: 'Hmm, the sky is overcast; ergo, my husband must be cheating on me.' Juno's thinking cannot tolerate the arbitrary or the contingent: she immediately sees all phenomena through the lens of Jupiter's unfaithfulness.[27]

But her monomania does not completely explain Juno's egregious cruelty to her rivals and their folk. If she is convinced that her husband's sexual victims are impediments to her happiness, why not simply eliminate them, as Apollo makes short work of the unfaithful Coronis (*Met.* 2.532–611), or as he and his sister Diana

---

[26] Inachus does not suffer as the others in this list do, but that conforms to the pattern of Juno tormenting her victims ever more extremely as the *Metamorphoses*' record of her vengeances progresses. Inachus does have to mourn his transformed daughter, and is even prevented from being near her, because Juno's servant Argus snatches her away (1.651–66).

[27] See John Peradotto's masterful analysis of myth and magic as exemplifying modes of thought that exclude the category of chance or accident (Peradotto 1992).

kill boastful Niobe's children (*Met.* 6.146–312)? Instead, Juno resorts
to torments she justifies by imputing to her rivals a deliberate desire
to antagonize herself, against all evidence. Before transforming Callisto, for example, she harangues the nymph as if she had deliberately
plotted Juno's disgrace:

> 'scilicet hoc unum restabat, adultera' dixit
> 'ut fecunda fores fieretque iniuria partu
> nota Iouisque mei testatum dedecus esset.
> haud inpune feres; adimam tibi namque figuram
> qua tibi quaque places nostro, importuna, marito.'
>
> (*Met.* 2.471–5)

'To be sure, it only needed this, you strumpet!' she said, 'that you become
pregnant and my betrayal be known because you gave birth, and that it
testify to how Jove dishonoured me! You won't get away with this! I shall
destroy your beauty, because of which you have pleased both yourself and
my husband, you bitch!'

Similarly, she accuses Semele of having deliberately plotted to get
pregnant by Jove ('mater, quod uix mihi contigit, uno | de Ioue uult
fieri'—'she wishes to become a mother by Jove alone, something that
has barely happened to *me*!' 3.269–70). Juno irrationally assumes
that Callisto's and Semele's pregnancies were the result of acts of will,
for which the two mothers ought to be blamed. Juno's hatred of her
rivals completely transforms them in her eyes: Callisto is Jupiter's
unwilling victim, Semele his naïve paramour, but Juno sees them
both as prepotent connivers at her unhappiness. Whence this distorted vision?

Juno's delusion points toward the connection between desire and
sublimation crystallized in Lacan's concept of anamorphosis. Lacan
borrows the term from the practice in painting of representing one
element in the picture from a distorted perspective. Viewed directly,
the object appears to be a meaningless blob, but seen from a particular angle, the distortion disappears and the image in the picture
looks normal. Lacan cites as his particular example Holbein's 1533
portrait of Jean de Dinteville and Georges de Selve. Known as *The
Ambassadors*, the painting shows two well-dressed men surrounded
by objects of learning such as astrolabes and books. The cuttlefish-
shaped grey mass in the lower half of the picture only becomes clear

to the viewer who has walked away at an oblique angle and then looked back at the picture over her shoulder; from this perspective, the amorphous mass reveals itself as a skull. Lacan is not the first to have seen the message behind Holbein's play with perspective—that all human wealth, whether material or intellectual, is *vanitas* precisely because subject to death and decay—but his inspiration was to grasp anamorphosis as summarizing the structure of human desire.

The sexual non-relation whose dissatisfactions goad Juno into misperceiving her rivals is structured around a central void conceptually equivalent to the anamorphic figure; that void is the asymmetry and instability of the positions Man and Woman. If this void becomes visible, reality falls apart. As discussed in Chapter 1, reality as a series of objects of recognizable permanence emerges with the subject herself, and with her identification with her own image as a discrete, stable entity. Both reality and selfhood are thus functions of the central lack round which subjectivity and the desire that is its quintessence are organized. The consistent edifice of reality—the significance and system that only desire can bestow upon the world's heterogeneous phenomena—depends upon this (w)hole. More precisely, reality depends upon the hiatus' invisibility: the subject avoids psychosis only insofar as her central abyss stays completely unavailable to representation, abiding as that magnetic void, the Thing. To prevent the hole's revelation, something must become the object elevated to the dignity of the Thing.[28] Looked at 'straight on', this object is merely one in a series of objects, but looked at 'anamorphotically', it assumes the office of the central explanation of phenomena. As such a sublimity not limited by quotidian logic, its influence can be perceived everywhere. The anamorphotic object thereby reproduces the logic that distinguishes melancholy from mourning: this sublime object is invested with a power that grants it non-pareil status, raising it above the welter of other objects seen as ordinary, interchangeable, and subject to mundane physical laws. To draw an example from the ancient world: in the fraught transition

---

[28] Cf. Lacan 1992, 112. In full, the French passage reads: 'Et la formule la plus générale que je vous donne de la sublimation est celle-ci—elle élève un objet—et ici, je ne me refuserai pas aux résonances de calembour qu'il peut y avoir dans l'usage du terme que je vais amener—à la dignité de la Chose' (Lacan 1986, 133).

between Republic and Empire, Cleopatra is but one of a number of opponents Augustus must face. Yet in the literary recapitulations of that period, she regularly becomes the Supreme Mistress of Intrigue, the woman behind the scenes manipulating her lovers and pulling all the strings to cause all the conflict.[29] Her metamorphosis into the single explanation of the Roman republic's final civil war marks her elevation to the status of an object treated as the Thing. Similarly, Juno invests her rivals—and eventually, their offspring, relatives, and acquaintances—with this 'dignity'. To anyone but Juno, her rivals are merely women, victims of Jove's desire; looked at from her perspective, anamorphotically, they become Mistresses of Cunning, manipulating Jupiter so as to alienate his affections.

It is telling that when Juno's *furor* increases between Io and Callisto, and again between Callisto and Semele, her objurgations against these rivals focus specifically on pregnancy as a special irritant (happily for Io, she conceives only after Jove concludes a temporary armistice with his wife). The anterior myths confirm Juno's complaints about her own difficulties in conceiving. Hera has at most four children with Zeus (Ares, Hephaistos, Hebe, Eleithuia)—not much for an eternal marriage. The only other married Olympian, Aphrodite, far outdistances Hera in childbearing, but significantly not with her husband Hephaistos. Rather, Aphrodite bears children to her various immortal and mortal lovers.[30] Hera also produces one monstrous 'child' without a father (Typhoeus), enviously emulating Zeus' production of Athena without a birth-mother (*HHAp.* 331–52).[31] Ovid seems to have noticed how comparatively paltry Juno's harvest is; in an era that made wedded motherhood a public duty and a prop of civic concord, he has the very goddess of marriage

---

[29] Cf. Wyke 1992.

[30] To name only the most obvious: Aeneas (by Anchises, *HHAphr.*); Deimos, Phobos, and Harmonia (by Ares, Hes. *Theog.* 933–7); Eros (by Ouranos, Sappho 198 LP; by Ares, Simonides 575 *PMG*); Priapos (by Dionysos, DS 4.6.1); Hermaphroditos (by Hermes, DS 4.6.5; cf. Ovid, *Met.* 4.285–388).

[31] Hesiod credits Hephaistos' birth to Hera's resentful parthenogenesis, while granting Ares, Hebe, and Eleithuia to Zeus and Hera together (*Theog.* 921–3). However, both the *Iliad* and the *Odyssey* contradict Hesiod on Hephaistos' genesis, since Homer's blacksmith god regularly calls Hera and Zeus 'mother and father' (e.g. *Il.* 1.577–9) and expresses resentment against his 'two parents' (*Od.* 8.312).

bewail her inability to meet such expectations. Especially in the light of the love-goddess's prodigious fertility and the infidelity that produced it, the complaints of the marriage-goddess make the ideal of conjugal romantic harmony seem farther away than ever (and all the weaker a reed to prop up community cohesion; no wonder the Olympians can so seldom accord). Juno's rebuke of Callisto makes it clear that her rivals' pregnancies infuriate the goddess because they publically advertise the central void in her marriage, the lack of complementarity that makes adultery attractive. To Juno, the children of her rivals relocate that fantasized fulfilment elsewhere, well outside the institution over which she presides.

But only one instance of that putative completion draws the full resources of Juno's wrath: Semele. Juno tortures Io to madness, yet accedes eventually to Jupiter's request that she allow the nymph to resume her human shape and an untroubled life (1.737–46). Perhaps this is because Io is not yet pregnant. But what about Callisto? Despite Juno's furious reproaches against the nymph's pregnancy, the goddess does not try to destroy her; she just changes Callisto into a bear (2.466–81). And albeit Juno fumes over Jove's catasterisms of Callisto and Arcas, regarding them as honours that dishonour herself (2.512–26), when she asks Ocean not to allow these constellations to bathe in his waters (2.527–30), she exacts an equivocal punishment at best. Her stipulation makes the pair constellations by which every seaman steers,[32] so that they become the cynosure of all mariners' eyes, and accordingly rise in importance. If Juno regrets the pair's exaltation, she does not deem it worth amending the fault. Of all supposed intriguers against her marriage, Semele angers Juno most. As noted above, not only Semele, but every Theban even remotely connected to her, must pay the price for her adultery. Juno can endure the mercies and even honours conceded to her other rivals, but she cannot let go of the 'wrong' done her by Semele. Why?

Semele's relationship with Jove appears to be based on affection, at least on his side. He is emotionally attached to her in a way he has been

---

[32] Arcas, or Ursa Minor, contains the present epoch's polestar, which indicates celestial north to navigators.

to no other of his paramours, visiting her repeatedly and appearing to love her in a lasting, conjugal fashion. Precisely that infuriates Juno. She indicates as much obliquely when she sarcastically pretends to invent an excuse for Semele: 'At, puto, furto est I contenta, et thalami brevis est iniuria nostri'—'But I suppose she is satisfied with dalliance and that the offense to my marriage bed was brief!' (3.266–7). In point of fact, this excuse goes ridiculously wide of Semele's case: neither she nor Jupiter give any evidence that either will make the affair brief. Far from being ready to tire of Semele, his wife's diabolical triumph over Jove depends on an affection for his paramour so deep that his wish to please her overcomes his caution. The sarcasm behind Juno's obviously counterfactual remark indicates wherein lies the particular source of her anger: each of the lovers seems to draw from the affair a fuller measure of pleasure than has ever been available to Juno. They come closest to the perfectly harmonious and complementary sexual relation of which she believes she has been cheated.

YOU BE DA MAN

Juno's envious reaction to Jove and Semele's affair casts not only her rival, but her poor outmanoeuvred husband, as sympathetic victim. Yet it also marks the first enlargement of Jove's role as Thebes' other primal father and affliction to match Agenor. Jove's sexual rapacity invites in its train destruction to equal the Tyrian king's pitilessness. Knowing as Jove does the history of his wife's scorched-earth policy toward her rivals, his persistent pursuit of other females compounds his lust with reckless disregard. It could perhaps be argued that, being objects of mere lust, their subsequent fate is of no moment to Jove. But Semele, the one woman he seems to love, fares no better. His thoughtlessness in binding himself irrevocably to grant Semele her wish before he even knows its content is astonishing, given that he himself had to repair the world-catastrophe wrought by such an oath when Helios bound himself to Phaethon's reckless whim (*Met.* 2.42–6, 304–18). The stupefying lapse of judgement toward his lover makes him appear morbidly possessed.[33] On the one hand, the parallel to Helios' loving if foolish pledge to his son implies a similarly genuine passion in Jove; yet that oath effectively continues the pattern of abandonment he had established with his other lovers. It is as if Jove now must rid himself of Semele without regard to emotion, operating *nolens-volens* under a compulsion to purge and destroy no less strong than his wife's. What and whence this drive?

From his and Juno's vain pursuit of totality, and the destructive negation of the other, *any* other, it entails. Taken together, the intertwined trajectories of satyriasis and reprisal that the heavenly couple describe illustrate their respective positions on the sexual non-relation, positions revealed by their bickering over the sexes' relative hedonic privileges. Jupiter and Juno act as if they aspire to the positions Man and Woman, the fantasies of perfect complementarity and fulfilment. When each position belies expectation (as it inevitably must, even for the gods), the heavenly couples' thwarted expectations underwrite a nightmare parody of erotic commerce. As mentioned, god and goddess blame each other for 'stolen' pleasure. Insofar as Juno sees Jupiter as the 'thief of enjoyment', she constructs

---

[33] It is true that Jupiter's predicament (like Helios') issues from a folktale motif well-established in some strands of the Semele myth: the unwitting request. However, that does not render insignificant Ovid's choice to have Jupiter bind himself in advance with an unbreakable oath, so that, knowing what his beloved's wish will entail, he must nonetheless fulfil it. There were other possibilities—for example, Diodorus' two versions of Semele's death. One version offers no explicit rationale for Zeus' compliance with her wish, leaving the door open to suppose the god ignorant of what will happen if he comes to his beloved in his full godhead (DS 3.64.3–4). Ovid has already shown his Jupiter to be very much less than omniscient or even forethoughtful: Jove vacillates over incinerating the world, fearing the flames could not be confined to earth, and recalling a prophecy warning of world conflagration (*Met.* 1.253–61). Moreover, despite his promises to his fellow Olympians to repopulate the world with a different race (by implication, a better one), Jupiter does nothing beforehand to ensure this. Deucalion and Pyrrha survive by pure chance; it is Jupiter's dumb luck that they are also reverent and good people (*Met.* 1.324–9). A Jupiter who burned Semele because he did not know what he was doing would be entirely in keeping with Ovid's general portrait of the feckless King of the Gods.

It is perhaps worth noting that Diodorus' other version of Semele's demise portrays in stronger terms the pattern of divine destructiveness I am suggesting controls Ovid's account. Diodorus records the Naxians as believing Zeus slew Semele deliberately—the god wanted his son to be born from himself, not a mortal woman, so the child would also be a god (DS 5.52.2).

him as the primal Father—the Father who balks all others' gratification by monopolizing it for himself, so that bliss becomes a purloined object. The *Metamorphoses* does indeed hold no greater amorous thief than Jupiter; like the patriarch of the primal horde, he enjoys 'all the women'. In addition to Europa and Semele, who inspire Juno's resentment against Thebes, his female victims are legion. More to the point, Jove has a perfect record: not only does he bed more females than any other lover in the poem, his efforts are never, ever vain. Jupiter always 'gets his woman' (or boy, in the case of Ganymede). No other god (and certainly no human) has a comparable record: Apollo fails of Daphne, Pan of Syrinx, Mercury of Herse.[34] Even Mars is frustrated of Venus by Helios and Vulcan's intervention, albeit only once (4.167–89). But for Jove, 'all' really means 'the whole, without exception'. Yet his unsatisfiable rapacity that compels him to sleep with a woman only once before abandoning her to his wife's tender mercies (Semele only temporarily excepted) reproduces another facet of the primal Father: His sadism and destructiveness in pursuit of monopolizing the all (all power, all enjoyment). Jove's annihilating progress through females is a recurrent failure traceable to the same root cause as Juno's marital dissatisfaction. Though seeming to 'have it all', Jupiter, like Juno, endlessly fails of the all in the form of a truly complementary relation between the sexes. Jupiter's perpetual search among the heterogeneous assemblage of women for complete fulfilment, for the totalizing object of his fantasy, yields nothing that lasts. What he seeks, and fails to find, in all these women is Woman.

And it is to that position, as Woman, that Juno's role in the *Metamorphoses* doubly tends. She first approximates Woman purely mathematically. Juno's reaction to Jupiter's lusts—getting rid of her rivals one by one, and eventually including in her purview all their relatives and associates—progresses toward one logical conclusion. At some point (albeit perhaps an asymptotic point attained only in

---

[34] I have excluded from consideration those gods who appear only once in the *Metamorphoses* as sexual conquerors (such as Vertumnus, 14.622–771), on the principle that *einmal ist keinmal*: such single conquests are statistically irrelevant next to Jove's crowded record.

infinity) she will be Woman qua the totality of women, because she will be the last female standing.[35]

That trajectory culminates in her annihilation of Semele and her kin. But it is at this point, after exterminating Athamas and Ino, that Juno the Destroyer vanishes as agent of her own anger, while the insubstantial idea of Juno takes the goddess's place and traverses another way toward becoming Woman. From the end of Book 4 onwards, Juno's vendettas appear only as memories conjured by other *dramatis personae*, or by the details of an ekphrasis,[36] and

---

[35] Of course, the irony in all this is that the ideal-impossible goals of Man and Woman toward which the paths of Heaven's King and Queen tend are asymmetrical, 'out of joint' with one another—another illustration of the fact that 'there is no sexual relation'. The idea of Man and Woman as complements turns on the fantasy that each would ratify the other's identity as not simply relational and contingent, but rooted in the bedrock of being. Jupiter's serial adultery is both the pursuit of his own lust and of proof of his power—in both respects, a quest that seeks to ratify his identity as omnipotent. This makes Juno singularly unsuited to be his complement, given that she strives always to rival Jupiter's power, not ratify it by giving way before it. Insofar as Juno strives to be The Woman—Jove's (largely infertile) wife, his only sexual outlet, bound to him by law, proof neither of his potency nor his charm—he cannot be The Man. The reverse is also true: the more he is The Man qua Lothario, the less she can be The Woman qua single, lawful object of his devotion.

By contrast, Semele's pregnancy, and her docile acceptance of her lover, ratify Jupiter's status as The Man, i.e. potent in every respect. Because Semele is not a rape victim (at least technically), Jupiter can flatter himself that charm, not force, has gained entry to her bed. And when he offers his beloved anything she wants, she does not demand he stop bedding other females. (Contrast the concession Jupiter must appear to make to Juno when bargaining for Io's rehumanization, as discussed earlier in this chapter.) Far from trying to curtail the god's power either in the number or magnitude of his sexual adventures, Semele asks for an even greater demonstration of that power: he is to embrace her with all his godly regalia as his sex toys. Juno, on the other hand, constantly tries to emasculate her husband, both by destroying his sexual objects and—in this instance—making his own divine potency an instrument of that destruction.

[36] Juno's wrath appears in *Metamorphoses* 5–15 in the following passages: the Ovidian narrator mentions that Athena's tapestry woven in the contest with Arachne shows the queen of the Pygmies changed into a stork, and Antigone transformed into a bird, both because of Juno (6.90–7); responding to the divine slaughter of all Niobe's children because of her pride, an anonymous Theban recalls that fear of Juno's wrath had made Latona flee Delos with her newborn babes (6.337–8); the dying and enraged Hercules mentions Juno as the cause of all his labours (9.198–9); Alcmene tells how Juno commanded Lucina to make birthing Hercules impossible, and how Juno (or Lucina—the text's *saeua dea* is ambiguous) transforms Galanthis into a weasel (9.281–323).

never again as dramas viewed directly by the reader without an internal narrator's mediation.[37] Narrative perspective on Juno's vendettas shifts from direct perception to mediated recollection. Instances of her wrath become a way to explain adverse events in the world by tracing them to a single source of evil. And when *dramatis personae* adduce Juno to explain the extraordinary, their explanations not infrequently tailor Juno's putative agency to their own idiosyncratic perspective. For example: King Aeacus blames the plague at Aegina on Juno (7.523–4); yet if this is the goddess's revenge for Jove's adulterously begetting the king, she has waited decades to take her revenge, showing a patience the poem nowhere else grants her. Moreover, everyone intially takes the plague to be a purely natural phenomenon (*Met.* 7.525–7); in a fit of overdetermination, Aeacus himself attributes the cause to pestilential winds and to serpents that both (apparently) poison the water resources (7.528–35). He never specifies when or why the revisionist theory of a divine curse arose.[38] Yet the King's story of the 'divinely inspired' plague paves the way to construing a new influx of Aeginetan population as Jove's supernatural intervention, which in turn allows him to claim divine parentage and tutelage in recounting the story to his Athenian guest Cephalus (*Met.* 7.652–7).[39] Minerva's use of Juno appears equally self-serving. The virgin goddess weaves into the tapestry she

[37] Juno's action of opening one of Rome's gates to the Sabines during their war with the Romans over the rape of the Sabine women is certainly peculiar, but is an exception more apparent than real. Juno has good reasons to support the Sabines. Titus Tatius, king of the Sabines, is supposed to have first established Juno's cult in Rome (Dion. Hal. 2.50.3—a legend that probably looks toward the syncretistic cross-contamination between the Latin *Iuno* and the Etruscan goddess *Uni*). And Ovid states flatly that Juno had given over her anger against the Romans generations before the Sabine–Roman conflict: at the time of Aeneas' death and apotheosis, the Trojan's own *uirtus* compelled Juno along with all the other gods to bring an end to long-standing resentment ('Iamque deos omnes ipsamque Aeneia uirtus | Iunonem veteres finire coegerat iras', *Met.* 14.581–2). After the conflict, Juno amply demonstrates her goodwill toward the Romans by reuniting the divinized Romulus-Quirinus with his wife Hersilia, now become the goddess Hora (*Met.* 14.829–51).

[38] Aeacus is well into adulthood when the plague strikes: his son Telamon is old enough to understand and announce the miracle of Aegina repopulated (7.648–9).

[39] Ovid has the 'miraculous transformation' of ants into people take place only in Aeacus' dreams; no one witnesses this wonder—Aeacus simply assumes that the magic of his vision explains the sudden influx of immigrants wishing to be his subjects (7.650–4).

creates in competition with Arachne instances of the queen of heaven's vengeance (the transformations of Rhodope and Haemus into mountains, of the pygmy queen into a stork, and of the Trojan princess Antigone into a bird, and of Cinyras' daughters into stone steps, *Met.* 6.85–100).[40] In each instance, Minerva makes the transformation result from a contest staged between mortal and goddess, an element that the mythical tradition nowhere else attests ('quattuor in partes certamina quattuor addit'—'in the four corners she adds four contests', *Met.* 6.85).[41] The way that Minerva's tapestry alters the myths' chains of causality reflects her own affront in being challenged by Arachne and positions her anticipated revenge on the Lydian in a history of precedent wherein the gods exact punishment owed by hubristic mortal challengers.[42]

---

[40] Ovid only mentions Juno as agent for the middle two punishments, but she would have suffered *lèse-majesté* from Rhodope and Haemon playing king and queen of heaven, so she is a logically apt avenger. That she also punishes Cinyras' daughters would fit the pattern of the tapestry's *certamen* vignettes, but it is by no means certain. Nonetheless, my argument does not depend on the number of instances in which Minerva has shaped Juno to her own ends; the fact remains that Minerva does so, whether twice or four times.

[41] Cf. Anderson 1972, 163–4. Admittedly, in the case of Cinyras, this is an *argumentum ex silentio*: we have no information on this myth, aside from the unhelpful and highly dubious gloss 'regis Assyriorum' (Ps.-Lact. Plac. *Fab. Ov.* 6.1). The story of Haemon and Rhodope is elsewhere that of a brother–sister pair whose arrogance prompted them to adopt not only the names, but the incestuous relationship, of heaven's ruling couple (Serv. Auct. Verg. *Aen.* 1.317; Ps.-Plut. *Fluv.* 11.3; Lucian, *Salt.* 51; Schol. Ov. *Ib.* 561; Ps.-Lact. Plac. *Fab. Ov.* 6.1). The Queen of the Pygmies simply scorns the gods, particularly Hera and Artemis (Anton. Lib. 16, 17.39; Eustath. *ad Hom.* p. 1322; Aelian, *Nat. Anim.* 15.29). Various sources give various reasons for the punishment of Antigone, the Trojan princess, daughter to Laomedon and sister to Priam: she boasts of her beauty, she vaunts it above Juno's, she had a liaison with Jupiter (Serv. Verg. *Aen.* 1.27; Mythogr. Vat. I.179, II. 69; Ps.-Lact. Plac. *Fab. Ov.* 6.1; Serv. *Georg.* 2.520). Many of the testimonia to these myths are late and sparse, so must be used with caution. Even so, nothing in them ratifies Minerva's tendentious intepretation of these mortals' fates as condign punishment for losing a direct challenge to a god. Bömer exhaustively lists the ancient sources on all four tales of vengeance (Bömer 1969–86, 3.32–5).

[42] This seems a particularly cynical modification of Juno's role in history—after all, as a goddess, Minerva ought to know the precise circumstances that called forth Juno's revenge. But that fits Minerva's pattern of self-serving mythical editing woven into her tapestry. For example, in depicting the contest between herself and Neptune to name Athens, she chooses the version most flattering to her power and sagacity in contrast to the god's. Whereas some variants rest Neptune's bid for the city on his creation of the eminently useful horse, Minerva follows the other versions that have

These are but the most dramatic examples of the way Juno's recollectors reduce the world's heterogeneous phenomena to a comforting intelligibility and order, insofar as they can trace the evils of a human life to divine intervention.[43] In so doing, they construct Juno as Woman qua conceptual totality. Just as Woman closes the set of women by representing the feminine as such, Juno is the rational principle whereby a heterogeneous collection (the egregious misfortunes of existence) can be closed into members of a set (examples of Juno's divine retribution). These theories appeal to their formulators' desire for a conceptual whole, an explanation without exception. Within such a coherent ideological edifice, the subject finds a place with which to identify, thus papering over her/his fundamental self-division with a seemingly unified identity. Now the Imaginary dominates the Symbolic: all the differences upon which the Symbolic is based dwindle before an underlying Truth. The perceiver privy to that eternal verity appears thus both unified and wise. Yet the slender or non-existent evidence behind Aeacus' self-aggrandizement and Minerva's cynical revisionism demonstrates the limitations of such a principle of intelligibility. The shortcomings of the king's and the goddess's accounts show why 'Woman does not exist', and why Juno as present agent of her own vengeance must disappear from the poem after Thebes. That Juno appears only in her recollectors' eyes as they formulate their metatheories of evil emphasizes the anamorphotic status of these speculations. Like Woman, such a totality does not exist outside their peculiar visions.

And yet Juno's expositors' view of her matches the goddess's perception of her rivals. Juno's trajectory of anxiety in Books 1–4

---

him uselessly and rather foolishly start a salt-water fountain on the Acropolis. She, on the other hand, provides the multifunctional olive tree.

[43] For example, the exchange between Alcmene and Iole in Book 9 after the death and apotheosis of Hercules implies the necessity of explanation, however grim, as a response to suffering. In the aftermath of losing Hercules as son and husband, the two women confide in each other, not telling stories of cheer and triumph, but tales of their own suffering because of divine retribution. Alcmene tells of her labour prolonged because of Juno's jealousy (9.281–323), Iole of her sister Dryope undone by Apollo's lust and the nymph Lotis' wrath (9.326–93). Having affirmed that Hercules' persecution is not a singular instance, but rather part of a general pattern both of Juno's vindictiveness and of divine callousness generally, they are drawn together: Alcmene ends the recitation by tenderly wiping away Iole's tears (9.394–6).

itself lent a comprehensible structure to the world and secured her place in it. Identified as the source of all her woes, the rivals 'make things clear', enabling Juno to perceive the world and her marriage as a closed and consistent space whose woes are the merely contingent expression of a single source of evil. Further, she gains an identity as her own champion against this evil. She indicates as much when she frames her revenge on Semele as proof of her selfhood—an identity at least partially dependent on constructing herself as Jupiter's complement (by blood, if less certainly by marriage):

> 'ipsa petenda mihi est; ipsam, si maxima Iuno
> rite vocor, perdam, si me gemmantia dextra
> sceptra tenere decet, si sum regina Iouisque
> et soror et coniunx—certe soror.'
>
> (*Met.* 3.263–6)

'I must seek out that very woman, yes, *her* I'll destroy, if I am rightly called "greatest Juno", if it is fitting that I hold the bejewelled sceptre in my hand, if I am queen and Jove's sister and wife—his sister, at least.'

Little wonder that persecuting her rivals and their kin affords the only occasions for her happiness and her laughter (she is happy (*laeta*, 4.479) and laughs (*risit*, 4.524) as she pursues her vendetta against Athamas and Ino). She is most herself when exterminating the other.[44]

From the perspective of the sexual non-relation, the concerns of Ovid's Juno assume an unexpected ethical dimension. True enough that—unlike Vergil's Juno—she does not fight for Carthage or for Turnus. But neither do her loyalties bend: she treats neither her enmities nor her affections as commodities with exchange value. The *Aeneid* closes upon a Juno prepared to forsake her hostility toward the Trojans for a price. She trades her favourite Turnus for Jupiter's promise that Troy will never rise again, and that native Latin culture will completely eclipse Trojan identity. Jupiter then summons

---

[44] Betty Rose Nagle has argued that the connection seen between revenge and identity in Juno's stories is part of a general pattern whereby the *Metamorphoses'* goddesses see intentional and unintentional affronts to their power as threats to their identities, reprisal as the means by which they may reassert who they are (Nagle 1984).

the Dira who paralyses Turnus and ensures Aeneas' triumph in the final duel.[45] The way Ovid words his Juno's declaration of war upon Semele underlines this contrast with Vergil's queen of Heaven. Ovid borrows the phrase 'regina Iouisque | et soror et coniunx' directly from the opening of the *Aeneid* (*Aen.* 1.46–7). There Juno bitterly reviews her inability to annihilate the Trojans despite her lofty status as Queen of Heaven, wife and sister of Jove. She appeals to Aeolus' power over storms to help her destroy the Aeneadae at sea. Yet when at the poem's end Vergil revisits the idea of Juno's status depending upon the persistence of her hostility, she is yielding Turnus and his cause because Jupiter has paid her off. 'Es germana Iouis Saturnique altera proles, | irarum tantos uoluis sub pectora fluctus' ('You are sister to Jove and Saturn's other child, you stir such great waves of anger in your heart!' *Aen.* 12.830–1), Jupiter exclaims. Ironically exclaims: his sister-wife has just conceded pursuit of the destruction she once thought would affirm her status.[46] By contrast to Vergil's political and politic Juno, Ovid circumscribes Juno's motives within the strict confines of sexual rivalry—and discovers a perverse integrity in the Queen of Heaven. Juno's demonic vengeance upon her *paelices* reveals itself as the 'dark underside' of loyalty. Her poisonous monomania is the verso to fidelity, the virtue that centrally structures her identity as goddess of marriage.

Long after her Theban campaign of annihilation, Ovid's Juno, like Vergil's, accommodates Aeneas; but it is *Aeneia virtus*, not bargaining, that finally persuades her to forsake her enmity. True to the (il)logic of anamorphosis, nothing about Aeneas has changed (least of all his exchange value). Only Juno's perspective has altered, for no specified reason—and her new vantage simply 'compels an end to old anger' (*Met.* 14.582). These observations must nonetheless fall short of a theodicy. Rather, Juno's divinely intensified woes write large a deadlock intrinsic to being human, outlining the logic whereby the subject's fundamental lack makes cruelty and constancy two sides of

[45] See Feeney 1991, 151–2 for a discussion of Jupiter's 'Junoism' at this moment.
[46] Of course, as Feeney notes, there is still the matter of Carthage to be settled (Feeney 1991, 148–9). Juno indirectly set in train Carthage's clash with Rome when she inspired Dido's love for Aeneas; the betrayed Carthaginian Queen calls down eternal enmity between the descendants of Carthage and of Troy. Juno has not so much forsworn as deferred some of her hostility to the Trojans.

the same coin. Far from redeeming Juno, this logic makes her demonic viciousness stultifyingly close and domestic. The history of her vengeances traces the mechanisms whereby the wish to abolish the grief of the impossible bewitches both intellect and conscience.

But her revenge, and the confirmation of her identity she repeatedly perceives crucially to depend upon it, also points to a relationship between self and enemy as intimate as that between fealty and ferocity. In the next chapter, we shall examine in the Narcissus story the logical extrapolation of this sinister interdependence between self and other. Ovid's version of the Narcissus story elucidates the paradoxical logic of Juno's wish to abolish the other, a logic that is capable of underwriting a tale of love, a tale of the self's realization and a tale of the self's destruction—and of making all these the same story.

4

Narcissus and Echo

The Arrows of Love's Errors

'Connais-toi toi-même': On n'a jamais exprimé en une formule
plus brève l'état de malédiction.

Emil Cioran[1]

Juno's acts of reprisal and their spectacular climax in Thebes essentially revolve around totalization perceived and desired. Juno and
Jupiter each see the other('s sex) as 'having it all' in the matter of
enjoyment. They loom in each other's regard as Woman and Man
respectively, icons without any lack. Moreover, their thrust and parry
over Jupiter's infidelities align both more closely with those positions
of totality, albeit by a crude mathematics. Like *the* Man, the primal
Father, Jupiter's heroic rapacity bids fair to have all (women). The
logical extrapolation of Juno's ever-widening vengeance not only
offers to destroy all (women), leaving the goddess alone as *the*
Woman, but conveniently explains all (whether accurately or not)
to those who posit her as *the* source of human evils.

The heavenly couple's skirmishes dramatically illustrate immortals'
expansive possibilities: they can with impunity seduce and destroy
at will. What, if anything, have they to say to mortal desire, to
the limited power and pathetic fragility of humans? The paired tales
directly spun from Juno and Jupiter's quarrel over sexual relations
pose just this question. Echo and Narcissus come together as

---

[1] Cioran 1997, 297.

nymph[2] and human respectively; neither enjoys the Olympians' powers or hardy immunity to harm, and at least Narcissus is mortal. They are also first of their kind in the *Metamorphoses*— Narcissus the first human lover,[3] Echo[4] the first desiring

---

[2] Euripides is the first writer who clearly regards Echo as a nymph. In his lost *Andromeda*, Andromache apparently engaged Echo in a dialogue (frg. 118 Nauck), a scene Aristophanes parodies in *Thesmophoriazusai* 1056–97.

[3] Studies of Ovid's Narcissus (with or without Echo) are far too numerous to list exhaustively. I consider here only a representative sample of purely literary analyses; I set aside completely those articles that, e.g., engage Narcissus as cultural anthropology, a reflection of such ancient cultural practices as scrying (Nelson 2000), catoptrics (McCarty 1989), or viewing art (Elsner 2000). Ovid's myth has attracted analyses from widely various methodologies, including narratology (Brenkman 1976), semiotics (Pellizer 1985), structuralism (Massenzio 1992), and psychology (Nicaise 1991, Milowicki 1996). For the widest swathe of his readers, Narcissus is a cautionary tale representing the dangers of self-referentiality and imagined autonomy, whether these be interpreted as pure egoism that renounces the sociality of life and love (Borghini 1978, DiSalvo 1980, James 1986, Massenzio 1992, and Anderson 1997); a fiction too little in touch with the 'laws of reality' to be sustained (Rosati 1983); the illusory primacy of voice/speech over the 'supplement' of writing (Brenkman 1976); or an allegory of psychological collapse into the other (Pellizer 1985, Nicaise 1991, Milowicki 1996).

The singularity of Heinrich Dörrie's amoral reading (Dörrie 1967) is instructive. He regards the story as a purely virtuosic intellectual and artistic exercise in paradox: 'Narziß is kein exemplum', 75. His outlier status illustrates how strongly Ovid's tale invites the opposite reaction: to see Narcissus' bizarre and unique fate as nonetheless generalizable to the human condition.

[4] Explanations of Echo's significance in the *Metamorphoses* run a much wider gamut than interpretations of Narcissus. The parallels between Echo and Narcissus lead some scholars to see the nymph solely as a minor complement to Narcissus. But among these, part consider her limitation to pure response to match the odiousness of Narcissus' self-absorption, part read her as throwing the boy's egoism into relief with her own self-erasure. Echo-as-auxiliary exemplifies everything from ultimate passivity ('Echo thus becomes a symbol of those pathetic but annoying females who are extremely responsive but have no initiative or originality of their own', Fränkel 1945, 84) to ultimate selflessness and compassion ('but selflessness makes a stronger appeal than selfishness, and Ovid shows Echo, even after suffering rejection, capable of sympathizing with and pitying the fate of Narcissus', Anderson 1997, 372).

The few scholars who have afforded Echo more attention see in her reflexive relation to language an allegory of the production or consumption of texts, although they still split over fundamental points of interpretation. For example, Joseph Loewenstein argues that her repetitiveness represents two opposite tensions in literary continuity: reverent emulation and anxious influence, so that Echo is handmaiden and emblem of the male poet's activity (Loewenstein 1984, 33–56). By contrast, Gina Bloom, Caren Greenberg, Claire Nouvet, and Shilpa Raval have all elucidated feminist perspectives from the Ovidian story, viewing Echo as circumvent-

female.[5] Ovid is apparently the first ancient writer to bring these two figures together. As such, their erotic vicissitudes enjoy paradigmatic status for earthly desire, and speak all the more loudly to Ovid's era, obsessed as its regime was with re-engineering the relation between the sexes into the model nucleus of civic harmony.

Ovid's version of Echo and Narcissus' tale is quickly summarized: the raped water-nymph Liriope bears Narcissus to the river-god Cephisus. When she asks the prophet Tiresias whether her son will enjoy long life, Tiresias replies with a clever play on the inscription adorning the pronaos of the Delphic oracle, 'gnōthi seauton'—'know thyself'.[6] Tiresias tells Liriope her son will reach a ripe old age 'only if he does not know himself' ('si se non nouerit', *Met.* 3.348). Beautiful but ultimately untouchable, the grown boy attracts and spurns a series of

ing masculine control to one degree or another. But where Bloom locates Echo's resistance in her body, Greenberg, Nouvet, and Raval find it in her voice. Bloom's nymph evades control by hiding, and eventually abandoning her body (*Met.* 3.371, 393–4, 396–8); an unlocatable body means an uncontrollable tongue (Bloom 2001, 134). Greenberg, Nouvet, and Raval instead focus upon Echo's reworking of Narcissus' words to express her own desire. For Greenberg, Echo models a rereading of male texts that converts them into expressions of feminine desire, outside the limitations of authorial intent, while for Nouvet, the nymph also undermines the speaker of the text: insofar as Narcissus cannot recognize her words as his own, neither can his words confirm his consciousness or his selfhood (Greenberg 1980, 307–9; Nouvet 1991, 107–10). Raval sees Echo's success in communicating her desire to Narcissus as a pyrrhic victory, so that (in direct contrast to Bloom's perspective) the loss of Echo's body is supreme punishment and constraint. Now Echo can only repeat, and she has no body with which to experience either desire or pleasure.

Both where scantly and lavishly attended, Echo inspires a gamut of contradictory interpretations. She is passive and active, witless and canny, slave and aspirant to literary forebears, feminine reader and masculine writer, victim and victor. These contrary analyses point to an irreconcilable incoherence at the centre of her portrait, a place where rational analysis cannot organize the details of her depiction into a whole. Seen from this perspective, her irregularity embodies ~~The~~ Woman, meaning, the non-existence of Woman as a totality organized by a single logical principle. Echo's seeming folly of self-sacrifice then parallels her linguistic canniness: each constitutes a resistance to 'reason' as a purely regulatory system that falls short of its own claims to subsume all phenomena. As I shall show in the following pages, Echo's passion is action, and she is most her own subject and agent when she is most the object of another's self-expression.

[5] As opposed to desired females, who have been legion in the first three books. Anderson notes that Narcissus is the *Metamorphoses'* first amorous human (Anderson 1997, 385).

[6] Pausanias records the inscription, which the extant ruins of the temple do not preserve (10.24.1).

lovers, among whom is Echo. Because the nymph's chatter beguiled Juno so that she failed to catch her philandering husband and his nymph-paramours[7] *in flagrante delicto*, the goddess limited the use of Echo's tongue to pure vocal reflection. After her punishment, Echo's unrequited love for Narcissus causes her to waste away until her only physical remainders are the phenomenon of the echo and her petrified bones—yet these witness Narcissus suffering a similar fate. Cursed by a rebuffed suitor with the words, 'sic amet ipse licet, sic non potiatur amato!' ('may he love what he cannot possess!' 3.405), Narcissus fulfils this doom when, seeing himself in a pool, he burns for what seems another beautiful youth. Eventually Narcissus wakes up from his delusion and realizes his error, but enlightenment does not quiet his passion, and he wastes away until he dies despairing (3.503–5). His kin can find no body, only a yellow flower; meanwhile in the Underworld, his ghost continues to stare at the waters of the Styx (3.505–10).

Virtually all the scholarship on Narcissus, and most of the attention to Echo, hold up both as cautionary exempla of what is to be avoided in human life and love. In the following chapters, I argue to the contrary that Narcissus and Echo—like the Real Father and Woman—are not 'bad, false' images of love, the self, the uses of language or of knowledge that we can avoid by being thoughtful, humble, wary, or discreet. Rather, Ovid deploys their paradigmatic primacy—first human, first female, to be enamoured, consequently first to suffer for it—because their cases illustrate what plagues intersubjectivity intrinsically and ineluctably, albeit *in extremis*. Narcissus and Echo exemplify the ways in which desire—and thus the subject founded by desire—revolves around a certain necessary ignorance, a 'gap' or 'blank space' in knowledge upon which fantasy is founded, and toward which the perpetual unrest of longing can surge.

My goal in the following two chapters is to answer the following questions: How do all the preoccupations of the Narcissus and Echo tale work together as a system? How do we draw the conceptual 'arrows' linking relations between the sexes to the paradoxes and ambiguities of identity and language, and to knowledge? How does

---

[7] These nymphs may well be rape victims, but since Ovid does not indicate whether these sex acts with Jupiter were consensual or not, I have chosen the more neutral term 'paramour'.

that entire system elaborate and complicate the central theme of
the Theban cycle—the identity, cohesion, and governance of the organized community? I address these puzzles in Chapters 4 and 5; both
engage the same narrative, but from different perspectives on the way
intersubjectivity fails. Chapter 4 revolves around Narcissus and Echo
both, elucidating how the failures of reason condition failed relations
between lover and lover. Chapter 5 asks how such noetic miscarriages
shape relations between citizen and community; it focuses on the way
Ovid moulded his Narcissus after Sophocles' Oedipus, whose self-
ignorance and self-revelation alike cursed his city and himself.

Prior to Narcissus and Echo's intertwined love-stories, *amor* has
been entirely an affair of lusting immortals and haplessly objectified
females; these Boeotians perplex desire with the mortal and the
feminine.[8] Before Narcissus, love has been fatal for only two of the
Metamorphoses' beloveds,[9] and none of its lovers. The epic's amorous
unfortunates have been doomed to transformation—grim, but not
fatal.[10] But so excruciating is Narcissus' love that he pines for the end
of desire itself in death, as no previous lover in this epic has done ('nec
mihi mors grauis est, posituro morte dolores', 3.471). As a minor

---

[8] Echo and Narcissus specifically rewrite the poem's very first love story: Apollo
and Daphne. Like Apollo, Echo loves at first sight, tracks her beloved, and longs to
address him with blandishments, while like Daphne, Narcissus steadfastly rejects any
advances (Keith 2002, 254). When Narcissus later sees himself in the fatal pool, he
reiterates the Apollo–Daphne narrative elements once more, but in compressed
fashion. Again the lover is immediately inflamed, shadows his beloved's movements
(perforce, since he unwittingly follows his own image), tries to persuade with
eloquent complaint. But Apollo is immune to attraction's fatality, and soon moves
on to other interests (such as the unfortunate Coronis, victim of his jealousy). The
god's desire is ultimately mobile, his objects exchangeable, unlike Echo's or Narcissus'
fixed, melancholic obsessions.

[9] The two ill-starred beloveds are Coronis (2.606–11) and Semele (3.308–9).

[10] Transformation is often offered in lieu of death, as an amelioration (e.g.
Arachne, 6.135–8; Daedalion, 11.339–43; Aesacus, 11.784–6). In each of these cases,
a god or goddess is said to have 'pitied' ('miseratus/-a') the mortal courting death,
effecting the transformation in order to prevent suicide. Of course, the gods more
often change human beings as punishment, especially when they see mortals as
challenges to their own status or prerogatives. A salient example drawn from the
victims of desire who precede Narcissus and Echo would be Diana's huntress Callisto,
Jupiter's rape victim. Juno gives the nymph a bear's exterior, while preserving her
human mentality. But as a beautiful huntress now become an ugly, hunted beast,
Callisto still avoids death (running and hiding from hunters and other predators, for

divinity, Echo is made of tougher stuff. Nonetheless, grief and longing reduce her physically to sound and petrified bones, so that her poor remainder differs minimally from the dead Narcissus (3.395–401).

These ghastly consequences follow a fidelity and a fickleness that Juno and Jupiter respectively embraced with impunity; Juno's unswerving loyalty to an object 'elevated to the dignity of the Thing'—her persecuted rivals—matches Jupiter's nonchalant serial exploitation of these same females. Echo and Narcissus replay the commerce between the heavenly pair: she is exclusively obsessed with him, he flits from one would-be lover to the next, until the very last. Narcissus' final object of desire underlines the difference between immortal and mortal in a different way. Whereas Jupiter can happily sustain his pattern of serial seduction and abandonment forever, Narcissus cannot. He eventually encounters an object that betokens the fatally attractive object that he (and every human subject) is utterly powerless to resist.

The previous chapter examined such fixation as constituting an ethical moment in its loyalty to the object of desire (albeit in Juno's case, an ethics lined with diabolical cruelty). The nymph and boy's devotions raise the stakes in this ethical hazard, since their desires seemingly demand everything of them, including life itself. In contrast to Juno and Jupiter's weightless exercises of will, these two lovers' fates fully discover the deadlocks that produce Man and Woman, the positions the heavenly couple pursue so energetically. The logical consequence of Echo and Narcissus' fixed desires spell the annihilation of the subject—not the end of desire, but the end of the commutation of desire. Their respective fixations threaten to foreclose the relations of substitution and exchange that produce the desiring subject and form the basis of intersubjective relations.[11] It is no mere coincidence that at the end of the tale, their tangible earthly remains are inert, inanimate (stones and a flower). For any being less than a god, the totalizations figured by Man and Woman offer to foreclose the subject as shifting, 'living' entity, constantly negotiating

example, *Met.* 2.491–5). The nymph apparently considers life even in her changed form preferable to dying.

[11] Miller deftly analyses this substitutive foreclosure as the fundamental subjective position of Ovid's exilic poetry, where Ovid himself occupies the position of the persistent, but inert, undead (Miller 2004, 210–36).

internal scission by addressing the Other's hollow-hearted promises of full measure. And yet neither boy nor nymph entirely succumbs to the inert petrifaction these positions threaten, just as their tangible remains are not all of them that survives the tale's end. Even after both abandon their bodies, they somehow manage to find voices with which to touch the living: all Boeotia learns their shared story despite a lack of witnesses who can break silence. The way their obsessions break off the metonymic relations on which the Symbolic depends, and implicitly collapse commerce between the Real, the Symbolic, and Imaginary, discovers a curious logic whereby the mute stones may speak.

HOW DO YOU KNOW?

Ovid organized Echo and Narcissus' shared amorous history around numerous puzzling details; this particular relation between the sexes unfolds questions even more enigmatic than those that have bedevilled the Theban cycle generally. I sketch the whole set of these narrative anomalies before attempting any analysis, in order to base exegesis upon a view of the entire perplexity.

First and foremost, what are Echo and Narcissus doing here?[12] Neither nymph nor boy are Thebans, yet their extensive intertwined

---

[12] The general approach to Echo and Narcissus' resident-alien status has been to ignore it. I know of no scholarly analyses that try to explain Echo's inclusion in the Theban cycle, only two—one by Philip Hardie, one by Ingo Gildenhard and Andrew Zissos—that attempt in a concentrated fashion to explain Narcissus' inclusion. Hardie, Gildenhard, and Zissos all base their arguments on the way Ovid aligns Narcissus with Thebes' most notorious native son, Oedipus (as do I: their essays I shall discuss in Ch. 5, where I take up this theme in detail). Scholarly analyses of Ovid's Narcissus that take no account of his presence in Thebes are too numerous to list exhaustively, but some from the last several decades are: Zanker 1966, Cancik 1967, Dörrie 1967, Brenkman 1976, Borghini 1978, DiSalvo 1980, Rosati 1983, Loewenstein 1984, Rudd 1986. Knoespel 1985 is an exception more apparent than real, in that he sees the thematic connection between Narcissus and the rest of the Theban cycle as *furor*. However, that thread could be drawn between any number of successive tales in the *Metamorphoses*, since its *dramatis personae* are habitually beset by destructive mental excesses.

tales intrude into the middle of Ovid's Theban-cycle.[13] Second, why are they here together? Ovid modified significantly previous versions of their tales in order to interweave the two plots. Different threads of Narcissus' mythical tradition contain all the elements of the Ovidian tale: lovers rejected, amorous vengeance inflicted supernaturally, a reflection desired (both as known, and not known, to be Narcissus' own), love frustrated and ending in death.[14] Yet the mythic tradition that had evolved both an ignorant Narcissus and a knowing Narcissus kept the one captured unwittingly by his own image separate from the one consciously smitten with himself. Ovid fused the two, even though the erotic logic of each strains against the other. Particularly puzzling about this melding is Narcissus' reaction to learning he loves himself: it makes no difference to his passion. How can he be so amorously fixated on the (putative) other one moment and so amorously self-absorbed the next? And though the revelation does not extinguish his love, it fractures his reason. That raises the question, How does this dénouement fulfil the doom Tiresias predicted if Narcissus knew himself? What specifically does Narcissus discover that drives him mad?[15]

Where Ovid cobbled his Narcissus from familiar if disparate elements, his Echo differs substantially from her other mythical instantiations.[16]

---

[13] The mythic tradition places Narcissus' origin in Boeotia, but in either Thespia or Tanagra rather than Thebes (Bömer 1969, 1.537); Echo has no homeland, as might be expected, since the phenomenon of vocal reflection to which she gives rise has none.

[14] Oxy. Pap. 4711; Conon, *Diegesis* 24; Pausanias 9.31.7–8. I shall have more to say about these witnesses to the Narcissus myth below ('The Sender Always Gets Back His Own Message in Inverted Form').

[15] That Narcissus loves himself does not by itself offer a sufficient explanation for his fatal despair: he never expresses revulsion for his self-love, only chagrin that he cannot fulfil his desire. Frustration alone can hardly account for his insanity. Both Cretan Iphis (9.669–797) and Pygmalion (*Met.* 10.243–97) believe their loves for a member of the same sex and an ivory statue respectively are unfulfillable. Iphis grows frantic at her own 'misplaced' desires (9.724–63), Pygmalion fantasizes wistfully about his love becoming real (10.254–69), but neither pines away, goes insane, or resolves to die because these wishes are unrealizable short of a miracle. Although they both happily obtain that miracle, it comes unexpectedly and after considerable waiting. In the meantime, unlike Narcissus, they betray anxiety, but no mental deterioration or suicidal despair.

[16] A full accounting of the sources on Echo can be found in the article by Otto Waser in Pauly–Wissowa, s.v. Echo.

Alternative sources portray her as rejecting love;[17] nowhere besides Ovid's tale is she said to pine away from unrequited passion, or to become incapable of initiating speech because of Juno. But Ovid's innovations logically stem from a question he is apparently the first one to pose: 'How did Echo become echo?' His answer—'by angering a god, and desiring in vain'—for once makes immortal wrath weaker than mortal yearning. Juno limits Echo's speech to response alone, but in the event Echo does not suffer much from the limitation. The nymph's exchanges with Narcissus express her desire quite capably, though she has no words but those of the notoriously cruel boy. Echo only becomes the disembodied repetition of sound when she cannot persuade Narcissus to reciprocate her love, and pines away in grief. What intelligence enables Echo to outwit a goddess in order to communicate her passion, but leaves her helpless against that passion's destructiveness?

The above summaries of the tales reveal that Ovid has moulded both around non-sense—around narrative features that 'do not make sense', from the principals' status as interlopers to Thebes, through the tales' contradictions of other mythic accounts, all the way up to the narratives' own internal contradictions. Within Echo and Narcissus' stories, ignorance and insight have precisely the same effect on emotion, illumination directly entails benighted lunacy, punishments do not punish. None of these paradoxes can easily be squared with a Platonic–Aristotelian notion of the laws of thought governing valid inference. Not by accident does Tiresias' prophecy to Liriope preface these tales. The seer's prediction that the boy's fate hangs on ignorance organizes the intertwined narratives around the limits of knowledge, around what cannot be an object of experience (at least, not without fatal consequences). Equally apt logically is Tiresias' function as the causal link between Echo and Narcissus' fates on the one hand, and Juno and Jupiter's quarrel over sex on the other. As noted in Chapter 1, transsexual Tiresias umpired the gods' dispute over sexual pleasure; Juno blinds him for pronouncing male pleasure

[17] Specifically Pan's. For example, Moschos attests that Pan loved her, but that she loved a Satyr instead, who in turn loved another nymph (*Idyll.* 6.1–3). Yet mysteriously, Echo also has two daughters by Pan, Iambe and Iynx (Iambe: Schol. Eurip. *Orest.* 964; Iynx: Tzetz. ad Lycophr. 310).

to be inferior, while Jupiter makes him a prophet. Unconvinced and unmollified, Juno continues to hound her husband's 'lesser' pleasure. The first instance of her pique recorded after Tiresias' decision is Echo's condition. For the first time, Juno expands her vengeance beyond Jupiter's actual sexual partners to one who aids their escape from the goddess's wrath; Tiresias' crass misunderstanding of female pleasure seems to have added considerable fuel to her fire.[18] The goddess makes of Echo a thief of language who must purloin her words from others, just as Tiresias painted Woman as a thief of enjoyment, stealing at Man's expense (Chapter 1).[19] Ironically, that limitation enables the nymph to read all the more sensitively the desire hidden in Narcissus' words and to make it frame her own, even if her stolen words do not warm his heart. No such amelioration accrues to Narcissus from Jupiter's intervention. The god grants Tiresias the power to predict Narcissus' doom, but no imperative of plain speaking to prevent it, so that the seer's enigmatic prophecy is simply dismissed (3.349). Ovid thus links the gods' tiff causally to Echo and Narcissus' encumbered loves through Tiresias, as a figure of preternatural experience and clairvoyance who nonetheless repeatedly, unwittingly stumbles over his own ignorance.

Tiresias articulates a supernaturally powerful conceptualization of knowledge when he foretells Narcissus' fate. Such knowledge can be lethal; Narcissus implies as much when, upon learning he loves his own image, he announces his own imminent death.[20] But then, he

[18] Raval sees Juno's anger as kindled both by Jupiter's and Tiresias' presumption to speak of women's pleasure (Raval 2003, 219–20).

[19] Raval also describes Echo as a 'thief of language', borrowing the phrase from Alicia Ostriker, who in turn takes it from Claudine Hermann's book *Les voleuses de langue*. Her point is that Echo 'steals' the language when she 'rereads Narcissus' negation of passion and recasts it into a narrative about female desire' (Raval 2003, 208). I agree with the second half of the statement, but am unpersuaded that Narcissus is so passionless.

[20] The two versions of the Narcissus story that most likely pre-date Ovid—Oxyrhynchus Papyrus 4711, attributed to Parthenius (Henry 2005), and Conon—have Narcissus shed his own blood violently. By contrast, Ovid makes the boy's death psychosomatic ('*La sua morte deriva direttamente dalla sua situazione psichica*, che è il vero centro d'interesse per il narratore romano', Barchiesi–Rosati 2007, 177, original emphasis). While still ignorant of the true nature of his object, Narcissus simply complains of his beloved's coyness for twenty lines (*Met.* 3.442–62). Only upon learning that he loves his own image—when he knows his love is truly hopeless,

lives in a world where the boundary between the noetic and the physical is strangely permeable. We saw in discussing the Diana/ Actaeon tale that Thebes' hallucinatory landscape strictly correlates to the paradoxical conceptualizations of law evident in the actions of the city's men and gods: Thebes' two fathers' (Agenor and Jove's) bizarre notions of *pietas*, and Diana's of offence against her modesty. Ovid sketches in Thebes a place where cognition and the objects of cognition behave as if they were part of a single ontological continuum, rather than securely divided between subject and object, mind and world. The Theban cycle poses in acute form the problem of the relation between the knowing subject and the world that she knows.

That blurring of the line between epistemology and ontology is precisely the basis of Kant's epistemic logic, and of Hegel's magisterial response to it. Ovid's anticipation of both philosophers' grappling with what we can know of anything, including ourselves, is such that their views deserve some review here. Kant pointed out that such concepts as space and time were not attributes of objects, but rather are a priori forms of intuition fundamental to perceiving objects— and by so doing changed the fundamental question of epistemology from, What is the world, and how may I know it? to, What must the world be in order that I may know it? Kant's 'Copernican revolution' (*KrV* B xvi) transformed the categories of traditional metaphysics into the categories of the transcendental ego through which knowledge is synthesized from the 'sensuous manifold', the array of subjective perceptions. Hegel pushed this revolution in epistemological thought even further. He rejected Kant's notion of the radically unknowable 'thing in itself' or *noumenon* (the term by which Kant designated the part of appearances that has no determinate relation to our cognitive faculties, but can only be posited in the mind). For Hegel, *no* object fell outside the limits of the knowing subject. The nexus of epistemic thought the two philosophers spun out between

since he cannot attain its object—does Narcissus speak of death, and of death as a surety (*Met*. 3.469–73). And he makes this calculation with surprising rapidity, a mere six lines after the fateful realization ('iste ego sum!', *Met*. 3.463). We might plausibly infer that Narcissus makes his own prediction come true by continuing to refuse food and sleep (*Met*. 3.437). Nonetheless, he only construes the love inspiring his starvation and wakefulness as fatal *after* he recognizes it as self-love.

them is thus especially fitted to addressing the peculiar fusion of knowing and being in Thebes.

But in addition, it is from Kant's epistemological innovation, or Hegel's critique of the same, that almost all subsequent continental or British philosophies of knowledge are derived. Although the generating spirit behind these subsequent epistemologies is frequently oppositional, Kant and Hegel ineradicably revised understanding of the essential terms of debate: mind and world, self and other, ground and conditions, identity and difference. Even European positivism, which eventually aligned itself strongly with empiricism rather than Kant's a priori epistemic principles, traces its roots to nineteenth-century German neo-Kantianism.[21] Apart from David Hume and the tradition of British empiricism, to which Kant was partly responding, no set of methodologies exists for studying the problem of knowledge in the modern world that does not follow in the wake of Kant and Hegel.[22] The problem of knowledge's synthetic relation to the world of perception and to things in themselves, and the critique of the concept of the thing in itself as separate from the limits of the knowing subject, are central to any meaningful philosophy of knowledge—including Freud's probing of unconcious knowledge. The lessons learned from both philosophers are evident in psychoanalysis's formulation of the symptom, wherein the spheres of mind and body are virtually coterminous, flesh expressing suppressed intelligence. For this reason, Lacan recognized the necessity of invoking both Kant and Hegel explicitly in his return to Freud. In particular,

---

[21] For example, Michael Friedman illustrates how the fundamental intellectual divergence between the two major genera of Western philosophy—the 'analytic' that has dominated the Anglophone world and the 'continental' that has obtained in Europe—is conditioned by different responses to Kant, which he illustrates in microcosm by parsing the famous 1930s disputations among the neo-Kantians Rudolf Carnap, Ernst Cassirer, and Martin Heidegger (Friedman 2000; see also Verene 1969, Frank 1949, Coffa 1993). Frederick Beiser draws a similarly catholic picture of the influence of Hegel (whose positions are unthinkable without Kant): 'Hegel remains the watershed of modern philosophy, the source from which its many streams emanate and divide. If the modern philosopher wants to know the roots of his position, sooner or later he will have to turn to Hegel' (Beiser 1993, 1). The details to flesh out Beiser's metaphor are not far to seek: see Löwith 1964, Sussman 1982, White 1983, Hylton 1993, Redding 1996.

[22] My thanks to Paul Allen Miller, who drew my attention to these Kantian influences.

Lacan's reception of the philosophers' epistemic logic and his redaction of it in his formulae of sexuation will in the following pages help explicate more fully how knowledge, rather than anatomy or biology, founds sexual relations—or more accurately, the complete *lack* of relationship between the sexes. When Juno and Jupiter each account for the failure of sexuality by fingering the other sex as the thief of enjoyment, their dour consensus exemplifies relations between the sexes as two matching blind spots. But their brief wrangle only outlines sex as a conceptual field. Ovid leaves it to Narcissus and Echo to elaborate the contours of these blind spots as two quite different 'holes' in reason that respectively structure the positions of Man and Woman, and ensure their mutual misfire in the sexual non-relation. The epistemic dialogue between Kant and Hegel on the one hand, and psychoanalysis on the other, will help us trace with precision the sticky shapes of (mis)understanding in which Echo and Narcissus find themselves enmeshed.

THE ANTINOMIES OF REASON

What troubles Echo and Narcissus are ultimately two forms of the perplexity round which every subject is organized. As we saw in Chapter 1, the emergence of subjectivity from the Real into the Imaginary and the Symbolic is a function of fracture, contradiction, and exclusion. The subject arises in the undecidable play between 'here' and 'there'—between the site of perception and the site of reflection in the Imaginary, between void and a fulfilment always deferred. Subjectivity's internal scission compels it to engage in the relations of exchange and substitution that subtend the Symbolic. Both the Imaginary and the Symbolic in turn rest upon the exclusion of the Real and its conceptual corollaries: *jouissance, objet a*, the Thing, the Real Father. Equally founded as the subject is on void and the unknowable Real, s/he is both ultimately insubstantial and unknowable—in essence, a Kantian noumenon.

Tiresias' dire warning to Liriope—that her son must remain radically unknowable to himself—does not, then, define a condition peculiar to Narcissus. And when Juno's pique at Tiresias' pronouncement on sex spills over onto Echo, neither does that render the nymph anomalous, even though the logical effect of limiting Echo's language would be to make her unknowable as an independent consciousness.[23] Rather, the words of the prophet and the actions of the goddess spin out between them a picture of the human subject's general obscurity to self and others. Yet the way Narcissus eventually stumbles into self-knowledge constitutes 'a new type of madness' ('nouitas furoris', 3.350). Equally, Echo's canny use of language to evade Juno's erasure is an unparalleled thwarting of the goddess's vengeance. The eye-catching novelty of these narrative elements throws into high relief two different modes of the failure of human knowledge (a failure that funds a partial success, in Echo's case): the male mode, and the female mode. As we saw in Chapter 1's discussion of the formulae of sexuation, Man and Woman are for Lacan two perspectives on totality, on the claims of the Symbolic to represent faithfully the whole of reality. Man's world emerges from the arbitrary imposition of limit (the 'all' constituted by the Real Father as the point of exception), while Woman cannot draw that limit, and thus fails to constitute any discrete, organized entirety of phenomena. The point of exception that constitutes Narcissus' world is (the core of) himself, the originary 'lost object' that organizes not only his final, fatal passion, but all the aborted loves that lead up to it. By contrast, Echo's refusal to regard language as a closed system of fixed meanings underwrites a porous cosmos, rich in pathways for her voiced desire. Moreover, Echo summarizes the way in which the world of the Symbolic compels us always to use the language of the Other.[24] Meaning is thus a constantly renegotiated commons rather than a private, bounded fiefdom.

The very nature of the knowledge Echo and Narcissus grasp thus radically fractures between more than one standpoint, and not just between nymph and boy. The moment wherein Narcissus recognizes the real nature of his beloved splits the truth of that perception irresolvably between lover and beloved, viewer and viewed, subject and object. Neither pole of the dyad can be dismissed as 'mere illusion', since the interaction of Narcissus-observer with Narcissus-

---

[23] Brenkman 1976, 299–302.

[24] As David Konstan pointed out to me (*per litteras*).

imago has already profoundly unsettled the ontological status of
both. For example, Narcissus complains of his beloved's aloofness—
the untouchableness that once characterized himself—because
he now feels a passion not only novel to the world, but to himself
(*Met.* 3.454–5). In this apocalypse, is it the watery image, or the flesh-
and-blood boy, who constitutes the 'self' against whom Tiresias
warned, whose trap is now sprung? This and other paradoxes of
Narcissus' coming-to-know I shall rehearse more fully below, and in
Chapter 5, but suffice it to point out here the novel contours of
the story's revelation. Ovid has introduced a 'crack' into knowledge,
wherein such basic distinctions as that between subject and
object disappear. In that respect, he anticipates Kant's fissuring of
the Universal: to posit the existence of the noumenal prevents the
totalization, the universalization, of phenomena beneath the aegis of
any unitary notion of knowledge. For Kant, as soon as a thing is
exposed to thought, difference saturates its identity, insofar as there
are two irreducible ways of conceiving of it: the way it is as an
appearance, a phenomenon, and the way it is 'in itself', a noumenon.[25] This irreducible 'split' in what exists Kant outlines by illustrating the fundamental ways human reason comes to grief in trying to
grasp the Whole of the world and thus to totalize, universalize,
knowledge. Kant's articulation of how reason goes astray warrants
some detailed review here, in order to articulate fully how its conceptual congruence with Ovid's notion of knowledge can shed light
on the poet's tale of doomed love.

The radically contrasting ways in which Echo and Narcissus each
grapple with knowledge and desire illustrate warring alternations
between the ordered world's dissolution and formation by limitlessness and limit. Respectively, they concede, and refuse to concede
(implicitly) that the desiring subject can be an all-knowing master
of meaning. They thus anticipate the unsettling images of fragment-
ing and cohering cosmic array that Kant uses in the *Critique of Pure*

[25] This is not a division between mere states of mind and actual objects. Rather, it
seeks to limit our cognition of real entities to their features that stand in determinate
relation to our cognitive faculties. Every appearance also has an existence in itself. Yet
to call an entity an 'appearance' refers to it as something intuited by us and standing
in relation to our faculties; to call it a 'thing in itself' designates it as it exists apart
from that relation (Wood 2005, 65).

Reason to illustrate the shortcomings of human ratiocination: if human reason extends the fundamental principles of thought beyond the limits of perception for purposes of theoretical knowledge, it garners only illusion. The *Critique* argues that the human mind supplies the conditions necessary for perceiving and understanding the world (such as space, time, and causality). These allow us to perceive the relations of dependency that obtain in the world, whereby each part is conditioned by another. This in turn gives rise to the idea of a world-whole, internally complete with regard to such dependency relations—each portion of space depending on the space that encloses it, each moment in time on the one that preceded it, each event upon its cause.[26] But regarding this theoretical cosmos, the question arises: do these dependent relations extend into infinity, or do they conclude in an autonomous first term unlike any other in the series? The contradictions generated from trying to grasp this world-whole from one side or the other, infinity or autonomy, instruct us that we cannot know the world as an absolute, an 'in itself', only as it is for us. Kant makes the world emerge qua collection of phenomena solely in virtue of the noumenon as limit.

Reason comes to grief in trying to apprehend noumena because of its drive to seek the unconditioned—to extrapolate a chain of ideas to its assumed completion even when that lies beyond the bounds of sense. But it does not always fail in the same way. Kant demonstrates the different ways that it blunders by formulating several seeming contradictions generated by pure reason. Both sides in each dispute, the thesis and antithesis, reflect different forms of reason's demand for something unconditioned, 'unlimited'. What conflicts with the limits of sensibility is the assumption that the rational grounds of the dispute are genuine rather than illusory. Kant organizes the four squabbles into two groups under the rubrics 'mathematical' and 'dynamical', resolving each half differently.

---

[26] Lucretius constructs a similar model of the infinite as an extendable, dependent finite in his famous thought-experiment of the spear-thrower: wherever one posits a limit to the universe, one can equally imagine someone standing there and throwing a spear beyond it (*DRN* 1.968–73; thanks again to Konstan for drawing my attention to the passage, *per litteras*).

The dynamical antinomies are:

THESIS: Causality according to the laws of nature is not the only causality operating to originate the world. A causality of freedom is also necessary to acount fully for these phenomena. (A446/B474)

ANTITHESIS: There is no such thing as freedom, but everything in the world happens solely according to the laws of nature. (A447/B475)

THESIS: There must be a necessary being as the cause of the whole sequence of contingent beings, either as its first member or underlying it. (A454/B482)

ANTITHESIS: No such being exists inside or outside the world. (A455/B483)

Kant answers the apparent contradiction by pronouncing both sets of thesis and antithesis to be true. The assertions of a causality of freedom apart from nature and of a necessary being may well apply to things in themselves, to noumena. On the other hand, declaring that the laws of nature link all things can apply to appearances, to phenomena. In this case both thesis and antithesis may be true (A532/B560). Because freedom and God are not possible objects of experience, theoretical reason cannot prove or disprove that either exists.

The dynamical antinomies correspond to Man's side of Lacan's formulae of sexuation that we saw in Chapter 1:

There is one x that is not subject to the phallic function.

Every x is subject to the phallic function.

Both Kant's and Lacan's formulae posit the existence of a realm of freedom and a being to inhabit it who enjoys complete power, as the First Cause—and yet He must be barred from the ordinary world of cause and effect, presumed as an exception (the First Cause) in order for reality as we know it to emerge. The lineaments of Kant's God correspond to those of the Real Father: the exclusion of God/the Real Father ('No such being exists' | 'There is one x that is not . . .') constitutes the regulatory, interdependent totality ('everything in the world' | 'every x . . .') wherein all happens according to rule ('solely according to the laws of nature' | 'subject to the phallic function'). In this realm—the realm of the Symbolic—the subject's power is limited, and most especially so when compared to the putatively limitless power of the excluded term. Nonetheless, this circumscribed world is comprehensible according to the dictates of Symbolic substitution, as long as its borders remain unbreached. Lacan pushes the borders of Kant's ordered world by making its integrity seem all but untenable. He elaborates Kant's point of exception into a collection of powerfully intrusive correlatives that regularly disrupt the ordered world of the Symbolic. These are the beguiling perditions of *jouissance, objet a,* the superego, and what shall be Narcissus' undoing, the Thing.

After embracing both sides of the dynamical antinomies as true, Kant settles the business more roughly in the case of the mathematical antinomies:

THESIS: The world has a beginning in time, and is also limited in regard to space. (A426/B454)

ANTITHESIS: The world has no beginning, and no limits in space, but is, in relation both to time and space, infinite. (A427/B455)

THESIS: Every composite substance in the world consists of simple parts, and there exists nothing that is not either itself simple, or composed of simple parts. (A434/B462)

ANTITHESIS: No composite thing in the world consists of simple parts, and there does not exist in the world any simple substance. (A435/B463)

Thesis and antithesis in each pair reflect different configurations of reason's search for the unconditioned: the thesis postulates the ultimate termination of a series, while the antithesis unfurls the series' unconditional extension. Kant denies truth to both sides; each simply marks an attempt to apply reason's demand for something unconditioned to space and time. Though both space and time are always indefinite in extent, neither is infinite. They are finite yet always extendible effects of our own cognition (A504–6/B532–4).

The mathematical antinomies point to the impossibility of determining the totality of a phenomenon where no limit can be drawn. There will always be another point in time or space, or another possible subdivision of matter, to dispute the boundary previously drawn—which is not the same as saying that either space or time or matter are infinite. These antinomies demonstrate the purely regulatory function of space and time. They are not things-in-themselves, but forms of intuition that allow us to locate different phenomena at definite places and times. We run aground when we use these concepts constitutively, as though they told us something about noumena.

Closure so foreclosed is precisely the point of Lacan's logical formulae on the feminine side of sexuation, also outlined in Chapter 1:[27]

> There is not one x that is not subject to the phallic function.
>
> Not all (not every) x is submitted to the phallic function.

The first formula may be translated as: no phenomena are exempt from the rules of reason solely capable of making them objects of our experience (for example, temporality and spatiality, which make discernment possible). The second recognizes the basic finitude of phenomena: being subject to the conditions of time and space, we must encounter them one by one. We cannot reach the endpoint where all phenomena would be known and we could constitute their totality. The world—the totality of all phenomena—is not a possible object of experience.[28] So too ~~The~~ Woman fails to form a totality because, like the world, not-all of Her can be grasped within the purely regulatory conceptual framework of the Symbolic. She thus summarizes the logical shortcomings of the Symbolic itself.

MASCULIN, FEMININ, BEVUE

With these correspondences between sex and the stumbling blocks of sense as background, we can now address the ways in which Narcissus and Echo's failed love story founders upon the bounds of reason. The forces behind the miscarriage of thought pertaining to Narcissus begin to reveal themselves when Ovid describes the adolescent's erotic magnetism:

---

[27] My discussion of the antinomies and their relation to the formulae of sexuation throughout this chapter is deeply indebted to Joan Copjec's masterful essay on the subject, 'Sex and the Euthanasia of Reason', (Copjec 1994, 201–36).

[28] Copjec 1994, 221.

> namque ter ad quinos unum Cephisius annum
> addiderat poteratque puer iuuenisque uideri.
> *multi illum iuuenes, multae cupiere puellae;*
> sed (fuit in tenera tam dura superbia forma)
> *nulli illum iuuenes, nullae tetigere puellae.*

> (*Met.* 3.351–5)

For to thrice-five years Narcissus had added one, and was able to appear either boy or young man. *Many youths desired him, many girls*; but (so unyielding was the pride in that lovely body), *no youths, no girls, had touched him.*

As often noted, these verses—especially 353 and 355, which I have italicized—draw upon Catullus 62, an amoebean epithalamium divided between a girls' and boys' chorus. Catullus' female chorus draws a sinister picture of marriage as a custom cruel to women, while his boys outline how wedlock benefits women. As one would expect from an epithalamium, matrimony has the last word, whichever chorus speaks the final lines urging the bride not to fight against her impending marriage.[29] But it is significant that Ovid structures his description of Narcissus' allure to correspond most closely, not with the boys' pro-union sentiments, but with the girls' despair over the consequences of wedlock. Both passages are below—the girls' chorus first, then the boys' response; I have italicized the verses that bear comparison with Ovid's:

> Ut flos in saeptis secretus nascitur hortis,
> ignotus pecori, nullo conuolsus aratro,
> quem mulcent aurae, firmat sol, educat imber;
> *multi illum pueri, multae optauere puellae:*
> idem cum tenui carptus defloruit ungui,
> *nulli illum pueri, nullae optauere puellae:*
> sic uirgo, dum intacta manet, dum cara suis est;
> cum castum amisit polluto corpore florem,
> nec pueris iucunda manet, nec cara puellis.
> Hymen o Hymenaee, Hymen ades o Hymenaee!

---

[29] If the last lines belong to the boys, they break with the rule of alteration in amoebean song; if they belong to the girls, they run counter to the girls' expressed cynicism about marriage. Thomas E. Goud offers a useful survey of scholarly debate on the question (Goud 1995).

> Ut uidua in nudo uitis quae nascitur aruo,
> numquam se extollit, numquam mitem educat uuam,
> sed tenerum prono deflectens pondere corpus
> iam iam contingit summum radice flagellum;
> *hanc nulli agricolae, nulli coluere iuuenci:*
> at si forte eadem est ulmo coniuncta marito,
> *multi illam agricolae, multi coluere iuuenci:*
> sic uirgo dum intacta manet, dum inculta senescit;
> cum par conubium maturo tempore adepta est,
> cara uiro magis et minus est inuisa parenti.

(Cat. 62.39–58)

[GIRLS] As a flower is born, hidden away, in an enclosed garden, unknown to cattle, torn up by no plough, [a flower] that the breezes caress, the sun strengthens, the rain draws forth—*many boys, many girls have wished for it.* The same [flower] droops when gathered by a slender fingernail; *no boys, no girls wish for it.* Thus a maiden, as long as she is untouched, so long is she dear to her own; when she has lost her chaste bloom because her body is defiled, she does not remain pleasing to boys, nor dear to girls.

[BOYS] As a lone vine that is born in a bare field never lifts itself up, never brings forth a ripe grape, but its delicate body bends down, slanting under its own weight. It all but touches its topmost shoot with its root. *This [vine] no farmer, no cattle tend.* But if by chance the same [vine] has been joined to the elm as husband, *that vine many farmers, many cattle tend.* Thus as long as a maiden remains untouched, so long does she wither untended. When she has obtained a worthy marriage at the proper time, she is the dearer to her husband and less of a nuisance to her father.

Ovid has *multi . . . multae* precede *nulli . . . nullae,* just as does Catullus' girls' chorus—an order Catullus' boys' chorus reversed. Ovid also places these substantives in the same metrical positions Catullus' female chorus did, different from the boys' structuring of their lines. Most strikingly, Ovid copies the girls' accounting for both female and male desiring and indifferent subjects, in preference to the boys' portrait of neglectful and devoted males alone. Ovid thus privileges as intertext Catullus' girls and their disenchanted perspective on desire over the boys' smug solipsism. And according to Catullus' girls' chorus, the desirability of the object-cause of desire is a *trompe l'oeil:* its charm depends not upon its objectively specifiable properties (which are not even described), but upon a trick of perspective. When beyond reach, both flower and woman kindle longing; when either is attained, in defiance of all logic, their charisma instantly vanishes—the flower withered,[30] the girl 'defiled' even in marriage.[31] The Catullan intertext thus outlines a species of anamorphosis, whereby a particular object of desire attains the status of *objet a*, an 'object elevated to the dignity of the Thing'. Ovid's reference to Catullus dramatizes in particularly stark terms just how the evidence of things not seen stands behind and funds *objet a*. The Catullan intertext shows a single object turned from gold to dross instantaneously and quite inexplicably—inexplicable unless, as in the dynamical antinomies, one posits some entity that stands outside all ordinary relations of cause and effect, whose operation is required to account fully for phenomena. Just as the dynamical antinomies made God visible only by virtue of a groping failure securely to include or exclude Him and His freedom of operation from a rational chain of causality, so this passage from Catullus illustrates how the value of any and every *objet a* sinks its roots into the incalculable. The Thing is the point of all-powerful exception that funds such objects, the divine and diabolical noumenon of desire. As the primordially lost object, the Thing subtends all subsequent objects of desire as refound objects; it remains not only beyond reach, but completely beyond representation or consciousness. As such, the object of desire described in Catullus 62 conforms to Lacan's formulation of masculine knowledge, or rather, of the masculine mode of the failure of knowledge. The desired only exists as a legible whole in virtue of an arbitrary limitation, the exclusion of the Thing construed as a phantasmatic realm of enjoyment the object only betokens. In that putative lost paradise, the subject was complete, like the very gods. Only detours around the visible object can make the

---

[30] It is true that real flowers wither after being plucked, just as Catullus describes, which makes them less desirable; but as one of my anonymous readers points out to me, 'that only points up the difference in the case of the virgin, who is not visibly different as an immediate result of defloration'.

[31] The boys' chorus does not articulate a direct refutation of this claim. The botanical metaphor for marriage that they choose is the vine 'wedded' to the elm. Such a union increases the vine's utility—to others, not to itself—but they remain silent on the topic of its desirability. As applied to the bride, the boys' chorus reaches the lukewarm conclusion that marriage to the right man at the right time makes the bride '*dearer* to her husband' ('cara', which also means more valuable in the monetary sense, as the vine has more use-value staked to the elm) and '*less of a nuisance* to her father' (Cat. 62.49–58).

outlines of that other, originary treasure of allness appear. In itself, the object-cause of desire is merely a nothing onto which desire is projected. To attain it is fatal to desire, insofar as it reveals the object-cause as a mere prosthesis.

Narcissus' story elaborates this eroticism of deferral. In a few broad strokes, Ovid alludes to a series of amorous admirers whom Narcissus attracts and then rejects, quickly disillusioned with each. What governs these swift tergiversations the poet sketches more fully in the first exchange between Narcissus and Echo. During a hunting expedition, chance separates the boy from his companions and—much to Echo's delight—affords her a chance for reflexive, but curiously apt, colloquy with him.

> dixerat: 'ecquis adest?' et 'adest' responderat Echo.
> hic stupet, utque aciem partes dimittit in omnis,
> uoce 'ueni' magna clamat; uocat illa uocantem.
> respicit et rursus nullo ueniente 'quid' inquit
> 'me fugis?' et totidem quot dixit uerba recepit.
> perstat et alternae deceptus imagine uocis
> 'huc coeamus' ait, nullique libentius umquam
> responsura sono 'coeamus' rettulit Echo
> et uerbis fauet ipsa suis egressaque silua
> ibat ut iniceret sperato bracchia collo.
> ille fugit fugiensque 'manus conplexibus aufer;
> ante' ait 'emoriar, quam sit tibi copia nostri.'
> rettulit illa nihil nisi 'sit tibi copia nostri.'

(3.380–92)

The boy had said: 'Is anyone here?' and 'Here!' Echo had answered. He is dumbstruck, and as he sends his glance in every direction, he cries in a great voice, 'Come!' She calls the caller. He looks behind him and again, when no one comes, he says, 'Why do you flee me?' and he gets back as many words as he has spoken. He persists and, deceived by the appearance of another's voice, he says, 'Here let us come together!' Never to respond more willingly to any sound, Echo returned, 'Let us come together!' and reinforces her words by exiting the woods and coming forth, so that she might throw her arms around the hoped-for neck. He flees and fleeing says, 'Take away your hands with their embraces! I shall die before you may have all of me!' She answered nothing more than 'You may have all of me!'

Echo changes the meaning of Narcissus' words so as to elucidate her own desire to unite with him. For example, Echo truncates Narcissus' exhortation 'huc coeamus' to 'coeamus'; dropping the adverb activates the amorous connotation of the verb, so that Echo's rejoinder means 'let us come together erotically, let us make love'. Or again, when they finally meet and he furiously rejects her embraces, he leads off his hysterical rebuff with a future indicative that emphatically subordinates the clause to his death wish ('ante emoriar, quam sit tibi copia nostri!'). By dropping the first two words, Echo changes the anticipatory subjunctive to hortatory, so that the utterance becomes a wistful if futile invitation to love.[32]

The logic behind Echo's ability to express her wishes contrasts sharply with the masculine logic that configures Narcissus' desirability, and will eventually shape his own fatal desire. Although she cannot initiate speech or choose words independently, she succeeds at communicating because of the stumble peculiar to feminine knowledge, here transformed into a fortunate fall. We saw Kant's mathematical antinomies mount a quarrel over the simultaneous necessity and impossibility of a limit, their mutual collapse forbidding the world, the totality of all phenomena, to come into existence. To apprehend this 'all' requires us to trace the series of phenomena in time and space either to no beginning point, in which case the series is incomplete and not all, or to a point in time or space preceded by nothing, from which nothing could arise. The world thus falls outside of the rules of reason that alone make anything graspable.

It merits specifying that this last statement is (to use Kant's terminology) an infinite judgement: having barred the world from our apprehension via reason, Kant stops short of pronouncing further on the world's existence. He thus crucially informs our reading of Lacan's statement 'The Woman is not-all', which (as Joan Copjec points out) Lacan insists be read as an infinite judgement.[33] Lacan makes ~~The~~ Woman a contradiction of reason, insofar as She, like the world, cannot be organized into a totality ruled by rational principle. But to say that She cannot be entirely subsumed by the purely regulative principles of reason that govern the Symbolic makes a space for

[32] Anderson 1997, 378.
[33] Copjec 1994, 224.

something else—for a feminine *jouissance* unable to be encompassed by these principles. To the degree that such feminine enjoyment marks reason's internal limit, it is unlocatable in experience, and thus incalculable. Tiresias, the one mortal who tries to assess such pleasure mathematically, pays dearly for it. Juno blinds him, Jupiter gives him a gift of prophecy that falls short of practical wisdom—as noted above, Tiresias' doomsaying never helps anyone avoid doom. But Echo can take advantage of the very same feminine indeterminacy in the Symbolic in order to negate the goddess's punishment. Echo exploits the ambiguity of language symptomatic of its irreducible incompleteness, an internal flaw that paradigmatically illustrates the limits of the Symbolic as a differential system.

In language, there are no positive terms, only relations of difference: a signifier means what it means only in relation to all other signifiers in the system. Meaning is thereby always ultimately suspended and deferred: another signifier will always come along to be added to the sum of signifiers, and that addition will change all previously established relations within the system. Without the totality of the system there can be no determination of meaning, and yet this very totality would prevent the successive consideration of signifiers that the rule demands. The same rule of language requires, and precludes, the completeness of the system of signifiers. As with the mathematical antinomies, we are foiled by needing limit and failing of it, insofar as we must—impossibly—determine the totality of an infinite progression.

This paradox leaves us with what Lacan calls *lalangue* ('llanguage'), the feminine, inconsistent, 'non-all' entity logically prior to *la langue* as totality—i.e. to language viewed as the abstract ideal of grammatical and syntactical rules.[34] Llanguage generates meaning effects that exceed conventional rules for interpreting language, contingent effects manifest in paronomasia, portmanteau words, antiphrasis, and other wordplay. Meaning is always sliding along the signifying chain, floating above whatever provisional unit of sense punctuation provides, rather than being tied to particular words. This *souplesse* of language, its dispersal into llanguage, affords Echo the power of self-expression in her colloquy with Narcissus, making a word or two

---

[34] On *lalangue*, see Lacan SXX (Lacan 1975, 126–127/1998, 138–139); Miller 1975.

judiciously dropped from the utterances of a boy-cynic produce the warmest expressions of a nymph's passion.

THE SENDER ALWAYS GETS BACK HIS OWN
MESSAGE IN INVERTED FORM

Yet, as Jacqueline Fabre-Serris has noticed, Echo's task requires adroitness, not brute contortion: a veiled eroticism in Narcissus' words lends itself readily to Echo's re-reading. His demeanour and behaviour confirm the latent content of his words. Upon hearing Echo's voice, he is 'transfixed' ('stupet', 381); the word and its paronyms often describe the effects of desire.[35] He looks for her in every direction, and summons her persistently. Much later, all the same details will characterize his passionate response to his own image in

[35] For example: 'quid *stupes*, Antiphila?' Terence, *Heauton Timorumenos* 404 (Bacchis wonders why Antiphila is thunderstruck when Antiphila has just caught sight of her beloved Clinia returned from lengthy military service abroad); 'Quid astitisti *obstupida*?' Plautus, *Miles Gloriosus* 1254 (Milphida addresses Acroteleutium, who is pretending to be stunned with disappointment because her beloved soldier is not within the house); 'Erus *stupidus* adstat: ita eius aspectus repens | Cor torporauit homini amore' ('the young master is standing by like an idiot; that's how fast the man's heart stupefied his face with love!' Sex. Turpilius, *Hetaera* 75 (= Nonius 182.4); Ribbeck 1898, 2:109); Ovid, *Heroides* 16.253: 'dum *stupeo* uisis—nam pocula forte tenebam— | tortilis a digitis excidit ansa meis' (Paris declaring the signs of his passion to Helen); Ovid, *Met.* 4.676 'trahit inscius ignes | et *stupet* et uisae correptus imagine formae | paene suas quatere est oblitus in aere pennas' (Perseus mesmerized by the sight of the naked Andromeda chained to a rock); Ovid, *Met.* 10.287: 'dum *stupet* et dubie gaudet fallique ueretur, | rursus amans rursusque manu sua uota retractat' (Pygmalion astonished as he sees his beloved *eburnea puella* come alive).

Of course, *stupeo* and its cognates do designate states of gormlessness induced by emotions other than love. But in erotic contexts (such as elegy and comedy, whose plots so often revolve about young men, and sometimes women, falling head over heels in love), the verb is regularly used to describe the effects of love. That association must at least shade how the reader perceives Narcissus' reaction to the lure of Echo's voice. Certainly when Ovid next describes the boy thunderstruck by his own visage, 'adstupet' (*Met.* 3.418) unmistakably describes erotic impact. The many details reproduced between the one scene and the other (particularly similar wording and word-positioning within the hexameter; see the discussion below of *Met.* 3.385 and 3.416) invite us to re-read Narcissus' encounter with Echo in the light of his encounter with himself, including the erotic fascination manifest in the later scene.

the spring. Narcissus is again transfixed—by himself ('adstupet ipse sibi', 418); though no longer perplexed by the need to look for his putative interlocutor, he calls to his reflection to join him as persistently as he had summoned Echo (3.454–62, 477–9). Ovid further underlines the symmetry between the two scenes by describing the source of fascination in each case as an *imago*, while structuring the two respective phrases in close parallel. Echo's voice astonishes Narcissus 'deceived by the appearance of another's voice' ('alternae deceptus *imagine* uocis', 3.385); later, he stares at the pond 'arrested by the appearance of perceived beauty/form' ('uisae correptus *imagine* formae', 3.416).[36] In both passages, participle and *imagine* are flanked by feminine adjective and noun, the pattern of the word endings identical except for the discrepancy between *uocis* and *formae*.

Although the details of Narcissus' encounter with Echo anticipate his captivation by his own image in the pool, his rejection of her—as of his other lovers—has usually been seen as unalloyed coldness. Yet that reading imposes upon Ovid what little his closest contemporaries had to say about Narcissus. Both Conon and Oxyrhynchus 4711 represent Narcissus as steadily scorning all his lovers prior to falling in love with himself.[37] However, both also report that Narcissus killed himself, where Ovid merely has him fade away (like Echo). Both make Narcissus the classic Greek paederastic *eromenos*, attracting only adult male lovers; neither mentions any female lover, much less Echo, still less the 'multae . . . puellae' Ovid records as longing for Narcissus. Moreover, evidence for a Narcissus who desires before he meets his own reflection exists, albeit postdating Ovid. Pausanias reports a variant of the tale wherein Narcissus conceived an incest-

[36] My description of the parallels follows closely that of Jacqueline Fabre-Serris (Fabre-Serris 1995, 183–4).

[37] If the attribution of Oxyrhynchus Papyrus 4711 to Parthenius is correct, that version of Narcissus' story might pre-date Ovid by as much as a generation. The papyrus was first published by W. B. Henry (Henry 2005). Subsequent scholarship on the papyrus includes: Reed 2006; Luppe 2006*a* and 2006*b*; Magnelli 2006. The attribution of Oxy. 4711 is not uncontroversial: Hans Bernsdorff dismisses the identification of the author with Parthenius (Bernsdorff 2007).

We can a little more securely, if only approximately, date the version in Conon (*Diegesis* 24, in Jacoby 1923, 197–8), because he dedicated his collection of 50 mythical narratives to King Archelaus Philopater of Cappadocia (reigned 36 BCE–17 CE).

uous love for his twin sister, who resembled him not only in features, but in dress. When she died, he sought consolation in his reflection in a spring, pretending that he saw his sister's face.[38] This Narcissus *has* experienced erotic longing before he encounters his own image—indeed, that very desire drives him to seek out his reflection. The differences between Ovid, Conon, and Oxyrhynchus 4711 underline the degree to which Ovid innovates upon his mythical inheritance; the desire that spurs Pausanias' grieving twin to seek out the mirroring spring, rather than surprising him there, reveals that other constructions of Narcissus were possible in antiquity. All this evidence cautions us against prematurely narrowing the scope of our interpretation of the *Metamorphoses'* beautiful boy.

Reading Narcissus as fickle rather than entirely cold—even if his fickleness is not present to his own consciousness—offers the advantage of better explaining the specifics of the boy's encounter with Echo, and why Ovid carefully foreshadows in that meeting Narcissus' eventual, unmistakable captivation by his own image. Lost in the forest and able only to hear Echo's voice, Narcissus is anxious to meet the person he cannot see. Yet Echo's voice must reveal her as a stranger, not a companion from his all-male hunting party, whom he might naturally wish to rejoin. She is a young female—i.e. another one of the 'multae...puellae' (*Met.* 3.353) Narcissus has always ended by scorning in the past. Why, then, is he so eager to join her, when to do so risks another amorous embarrassment? The verbal parallels Ovid draws between Narcissus' meeting with Echo, and the boy's subsequent rencounter with his image, sketch the first convergence as paradigmatic for the second, and crucial to the interpretation of both. The structure of that first failed encounter with a tantalization outlines the nature of the boy's desire, thus the reasons behind its repeated failure. Echo makes Narcissus' captivation by the ultimately unavailable image of himself more understandable.

Until the moment he comes across his image in the spring, Narcissus' erotic fascination accrues purely to the object in prospect, not attained (just as the girls' chorus of Catullus 62 would predict). Lost in the forest and able only to hear Echo's voice, he is anxious to meet

---

[38] Pausanias 9.31.7–8.

the person he cannot see, enthralled and eager just so long as she is a (visual) nothing. Once she reveals herself as tangible and available, Narcissus rejects her: his object's sudden, disconcerting visibility and availability makes her *ipso facto* undesirable. (Curiously, he desires what she will be later, once her sorrow at his rejection wastes her physical being: a disembodied voice, infinitely captivating in its elusiveness.)[39] His subsequent history repeats this pattern of wanting only the unavailable. Narcissus is described as 'deceiving' his would-be lovers ('sic hanc, sic alias undis aut montibus ortas | *luserat* hic nymphas, sic coetus ante uiriles'—'and so he had *deceived* this nymph, so he had *deceived* others risen from the waves or the hilltops, and so, before that, the embraces of men', *Met.* 3.402–3). Whether he does so consciously or not, he acts the coquet rather than Vestal Virgin; *ludere* implies he gives his pursuers some hope, delighting to bring them closer, but never to let them close upon him.[40]

Narcissus' desire only for the occluded (such as the hidden Echo, or his yet-distant would-be lovers) constructs his objects as blank screens onto which he is free to project his own imaginings. Seen clearly and directly, the focus of his fascination reveals its distance from the noumenon that produces a discrete, coherent object of desire. Like the dynamical antinomies, Narcissus' desire depends for its very existence upon an exception to a causal series. The dynamical antinomies both declared and denied that the chain of cause and effect accounting for phenomena was supplemented by a free cause predicated upon no other. Their conflict revolved around the idea of an uncaused cause unconditionally precipitating all other phenomena. These antinomies are both pronounced true because they draw the limit needed to close the series of phenomena and render it whole ('all') by passing negative judgement on what cannot be included within the series. Freedom and God appear either as supplements not subject to the laws that generated the series ('a causality of freedom is also necessary/there must be a necessary

---

[39] Konstan, *per litteras*.

[40] The *Oxford Latin Dictionary* cites as among the meanings of *ludo* the following: 'to treat (a person, his feelings, etc.) without due seriousness, trifle with, baffle, tease, tantalize, or sim.' and cites this very passage from Ovid, *Met.* 402–3 as one of its examples (*OLD* s.v. *ludo*, 9a).

being') or as what is prohibited from becoming visible within it ('there is no such thing as freedom/no such being exists'). The inconceivability of freedom and God is thus conceptualized as an occlusion: the cause is made to disappear from the field of its effects.

Insofar as such a vanishing principle appears to structure the waxing and waning of Narcissus' desire, it moulds that desire according to the masculine (il)logic of sexuation. Man considered as a whole ('every x') is made to appear in the formulae of sexuation only by virtue of a delimitation. What draws the boundaries around that set and thus makes it visible is a supplement that is also a subtraction. The set of all subjects is produced by the phallic function, meaning, the imposition upon the living being of the Symbolic, whose regulatory function the phallus represents. To say that is to say, 'the set of all subjects is constituted by the one that got away'. 'There is at least one x' construed as the locus of Being insofar as it cannot enter this rule-based system. Being is a noumenal point of plenitude and freedom barred from representation within the Symbolic. What its absence leaves behind is an 'idea of reason': the object of desire as a pure conceptualization devoid of Being, a concept that nonetheless depends for its unity upon the Being it excludes. The different manifestations under which various objects of desire appear are reduced to order only in reference to this original object as lost—as referenced to the Thing, the noumenal guarantor of all value.

The figure of the primal Father and his relations with His primal horde (Chapter 1) exemplify this set of ideas marshalled under Lacan's masculine formulae of sexuation. The primal Father is the exception to law whose excesses eventually produce a rule-based system. Considering all women sexually accessible, all men His sexual rivals and slaves, the primal Father acts unchecked by familial regard of any kind. Not subject to any law, He is His own law—until his excesses inspire his sons' bloody revolt, followed by their guilty institution of rule-based relations within the tribe, including the incest taboo. As remarked in Chapter 1, the primal Father's effects continue to be felt by his now-regulated sons and daughters even after his murder: the prohibition upon incest marks the sons' renunciation of the Father's ungoverned desire, so that His limitless licence continues to shape their desire *per viam negativam.*

The idea of an unthinkable, lost plenitude informing quotidian desire (*à la* primal Father and epigone sons) seems to inform Narcissus' punctual erotic ennui, but maximally extrapolated: this is an alienation and belatedness so extreme that the splendour shed by that lost bliss punctually fails. The boy repeatedly enacts losing the perspective from which that original, ineffable loss illuminates the object of desire. Failing of the glory shed by the absolute, his vicarious objects collapse once more into nothing intelligible to his desire. When the face in the pool finally captivates him permanently, he falls in love with an image of what cannot be weighed and found wanting—the untouchable and inhuman. The narrator gives the image stars for eyes and hair of the immortals,[41] implying a physical inaccessibility Narcissus also soon discovers, as he snatches in vain at the water's surface. Only this object of desire, the one upon which he can never close, holds his interest. And it continues to do so even when he knows what he sees is himself.

But as noted, though the enlightened Narcissus keeps his passion, he loses his wits and his life. Kant and Lacan's shared epistemic framework helps us to unfold the nature of this fatal knowledge, and how its medium (the spring) grants Narcissus both unique captivation and destruction. After all, this cannot be the first reflection of himself that Narcissus has ever seen. How could an active hunter born from a water nymph never in sixteen years have bent over any stream, looked at a rain puddle, glanced at water held in his own cupped hands? But if this is where desire for what he saw up close overtook him, then this can be no ordinary spring—and indeed, the poem marks these waters as uncanny, unreal, weird.

> fons erat inlimis, nitidis argenteus undis,
> quem neque pastores neque pastae monte capellae
> contigerant aliudue pecus, quem nulla uolucris
> nec fera turbarat nec lapsus ab arbore ramus;
> gramen erat circa quod proximus umor alebat,
> siluaque sole locum passura tepescere nullo.
>
> (*Met.* 3. 407–12)

---

[41] 'spectat humi positus geminum, sua lumina, sidus | et dignos Baccho, dignos et Apolline crines', 3.420–1.

There was a spring free of mud, silver with shining waves, which neither shepherds nor goats pastured on the mountain or other cattle had touched, which no bird nor wild beast nor branch fallen from a tree had disturbed. There was grass round about, which the water close by nourished, and the woods would not allow the place to grow warm because of the sun.

The spring is unnaturally pure, clear, secluded, untouched either by man or beast. Even time stops in this place. The natural process of deterioration, such as trees ageing and losing branches, is suspended; the sun cannot penetrate the foliage so as to mark either the passage of the day, or the succession of night to day. The pool's timeless impeccability and seclusion embody the logical perfection toward which Kant's antinomies strain, as they grapple with the eternal, the absolute, and the infinite. Yet the fount also realizes the threat behind the nonpareil: everything freezes in the absolute. All relations of commutation, cause and effect, commensurability—relations that subtend thought and the subject of thought—come to a halt. Lacan conceptualized this domain of absolute zero in the Thing: as the noumenal object behind the lure of all phenomenal objects, the Thing's value is incommensurable. Exchange and substitution are impossible within its sphere, just as the glade discovers to Narcissus the one object that nothing can supersede. And it discovers it to him at what Ovid marks as a *kairos* of one in his own life: the poet records the boy's age as 'thrice five plus one', his last year expressed as an anomalous surplus added to the neat multiple. This is the year in which Narcissus' own time will be suspended: he will never pass beyond the boundaries of his adolescence into the world ruled by displacement and succession.[42]

The spring's cool shade and seclusion underline how baleful is his encounter with its timelessness in the Year One. Chill privacy ranges the fount with the other sinister bodies of water dotting the *Metamorphoses*' landscapes.[43] Its virginal status aligns it especially with two other pools that significantly punctuate Thebes' environs and Thebes' history: the spring in the inviolate woods where Cadmus'

---

[42] Konstan, *per litteras*.

[43] Hugh Parry (Parry 1964, 275–80) and Charles Segal (Segal 1969, 23–33) discuss the role bodies of water play in the *Metamorphoses*; both see water as marking loci of sexual violence.

unfortunate followers find the monstrous serpent and their deaths, and the spring wherein Diana bathes and disaster overtakes Actaeon. The similarity and geographic proximity of all three founts urge the reader to consider them as mutually referential. Each of the other two springs contains a hidden threat traceable to a specific agent.[44] For Cadmus and his men, it is the monstrous snake, hidden in the cave adjacent to the spring; for Actaeon, it is the goddess Diana, quick to anger and punishment for being surprised at her bath. The *monstrum* in this water is an image of what Narcissus truly desires; by offering him this captivating vision, the spring realizes Narcissus' innermost longings without his having to articulate them. That short-circuit effectively collapses the distance between the Symbolic and the Real. The spring bypasses the Symbolic as Other, as the purely virtual order that frames both knowledge and the communication of that knowledge—including what of the self can be known without destroying the epistemic basis of that self. In this strange place, forbidden knowledge comes to exist as noumenon made phenomenon, a Real Thing that is no longer purely virtual, but concretizes the primordial loss behind all desire.[45] Although the mysterious pool eventually destroys Narcissus, it is even more his self than he is, insofar as it stages directly, as a sensual object, an Otherness that is the fantasized core of his being.

What allures Narcissus is an image in the water that (as he remarks) mimics his every gesture. This logically extrapolates his previous habit of bestowing interest only upon objects that offer themselves as blank spaces for his imaginings. By making them the screens onto which he casts his fantasies, Narcissus projects himself onto his would-be lovers: the fantasies he paints onto his admirers revolve around the core of himself. His imaginings parody the erotic ideal, 'we two are (as) one', just as if he had climbed into his lovers' bodies and animated them in a species of erotic takeover. Nonetheless, his initial desire for the image in the water arises from the delusion that what he sees is not himself—i.e. from an implicit denial that he is, in fact, facing the actuality of the fantasy his erotic history sketches. Narcissus has to err in his perceptions, and to err badly, in

---

[44] As often in the *Metamorphoses* (Segal 1969, 23–33).
[45] Žižek 2000*b*, 236.

order to maintain this denial. At first he believes that he sees a time lag between his gestures and the image's 'responses', as though a real person were answering his gesticulations and exclamations. Once he loses his grasp upon that difference, realizing that the image is himself, the object of his desire becomes deadly to him. Although no less fascinated by the image, Narcissus begins to talk of death as his inevitable end, and to lose his reason. The image was acceptable insofar as it did not align exactly with his innermost desire as evidenced in his previous fascinations; revealed as the instantiation of his core fantasies, it drives him to insanity and death.

His despair marks the coincidence of what is utterly Other and foreign to any human experience, and the innermost core of himself qua human. The spring's alien status and power disclose to him what in the human subject must remain at a distance if he is to sustain the consistency of his Symbolic universe: his innermost, categorically repressed core fantasy, the shape of the lost paradise whence his subjectivity is supposed to have sprung—in short, the Thing.[46] The fact that the image in the spring is Narcissus' own throws into relief the core fantasy's fundamental threat: the reflection essentially presents Narcissus with the message, 'there is no Other'—i.e. there is no network of relations of commutation to confirm Narcissus' status as a subject who has emerged from the homogeneous Real. His innermost fantasy, his Thing, turns upon being enclosed in himself.

Significantly, what alerts Narcissus to the fact that he has come too close to the innermost object of his desire is that the image in the spring cannot speak (by contrast with Echo, who could be heard, but not seen, and caused the boy no such existential crisis). Although Narcissus can see the *imago* mouthing words, no sound reaches him. The image is thus marked as not properly integrated into the differential system of language, whose elements and order are the currency of reason. The moment Narcissus realizes how his beloved's participation in the Symbolic is strangely barred—marked as alien to that system, something that does not properly belong in the Symbolic but must rather be excluded—his world begins to disintegrate. The necessary exclusion of the Thing qua primordially lost object ceases to organize Narcissus' universe. Face to face with his own image, he

---

[46] Žižek 2000*b*, 236.

discovers only indifference (in every sense of that word). He despairs, is certain that he must die, goes insane.

Narcissus' plight underlines the fact that, like the contradictions of the antinomies, the Thing marks the limits of reason. But the limits that for Kant skirt infinity, eternity, and omnipotence, for Lacan also border psychosis.[47] Propelled toward this wasteland by the knowledge of his core fantasy, Narcissus is possessed by a desperate insanity focused on denying that his beloved is in fact himself. Shortly after he fully recognizes his plight, he again addresses the image as if it were another lover who threatened to leave him. His ravings fictively re-install difference between himself and his innermost desire, as if he could thus abolish its threat to his subjectivity.

Narcissus' increasingly deranged suicidal thoughts all gesture wistfully toward the idea that death could befall either him, on the one hand, or his beloved on the other, as if they were two separate entities:

> 'iste ego sum! sensi, nec me mea fallit imago.
> uror amore mei, flammas moueoque feroque.
> quid faciam? roger anne rogem? quid deinde rogabo?
> quod cupio mecum est; inopem me copia fecit.
> o utinam a nostro secedere corpore possem!
> uotum in amante nouum: uellem quod amamus abesset.
> iamque dolor uires adimit nec tempora uitae
> longa meae superant primoque exstinguor in aeuo.
> nec mihi mors grauis est posituro morte dolores;
> hic qui diligitur uellem diuturnior esset;
> nunc duo concordes anima moriemur in una.'

(*Met.* 3.463–73)

'That one [of yours] I am! I perceive it, and my own image does not deceive me. I burn with love for myself: I inspire and suffer the same passion. What shall I do? Shall I be asked, or ask? For what shall I ask? What I desire is with me: my abundance makes me poor. Oh would that I were able to withdraw

---

[47] Fabre-Serris offers an alternative Lacanian reading of Narcissus' encounter with the pool. She points out that, being the son of Liriope, a beautiful water nymph, Narcissus' sight of an alluring image in a body of water aligns this *fons* with his mother. Fabre-Serris develops the significance of this encounter by drawing upon Lacan's concept of the Imaginary; she sees Narcissus' story as an allegory of subject-formation, to which 'narcissism' is necessary and normative. Her analysis, while canny and persuasive, does not explain why Narcissus' perception of his own image results in insanity and death rather than normality (Fabre-Serris 1995, 185–9).

from our body! A novel prayer in a lover, that I would wish what we love to be far away/destroyed! And now the anguish saps my strength, and no long extent of life remains for me, and I am dying in my early youth. Nor is death burdensome to me, when it will abolish my sufferings. This one, who is beloved, I would wish to be longer-lived; now, our hearts in harmony, we shall die in the same breath.'

His first words of revelation both acknowledge and deny his dilemma. He begins with the distancing demonstrative 'iste' ('that one of yours'), which marks what it modifies as separate from the speaker and relegated to his addressee. However, what it modifies is the principle marker of self, 'ego' or 'I'. 'Sum' patches together an uneasy truce between these bickering gestures of distance and identification, but not one that lasts.[48] His lament over his 'abundance' (*copia*) making him 'poor' (*inopem*) indicates a suffocating proximity to his beloved object, with whom he is one not only in body, but in mind and soul, in every particular. That conflux of desirer and desiring object—a state in which the desirer really does overtake the object of desire—reveals the object to be radically empty, 'poor'. From the black hole of primordial loss, he has mined a gold that necessarily turns to dross in his hands.

His first thought of a solution, 'would that I could depart from my body' (467), refers ambiguously both to death and to a supernatural answer to his problem. His exclamation can be read either as wishing that the life depart from his flesh, or that his one self were magically twinned. However, the next line veers closer to the idea of abolishing the beloved object: 'abesset' (468) means 'not be present, disappear', not just 'be separate [from me]'.[49] Narcissus next speaks unambiguously of death—which he now embraces, though paradoxically he has swung from wishing the *imago*-beloved to go missing to wanting it to survive himself. But either pole of his wish encapsulates the idea of sacrifice: either he wills the *imago*'s destruction, or welcomes his

---

[48] My thanks to Alessandro Barchiesi and Susanna Morton Braund for pointing out to me these aspects of the verse (*per verba*, Stanford University, 12 Feb. 2005).

[49] See *OLD*, 'absum'; common to the definitions the *OLD* gives that pre-date or are contemporaneous with Ovid is the idea of an object or person distant in space or time, unavailable or derelict in duty. Simply being a separate entity falls outside the purview of these usages.

own. The impossible-ideal death he envisions—the death either of himself or his *imago*, but not both together—would re-establish the distance between Narcissus and his innermost object that the reflecting pool has collapsed.

In the event, death cannot amend Narcissus' dilemma, insofar as he cannot disentangle himself from his *imago* even in the Underworld: he still stares at his reflection in the Styx. Monstrously bewitching desire captivates even his Underworld spirit. The sacrifice of his living self, his body, to his love has not worked, in the sense of putting distance between Narcissus and the unbearable image of his innermost desire. His world and his self unravel: before death, he loses his sanity; after death, he loses himself. We cannot determine what of Narcissus persists in the yellow and white flower left behind at his death, or in his Underworld spirit, or in the reflection in the Styx at which the spirit stares. But his human subjectivity disintegrates, insofar as its ability to be located as an organized entity disappears.

NOT THIS ONE

The failure of Narcissus' dreamed-of solution in death (either his own, or the *imago*'s) leaves us with the image of being entrapped by a literal realization of the erotic cliché that subtends the sexual relation, 'we two are (as) one'.[50] Narcissus' doom reveals the flaw in conceiving

---

[50] Of which the chief ancient example is Aristophanes' speech in the *Symposium*, which posits that what drives true lovers to seek each other out is their status as the surgically separated remnants of an original whole entity; Aristophanes even imagines the lovers wishing to live welded together physically, and to die together. Propertius glories in that particular fantasy of *Liebestod*: he imagines himself and Cynthia navigating the Underworld rivers together (Prop. 2.28.39–42); praises the Eastern custom of suttee, whereby the wife demonstrates her devotion by immolating herself upon her husband's funeral pyre (Prop. 3.13.15–24); even threatens to kill both himself and Cynthia together in a *crime passionel* (Prop. 2.8.21–8). Ovid's Thisbe glances at this notion of two becoming one in death in her dying request that she and Pyramus be mixed in one urn, as though they were the ashes of one body (*Met.* 4.154–7). Duncan Kennedy has a particularly sophisticated discussion of the erotic tension between 'two' and 'one' in the ancient discourse of sexuality, and he brings this to bear upon the Narcissus episode (Kennedy 1993, 69–70).

the erotic as a relation between two complementary entities.[51] That Imaginary ideal construes Man and Woman as two symmetrical halves that together make up a whole. Yet as noted above, conjuring from particular, contingent men the conceptual totality that is Man depends upon a constitutive exception, upon what is forbidden to enter into the all (e.g. the primal Father). By contrast, the totality of Woman is simply impossible to produce on the basis of a single logical principle: in contrast to the sleight of hand that produces Man by disappearing the embarrassing anomaly, Lacan's notation ~~The~~ Woman simply confesses that no 'essence of Woman' can be wrung from the generality of women. It follows that the logic governing the two positions, Man and Woman, is asymmetrical, uncomplementary.[52] Yet from this mismatch of a prohibition and an impossibility, ideology weaves the illusion of a (barred) whole. It converts an impossibility into the semblance of a (theoretically superable) prohibition: 'We could be one, if only this or that circumstance were changed.' Ideology thus provides the explanation for 'why things went wrong', and for how they could, in theory, go right.[53]

Narcissus and Echo together unravel the operation of such erotic ideology. Ovid extrapolates the idea of complementarity to its logical conclusion, such that its inherent impossibility becomes obvious.

---

[51] The mysterious status of the flower Narcissus leaves behind raises a question regarding the sexual relation that its intertext, Catullus 62, had only suggested. Ovid changes Catullus' question from 'what is this object worth?' (the intact flower versus the 'plucked' flower) into 'what is it?' ('is this flower Narcissus, or is his being located elsewhere?'). Ovid sees how Catullus' flower already raised a deeper question of identity. To characterize the virgin as 'defiled' even in marriage demands the further query, 'What is a wife—the fulfilment, or the degradation, of Woman?' The stark divide between the boys' and the girls' valuation of the bride points to an internal contradiction in the way the ancients construe relations between the sexes (as Roman comedy attests, the cynicism of the girls' chorus regarding the unattractiveness of wives has solid cultural grounds; Terence even reflects sardonically on this theatrical cliché by making the eponymous 'mother-in-law' of the *Hecyra* a completely kind, accommodating, amiable wife groundlessly blamed by her husband for everything that goes wrong in his life). The choruses' division of opinion thus points to a logical shortcoming in the Roman Symbolic itself—in short, to ~~The~~ Woman lurking behind the promise of completed identity that Rome's Woman dangles.

[52] Copjec 1994, 235.

[53] Žižek 2000*b*, 248.

Narcissus' dilemma illustrates why erotic fusion is not the solution, but rather the problem, insofar as the ideal entails a subject collapsing back into himself and into the pre-subjective in-difference from which he came. Narcissus, the paradigmatic human lover, will never enjoy his beloved; when confronted with the reality of his innermost desire and the animating fantasy of *amor*, 'being one with the beloved', he can do nothing but die. Echo enacts an equally instructive version of this doom. Her versatile use of language is not matched by an equal mobility in her objects of desire: she fixes upon the unattainable Narcissus and so dooms herself. But Ovid's description of her physical evanescence makes the exact nature of her end much more difficult to determine than in Narcissus' case.

> attenuant uigiles corpus miserabile curae,
> adducitque cutem macies et in aera sucus
> corporis omnis abit. uox tantum atque ossa supersunt:
> uox manet; ossa ferunt lapidis traxisse figuram.
> inde latet siluis nulloque in monte uidetur,
> omnibus auditur; sonus est qui uiuit in illa.

> (3.396–401)

Her wakeful cares thin out her pitiable body, and thinness draws tight her skin, and all the moisture of her body vanishes into the air. Only a voice and bones remain. The voice remains; they say that her bones took on the appearance of stones. From then on, she hides in the woods and [though] she is seen on the mountain by no one, she is heard by all. *sonus est, qui uiuit in illa*.

Her flesh melts away, her bones turn to stone, some kind of sound survives—but where is Echo? Ovid's description pulls her apart in a way that defies rationality. As Joseph Loewenstein points out, the two possible translations of the last half-line point in opposite directions: 'There is a sound that lives in her' or 'She is sound, which lives in her.' The first makes the sound an alien entity cohabiting with Echo; the second makes it coterminous with herself—and yet not so: if she is the sound, how does it 'live in her'? The Latin fractures among ambiguities that do and do not equate Echo with echo, that do and do not make her a formal vessel for a physical phenomenon. Ovid seems to forget all this when he brings her back to witness Narcissus' death as if she were a sentient being. She sees Narcissus, she feels pain at the memory of his rejection of her, but she behaves like a simple echo, repeating back his, and eventually his sisters', expressions of grief (3.494–507). But that simplicity fragments again upon Ovid's description of Narcissus' dying words:

> 'heu frustra dilecte puer!' totidemque remisit
> uerba locus, dictoque 'uale' 'uale' inquit et Echo.   (3.500–1)

'Alas, boy beloved in vain!' and just as many words the place returns, and when he says 'farewell!', Echo says it, too.

Not Echo, but the glade itself repeats Narcissus' dying words; Echo only repeats his last 'farewell!' If she is now fully echo, why do the environs, and not she, repeat his 'alas, boy beloved in vain!'? And if the place can produce an echo apart from her, then what is she? This final picture of Echo revives the problem posed by the earlier description of her wasting away into bones and sound: something that hints of agency and of an existence exceeding the physical phenomenon of echo persists, but cannot be securely established as such. Ovid closes Echo's history by dispersing the ambiguous signs of her existence over the landscape of Thebes. No totality construable as a subject, or even a living being, can unambiguously be coaxed from these signs. But neither can it be denied: as with the world conjured in the mathematical antinomies, as with The Woman, the judgement on Echo is infinite. Ovid refuses to pronounce definitively upon her existence.

The misapprehensions round which Echo and Narcissus' amorous history is structured demonstrate why, even for the gods, the sexual relation does not exist. The two would-be lovers exemplify Man and Woman, two distinct models of the desiring subject whose mismatched rationales cannot be made to overlap or cohere. But they also show that the sexual relation's non-existence, the void round which its deadlock is structured, animates desire and underpins the existence of any desiring being. The fault is radical, inherent to the status of any subject, and correspondingly insurmountable. That is why human beings continue to stumble across it in these two different, asymmetrical modes of failure exemplified by nymph and boy.

THE MUTE STONES SPEAK

Ovid remarks that Narcissus' story became widely known (and presumably Echo's also, since the poet makes her inextricably part of
Narcissus' tale), redounding to Tiresias' credit as a prophet. But how
is this possible, without any speaking witnesses to disseminate it?
Echo is the only observer of Narcissus' fate, and she cannot communicate autonomously. What disseminates the story? The sole earthly
aftermath resides in objects: a yellow-and-white flower, a pool in a
glade. True, in the miraculous world of the *Metamorphoses*, even
animals can sometimes communicate, as Io-cow manages to spell
her name in the dirt for her father. But since Ovid carefully specifies
that no one and nothing visits this pool—not shepherds, not even
goats, birds, or animals (3.408–10)—he leaves us with a 'locked-
room mystery'. To paraphrase Sherlock Holmes,[54] once the poet
has specified the impossible, whatever he has left, however improbable, must be the reader's truth. Somehow the collection of mute
objects round the fatal pool communicates a story of thwarted
desires. Reversing the direction of Narcissus' doom, whereby unconscious desire bypassed the Symbolic to emerge in the Real, the Real
now obtains its own voice, becomes directly 'Symbolified'.[55]

   Which means, appropriately enough, that Echo has the last
word: she set the pattern for this miracle. When she was reduced to
petrified bones and became echo, the phenomenon of vocal reflection, this stone, *mirabile dictu*, produced intelligible sound. The

---

[54] From 'The Adventure of the Beryl Coronet': 'It is an old maxim of mine that
when you have excluded the impossible, whatever remains, however improbable,
must be the truth', Doyle 1892, 278.

[55] Yet another bizarre change in perspective on the Theban landscape, a change
that conforms to a pattern of such bafflements within the *Metamorphoses*. As O'Hara
shows, Ovid's epic repeatedly stages contradictions whereby one passage cannot
logically be reconciled with another without some extraordinary assumption not
given by the text—e.g. Jupiter's strange assertion that Lycaon tried to murder him as
he slept, and served him human flesh, at which point Jupiter used his lightning to
destroy the palace. How is it that we can plausibly reconcile the god sitting down at
the table of a man who had just tried to murder him? And why does cannibalism
unleash the lightning that Jove's own attempted murder could not? (O'Hara 2007,
116–17).

spring spreads its supernatural influence and finds a way to communicate Narcissus' story, through dumb objects that have no voice at all and yet speak. Like Echo, the Real has found a voice that seemed to be denied it.

The story of Echo and Narcissus continues the pattern of the Real emerging more and more forcefully from within Thebes' Symbolic, a pattern that began with the hallucinatory landscape evident at the city's origins (Chapter 2). The Theban Real usurps the powers of the Symbolic, discovering meaning and a shadowy, ambiguous subjectivity precisely where the rules break down that govern speaker and speech, sentience and brute matter, knowledge and the impenetrable, phenomenon and noumenon. Thebes' Real begins to assume the contours of 'contentful' noumenon. The contentful noumenon—Hegel's response to Kant's conceptualization of the radically unknowable—organizes the next chapter. Chapter 5 examines Narcissus' status as a substitute for Thebes' most famous, and most egregiously absent, son—Oedipus.

5

'Through a Glass, Darkly'

Narcissus as Oedipus

The Death of ~~a~~ Saint Narcissus

Come under the shadow of this grey rock—
Come in under the shadow of this grey rock,
And I will show you something different from either
Your shadow sprawling over the sand at daybreak, or
        behind
Your shadow leaping ~~by~~ the fire against the red rock:
I will show you his bloody cloth and limbs
And the gray shadow on his lips.

He walked once between the sea and the high cliffs
When the wind made him aware of his limbs smoothly
   passing each other
And of his arms crossed over his breast.
When he walked over the meadows
He was stifled and soothed by his own rhythm.
By the river
His eyes were aware of the pointed corners of his eyes
And his hands aware of the tips of his fingers.
Struck down by such knowledge
He could not live men's ways, but became a dancer before God.
If he walked in city streets

         ive
He seemed to tread on faces, convuls~~ed~~ thighs and knees.
So he came out to live under the rock.

P.T.O.

First he was sure that he had been a tree,
Twisting its branches among each other
And tangling its roots among each other.

Then he knew that he had been a fish
With slippery white belly held tight in his own fingers,
Writhing in his own clutch, his ancient beauty
Caught fast in the pink tips of his new beauty.

Then he had been a young girl
Caught in the woods by a drunken old man
Knowing at the end the taste of her own whiteness
The horror of her own smoothness,
And he felt drunken and old.

So he became a dancer to God.
Because his flesh was in love with the burning arrows
He danced on the hot sand
Until the arrows came.
As he embraced them his white skin surrendered
    itself to the redness of blood, and satisfied him.
Now he is green, dry and stained
With the shadow in his mouth.

T. S. Eliot[1]

The preceding discussion of Narcissus and Echo's intertwined stories revolved around the sexual non-relation, and how the two different ways in which reason fails shaped its disaster. However, another significant aspect of Narcissus' story also pivots on epistemic failure that accrues to him alone and cannot be explained within the framework of his exchanges with Echo. Ovid's Narcissus evokes another story also organized about knowledge gone awry—the Oedipus myth, that notorious Theban whom the poet refuses to discuss.[2]

---

[1] Eliot 1971, 93–5.

[2] 'Behind the Narcissus story there hovers the figure of the Sophoclean Oedipus, the glaring absence from the narrative surface of Ovid's Theban books' (Hardie 1988, 86; reiterated in Hardie 2002*b*, 164); 'The absence of any extended reference to the myth of Oedipus in Ovid's otherwise rather comprehensive mythological compendium is a remarkable silence, and one that merits investigation' (Gildenhard–Zissos, 2000, 130). It is true that Oedipus' story within Thebes proper featured no metamorphosis—but neither does Phaethon's story, nor the tale of Mars and Venus' adultery, or of Pentheus' downfall. Into the first Ovid inserts a throwaway line

Cadmus, Actaeon, and the transsexual Tiresias have all prepared the way for Narcissus, insofar as their mishaps have reproduced the juridical logic of Oedipus' doom, the empty law (Chapter 2). But as Philip Hardie, Ingo Gildenhard, and Andrew Zissos have described, Ovid moulds Narcissus' story around the most striking elements peculiar to Oedipus' myth.[3] The poet particularly draws upon Sophocles' *Oedipus Tyrannus*, a powerful version of the myth that became authoritative for its successors. As in addressing Sophocles' king, the prophet Tiresias ambiguously links continued thriving to ignorance (*OT* 316–18, 320–1, 332–3, 440–1 cf. *Met.* 3.348). When Liriope asks Tiresias whether her son will attain a ripe old age ('maturae . . . senectae', *Met.* 3.347), his answer specifically echoes Jocasta's despairing cry to Oedipus when she has grasped the truth of his birth before he does, and warns him against further inquiry:

fatidicus uates 'si se non nouerit' inquit. (*Met.* 3. 348)

The doomspeaking prophet answers, 'Only if he does not know himself.'

'O duspotm', eithe mēpote gnoiēs os ei' (*OT* 1068)

'Oh, ill-fated man, may you never know who you are!'

Both Ovid's prophet and Jocasta echo the inscription at the temple of Delphi ('know thyself')—the temple where Oedipus heard he would kill his father and marry his mother, and fatefully miscon-strued the disclosure. Narcissus' fate, like Oedipus', revolves around

about the Ethiopians burnt to their current dark colour when Phaethon brings the Sun's chariot too close to earth, and a coda that involves his mourning sisters transformed into amber trees (why is not made clear). The second apparently qualifies for inclusion because its author undergoes transformation into a bat, along with her sisters (one could imagine a similar justification for the Oedipus tale—a transformed narrator rather than changed *dramatis personae*, along the lines of Callirhoë's transformation into a horse after prophesying about Achilles). Into the third, Ovid inserted the tale of Dionysus' sailor-infidels transformed into dolphins, a story borrowed from the *Homeric Hymn to Dionysus*. Also, given that Sophocles' *Oedipus Coloneus* involves the exiled king's dramatically supernatural transformation into a hero whose mere post-mortem presence outside Athens protects the city, some notice of that radical change could have found its way into an Ovidian version.

[3] Hardie 1988, 86. Hardie later cited Joseph Loewenstein for this same observation (Hardie 2002*b*, 165 n. 42, referencing Loewenstein 1984, 41–5). However, Loewen-stein does not develop its implications with Hardie's thoroughness. Inspired by Hardie's essay, Gildenhard and Zissos went further and exhaustively analysed the correspondences between Ovid's Narcissus episode and Sophocles' *Oedipus Tyrannus* (Gildenhard–Zissos 2000).

self-knowledge and ignorance. Thematic parallels also tie the Latin epic vignette to the Greek tragedy. Gildenhard and Zissos observe that, like the Theban king, Narcissus 'sees double'. Oedipus begins his investigation of Laius' murder believing he seeks a bloodstained stranger, an other, unaware that in fact he seeks himself. So, too, Narcissus gazes at his reflection in a pool and conceives love for an elusive being who—he realizes too late—is himself.[4] Theban king and Boeotian boy also share an excessive erotic attachment to their own flesh and blood; Oedipus' unwitting love for his mother, Jocasta, is paralleled and redoubled in Narcissus' love for himself.

But if Ovid is so concerned to evoke Oedipus, why not just use the king himself? The tragic plot would have been logically apt in a story-cycle centred on the decay of Oedipus' hometown. It is true that strict chronology would have required postponing Oedipus' story until well after Bacchus' incursion into the city. But given the way the *Metamorphoses* regularly uses prophecy to look forward in time, this need hardly have been a hindrance to touching upon Oedipus in some fashion within the Theban cycle. And chronological awkwardness does not explain why Ovid never addresses the tale at all within his epic poem, even though he returns to Thebes more than once.[5] Ovid's banishment of all the Labdacids is made more peculiar by his

---

[4] Cf. Gildenhard–Zissos 2000, p. 136; as they acknowledge, Froma Zeitlin coined the idea and the phrase 'seeing double' in her analysis of Thebes in Athenian drama (Zeitlin 1986, 111). Hardie also observes Narcissus' double-vision (Hardie 2002*b*, 170–1), but develops its thematic pertinence to Bacchus. For Hardie, Narcissus' striving to know his (mirror) self epitomizes the beguilement that haunts Thebes. Ovid's Thebans enact a desire for presence—for the tangible, the immediately intelligible, the securely identifiable—that is repeatedly baffled by illusion. These *phantasmata* are chiefly (and appropriately) orchestrated by Bacchus, the god of theatre.

[5] Narcissus' story does suit the theme of the reception of visual images that is a particularly prominent strand in all of the Theban stories. However, Thebes is not the only venue the boy would fit thematically: the story-cycle related by the Minyeides also emphasizes vision and delusion. Narcissus' story would fit at least as well, if not better, among the stories of erotic desire gone awry illustrated by Pyramus' and Thisbe's mutual inability to interpret visual clues accurately (*Met.* 4.107–18, 131–6); Mars and Venus' embarrassment when caught *in flagrante delicto* seen very differently from the perspective of Vulcan and of another god ('aliquis de dis non tristibus optat I sic fieri turpis'—'one of the gods, not a puritan, wished *he* could become a scandal that way', *Met.* 4.187–8); Salmacis' voyeurism of Hermaphroditus (Narcissus-like in his beauty and ultimate unassailability, *Met.* 4.339–55, 368–9); the disturbance

fully detailing the fates of Labdacus' cousins Actaeon, Pentheus, and Dionysus. Labdacus alone goes missing from Cadmus' grandchildren; with him go his descendants, a *damnatio memoriae* most achingly noticeable in the case of Oedipus, the family's greatest gift to the drama of malign fate.[6] Why?[7] What can Liriope's son say to Rome that Laius' son and all his kin cannot?

Answering these questions requires that we expand our interpretative framework beyond the sexes' mutual misconceptions. Seeing Juno and Jupiter's quarrel over sex as the narrative mainspring behind Narcissus and Echo's story helped explain why the non-Thebans were in the Theban cycle, and the precise nature of their epistemic errors (Chapter 4). But when Oedipus' shadow falls on Narcissus, it points to knowledge and ignorance not exhausted by reference to a lover, or to any single other. Insight and blindness condition Oedipus' relationship to an entire city, subsuming all his complicated history with Thebes. The king's tragedy is political as well as personal, so that discerning his figure in Narcissus invites another interpretation of the boy's story, one that accounts for the way epistemology structures relations not only between subject and (beloved) object, but also between individual and society, citizen and polity. Reading Narcissus from this vantage elucidates how knowing both weaves and ravels the polity; that perspective will in turn clarify how the Boeotian boy fits the Theban cycle's response to the premier political epic, the *Aeneid.*

---

of Helios' regular path across the sky and of his brightness, because he is so absorbed in gazing upon Leucothoë and pales with love (*Met.* 4.192–203).

[6] Or so Oedipus was in Aristotle's eyes, judging from the lavish praise the *Poetics* heaps on *Oedipus Tyrannus* as the paradigmatic tragedy.

[7] Gildenhard and Zissos argue that Ovid substituted Narcissus for Oedipus because he did not want to focus on 'the fate of the city as such' as opposed to individual members of Cadmus' family. Aside from the question of how exactly the city's destiny could be strictly distinguished from that of its ruling family, this statement does not explain why, if Ovid's focus were the royal family exclusively, he would have made both the Theban citizenry and the fate of the city such prominent features of, e.g., the Bacchus–Pentheus story. The way Pentheus' Theban subjects gaudily celebrate the god who has just come to town is the focus of the king's concern (3.528–63)—as well it ought to be, since it ultimately destroys him. The frenzied Bacchants who rush upon him as he spies upon their rites and tear him to bits are not just his royal family, but a whole crowd of Thebans bent on murder ('ruit omnis in unum | turba furens', 3.715–16).

THE WIDENING GYRE

We need to understand just how *Oedipus Tyrannus* conceives ignorance and knowledge in order to illuminate the Sophoclean Oedipus' significance to Ovid's Thebes. Mystery catalyses the plot of Sophocles' play, which opens on one all-consuming question: Why does plague afflict Thebes? No earlier extant version of the myth mentions the epidemic; whether Sophocles invented it or not, it allows the Theban subjects to appeal to their king for remedy on the basis of his previous intellectual triumph over that other plague, the Sphinx. He must use his powers of discernment to discover a solution for this present bane, whether from man or god (*OT* 35–43). At least initially, Oedipus chooses the latter: he informs his agonized subjects that he has sent his brother-in-law Creon to consult the Delphic oracle (*OT* 69–72). Creon seeks what the gods know. Insofar as the oracle's knowledge lies beyond human ratiocination, his object is a Kantian noumenon— the first link in a chain of such noumenal intelligence that eventually includes Apollo's earlier oracles to Laius and Oedipus. When the oracle blames the pestilence on Laius' murderer, but declines to name the culprit, Oedipus must again appeal to an extra-logical source of knowledge, to the prophet Tiresias (*OT* 287–9). But the answer prised with huge effort from the reluctant seer, that Oedipus himself is the murderer, goads the king to accuse first Tiresias, and then Creon, of conspiring for power through Laius' murder (*OT* 380– 9). Oedipus ridicules Tiresias' clairvoyance, pointing out that he, not the diviner, solved the Sphinx's riddle and thus released Thebes from the monster (*OT* 390–403). His angry scorn for Tiresias effectively rejects the idea of a realm of knowledge not susceptible to reason. He is not alone: accepting such information exceeds everyone's powers of credence. The Chorus (500–10), Creon (525–6), and Jocasta (707–25) all dismiss Tiresias' accusation as incredible.

So how does Oedipus find the answer? By refinding it. At the end of the play, Oedipus has again arrived at Tiresias' truth, but through reason rather than revelation; the king manages by the same route to make sense of the Delphic prophecies his father and he had heard before. Only Oedipus' detective work makes the answer he already has credible to him, conferring the status of knowledge upon the data (the four divinely inspired pronouncements, three from Apollo and one from Tiresias). Contradiction—what does not fit in the clues—propels him toward that recognition. Jocasta's tale of how Laius died makes the mystery pivot on whether the late king and his party were beset at the crossroads by many men or only one (842–7). The Corinthian messenger's surprise tale of Oedipus' adoption further transforms the question, Who committed the crime? into, Just what crimes were committed? Now the inquiry must establish whether the wounded, exposed infant Oedipus was merely of Laius' household, or Laius' own child (1016–50). The irreconcilable differences in the various accounts of violence against murdered king and exposed child drive Oedipus to investigate relentlessly until he has a rational, terrible chain of causality in which to fit Apollo's and Tiresias' vatic pronouncements. Yet even that does not entirely lay contradiction to rest. When Oedipus has finally established his genealogy and his role in Laius' murder, the intelligence only creates further paradoxes he must probe: his exact relation to his sibling-children (1403–8, 1480–1), to gods and men (1340–3), even to the elements of earth and sky, which Creon avows both reject the fallen king (1424–8). At the end of the play, although we understand more, we still have no definitive answers to the play's central questions: who is Oedipus and where does he belong?

The conceptualization of knowledge in the play drifts away from a model delimited by what passes human understanding to one driven forward by that limit. The first epistemology conforms to the Kantian terms that we saw organized Narcissus and Echo's blind missteps in love, the second anticipates the way Hegel frames understanding. Although *Oedipus Tyrannus* begins with the crucial unknown conceived as a noumenon, it remains available only to the divine (or divinely inspired) mind and is roundly rejected by all ordinary mortals. What makes it knowledge for humans is a Hegelian dialectical process spurred onwards by internal contradiction that is never entirely abolished. Crucially, Hegel locates that obstinate contradiction, that productive enigma, not in what entirely escapes the knowing subject's ken (as Kant does), but in the very heart of what constitutes both the subject and her world. Therein lies the key to parsing Oedipus as the palimpsest beneath Ovid's portrayal of Narcissus: Oedipus throws into relief not what or why the boy loves, but what he becomes. The epistemological principles that found Narcissus' identity on what is ultimately unassimilable within that identity look beyond the boy's story. They glance backwards to Oedipus, but also forward to Thebes' increasing civic incoherence, and ultimately beyond Thebes' decline to Rome's.

But to illustrate fully what Oedipus and his incognizable knowledge bring to the *Metamorphoses*, I must first train my attention a little longer upon *Oedipus Tyrannus*, so as to detail how the play's noetic patterns bear upon Ovid's Narcissus. The questions that spur Oedipus' inquiry into Laius' murder and his own origin (many assailants or one? blood-kin or adopted? king's child or slave's child?) are not resolved into the simple choice of one alternative over the other. Oedipus slew Laius, but not alone: in his blinded agony at the play's end, he proclaims to the Chorus that while his hand dealt the blow, 'Apollo, friends, Apollo—he it was that brought these evils to pass!' (*OT* 1329–31). Though born to inherit Thebes' throne, his parents treat him in infancy as abject, alien, and anathema; they mutilate him, cast him out of the city, and leave him for dead. Rescued and brought up as heir to Corinth's throne, with no memory of his Theban past, his estrangement from his native town makes the rest of his tale possible. But his story illustrates his incomplete assimilation to either city, vulnerable as he is to doubt cast on his Corinthian paternity. Oedipus lives the history of a foreigner *and* a native, a stranger *and* blood kin, the lowest *and* the highest in his polity.[8] In sifting these key terms of Oedipus' life, we

[8] These contrasts are shadowed forth in the very terms with which others address Oedipus: before the revelation of his true identity, he is called *tyrannos* ('absolute ruler'; *OT* 514, 925); afterwards, he is *basileus* ('hereditary king'; *OT* 1202). The two words primarily contrast one who comes to power irregularly, as opposed to one who inherits the throne. Although the former could be a native, Oedipus in describing his obligation to discover the murderer of Laius (he calls the dead king *basileus*, *OT* 257) emphasizes his own status as a *xenos* ('foreigner') who came to Thebes relatively late in life (*OT* 219–22). The word *tyrannos* can be used neutrally, referring to the manner of gaining power rather than the mode of its exercise. But on at least one occasion the chorus in Sophocles' play associate the word with an arrogance that ensures a precipitous rise and fall. 'Violent pride (*hubris*) engenders the *tyrannos*', the chorus sing; they proceed to describe how, surfeited by riches, the *tyrannos* scales the heights (*akrotaton*) and then, unable to find purchase, falls down to his ruin (*OT* 872–80). Their ominous words unwittingly point to Oedipus' past and future that together will disclose how Thebes' saviour is also her curse. (For the signficance of *basileus* and *tyrannos* in the play, I am greatly indebted to Bernard Knox's classic analysis (Knox 1954).)

find ourselves in the realm of Hegelian negation, where meaning inheres, not in any concept considered as a discrete, isolated whole, but in the web of dynamic relations woven among these terms.

Hegel's enchainment of antithetical but related terms in dialectic (terms such as 'foreign/native') is typically conceived as commerce between complementary pairings, as if the halves of the dyad together made up a Whole, effectively abolishing the initial negation (the 'no X without Y' model). To the contrary, Hegel roots the dialectic in the attempt to grasp the initial term in isolation; that attempt itself propels the passage from one extreme over into its opposite. The first extreme, in its abstraction from this other, is the other itself. Hegel paradigmatically illustrates this principle by considering what it would mean to grasp the concept Being on its own terms.[9] Being as bare, isolated concept is so utterly devoid of positive characteristics as to be a conceptual vacuum. It has thus already effectively 'passed over' into its opposite, Nothing.[10] The move from Being to Nothing is the mark, not of comprehending Being, but of a failure to comprehend, a failure that propels the next move in the dialectic. The original negation contained in the first extreme term propels the passage over into its antipode. That internal 'gap' or 'flaw' in the first term's conceptualization is both transformed and its essential characteristics preserved in its opposite, but that negation is not resolved, nor is it abolished by being subsumed into some greater Whole.

Sophocles turns Oedipus' investigation of Laius' murder into a similar striving to determine the younger king's own being, as Oedipus strips away the weight of determinate properties conferred upon himself by the cultural mandates of kingship, marriage, and fatherhood. Behind all these, he discovers the naked lump of crippled flesh that negates them all. Oedipus' investigation of the brutal clues to himself describes a Hegelian epistemological model wherein knowledge spirals upward around its own failure to comprehend. To that degree Sophocles' play turns toward Hegel's modification of Kant's epistemology. The paralogisms exemplified in Kant's mathematical and dynamical antinomies mark the place of an impassable

---

[9] Hegel 1977, 58–79; Hegel 1969, 82–108.
[10] Žižek 1993, 122–3.

void, opening up a chasm between phenomena on the one hand, and noumena on the other. The noumenal locates the unknown and the unknowable 'out there', beyond whatever can be perceived or intuited by the subject. But when Hegel rejects the noumenon, he moves inside the mind the gap Kant had previously established between cognition and objects in the world; that gap now fissures both poles of the subject–object relation. The contradictions that for Kant divided mind from the world of objects 'as they are in themselves' for Hegel unite the two realms. Within Hegelian dialectic, the inadequacy of a conceptual framework drives philosophical consciousness through negation to expanded understanding, transforming both consciousness and object in the process.

Apollo's dire prophecy to Laius that his own child will kill him constitutes just such a point of negation (*OT* 711–14). At the hour Apollo speaks, Laius' son does not yet even exist. But the god's mysterious words inject an unassimilable remainder into the concept 'beloved heir to the Theban throne'. That remainder causes the concept of Theban crown prince to pass over into its opposite: 'estranged enemy of Thebes'. The infant-to-be's predicted properties as regicide and patricide make him a counter-moment in Theban identity. Even before he is born, the foretold son becomes the indigestible piece of grit that his polity strives—in vain—to expel.

However, two things are important to grasp here: first, the negation, or fissure, in the identity 'Thebes' royal heir' is strictly correlative to a fissure in Thebes' collective identity, to the social antagonisms that plague the city even after Oedipus' exposure on Cithaeron. Oedipus merely positivizes this failure, becoming the object designated to cover over the polity's internal failure. If baby Oedipus is potentially guilty of kin-murder, his father has already tried it (only a slave's disobedience prevents Laius from succeeding at infanticide). Moreover, Laius' transgressions, not Oedipus', bring the next plague to the city. The *Phoenissae* Peisandros scholion tells us that Hera sent the Sphinx to decimate the youth of Thebes because the city had failed to punish Laius' abduction of Chrysippus, the son of King Pelops (*Σ Pho.* 1760). The plague that visits Thebes in the last year of Oedipus' own reign as her king makes all its women barren (*OT* 26–7), but as such it simply mirrors Thebes' inveterate status as the place that fails to nurture youth, as indicated by Oedipus' exposure and Chrysippus' rape.

What is crucial to notice here is how that initial negation is never resolved, and remains as unresolved for Corinth as for Oedipus and for Thebes. When the adult Oedipus painstakingly reconstructs the circumstances of Laius' murder and of his own birth, he does not discover himself simply to be true Theban and true kin to Laius and Jocasta. Rather, his revelation preserves the initial negation driving his entire history: the Heir as the Enemy. That alienation runs like a black thread through the complex of differential relations that make Oedipus' life intelligible. Although royal Corinth raised as its heir what royal Thebes had rejected, Oedipus is at home in neither city; his Corinthian princely identity never quite 'takes hold'. The very fact that a drunk at a banquet can taunt the crown prince with bastardy and get away with it indicates the open secret of Oedipus' adoption does not sit well with all Corinthians.[11] Apparently, neither do King Polybus and Queen Merope feel their position strong enough to retaliate. They simply get angry; while Oedipus finds that consoling, it is not enough to dissuade him from investigating further. His

---

[11] David Konstan elucidates a similar unresolved negation in the Oedipus myth when he asks why the horror accruing to murdering, or sleeping with, a blood-parent should be any greater than that of either transgression with an adoptive parent (Konstan 1999). Konstan demonstrates how Sophocles' play elucidates an unacknowledged point of contradiction within the *polis* ostensibly comprising citizens organized by *dēmoi* and connected by law, rather than members of *oikoi* who are connected by blood. The audience must believe that—despite Laius' two attempts to kill his child (the second time at the crossroads, which makes Oedipus' reaction legitimate self-defence) and his mother Jocasta's acquiescence in the first attempt, his 'offences' against these two vicious people are horrific crimes simply because blood trumps every other consideration. As Konstan reasonably notes, murdering or sleeping with his loving foster parents, Polybus and Merope, surely ought to count as a greater offence to justice, by any measure of desert. Yet the play does not allow us to believe that: the secret spring of its emotional impact implies that Athens—like Oedipus' Corinth and Thebes—is vitiated by the Real. Athenian citizens and playgoers must react to the play under the spell of the element unintelligible, unaccountable within the city's contemporary Symbolic. 'Violence/offense against one's own fellow citizens', in despite of the bonds of citizenship, is the radically repressed within the deme system, what it cannot acknowledge without unravelling the idea(l) of the harmoniously integrated *polis*. That repression comes back to haunt the city in the staging of Oedipus' incestuous and murderous actions, at the same time the play's concentration on the blood-relation as the crux of the problem distracts attention from the return of the repressed.

reaction indicates the degree of his anxiety. He travels overseas and ascends the narrow mountain tracks to consult the oracle at Delphi—a far from trivial undertaking, especially since he must conceal his departure from his parents.[12] There he hears the prophecy that confirms his unease; he flees Corinth forever, fearing to be a criminal (779–97).

Years later, when he discovers his Theban royal birth, he re-enacts the Delphic moment of civic alienation as the *verso* to his civic exaltation. No sooner discovered to be his new city's rightful prince of the blood, its *basileus*, Oedipus becomes what is unassimilable to the polity, its excremental remainder. He is 'unclean' (*anagnos*, 1383), a 'stain, defilement' (*kelida*, 1384). Far from forming some harmonious resolution of opposites between Corinthian and Theban, foreign and indigenous, stranger and kin, Oedipus' existence worries the unbridgeable fissure at the heart of each term within each dyad. His passing over between one identity and the other elucidates the failure of both. Neither term of any of these dyads can subsume Oedipus completely as subject; each identity only papers over his split subjectivity. Nor can these terms produce even themselves as discrete conceptual wholes firmly rooted in ontology. Sophocles' dramatic chain of events unfolds no kernel of identity that was always-already present in Oedipus, nor present in the cities of Corinth and Thebes. The tragedy cannot be reduced to any series of simple static oppositions imagined to summarize the king or his two polities. Rather, we see Oedipus *and* Corinth *and* Thebes produced by their positioning within a web of differential relations, forcing us to think those differences in their complex, dynamic relations to one another.[13]

---

[12] Oedipus would have to make his way from Corinth to the port at Lechaion (about 2.5 miles) to commence a journey north-west along the Corinthian Gulf of at least fifty miles overseas to the ancient port of Kirra. Thence he would walk the Krisa plain and make an ascent of some 1,500 feet straight up to Delphi by way of zigzag trails that were nothing more than mule-tracks. (My thanks to John Younger for his guidance regarding these ancient travel logistics.)

[13] It is exactly this insight that Paul Allen Miller brings to bear upon Foucault's portrait of Graeco-Roman male, aristocratic identity in *Le souci de soi* (*Histoire de la sexualité*, vol. 3). Miller argues persuasively that the notorious 'flatness' with which Foucault portrayed the ancient male citizen, reducing him to a static collection of positivities, is the result of excluding the Hegelian concept of negation from *Le souci de soi*'s account of historical forces and conditions (Miller 1998).

UPON REFLECTION

Oedipus, Corinth, and Thebes, figured as nothing but the breaches in their own selves, all lay the conceptual ground for understanding Ovid's Narcissus—specifically, for grasping what the boy split between flesh and reflection has to say to the concept of identity as caesura. He speaks both to individual and collective identity; I address the former first, since that will smooth the way for understanding the latter. The next section of this chapter ('Narcissus, Aeneas') engages collective identity, and will elucidate what Narcissus signifies for Thebes as *alter*-Rome.

Like Oedipus, Narcissus comes across his own negation, not in opposition, but in his own identity and the grasp thereof. But just what that means is no simpler to parse in Narcissus' case than it was in Oedipus'. Consider, for example, the moment when Narcissus stares into still waters and knows his own image. Does he then fulfil Tiresias' prophecy—does he, at last, 'know himself'? I concluded in the last chapter that what he saw when he gazed at the reflected image was his core fantasy, an earnest of the Thing—more his self than himself, yet paradoxically unknitting that self. But to say that does not specify which self is known—nor the corollary, to which self that fatal knowledge accrues. Is it lover or beloved, viewer or viewed, subject or object, who knows? And which element of these pairs is then known? And when Narcissus wastes away and dies, weighed down by unrequitable love, does death change the answers? Is it Narcissus, or another, who remains gazing at his reflection in the river Styx at the tale's close? At whom (or what) does he stare? And what is the status of the yellow flower his grieving relatives find in place of his body—is that (also) Narcissus?

The internal contradictions of the story itself press these questions, as Ovid obsessively thematizes the way that doubling fissures identity. Hegel's model of knowledge dynamically mediating between subject and object can answer them, while also preserving the conceptual tensions produced by the data, such as the way Narcissus-in-the-flesh and Narcissus-in-the-water repeatedly and variously negate one another. For example, the Narcissus we first meet acts the coquet (whether consciously or not). His interaction with Echo and the narrator's description of his previous history indicate that the boy gives his potential lovers grounds for hope, then refuses them, until the prayer of his last disappointed suitor gains Nemesis' ear (*Met.* 3.379–92, 3.402–6). But it is unclear whether the scorned would-be lover revenges himself on the right person; the image in the pool that fulfils this curse transforms the cold, aloof, corporeal Narcissus into someone else entirely, the opposite of his old self. For the first time in his life, Narcissus loves passionately and even puts his beloved's interests ahead of his own: he wishes his darling to live longer than himself (472). By contrast, the object of his affection, his reflection, now embodies the former Narcissus. Its gestures indicate reciprocal desire, but they evade contact; it flirts with its desiring audience while remaining aloof and untouchable. Like the old Narcissus, the image is cold—cold both figuratively and literally, because the sun never warms the impenetrable shadow surrounding the spring (412). Yet if the frigid Narcissus-image reflects the now loving Narcissus-in-the-flesh, the reverse is also true: the corporeal Narcissus-lover is unthinkable without Narcissus-image to spark his desire. How do we think through these two impossibly implicated existences so as to find Narcissus?

The key question that Narcissus' predicament poses—whether and how being captivated by his reflection constitutes 'knowing himself'—matches the deadlock we encountered above when trying to grasp Being entirely in terms of itself. That attempt to comprehend an entity solipsistically amounts to a tautology: 'A = A', subject and (defining) predicate either side the copula being identical. Just that relation obtains between Narcissus and his beloved when the trap of Tiresias' prediction snaps shut. Or so it seems at first glance; closer inspection reveals the absurdity of this strictly formal representation of identity, as Hegel demonstrates in his discussion of 'reflexive determination':

If anyone opens his mouth and promises to tell what God is, namely God is—God, expectation is cheated, for what was expected was a *different determination*; and if this statement is absolute truth, such absolute verbiage is very lightly esteemed; nothing will be held to be more boring and tedious than conversation which merely reiterates the same thing, or than such talk which yet is supposed to be truth.

Looking more closely at this tedious effect produced by such truth, we see that the beginning, 'The plant is—', sets out to say *something*, to bring forward a further determination. But since only the same thing is repeated, the opposite has happened, *nothing* has emerged. Such *identical* talk therefore *contradicts itself.* Identity, instead of being in its own self truth and absolute truth, is consequently the very opposite; instead of being the unmoved simple, it is the passage beyond itself into the dissolution of itself.[14]

Discovering tautology in the predicate cheats expectation, delivers nothing upon the promise of defining the identity of God (or plants), despite the fact that the proposition seems the purest formal expression of identity. From this perspective, the still waters' purest reflection appears to be nonsense, to tell us nothing at all about Narcissus' identity.

But the reflection never really is pure. As Slavoj Žižek observes of Hegel's tautology:

More precisely, instead of encountering itself, the initial moment comes across its absence, comes across itself as empty set. If the first God ('God is . . .') is the positive God, the genus which encompasses all species, all His particular content, the God of peace, reconciliation and love, then the second God ('. . . God') is the negative God, He who excludes all his predicates, all particular content, the God of hatred and destructive fury, the mad God.

It is no accident that the phrase 'God is God' tends to be invoked just when some putative divine precept or action seems most cruel, unfair, 'ungodly' (just as, in a more purely juridical context, 'law is law' is offered to excuse statutory injustice). Žižek notes as much, drawing out the logical implications of this perversion as identity's defeat in tautology:

We come across identity when predicates fail. Identity is the surplus which cannot be captured by predicates—more precisely (and this precision is crucial if we want to avoid a misconception of Hegel), identity-with-itself is *nothing but* this impossibility of predicates, *nothing but* this confrontation of an entity with the void at the point where we expect a predicate, a determination of its positive content.[15]

---

[14] Hegel 1969, 415; original emphases.
[15] Žižek 1991*a*, 35–6; original emphases.

Just as the negation of all predicates in pure abstraction compelled Being to pass over into its opposite, into the void of Nothingness, so it is with pure identity. Identity is nothing more than a name for a certain radical and double impossibility: the impossibility, on the one hand, of achieving a set of properties that would exhaustively define identity, and, on the other, of remaining in the void bereft of all determinate properties. Narcissus and his beloved self, as mirror-reversals of one another, stand on either side the split opened up in identity by this 'missed encounter' with the self. On the one hand, the flesh-and-blood lover Narcissus encompasses all the wealth of his human properties, including altruism; on the other, the watery beloved Narcissus excludes all that particular content in favour of an icy vampirism, draining the life of his lover.

And yet the complications of Narcissus' identity do not stop there. The analysis above grants the fleshly Narcissus ontological priority as the first term of the tautology, while reading the image in the pool as the second term, the predicate. But the relation between the two also scans the other way. In Ovid's version of Narcissus' history, the boy was aloof before he was loving; his watery reflection therefore enjoys temporal priority over his corporeal self, since it embodies the 'original' Narcissus. And who transformed the original? The reflection, which thus becomes (primary) cause to the changed Narcissus as (secondary) effect; his altruism is a new-found trait, not part of his original personality. Ovid's own description of the scene implicitly acknowledges these slippery, reversible relations between the doppelgängers. Although the Ovidian narrator gleefully rings changes on the theme, 'You silly boy, you have fallen in love with (an image of) yourself!', he does not always clearly distinguish original from duplicate. In the midst of taunting Narcissus for mistaking his own mirrored gestures for another's signs of love and coquettishness (432–6), the narrator himself blurs the ontological status of the two Narcissi. He says, 'Ista repercussae, quam cernis, imaginis umbra est' ('That which you see is the shadow of a reflected image', 434). The terms of this equation appear reversed, since they make the flesh-and-blood boy clinging to the pool's edge a mere 'reflected image'. The face in the pool is an even more impalpable, but oddly unreflexive, 'shadow' of this image.[16]

Not even death unambiguously resolves the dilemma of who (or what) Narcissus is. Ovid says of the boy's end on earth that 'lumina mors clausit domini mirantia formam' ('death closed his eyes, marvelling at the beauty of their owner', 503), but it is not entirely clear what that means. The boy's family can find no body for the funeral pyre, only a yellow-centred flower with white petals (508–10). Meanwhile, Narcissus enters the Underworld—but which Narcissus? The narrator had called the image in the pool an *umbra* (417, 434), a word that can also mean 'dead spirit' (*OLD*, s.v. *umbra* 7). As a shade in the Underworld, Narcissus has assumed the ontological status of his erstwhile reflection. He still apparently casts his own reflection (even though the *umbra* in the earthly pool did not), another image in yet other waters; even in Hell he continues to gaze fixedly upon the waters of the river Styx (505). At the end of the story and of its protagonist, we must again ask: where is Narcissus now? Up by the shaded pool on earth, as the yellow narkissos, or in and by the Stygian waters below, as captivated shade and captivating image? Whether or not Narcissus knows himself—before or after death, on or below the earth—can we?

Yes, we can make sense of all these refracted (and refractory) pieces of Narcissus, and in the same way that we comprehended Sophocles' Oedipus. Narcissus, like Oedipus, like the other intricate dialectics we have surveyed as epistemology grasps after ontology, is all the enchained moments that make up his refractions between self and other, boy and flower, living body and insubstantial spectre. The *telos* Tiresias sketched for him so obscurely turns out to be less a fixed point than multiple bridges between spiralling strands of understanding. But the understanding Narcissus underwrites pertains to more than his peculiar history: the Boeotian's multilocal mortality illustrates what it means for any subject to know oneself. Mapping

---

[16] Cf. DiSalvo 1980, 19. It is also possible (as one of my anonymous readers points out to me) to take *imaginis* as a defining genitive, thus glossing the Latin as 'what you see is the shadow of (consisting in) a reflected image'. But there is no way to eliminate entirely the ambiguity of *imaginis*, the way its semantic range conjures up the shade of a shade.

onto human subjectivity the contradictions that split the self reveals not only the self's multivalence, but the antagonism in which the fracture is rooted. The discordant tautology that cleaves identity into self and the dark lining of that self reproduces Hegel's Master/Slave dialectic. As noted in Chapter 1, the relation between Master and Slave roots the subject in the other, in the desire for recognition as autonomous subject by autonomous subject. That paradox is as impossible to untangle logically as Narcissus' implication with his own alluring, frustrating, and destructive image. The Master and Slave's struggle to find a self-consciousness reflected in the other's consciousness makes the other both an admired extension of the self, and a detested rival to be subjugated and eliminated, because his very existence negates the self's putative independence. Each conscious-ness looks for final appeasement in destruction. Abolishing the other seemingly ensures the autonomy and majesty of the self, but mutual dependency makes the desire suicidal. Moreover, this dialectic obtains even in the absence of another human being, since self-consciousness internalizes the categories of independence/depend-ence, subject/object.[17] Narcissus dramatically illustrates that the enemy is always ultimately the enemy within myself, and no less an enemy for being also an object of desire.

The only thing Narcissus leaves behind on earth is the yellow narkissos, an ill-omened bloom of oblivion (*narkē*). The flower's history points again to a subjectivity founded on fatal attraction that spells the loss of self: it figures crucially as a plot-spring in the *Homeric Hymn to Demeter*, a poem that greatly influenced Ovid's own two versions of the Demeter–Persephone story, and with which his audience would have been familiar.[18] The narkissos ensnares Persephone for her rapist-bridegroom, Hades; Gaia puts forth the flower as a 'deception' (*dolos*) for the flower-like maiden (*HHDem.* 8–9). The 'wondrous' (*thaumaston*, 10) flower enchants Persephone

---

[17] Hegel 1977, §§ 178–81 (p. 111). See also Adelman 1998, 162–3; Kelly 1998, 178–80.

[18] Stephen Hinds masterfully elucidates the way both the version in Ovid's *Fasti* (*Fast.* 4.417–620) and his *Metamorphoses* (*Met.* 5.341–661) reflect the *Homeric Hymn to Demeter* (Hinds 1987, 51–98). Alessandro Barchiesi analyses with equal cogency Ovid's probable debt to the *Homeric Hymn to Aphrodite* specifically, and also makes a compelling case for Ovid's 'unique degree of interest in the Homeric Hymns' as a whole (Barchiesi 1999, 123).

so that she reaches forth her hand to pluck this 'delight' (*athurma*, 16), whereupon Hades snatches the distracted girl away to the Underworld (16–18). Her mother Demeter blights the world with barrenness in her grief, eventually forcing a compromise: Hades can immure Persephone in the Underworld as his bride, but only for a third of each year (*HHDem.* 445–6). Like Ovid's Narcissus' tale, the hymn contemplates the sinister consequences of desire, including the radical transformation of the individual erotic subject (Persephone) and of the whole human community (which knows starving winter for the first time). Figured in this flower that replaces Ovid's Narcissus when he himself slips down to the realm of the dead is another story of existence mortgaged to the lure of desire, besieged by an intimate enemy, and ultimately in thrall to death.

NARCISSUS, AENEAS: ἐχθρὸς ἄλλος ἐγώ

The flower is the only material remainder of Narcissus' misery: apart from it, Narcissus is come to dust, his identity at its tautological purest fissuring into itself and its sinister obverse split along multiple fault lines. His irrecoverable dispersal among various selves makes most visible, and most logical, the politically significant spectre of King Oedipus haunting Ovid's anti-*Aeneid*. That Narcissus cannot ultimately be made coterminous with a fixed positivity, a set of properties, or a transcendant Idea exemplifies how, on either side the divide between subject and object, each term fails to constitute itself as an organic, self-enclosed Whole. The coherence of both depends, not on identity, but rather on difference. The identity of each element within a differential order consists in the array of features distinguishing it from all the other elements; each is the complex tissue of relations binding it to all its counterparts. But for finite, historical beings, no completion of the system, no final element, can yield that 'all' to synchronic contemplation, and allow us to grasp the nature of any one element as permanent and stable. Hence the fissure, the incompleteness, that vitiates both cognition and what it contemplates. The reconciliation of consciousness and world rests not upon the integrity of either, but rather upon the split that traverses both and thus unites them. They are reconciled by being posited as differential, i.e. united by their common insufficiency, their common lack.[19] Read from this perspective, the relation between 'individual' and 'society', 'citizen' and 'polity', 'compatriot' and 'nation' is not a complementarity, but instead rests on what is ultimately unassimilable within the conceptual frame of either: on the one hand, the divided subject restlessly revolving about its own self-alienation, and on the other, the social antagonisms that sunder the collectivity.

That mirroring dehiscence between self and Other certainly matches Oedipus' relation to Thebes. But it also reflects the complicated failures of individual and collective identity traced in the *Aeneid*, the most obvious intertext for Ovid's Theban city-founding (as Philip Hardie has shown).[20] From this perspective, Sophocles' Oedipus, Vergil's Aeneas, and Ovid's Narcissus are structurally homologous. Narcissus is a fulcrum between the two rulers and their polities, poising the Theban king and the lurching disintegration of the polity he rules against the proto-Roman leader and the latent incoherence of the polity he founds.[21]

The *Aeneid*'s self-proclaimed theme is how 'the lofty walls of Rome' originated and how difficult it was to 'found the Roman race' (*Aen.* 1.6–7, 33). Vergil traces the transformation of Aeneas' Trojans into proto-Romans through confrontation with the other, like a collective version of the Master/Slave narrative. He contrasts the Trojans with their corrupt vanquishers, the Greeks;[22] with their morbidly emotional vanquished, the Italians;[23] and with a series of

---

[19] Žižek 1993, 30, 122, 124.

[20] See above, the discussion of Hardie 1990, in the opening pages of Ch. 1.

[21] My thanks to Paul Allen Miller for pointing out this aspect of Narcissus to me.

[22] The substance of *Aeneid* 2, which regularly contrasts the vicious Greeks who treacherously invade Troy with their honourable victims, the Trojans.

[23] Turnus figures such emotional lability most dramatically. His encounter with Allecto confronts divine *force majeure*, so that his consequent rage for war is a not-unambiguous index of his native excitability (*Aen.* 7.415–70). But Juno dismisses Allecto two-thirds of the way through *Aeneid* 7 (7.552–60), refusing the Fury's explicit offer further to bend minds to war ('accendam animos insani Martis amore'—'I shall kindle minds with passion for insane warfare', *Aen.* 7.550). We see Turnus thereafter readily take fire under circumstances wherein no godly manipulation is mentioned. For example, Lavinia need only blush to stoke his will to fight

figures in between, such as the fatally nostalgic denizens of Buthro-
tum (*Aen.* 3.294–505). These tableaux of opposed *ēthē* organize the
epic's narrative of nascent identity around the inveterate Roman
fantasy of abolishing the other.[24] The contours of Romanness imagined as a conceptual totality arise from identifying and eliminating
elements construed as anathema to Rome. Such elements are per-
sonified in Carthaginian Queen Dido and Rutulian Prince Turnus
most dramatically, but also in the native Italians Camilla and Amata,
and the erstwhile Etruscan king, Mezentius (among others).[25] These all

---

Aeneas to the death (*Aen.* 12.64–80). Yet he is not the only Italian indigene with
quicksilver emotions. A great many native peasants join him in his fight against the
Trojans because Trojan Ascanius wounded Italian Silvia's pet stag, though it is not
even clear the wound was fatal (*Aen.* 7.477–510). As Vergil drily remarks of the stag's
shooting: 'prima laborum | causa fuit, belloque animos accendit agrestis'—'That was
the first cause of trouble, and kindled rustic minds to war', 7.481–2.

[24] Rome's punctual demand for a scapegoat stretches all the way from Romulus'
mythic fratricide of Remus to Augustus' crushing defeat of his former colleague and
brother-in-law Antony (leaving Antony no option but suicide). Repeatedly, across
Roman history, the need for an other uncannily close to the self arises—an other to be
constructed as evil, then expelled and/or killed. Aside from Remus, other examples
from Rome's mythic history would be: Tarquinius Superbus, expelled from Rome
after his son Sextus rapes Lucretia (Livy 1.60.1–2); Lucretia's husband Collatinus,
exiled merely because he was related to the Tarquins (Livy 2.2.10–11); Genucius
Cipus, self-proscribed because as he left Rome a portent marked him as king should
he return to the city (Val. Max. 5.6.3, Ovid, *Met.* 15.565–621). With regard to
historical examples, see Habinek's excellent discussion of Cicero's Catilinarian
speeches as exemplifying 'the problem of the excluded other and of rivalry between
peers [that is] fundamental to Roman identity' (Habinek 1998, 85). That essay
adduces the exiled Ovid himself as an example of the excluded other (Habinek
1998, 151–69).

[25] Prophetic texts of various kinds within the epic foretell the Aeneadae's melding
of bloodlines and culture with the Latins', their alliance with the Italians. But these
assimilations and alliances between Trojans' descendants and the natives of Italy are
fraught with nearly as much antagonism and contest for dominance as Rome's open
enmities. For example, Amata and Turnus both portray Lavinia's prospective marriage to Aeneas as an abduction about to happen or already accomplished (*Aen.*
7.361–2, 9.138–9). While tendentious, that characterization anticipates the rape of
the Sabines as depicted on Aeneas' Shield ('raptas sine more Sabinas'—'the Sabine
women lawlessly carried off', *Aen.* 8.635). The aspect of violent crime thus links the
first melding of distinct nations at Latium (Trojan with Latin) with the first melding
of distinct nations at Rome (Sabine with Roman). And when Juno and Jupiter
adjudicate the melding of Trojan with Latin, they weigh Latin *against* Trojan elements
in the Roman descendants (*Aen.* 12.821–37; Dench 2005, 24, 203). Finally, it is not
even clear the Alban kings who will preside over this hybrid future themselves fully

figure qualities that incipient Rome has rejected, and upon whose exclusion it depends: the feminine, the erotic, the emotional, the cult of personal honour and individualistic heroism. For example, the final books of the *Aeneid* frequently contrast Turnus and Aeneas as leaders of their respective nations. Turnus involves his people and allies suddenly and rashly in war because the Fury Allecto infects him with frenzy (*Aen.* 7.445–66); Aeneas enters the conflict reluctantly and with deliberation, but also with Olympian aid and arms (*Aen.* 8.18–25, 70–453, 608–731). By contrast with Aeneas' regular attention to strategy and the corporate welfare of his troops, Turnus conducts himself in battle as if he were a lone hero rather than commander-in-chief. This trait increases his personal glory, but repeatedly lays the Rutulian open to deception, and sacrifices tactical advantage for his side. Turnus throws away his chance to take the Trojan citadel when he will not open the gate to admit his troops, but insists on fighting unseconded (9.756–61). Juno later abducts Turnus from battle by tantalizing him with the prospect of single combat with Aeneas (10.636–88). Opposing Turnus to Aeneas provides the Trojan with a foil against which he can emerge as statesman and martial champion. The images splashed across Aeneas' immortal Shield that he hefts upon his shoulders just before he enters upon hostilities with Turnus project this antipodal pattern into future Roman history. They culminate in the grand tableaux of the Battle of Actium: Vulcan's depiction translates a battle between Caesarian factions into a titanic struggle between West and East, Olympian and theromorphic gods, homogeneity and heterogeneity. All the first terms triumph under the aegis of the Romans, while Rome destroys or subordinates all the 'foreigners' and their unwanted associations.[26]

Yet it is also true that Vergil repeatedly undermines the idea that Roman identity can be conjured as a whole, discrete, organic entity

---

participate in it. The *Aeneid* implies variously that Ascanius, the purely Trojan son of Aeneas and Creusa, will rule Lavinium and found the royal bloodline, and that Silvius, Aeneas' mixed-blood son by Lavinia, will do so (O'Hara 1990, 145–7; 2007, 88–90). On the complex issue of national identity in the *Aeneid*, see now Syed 2005, Reed 2007, both of which provide useful bibliography to past scholarship on the question.

[26] Quint 1993, 21–31.

by any means whatsoever, including ruthless surgery. This is most dramatically evident at the epic's problematic close. Over Aeneas' final confrontation with the defeated, suppliant Turnus, when the Trojan must decide whether to spare the Rutulian's life, oceans of ink have spilled in radically opposed interpretations.[27] The irreconcilable divergence of opinion demonstrates what in this textual moment is 'impossible', unassimilable to any all-encompassing conceptual framework of legitimation. For one thing, Aeneas' attachment to Pallas that leads him to kill Turnus uncannily mirrors—in its passionate unreason, erotic colouring, and inflexible definition of personal honour—Turnus' own attachment to Lavinia that began the war.[28] The reflexive relationship between Turnus' and Aeneas' motivations indicates Turnus' status as a projection outward of what is always-already mutilated, truncated, impossible, and antagonistic about Roman identity.[29] But a further step is required here: we must fully account not only for how the two men reduplicate each other in discord, but for how Aeneas antithetically reduplicates himself. Aeneas can be read as the pious avenger killing the slayer of his friend and ally Pallas, as the prudent statesman eliminating a potential future enemy to his fledgeling nation—and *at the same time* as ruthless, bloodthirsty avenger disobeying Anchises' formula for Roman imperialism, 'parcere subiectis' ('spare the fallen', *Aen.* 6.853). Once again, as with Agenor exiling his son Cadmus for his daughter Europa's sake, we encounter the inherent duplicity of the rule-bound act, of the law. The *pietas* that founds Thebes and Rome both causally and conceptually, in its paradoxical astriction of justice to sadism, moulds a foundation of sand.

---

[27] The literature on the question is far too vast to survey comprehensively. Worthy of note among more recent publications are: Smith 2005, 128–75; Nicoll 2001; Putnam 2001; Warren 2001; Spence 1999; Mitchell-Boyask 1996; Horsfall 1995, 195–216; Putnam 1995, 27–49, 152–200; Stahl 1990. Burnell 1987 and Lyne 1983 not only discuss the question of Aeneas' act, but also usefully survey previous scholarship.

[28] Putnam 1985, esp. p. 16.

[29] Cf. J. D. Reed on national identity as portrayed in the *Aeneid*: 'The poem constructs the self as empty of nationality except as defined against a foil, or a series of foils...There is no essence, no absolute center, no origin that exclusively authorizes Romanness' (Reed 2007, 2).

Yet we can also now see how juxtaposing these two key moments—Aeneas' final confrontation with Turnus and Agenor's banishment of Cadmus—reveals the way in which citizen and state are ineluctably organized around additional sites of conceptual fissure. The vitiation of *pietas* that Agenor/Cadmus and Aeneas/Turnus together embody reproduces the internal, inevitable negation of the concept considered as pure abstraction: the slippery unfolding of *pietas* into cruelty reproduces the passage of Being into Nothing, of God into Ruthless Avenger, of 'A' into a demonic parody of 'A'. The two confrontations also dramatize the paradox of the Self, based as it is on the futile, internecine struggle of the Master to establish his identity on the grave of the Slave: the wrath that possesses both Agenor and Aeneas against the weaker party undoes their identities as neutral heads of state, as 'Names of the Father'. Taken together, the inability of either rule-based concept or ruling self to cohere as organic entities makes it impossible to conceive the polity as organic nation-state organized by a transcendent self-concept and ruled by a just sovereign. The contradictory founding moments of Thebes and Rome ensure their failures as collectivities, failures manifest in two civic histories punctually marred by internal strife. The fact that these moments are organized around facing the other makes the inclusion of Narcissus in the Theban cycle both legible and inevitable. Thinking through the boy's confrontation with himself and all its malign sequelae rooted in the failures of identity draws an epistemic path from Sophocles' Thebes to Vergil's Rome through a pool in Ovid's Boeotia.

As recorded in the *Aeneid* and the *Metamorphoses*, both Rome and Thebes attempt to organize themselves as collectivities centred upon interlocking conceptual totalities—upon law, sovereign, nation-state—yet such effort always stumbles upon the other surface of these totalities: sadism, despotism, and xenophobia are their unassimilable remainders. The impossible coincidence of opposites elucidated above in law (*pietas*), in the sovereign (Agenor/Aeneas), and in the nation-state (Thebes/Rome) in each case exactly coincides with another facet of the impossibility that is Theban, and Roman, identity.

THE TRUTH IS NOT OUT THERE

I began this chapter by noting that the antinomies of reason, though they make legible Narcissus' failed relations with Echo, cannot parse why Ovid figures Oedipus behind Narcissus. For that, we needed to move from a Kantian to a Hegelian perspective on knowledge, to see why the clever-benighted king shadows the fascinating-fascinated boy. That move might appear to dismiss or negate whatever clarity Kant brought to Echo and Narcissus in the last chapter: if Hegel's epistemology disagrees with Kant's, surely we must choose one over the other, no? Kant says that there is a noumenon, while Hegel denies it, instead imagining a negation purely internal to the phenomenal world; does that not constitute an irreconcilable difference—a difference on which stands or falls either the validity of the formulae of sexuation, or of reflexive determination? On the contrary: as the most consequential of Kantians, Hegel has merely taken the lesson of the antinomies and extrapolated it to its logical conclusion (as Žižek shows). Where Kant takes the paralogisms the antinomies demonstrate to indicate the Thing-in-itself as positively given beyond the field of phenomenality, Hegel construes Kant more literally, heeding the fact that what alone is positively given in the antinomies is the entanglement of reason itself. That nullity—the measure of the inadequacy of the phenomenal world—correlates to the nullity, the non-existence, of the Thing-in-itself as a positive entity. The masculine and feminine failures of reason demonstrated by the dynamical and mathematical antinomies respectively are simply two different perspectives on this radically non-substantial Thing, which is produced solely by the limits of the phenomenal.[30]

The figure of Narcissus himself demonstrates this. As shown above, a plethora of phenomena compete to be construed as Narcissus: the passionate flesh-and-blood boy, his cold reflection in the earthly pool, his ghost, the reflection of that ghost in the waters of the Styx, the yellow flower that supplants his body on earth. Saying that

---

[30] Žižek 1989, 205–6.

he was all these and their complex relations together, I embraced these different sites of Narcissus in one complex, shifting web under the aegis of dialectic. Yet such a resolution simply embodies the feminine (or 'mathematical') perspective on Narcissus' identity, as a not-all set of heterogeneous elements that ultimately cannot be closed under a single logical principle. The irreducible antagonism-in-equivalence of Self and Other that the various Narcissi describe ensures that no discrete, stable entity can emerge from this quarrelling congeries—but precisely that deadlock, that 'piece of grit' ensuring the forward movement of the dialectic, is the human, desiring subject.

It is not, however, the only possible perspective on the subject of desire. As remarked in the previous chapter, the dénouement to Narcissus' life becomes known and increases Tiresias' reputation as a diviner ('Cognita res meritam vati per Achaidas urbes | attulerat famam, nomenque auguris erat ingens'—'the affair became known and spread the prophet's reputation deservedly through the Greek cities, and the augur's name grew in importance', 3.511–12). This can only mean that the rumour of Narcissus' vicissitudes reads the boy's disastrous end as proving that he did indeed come to 'know himself' and thus to inherit the ill-effects the prophet foretold. Passing over the perplexities of identity posed by the scattered sites of Narcissus, rumour implicitly affirms that there was a self here to be known (for if not caused by knowing himself, Narcissus' unhappy end cannot measure Tiresias' prophetic powers). This is the masculine ('dynamical') perspective on the phenomenal limits posed by Narcissus' complicated history, a perspective not so much false as partial. It closes the set of phenomena performatively and arbitrarily, by simply declaring Narcissus' end to be the last in a series of dependent events—a rule-based series whose organizing principle, its 'uncaused cause', Tiresias' prophecy articulates ('knowing oneself').

Hegel's patient coaxing of the noumenal back from some conceptual borderland into the heart of the phenomenal itself lays the ground for answering the question with which I began this chapter. Why does Ovid replace Oedipus with Narcissus (and in fact eliminate all the Labdacids)? Because he, like Hegel, rejects the idea that 'the

truth is out *there*—that the phenomenal field is conditioned by
something substantial and radically exterior to that field. On this
point, the *Metamorphoses'* Thebes differs significantly from Sophocles'
Thebes. Despite all the complicated fissuring of knowledge and identity that we have traced above in Sophocles' portrayal of the Theban
king, and even allowing for the fact that Creon defers Oedipus' final
despairing wish to be exiled (*OT* 1436–45), the Sophoclean
Thebes does eventually yield to the illusion that she can (re)constitute
herself as whole, complete, and uncontaminated by excluding the
despised and dangerous other. By the beginning of *Oedipus at
Colonus*, Thebes has expelled her former king as polluted, accursed
transgressor (*OC* 356, 944–6, 1298). He is, in fact, the one reprobate
son of whom Thebes manages to make a successful expiatory offering
(at least temporarily successful: a brief period of sanity and peace
obtains after his exile, when even Oedipus' sons give over their destructive love of power, *OC* 367–73).[31] As René Girard points out,[32]
Oedipus assumes the dimensions of the paradigmatic scapegoat-sa-
viour who returns the community to itself by being excluded and
symbolically bearing away the city's internal disharmony. Thebes can
rid itself of its intimate discord and continue, cleansed and redeemed,
if only for a time. Even the exiled Oedipus himself attains a state of
grace at Colonus.[33]

[31] *Oedipus Coloneus* also concludes on a hopeful note, with Antigone and Ismene
planning to try to heal the rift between their brothers, and Theseus promising to aid
them in any way he can. Of course, Sophocles' *Antigone* records the complete failure
of this plan. Since *Oedipus Tyrannus* takes special notice of the king's daughters and
their precarious future at its conclusion, it can be seen to point ambiguously to both
of Sophocles' other Theban plays—to a future of hope in *Oedipus Coloneus*, and to
the dashing of that hope in *Antigone*. But even taking account of this irreducible
ambiguity in Sophocles' plays as intertexts, it remains the case that Sophocles' Thebes
enjoys a respite from disaster after Oedipus' exile that has no parallel in Ovid's
Theban cycle.
[32] Girard 1977, 68–88.
[33] In *Oedipus Coloneus*, Oedipus bears blessings rather than curses for Athens. Yet
he firmly excludes himself from the city, as though he were still constrained to operate
within the scapegoat status Thebes assigned him. The later play shows him taken
under Athens' aegis, redeemed as his newly-adopted city's benefactor (*OC* 631–41),
but refusing Theseus' kind offer to accompany him—presumably to Athens (*OC*
639)—and clinging to the outskirts of Colonus. No less than at Thebes is the bearer of
Oedipus' cursed history firmly self-consigned outside Athens' borders, however

By contrast, Ovid's Thebes never solves anything by extirpating the other: Cadmus killing the monstrous serpent, the Spartoi killing each other, Pentheus violently opposing Bacchus and his followers, each but turns the screw. Epitomizing this pattern, Narcissus' story emphatically forecloses the possibility of resolving the crisis by designating a scapegoat. His story concerns an other who not only cannot be cut off from the self, but whom there is no desire to repudiate. Narcissus supplants Oedipus, and reverses the whole history of murderous intrafamilial violence that plagues the Labdacids (indeed, mythic Thebes generally). Oedipus' patricide, his father's filicide, and his sons' mutual fratricide—all their black hatred of the other who is also (wittingly or unwittingly) their own flesh-and-blood—find no overt parallel in Narcissus' history. Only their internecine destruction finds its match: with Narcissus, excessive hatred of the other-who-is-the-same becomes (equally deadly) excessive love for him, a mirror-reversal sketching fatal fascination with the intimate enemy rather than despite. Narcissus is ultimately a symptom within the Theban cycle. Through him, Ovid can introduce the Oedipal narrative into his Thebes without entailing the complication that Oedipus' myth trails—the illusion that the polity's negative moment can be positivized and successfully rejected.

Let me be perfectly clear: my analysis in no way demonstrates a sanguine Ovidian embrace of 'diversity' *avant la lettre*. On the contrary: the other whom Narcissus cannot, will not, reject eventually destroys him, just like the internecine combats of Sophocles' Labdacids and Vergil's proto-Romans. The logic of Ovid's tale does not domesticate Narcissus' dark underside by portraying its intimate imbrication with the boy's self; rather, that underside becomes suffocatingly close, oppressive, and inescapable. The accursed telos anticipated by Tiresias' dark prophecy at Narcissus' birth requires the boy to become an other to himself, graphically

generously welcomed, and even when he promises blessings for *that* city. The same dynamic of exclusion obtains in Athens, Oedipus' ultimate saviour, albeit gentled. The city accepts Oedipus' benefits only at arm's length.

illustrating how the impossibility of being fully coterminous with oneself is the internal 'flaw' or 'void' that itself constitutes identity. Narcissus—like Thebes, like Rome—is precisely where, and when, he fails to be.[34]

[34] Paul Allen Miller has shrewdly observed that Ovid sketches this same logic of identity-as-non-coincidence in his exile poetry. Miller analyses the complex inter-textual references of the *Tristia* and *Epistulae ex Ponto* in order to show that Ovid's voice is most truly his own when it is not his own at all (Miller 2004, 210–36). In *Tristia* II, for example, Miller argues that Ovid most forcefully 'speaks truth to power' precisely when he frames his trenchant criticisms of Augustan power in words and images borrowed from Horace and from the neo-Callimachean tradition of *recusatio*. Moreover, this indefatigably allusive Ovid spouts an adulation so excessive and cloying as to imply criticism of his addressee. In this way, too, Ovid is 'most fully present where he is absent' and when 'he means the opposite of what he says, while saying what he means' (Miller 2004, 225).

6

Pentheus Monsters Thebes

Behind the time when dogwood starts to flower
I work and dance inside long changing days
to find the taste, the marrow of the hour
and twist it like a snake into a phrase
that stings with all the passion of a kiss
and smiles with anger in a lying mask
behind your back and turning in your wrist:
I give you back in blood the thing you ask.

And while you climb the mountain like a child,
expecting pleasures and a pretty dance,
I'll screw your trouble into a spring wild
and deadly in the hidden trap of chance.
Under your well-laid palace stones I've cracked
and wriggled like a rooting lightning-gale
and gently, sweetly in bright birds of fact
I'll wind fat songs of fancy up your trail.

Go loudly, grin behind your mask as dead
as I will make you in a ringing glade.
I take joy in the sour blood I've said
into your ignorant ears. Now fade
and take my phosphor in your vein
as suddenly as it has ripped your sky.
Hear as you die the innocent refrain
of birds inside your blue unseeing eye.

Colin Way Reid[1]

---

[1] 'Go Loudly, Pentheus' (Reid 1986, 50).

Divine vengeance has been the crucial lever in each of the Theban tales discussed so far; I have generally emphasized the Real aspect of that vengeance as its lurid effects irrupted into the Symbolic. This last chapter takes up the same fundamental theme, but reverses vantage so as to concentrate more fully on what it is within the Symbolic and Imaginary that these Real intrusions precipitate. My fundamental question is this: if the Real is that upon which the Symbolic and Imaginary cannot gain a foothold, how does it nonetheless create such devastating effects within both corollary orders? Upon what in them does the Real fasten, and how? I pose these questions to the final stories of divine vengeance in the Theban cycle.[2] These comprise the narratives of King Pentheus' opposition to Bacchus, Cadmus, and Harmonia's transformation into snakes, and the conversion-tale of Bacchus' disciple Acoetes—respectively, the longest, the last, and the most miraculous tales of the cycle. Taken together, they engage the chief thematic threads that we have traced through Thebes' history as the effects of the Real: the slipperiness of identity, the savagery of law, masculine and feminine epistemology, the subject's ambivalent dependence on the other, the necessary-impossible scapegoat. The discussion of these themes in previous chapters has broadly traced the tense play between fantasy and aporia. On the one hand, we have Thebes imagined as the ideal of the polity—a transparent, organically united community, to which the subject relates as harmonious, self-determining agent. On the other, we see Thebes as embodying the antagonism fundamental to civil society, matched by a subject caught up in the blind automatism of self-destruction. The regulative orders of law, identity, and knowledge evoked in our analysis of Thebes all offer to bridge this gap between utopia and dystopia, insofar as they promise answers to the problems of evil and suffering, the dialectic of desire and disappointment, the perplexing flux of phenomena. Hitherto we have concentrated on just how and why these promises fell short; that shortfall was often dramatized as the gods' abortion of earthly ambitions, but always wrought upon a passive, inert subject. For that reason, though this chapter also addresses default, it poses to it the following question: if the lures of order, wholeness, and logic

---

[2] Except for Athamas and Ino, who, as Juno's victims, were included in Ch. 2's analysis of the goddess's vengeance.

are mere fantasy, what nonetheless brings them to bear upon the subject? What transforms the evidence of their pitiful imposture into glorious corroboration? The answer (I argue) is ideology—that aspect of the Symbolic whose office it is to articulate 'the Imaginary relationship of individuals to the Real conditions of their lives'.[3] The specific instrument through which ideology accomplishes that is the *point de capiton*, or 'quilting point', whose operation in these final Theban tableaux will converge our discussions of them.

I begin with the Pentheus–Bacchus episode, eclipsed in scholarly attention of late. A survey of the last fifty-six years (1949–2005) of *L'Année Philologique* reveals only three articles that address the episode more than tangentially.[4] Many books on the *Metamorphoses* do not discuss the story at all, or confine themselves to a sentence or two of observation.[5] Franz Bömer's and W. S. Anderson's commentaries make conscientious and often imaginative efforts to give the story its due, but the surrounding silence is still puzzling.[6]

Perhaps the story's less than beguiling protagonist, the blustering martinet Pentheus, repels interest. Anderson articulates representative distaste for Pentheus when he characterizes him as a petty tyrant.[7] Nonetheless, his keen ear for Ovidian borrowings detects the distorted reflection of the *Aeneid* and its exemplars of governance

---

[3] Althusser 1971, 162 ('L'idéologie représente le rapport imaginaire des individus à leurs conditions réelles d'existence', Althusser 1976, 114).

[4] James 1975; James 1991–3; Feldherr 1997. Even among these, A. W. James's comparative study confines itself to matching only the middle episode of the Bacchus–Pentheus story, Acoetes' tale of the Tyrrhenian sailors, with other versions of the myth.

[5] Notable exceptions are: Lafaye 1904, 144–6; Otis 1970, 139–41 and 371–2; Glenn 1986, 38–9; Spencer 1997, 41–63; Hardie 2002*b*, 167–70; Keith 2002, 262–7; Fantham 2004, 40–3; Salzman-Mitchell 2005, 53–6.

[6] Bömer 1969–86, 1: 570–87; Anderson 1997, 388–409. Anderson 1993 also addresses the Pentheus–Bacchus episode briefly (114–17), but for the purposes of this chapter I have generally preferred the more detailed reflections on the story contained in his 1997 commentary.

[7] Anderson 1993 and 1997. Among the few authors who engage the Pentheus episode and the even fewer who record their opinions of the Theban king, nearly all disparage him. Edgar Glenn also finds Pentheus repellent ('[Pentheus] comes to seem insensitive, violent, inflexible and obtuse, and, hence, unlikable'—Glenn 1986, 38), as does A. A. R. Henderson, who summarizes the plot as 'the bullying blasphemer gets his just deserts' and characterizes the king as 'choleric and prejudiced' (Henderson 1981, 9, 112). Stephen Wheeler describes the king as 'impious' and drily notes his

in the story Ovid organizes round the Theban king.[8] Naturally, he notes that both narratives are grounded in exile, since Pentheus, like Aeneas, rules over a city established by refugees forced from their native land.[9] Moreover, they discovered the site of that city courtesy of an oracle that mirrors Aeneas' own divine guidance to Alba Longa (as Philip Hardie notes in an essay Anderson cites).[10] Apollo's command to Cadmus to found a city where an animal reclines (the untouched heifer) parallels the seer Helenus' prophecy in *Aeneid* 3 (388–93): through Helenus, Apollo informs Aeneas that he will found Alba Longa where he finds a newly farrowed white sow. The river-god Tiber repeats and expands the same prophecy regarding Rome's precursor city through a dream-revelation (*Aen.* 8.42–8). These resemblances between Vergilian Rome and Ovidian Thebes notwithstanding, Anderson considers Cadmus' descendant Pentheus to be 'a Mezentius, not an Aeneas' who is 'psychologically and morally warped'[11]—and not without cause. Anderson notes that Ovid avoids the tragic pathos embodied in Euripides' *Bacchae*, where the cruel god lures the arrogant but pitiably young king to his death.[12] Ovid's Pentheus is simply arrogant.

---

cruel orders to torture and kill Acoetes (Wheeler 1999, 182). Brooks Otis deplores Pentheus, but considers the god's punishment of the king 'excessive' (Otis 1970, 140–1). Paula James offers an unusually sympathetic reading of Pentheus, seeing his obduracy and irascibility as determination (James 1991–3, 88, 92), albeit a determination misapplied. Yet even she concludes that 'the *ira* which gave him his initial strength threatened to turn him into a destructive force with no redeeming quality of joyous redemption ... he fulfils his hereditary potential as *contemptor superum*' (James 1991–3, 92). I have chosen to focus on Anderson's analyses of the Pentheus–Bacchus episode because they represent the fullest, most thoughtful, and most articulate summations of the case against Pentheus. What is maddening and repugnant about Pentheus is (I shall argue) the key to his significance in Ovid.

[8] Spencer 1997, 8–9, 42–4, elaborates on the theme of Ovid's Theban cycle replying to Vergil's *Aeneid*, but he makes few points not already observed by Anderson. None of these concern the Pentheus–Bacchus episode's relation to the *Aeneid*.

[9] Anderson 1997, 392.

[10] Hardie 1990, 226.

[11] Anderson 1997, 392, 389.

[12] Cf. William Arrowsmith's observations that preface his own translation of the play: 'Yet as [Pentheus] makes his entrance, breathing fury against the Maenads, I think we are meant to be struck by his extreme youth. Just how old he is, Euripides does not tell us; but since he is presented as still a beardless boy at the time of his

But what exactly stirs the ire of this Mezentius *avant la lettre*? Disruptive alien religious rites subtly different from what any ruler faced in the *Aeneid*. Against a broad background of semblance, the differences loom the larger. First, the semblances: Vergil's Queen Amata acts out a false Bacchic possession ('simulato numine Bacchi', *Aen.* 7.385) to prevent her daughter Lavinia's betrothal to Aeneas. Whether or not she is conscious of its falsity, she thus impedes founding Rome as an amalgam of Trojan and Latin bloodlines.[13] Furies rather than Dionysus drive the Latin matronae to join her imposture (*Aen.* 7.385–405). The same air of counterfeit and misdirection disrupting an incipient city shadows Ovid's Bacchanalia. At first it seems that Pentheus is the only apostate; while the Thebans 'are borne toward unknown rites', Tiresias warns the king he will be torn in bits unless he, too, honours the god (3.519–23). But when Pentheus actually suffers *sparagmos*, Ovid remarks that the Theban women in particular throng Bacchus' rites because they have been warned by the dire example of the king's fate (3.732–3). Immediately thereafter, a priest compels Thebes' near neighbours,

---

death (see ll. 1185 ff.), he cannot very well be much more than sixteen or seventeen. And this youth seems to me dramatically important, helping to qualify Pentheus' prurient sexual imagination (for the voyeurism which in a grown man would be overtly pathological is at most an obsessive and morbid curiosity in a boy) and later serving to enlist our sympathies sharply on the side of the boy-victim of a ruthless god' (Grene–Lattimore 1968, 5: 147).

[13] Whether 'simulato numine Bacchi' refers to Amata's or Allecto's intention to deceive, or to no one's, is a matter of dispute. As Fordyce points out, 'simulatus' need not imply intent (Fordyce 1977, 133). But even if we read the participle strongly, as indicating fraud, the degree to which Amata is capable of agency while being harried by Allecto is assessed variously by different scholars. The spectrum of debate ranges roughly among the following positions (I cite the scholarship only very selectively, as exempla of opinion): deliberate fraud on Amata's part (Otis 1963, 324; Burke 1976, 24); madness entailing Amata's complete incapacity for *mens rea* (Quinn 1968, 181); madness exacerbating Amata's inherent character flaws, so as to exert pressure upon the queen, but not determine her choices—she is still culpable (Rabel 1981). Feeney exemplifies a quite different approach; he delicately lays out the way the clues the Amata episode offers point in opposite directions, which he regards as a deliberately aporetic textual strategy: 'By laying bare the impossibilities of adequately narrating such extremes of behaviour, this technique involves the reader in the recognition of our inability to understand madness in others, or acknowledge it in ourselves' (Feeney 1991, 168).

the Orchomenians, to worship Bacchus by again warning of the god's 'savage anger' if scorned (4.4–9).[14] If the Thebans and Orchomenians need bloody examples and menace in order to honour Bacchus, then a reign of terror rather than religious conviction is spreading the god's worship—odd for a god quintessentially associated with ecstatic possession of his faithful.

To be sure, the mythological tradition regularly makes fear the other side of the god's kindlier nurturance. But when set against Ovid's closest literary intertexts, the *Homeric Hymn to Dionysus* and Euripides' *Bacchae*, the poet can be seen to highlight grounds for fear while diminishing signs of benevolence. Ovid offers more monsters and fewer wonders than either Greek text: where just two beasts attack the infidel sailors of the Homeric Hymn (the god as a lion, plus a bear; *HHDion.* 44–6), a multitude of tigers, lynxes, and panthers terrorize Ovid's sailors (*Met.* 3.668–9). Euripides' Bacchants are violent (*Bacch.* 735–47)—they tear apart cattle with their bare hands—but their observers also report the women 'a marvel of orderliness to behold' ('thaum' idein eukosmias', *Bacch.* 693). No such word returns to Ovid's Pentheus from his slaves bloodied by Bacchus' devotees (*Met.* 3. 572–3). Neither does anyone in Ovid witness wine miraculously flowing on shipboards (*HHDion.* 35) or springing from a vine; no Bacchants suckle animals, or coax cool water from rock, honey from thyrsi, milk from the ground (*Bacch.* 699–711). All these paradisal details complicate the picture of the god and his devotees in the older texts. One could be forgiven for wondering what Ovid's god has to offer Thebes and Orchomenos aside from fear. And a Bacchus who cannot command fealty by enthusiasm, but only through terror, gives credit to Pentheus' allegation that the rites of this 'uanum numen' are 'magicae fraudes'

----

[14] 'Talibus exemplis [viz. the death of Pentheus] monitae noua sacra frequentat | turaque dant sanctasque colunt Ismenides aras'—'Warned by such examples, they throng the new rites and the Theban women burn incense and worship at the holy altars' (*Met.* 3.732–3); 'festum celebrare sacerdos... | iusserat, et saeuam laesi fore numinis iram | uaticinatus erat'—'the priest had commanded that they throng the feast, and had predicted that the anger of the divinity would be savage if he were offended' (*Met.* 4.4, 8–9).

(3.534, 559–60)—just like the meretricious exercises Amata undergoes and their Dirae demagogues.[15]

But Ovid departs significantly from Vergil when he makes his
Theban Bacchants a motley of women and men, slave and free,
low-born and high-born (3.529–30, 538–42).[16] The mixture of
sexes in particular contradicts Greek practice—counter-intuitive for
a cult supposed to arise on Boeotian soil. In this detail, Ovid reflects
Rome's more recent history. Mixed-sex thiasoi conform to what is
known of Italian Bacchic cults, the most notorious example of which

---

[15] Ovid's emphasis on Bacchus' cruelty and reign through fear over his benevolence engages a question much-debated in antiquity: can the gods be understood and
evaluated in human terms? Against the cultural prestige accorded to the Homeric
epics as the models for all excellence—a paragon status implicitly condoning the
behaviour of the gods in the poems, or at least exempting them from human
assessment—arise voices of criticism directed at those very portraits of the gods
and the ways they fall short of human morality. Some attack the problem of
misbehaving gods by denying categorically the truth of such reports. Pindar refuses
to believe any god could be a cannibal, so the story of the gods consuming Pelops as a
dish his father proffered must be false; rather, that rumour was started by an 'envious
neighbour' (*Ol.* 1.35–55). Xenophanes also rejects stories of miscreant gods, because
the divine is perfect, therefore without desire and without the motor force behind evil
action (fr. 12, 24, 26). Plato exiles such stories from his ideal city on the grounds that
they are both false and corrupting (*Rep.* 377e–383c). On the Roman side, Lucretius
imports into the Latin language Epicurus' notion of the divine as benignly indifferent
to mortals (*DRN* 1.44–9). Cicero's discussion of Stoicism reflects a god immanent
within the universe and (unlike Epicurus' *fainéants*) directing its development
meticulously; there is no room in this entirely rational divine for cruelty or caprice
(*De Natura Deorum* 2.16–22).

Yet it is not irrelevant that Greek tragedy looms even larger than philosophy among
Ovid's important intertexts for the Bacchus–Pentheus tale. As Martha Nussbaum has
shown, the tragedians regularly dramatize godly cruelty, violence, and enslaving
imposition upon human beings. They equally assume a universe to which moral
assessment is crucial, and so refuse to accept divine transgression blandly. They will
not make the abusive gods disappear, as, say, Pindar and Plato would like; rather, the
abuse of power poses an ethical problem within the tragic universe, no matter what
the status of the abuser (Nussbaum 2001, xxviii–xxxvii, 25–50). For an Augustan poet
such as Ovid, the divine status accorded to Julius Caesar and the beginnings of
imperial cult would have sharpened questions about the gods' humanity and the
standards by which they could appropriately be judged (cf. Severy 2003, 96–139).

[16] The rites at Orchomenos, whose description immediately follows the end of the
Pentheus episode, similarly mix classes and ages, though the rites there seem to be all
female (4.5–12). Orchomenos' gender discrimination makes the co-educational
Theban rites all the more eyecatching and significant.

the Roman Senate ruthlessly suppressed in 186 BCE.[17] In Livy's account of the episode, the lone eye-witness to the cult tells the Roman consul Postumius that the cult was originally for women only; the trouble started when a new priestess started initiating men (Livy 39.13.8–14). This is the most specific charge Postumius levels against the Italian cult, that mingling with women has effeminized the rite's male devotees, making them unmartial, and thus unfit citizens of their state (Livy 39.15.9–14). Pentheus also catechizes his Thebans by linking gender-propriety to citizenship: the effete trappings of Bacchic worship—thyrsi, strange foreign musical instruments, drunkenness, and 'female caterwauling' (*femineae uoces*, 3.536)—conquer a people previously unmoved by the face of war. Those who should defend Thebes yield without a fight to a divine pretender, whose boyish beauty, perfumed and garlanded hair, rich costume, and allergy to arms also feminize him (3.533–42, 553–6). These echoes between 'official response' to the Bacchanalia in Livy's Roman history and in Ovid's Theban myth deepen and complicate Thebes' mirroring of Rome.[18] Both cities' leaders locate what is chiefly wrong with this 'wild religion' in the way it breaks down categorial distinctions between Man and Woman.[19]

Pentheus' attempt to address that breakdown propels the story away from Vergil's high drama, even beyond Livy's melodrama, into burlesque; he tries to turn his Thebans from worshipping Bacchus with an absurd harangue. Its absurdity lies in exhorting his frenzied subjects to forsake the new god in favour of another role model—the

---

[17] *OCD*³ s.v. 'Bacchanalia'; Bouvrie 1998 (with useful bibliographical references); North 1979, 89.

[18] On the relations between the Bacchic episode of 186 BCE and Ovid's Pentheus story, see now Barchiesi–Rosati 2007, 210, 218, which also offers helpful bibliography on the Roman Bacchanalian cult's 2nd-cent. suppression.

[19] A theme that Ovid, at least, probably borrows from Euripides' *Bacchae* to shape to his own purposes. True to actual Greek practice, Euripides' play represents the thiasoi of maenads as exclusively female, with Dionysus as the only allowable male (*Bacch.* 115–19). Yet Euripides repeatedly underlines both the ambiguous gender of Dionysus himself, and the way the god moulds the pixilated Pentheus into a similarly epicene figure. For example, the disguised Dionysus persuades Pentheus to wear women's clothing, so the king can in theory spy on the maenads undetected (*Bacch.* 810–46, 912–44). For more on the dissolution of gender boundaries in the *Bacchae*, see Segal 1997, 158–214; Bremmer 1999.

monstrous serpent that Cadmus slew after it had killed several of his
men and nearly prevented the city's founding:

> 'este, precor, memores, qua sitis stirpe creati,
> illiusque animos, qui multos perdidit unus,
> sumite serpentis. pro fontibus ille lacuque
> interiit; at uos pro fama uincite uestra.
> ille dedit leto fortes.'
>
> (*Met.* 3.543–7)

'I pray you, be mindful of the stock from which you were created! Take on
that serpent's courage, who being one, destroyed many! He died for his
springs and his pool; you, conquer for the sake of your reputation! He gave
strong men over to death.'

Pentheus' speech on the snake's hypermasculine virtues invokes the
chief ideologemes of Augustan propaganda: manliness and martiality, proper to the compatriot, against the effeminacy and demonism
of the foreigner ('aduena', 3.561). But by what logic does the king
place on the side of the angels Thebes' aboriginal enemy, the serpent
who nearly destroyed her inception?

Pentheus' tirade generally repels those scholars who attend to
it specifically.[20] Yet only W. S. Anderson and Andrew Feldherr
articulate the unease the speech inspires as a specific function of its
distorted relation to Roman virile *Gemeinschaft*. Feldherr places the
speech in the context of historicizing Augustan rhetoric represented
in Livy and Vergil. He sees Pentheus as mirroring the exhortations of
Livy's Roman generals to their troops to have contempt for their
enemy's effeminacy. Pentheus matches even more closely the ironic

---

[20] For instance, Pentheus' wild assertion that he would rather see the city destroyed by war than submit to the god strikes Glenn as evidence that 'Pentheus and
Bacchus, or Liber, manifest the same aspect of the human psyche, its dark, bloody and
irrational traits' (Glenn 1986, 38). Paula James concurs, seeing Pentheus' speech as an
invocation of the serpent's spirit that manifests itself in the king 'lashing out blindly at
all opponents and thrusting aside all obstacles in his rage' (James 1991–3, 87).
Andrew Feldherr notes that Pentheus hamhandedly manages to exhort his Thebans
to mutually contradictory and equally bloody goals: the aged colonists who arrived as
exiles are to defend their new land, while the younger natives must emulate their
ophidian ancestor's slaying of foreign invaders. Which is the enemy in this paradigm,
the Foreign or the Native (Feldherr 1997, 50)?

objurgations levelled by the *Aeneid*'s Italians at the Trojans. Italy's denizens regularly task the immigrants for effeminacy and unmartiality; they thus unwittingly scorn the race with whom they shall merge, their future fellow Romans. And while hecklers such as Numanus Remulus may have *Blut und Boden* on their side when decrying the Trojans as exotic foreigners—'Phrygian women, hardly Phrygian men' (*Aen.* 9.614–20)—the Argive ancestry of Numanus' brother-in-law Turnus (*Aen.* 7.371–2, 9.593–4) does not prevent him from also indulging in mannish nativism. He scorns Aeneas specifically as a 'Phrygian half-man' sporting perfumed ringlets, easily to be bested by Turnus' own spear (*Aen.* 12.97–100). But Turnus and Pentheus are both on weak ground in their rejections of the immigrant: as Feldherr remarks, the effeminate, anomalous Eastern invader can in each case claim to be returning to his native land.[21] I would add that Ovid draws Pentheus and his ill-conceived sexist xenophobia even closer to Turnus' folly when Pentheus cites Acrisius as his role-model for opposing Bacchus (3.559–61). No other extant mythic source records Acrisius' violent opposition to Bacchus, though Ovid notes that he lived to rue it (4.612–14). Whether invented, or simply from an unknown tradition, the reference to Acrisius reminds us that Turnus is the Argive king's distant descendant (*Aen.* 7.372). Ovid's portrayal of Acrisius snatches paradigmatic status-priority from Turnus as xenophobe opposed to divine will. Ovid makes Vergil's Turnus silently emulate Acrisius in opposing louche foreign influx, whereas Ovid's Pentheus, Acrisius' contemporary, explicitly lionizes the truculent Argive. Literary one-upsmanship notwithstanding, all three rulers reap disaster.

   Feldherr's analysis makes excellent points, but does not engage the weirdest feature of Pentheus' speech, the king's rehabilitation of the monstrous serpent. Rather, Feldherr glosses the snake as Pentheus' unwitting use of an oblique emblem of his future suffering, insofar as the snake's fate conforms to a general pattern of the *Metamorphoses*: victors become victims. His argument, though subtle and sharply observed, nonetheless falls into a pattern among *Metamorphoses* scholars of explaining away the epic's most jarring features, including

---

[21] Feldherr 1997, 44–6.

this embarrassing serpent-icon.[22] The sheer *bizarrerie* of Pentheus' speech is (I shall argue) essential to its significance. For this reason, Anderson's pungent reaction to the speech usefully compels us to focus on its shock value. He assimilates Pentheus' rehabilitation of the snake to a pattern of patriotic distortions the king visits upon Theban history. Recreating the monstrous serpent Cadmus dispatched as the Theban *beau ideal* is (for Anderson) still more evidence of the king's queer jingoism:

By turning the snake into the Founding Father of Thebes and urging the populace to be mindful of its heritage, Pentheus patently abuses Augustan rhetoric. It is as if a Roman orator should hail as a foundation-symbol the wolf that raised Romulus and Remus.[23]

Yet to this one must reply: precisely. As Hardie points out, what Anderson posits as the *reductio ad absurdum* of nationalist rhetoric is in fact elaborately realized in the *Aeneid*.

Virgil's scenes of Roman history on the Shield of Aeneas open with Romulus and Remus and their 'mother', the she-wolf, also an animal of Mars (8.630–4): what is it that they suck in with their mother's milk? This origin is not put away with childish things: at *Aeneid* 1.275 Romulus makes his entry into the poem in the disguise of the wolf, clad in his nurse's hide.[24]

---

[22] Kenneth Knoespel regards Pentheus' exhortation to his people to be more like the dragon that threatened their founder to be evidence that 'a book that begins with coherence unravels into incoherence' (Knoespel 1985, 20). Richard Spencer considers the speech 'marvelously shocking irony' that Ovid uses to ridicule Pentheus and to emphasize the dissimilarity between Pentheus and his grandfather, Cadmus (Spencer 1997, 48). Bömer takes no explicit exception to Pentheus' rehabilitating the serpent as a model of patriotism, but considers the parallels the Theban king draws between the serpent's behaviour and the behaviour he wishes from his subjects 'eigenartig frostigen und auch gewaltsamen' ('weirdly cold-blooded and yet also violent', Bömer 1969–86, 580). Paula James takes partial and notable exception to the *communis opinio* on Pentheus' use of the serpent in his speech (James 1991–3). She sees Pentheus' redefinition of the snake as justified by the Theban king's groping for a role model of infuriated strength (James 1991–3, 86–91). Yet she never explains why the wrath is so important, nor why the image of Cadmus' calmer, triumphant strength would not better serve his grandson (the serpent ultimately lost to Cadmus, after all).

[23] Anderson 1997, 392–3.

[24] Hardie 1990, 229–30.

On the Shield, the she-wolf not only demonstrates maternal tender-
ness, she measures the infants' virile courage: they suck their foster
mother's dugs 'fearlessly' ('impauidos', 8.633); Romulus appears
wearing her hide in Jupiter's first prophecy of the Romans' future
greatness. In both instances, Ovid's chief predecessor in Latin epic
deploys the wolf in contexts of proud reflection on Roman origins.[25]
Orators may have scrupled to use the *lupa* as a sign of Rome's origins,
but the *Aeneid*'s poet did not.[26]

By adducing the *Aeneid*, I do not mean to argue that Anderson's
outrage is misguided—quite the opposite. Anderson is right to draw
a difference. Vergil evokes *amor patriae* with the nurturing wolf who
is nonetheless *experimentum crucis* of the boys' *uirtus*; Ovid, making
the monster snake into an icon of macho patriotism, stretches
Pentheus' speech into satire. The she-wolf succoured Rome's founder; Thebes' king cites as proud icon of Thebanness the beast that

---

[25] Not that Vergil was likely to be blind to the irreducible ambiguity of such a
symbol.

[26] Nor, for that matter, did Propertius: he hails the she-wolf as the nurse of Rome's
walls ('optima nutricum nostris lupa Martia rebus, | qualia creuerunt moenia lacte
tuo!', Prop. 4.1.55–6). Yet the *Aeneid* holds pride of place for the *Metamorphoses*, as
the only Augustan epic prior to Ovid's and as the definitive dramatization of the
Augustan view of Roman history (albeit a view that Vergil persistently interrogates
and problematizes). O. S. Due states the case most clearly: 'No model, however, was
more important to Ovid and his readers than Vergil, especially the *Aeneid*. As a
matter of fact, Vergil is ubiquitous in the *Metamorphoses*. It seems impossible that he
should not be. But the *Aeneid* was a unique achievement which could by no means be
repeated . . . The *Metamorphoses* recalls the *Aeneid* almost everywhere, but the Vergilian element seems always to be varied, surrounded by a different context, and given
a new meaning so that the result is extremely Ovidian' (Due 1974, 36, 37). In support
of these statements, Due cites Rosa Lamacchia, who writes: 'L'imitazione di Vergilio,
che si estende com'è noto al di là della sezione "Virgiliana" del poema, fino a investire
l'intera opera di Ovidio, assume tuttavia nelle *Metamorfosi* un carattere e un sig-
nificato tutto particolare: essa risponde ad un intento programmatico da parte del
poeta, ed è intesa a garantire dal punto di vista formale e tradizionale l'epicità stessa
dell'opera' ('The emulation of Vergil, which extends, as noted, far beyond the
"Vergilian" section of the poem [= the *Metamorphoses*], until it pervades the whole
of Ovid's oeuvre, nevertheless assumes in the *Metamorphoses* a character and a
significance all its own: this answers to a programmatic intent on the poet's part,
and it is intended to guarantee, from the formal and traditional point of view, the
very "epicness" of the work', Lamacchia 1969, 18). Vergil had defined what 'epic'
meant to the Augustans, Propertius had not; for that reason, I focus my attention on
the *Aeneid*'s use of the wolf symbol.

destroyed the first Thebans rather than fostering them. Yet it remains true that Pentheus' rehabilitation of the serpent is *both* scandalous *and* oddly in conformity with the Roman use of myth; the point of the snake-as-patriotic-symbol lies in this tense duality.

Satire's efficacy lies in presenting to us a *verkehrte Welt* that, in its absurdity, reflects back to the reader what is already 'topsy-turvy' in the 'normal' world she inhabits. I use deliberately Hegel's expression for the way in which the dialectic turns the subject's accustomed world-view upside down,[27] because here in the Pentheus story, as in the Narcissus episode, Ovid stages an epistemological upset of received ontology. The way the dialectic ruthlessly pursues reality in the shifting logical sequelae of contradiction conjures a world forever in process; not only are its phenomena mutable, so are the rules governing those phenomena. The dialectic shatters the idea of reality as a rule-bound, unchanging supersensible world—as 'the tranquil kingdom of laws' ('das ruhige Reich der Gesetze', *PhG* 157) whose eternal reality trumps the flux of the sensible world. Although Hegel's immediate source for this static picture is Kant's noumenal realm, the idea that what really counts as real lies immutable beyond our senses stretches back to Plato. Pentheus' stupefying appeal to the Thebans' 'venerable' heritage in the bloody snake merely foregrounds what is already present in the Augustan construction of the Roman national myth—the idea that the nation's mythohistorical genesis in bloodshed reflects its own tranquil kingdom of laws. Violence is regrettable, but necessary, because 'it has always been thus, it is in our nature, that's the way the world is'. Vergil's *Aeneid* crucially stages both this ideology of necessary carnage, and its internal paradoxes. As Hardie has shown, the *Aeneid* sets the terms for a Latin epic tradition that regularly engages the slippery duplicity of violence.[28] He reads the *Aeneid* and its successors through the lens of René Girard's idea of 'sacrificial crisis', whereby a community's agreement to designate and sacrifice a victim circumscribes the breakdown of social order and the concomitant threat of rampant social violence. Though violence be an unavoidable law of the world, ostensibly

---

[27] Hegel 1999–2000, 3: 129/Hegel 1977, §158.
[28] Hardie 1993.

'good violence' combats 'bad violence'. Citing Girard's *Violence and the Sacred*, Hardie contemns this solution as specious:[29]

For Girard, the accepted practices of sacrifice, 'beneficial violence', are a mask for the harmful violence that without sacrifice would rage uncontrolled. The killing of Turnus is the act on which the Roman cultural order is founded; Virgil narrates a senseless vengeance-killing which is masked, in the words of the killer, as a sacrifice, but whose true nature many readers experience as quite other.[30]

Ovid's juxtaposition of 'bad violence' and 'good violence'—with which we may align the snake's massacre, respectively before, and after, its Penthean reconstruction—is even more jarring than Vergil's (as Anderson's scandalized comments illustrate). Yet the very scandal of Pentheus' sophistic revisionism emphatically illustrates how the two kinds of violence are reverse and obverse of the same coin.

Girard's insight on the inherent duplicity of violence is useful. However, the exact mechanism that converts rage into (apparent) redemption remains undertheorized in the Girardian paradigm. How does Pentheus try to persuade his ensorcelled Thebans that Bacchus and his Bacchants are the enemy, ripe candidates for butchery to match the ancient serpent's carnage? Through impassioned rhetoric—through speech. Yet Girard's theory of sacrificial crisis takes no specific account of language's role in converting bloody outrage to propriety. Such a theory can certainly shine light upon the operation of violence in epic, but cannot be adequate to a sophisticated linguistic artefact such as the *Metamorphoses*. Moreover, language is the material out of which intersubjectivity, and hence sociality, is necessarily constituted. In his parody of Roman patriotic oratory, Pentheus invokes an ideology of identity that only exists in and through the linguistic categories that make it possible.

Notwithstanding, we can build upon Girard's model by retaining its roots in Hegel's dialectic, and articulating the role of language in

---

[29] Girard 1972. As Carl Rubino points out, the theories articulated in *La Violence et le sacré* were not new to Girard's work, only most fully elaborated there. They had been building in Girard's work for years, beginning with Girard 1961, and stretching through Girard 1963, 1968, and 1970 (Rubino 1972, 987 n. 4).

[30] Hardie 1993, 21.

this process.[31] Language mediates sublation (*Aufhebung*), the up-ward-spiralling, inverting movement between antipodes inspired by negation; sublation is negation that retains the essential principles of the cancelled term in the negation. The power of language to broker such contradiction figures prominently in the way Lacan accounts both for culture and for cultural crisis. Specifically, his analysis of the power of ideology both to map troublesome social reality and help forge collective conscience rests upon seeing ideology as a linguistic function. For that reason, Lacan's thought can rigorously parse what is operating in the satiric exaggeration of Pentheus' speech.

As noted previously in discussing the Lacanian divided subject (Chapter 1), language is one of the metaphorical mirrors that, by granting the subject an extrinsic representation of selfhood, an 'I', also installs intrinsic division. The subject who speaks ('le *je* qui énonce') is never exactly coincident with the subject of the speech ('le *je* de l'énonciation'). The person who says 'I laughed' may or may not be laughing at the moment of speaking, and thus ob-viously differs from the subject, the 'I', of the sentence. We are both

---

[31] Rubino offers a particularly lucid sketch of the debt Girard's thought on violence owes to Hegel (Rubino 1972, 986–8), most particularly to Hegel's analysis of the development of self-consciousness in the Master–Slave dialectic, wherein (as we have seen) each individual self-consciousness seeks to negate any rival claim to self-consciousness, sparking a life-and-death struggle to annihilate the other in order to assert the self. Girard draws a similar theory of 'mimetic rivalry' from his reading of the major characters of Cervantes, Stendhal, Flaubert, Dostoyevsky, and Proust (as articulated in *Deceit, Desire, and the Novel*). He sees the desire animating these characters as imitative rather than spontaneous or need-based, copied from another's longing for an object. Such triangulation necessarily draws both desiring subjects into competition for the fascinating object. In *Violence and the Sacred*, Girard expands that model of longing based on rivalry into a general account of social violence.

Eugene Webb notices not only Girard's obligation to Hegel, but even more particularly to Alexandre Kojève's interpretation of Hegel. In a personal conversation, Girard acknowledged to Webb that he was studying Kojève's *Introduction to the Reading of Hegel* while articulating the idea of mimetic rivalry in *Deceit, Desire, and the Novel*. Curiously, in the same conversation Girard denied that either Hegel or Kojève contributed to his theory that sacrifice—the elimination of a victim upon whom the whole community can agree—resolves violence, claiming that both Hegel and Kojève remain bound to the idea of a perpetual dialectic of violence (Webb 1993, 116 and n. 14). While that may be true, it is impossible to miss the fact that Girard's model of bad violence converted to good violence reproduces the logical structure of sublation, insofar as sacrifice combats destruction with destruction.

constructed in and alienated by our relation to language[32]—a warped
reflexive relationship Lacan articulated in precise linguistic terms:

A signifier is that which represents the subject for another signifier. This
signifier will therefore be the signifier for which all the other signifiers
represent the subject: that is to say, in the absence of this signifier, all the
other signifiers do not represent anything, since something is represented
only for something else.[33]

The graphemes Lacan employed a few years later to represent the
discursive subject[34] can economically summarize this as follows: a
signifier (S1) represents the subject ($) for another signifier (S2).[35]
Yet the split between the subject who speaks and the subject of the
speech means that something always escapes this process of representation. As Žižek observes,[36] the subject has no 'proper' signifier
that would fully represent her. Every signifying representation, however imperceptibly, displaces and distorts the subject. Every signifier
thus *mis*represents the subject—a failure that compels the movement
of representation always to grasp after the next signifier in search of
an ultimate 'proper' signifier. The result of this restless groping is a
non-totalized infinity of signifying representations, a confused array

---

[32] Cf. Lacan 1973, 127–30 (= 1981*b*, 138–42), where Lacan illustrates this concept
by means of the Liar's Paradox ('I am lying').

[33] Lacan 1966, 819. I have reproduced Slavoj Žižek's translation of Lacan's rather
elliptical French (Žižek 1991*a*, 21); Sheridan's English translation makes nonsense of
the passage (Lacan 1977, 316).

[34] Lacan 1991.

[35] Lacan's formulation bats against the communicational model of language,
whereby the sender transmits a message to a receiver; ideally, that transaction directly
communicates 'self' or 'pure, original meaning' between two transparent subjects. By
contrast, Lacan sees the subject's constitution by, and enmeshment within, language
as an endless groping after meaning, after 'wholeness' (of self and of understanding).
Ultimately, that search is addressed not to another subject, but to the Symbolic itself.
Even in the case of a speaker like Pentheus, who directs his speech to his fellow
Thebans, his addressees become visible, legible—and thus 'addressable'—only by
virtue of their participation in the categories of understanding defined by cultural
symbolization systems: 'snake-born offspring of Mars' (*Met.* 3.531–2), 'elders who
founded the city' (*Met.* 3.538–40), 'youths of military age' (*Met.* 3.540–2), etc.
Pentheus tries to turn each group away from the worship of Bacchus by appealing
to the mores expected of their class, whether that be bellicosity, the necessary
toughness of the colonizer, or youthful machismo.

[36] Žižek 1991*a*, 24.

of signifiers that 'do not represent anything'. The failure of the signifier S1 to form a complementary relation with another signifier S2 that transparently and fully represents the subject mires every subject in meaninglessness—or would, if this very aporia did not open the door to elevating any other signifier to the place of S1. Thus promoted and reflexively constructed as the One signifier that can totalize the battery of other signifiers, this new Master-signifier makes a legible totality out of the meaningless pullulation of 'all others'. Identifying with this miraculously concatenating signifier 'sutures over' the gap in the subject, the gap that inspires the desire for wholeness and the endless, futile pursuit thereof. The subject's internal scission can be closed and himself rendered whole insofar as he reconciles or opposes himself to what constitutes, e.g. a 'brave man', a 'good warrior', a 'true Theban', and the like. The divided psychoanalytic subject can thus function as a coherent whole (as 'I'), but only via ideological commitment to the narratives various master-signifiers produce; these narratives appear to make the various parts of being (anatomy, intellect, desire, cultural ideals) cohere in a natural fashion. The ordering signifiers that organize these commitments Lacan calls 'quilting points' (*points de capiton*).[37]

Tracing the vicissitudes of the subject's relation to the signifier brings us via an unexpected path back to the formulae of sexuation. The failure of S1 and S2 to form a symmetrical complementarity produces as its symptom an inconsistent multitude of signifiers—a feminine 'non-All'. Only the exception of one element (the Master-Signifier) can totalize that multitude; the intervention of that single element raised from the status of one-among-many to the One produces the masculine All. This exactly corresponds to the function of the Lacanian phallus as noted in Chapter 1. The phallus construed as empyrean exception—as the single unattainable point of plenitude, without division or lack—anchors the mundane conceptual boundaries of the Symbolic, the battery of differences upon which meaning and identity depend. So when Pentheus proposes the monstrous serpent as the perfection of Theban identity, the lodestar to guide his citizens' reflections on their history and on themselves, he opposes to their Bacchic feminization a phallic symbol in more senses than one. As noted, an indiscriminate heterogeny marks the Theban Bacchants: they are a 'feminine' multitude not just because the men in the group have softened in step with their female fellow-devotees and their degenerate god (as Pentheus sees it). Rather, Bacchus' Theban celebrants have broken down criteria of discrimination on all fronts: young mix with old, slave with free, low-born with high-born. City-dwellers throng the wild places, and dress in animal skins rather than civilized clothing (3.702, 4.6). To all appearances, a mere boy commands obedience from his elders; this stripling's outlandishly luxuriant, perfumed costume makes it even harder to take him seriously. No consistent, organizing principle can be found to make either this mob or their god legible to Pentheus.

Against this imbroglio Pentheus sets the monstrous serpent as a point of exception (S1): he focuses on the chief scandal of Theban history in order to rewrite it. This vicious, instinctively territorial, lethal serpent is literally the forefather of the Thebans. As mentioned in Chapter 1, the dead serpent's teeth sown by Cadmus produce the internecine Spartoi. These warrior-fratricides were the first autochthonous Thebans; their strife marks the very origins of Thebes with the obscene antithesis to citizenship and to harmonious polity. The covetous territoriality and mutual murder that the serpent and serpent-born embody eventually surface again between Eteocles and Polyneices; then it destroys the last mythic Theban dynasty, and soon Thebes itself.[38]

LA PEAU DE CHAGRIN

Nonetheless, a few generations before Oedipus' sons, Pentheus succeeds in sloughing the symbolic burden of Thebes' history via an ideological sleight of hand: he does not deny Thebes' past, but

---

[38] The mythic history of Thebes ends with her sack by the Epigonoi, the sons of the seven heroes who enlisted in Polyneices' cause to retake the city from his brother Eteocles. The 'After-born' set out to finish what their fathers left incomplete at their deaths (Hom. *Il.* 4.405–10). Polyneices' and Eteocles' quarrel thus indirectly inspires this group's destruction of Thebes.

completely transvalues its chief terms. Everything that ought to be a source of shame he transforms into a model for emulation: the One (the serpent) saved at the expense of Many (Cadmus' followers)[39]— and a multitude sacrificed who were fellow citizens, if (as Pentheus reasons) the serpent is the proto-Theban *par excellence*;[40] the bestial origin of the Thebans, and their internecine propensities; the supernatural powers that haunt their environs and make Thebes a noisome place. He makes the serpent the interpretive anchor of that revaluation. The ease with which Pentheus miraculously reverses the discursive field by adducing the monster points to the supremely convertible quilting point.

The usefulness of the quilting point's conceptualization lies in it having no intrinsic, stable value, and being therefore infinitely adaptable. It simply grants momentary coherence and stability to the other signifiers floating in the discursive field by 'quilting' them into an intelligible unit, rather as punctuation marks can organize otherwise random words into comprehensible sentences.[41] The monster snake's facile conversion from *bête noire* to paragon points to its status as just such an empty, but structurally crucial, element.

Strictly speaking, the serpent-as-quilting-point does not differ essentially in this respect from any other signifier: every signifier is empty of content before construed in relation to its context. Meaning is numinous and immanent in the concatenation of signifiers grasped as a whole.[42] Yet there exist in discourse more explicitly symptomatic signifiers, that draw attention to the arbitrariness of

---

[39] Spencer notes the contrast between the serpent as one, his victims as many, but does not see this violence as a type of civil war (Spencer 1997, 48).

[40] 'Many sacrificed for one' is, of course, the opposite of the *Aeneid*'s controlling formula of heroism, which emphasizes saving the collectivity even at the expense of the individual. See Quint 1993, 83–96.

[41] For more on the concept of the quilting point, see Janan 1994, 25–6, with references.

[42] Lacan arrives at this model of language by taking Ferdinand de Saussure at his word. Saussure argued that language was a purely differential system: every signifier gained its meaning only in relation to all other signifiers in the system (see e.g. Saussure 1959, 120). Rigorously applied, that thesis contradicts Saussure's assertion that the relation between signifier and signified resembles that between two sides of a piece of paper—synchronically rigid and stable, though it may gradually change diachronically (Saussure 1959, 113). Lacan illustrates the way in which meaning cannot be assigned to individual signifiers, but only to the semantic unit as a

their own operation. For example, Tacitus famously deconstructs the way Augustus' ruthless and deadly pursuit of his enemies, and expropriation of their properties, is glossed as the supreme Roman virtue, *pietas*.[43] The princeps-to-be 'avenged' his adoptive father, Julius Caesar, by hunting down Caesar's assassins[44]—in the process conveniently eliminating many of his own potential rivals (*Ann.* 1.9–10).[45]

Pentheus' 'magical inversion' similarly ameliorates the scattered and disorganized memories that chronicle the city's origin in bloodshed and shame. Without introducing any new evidence, without contradicting a single fact, he quilts them into a narrative that reconfigures the serpent. Now the beast is not only *not* anathema, but is in fact the very icon of Theban identity at its best. Most surprising of all, Pentheus fashions this national anthem out of the very data

---

whole, by analysing a line from Victor Hugo's '*Booz endormi*': 'His sheaf was neither miserly nor spiteful' ('Sa gerbe n'était pas avare ni haineuse'). The word 'sheaf' is a metaphor for 'Boaz', yet bears no logical relation to 'Boaz', no Aristotelian relation of similarity that legitimates the substitution. Only the line taken in its totality allows the substitution to work, making 'sheaf' (as grammatical subject) produce 'Boaz' (as conceptual subject). See Lacan 1966, 506–9 (= 1977, 156–8).

[43] Tacitus records this as a division of opinion among the *prudentes* on Octavian's pursuit of his adoptive father's assassins. The meliorists' judgement is that 'pietate erga parentem et necessitudine rei publicae, in qua nullus tunc legibus locus, ad arma civilia actum, quae neque parari possent neque haberi per bonas artis; multa Antonio, dum interfectores patris ulcisceretur, multa Lepido concessisse' (*Ann.* 1.9) ('filial duty and the needs of the republic, which at that time had no room for law, had driven him to civil war—and that can neither be begun nor sustained by ethical means; for the sake of avenging himself upon his father's murderers, he had tolerated much in Antonius, much also in Lepidus'). By others 'dicebatur contra: pietatem erga parentem et tempora rei publicae obtentui sumpta' (*Ann.* 1.10) ('the opposite view was articulated—that filial duty and the exigencies of the republic had been used as mere pretexts'). Vengeance is, in this view, an excuse to consolidate Octavian's power.

[44] It appears from Cicero's letters that Octavian swore publicly on at least one occasion to take revenge for Caesar as if it were filial duty. Cicero reports the following words from Octavian's November 44 BCE speech: 'Iurat, ita ibi parentis [sc. Caesaris] honores consequi liceat, et simul dextram intendit ad statuam' (*Att.* 16.15.3) ('He swears by his hopes of attaining to his father's honours, and at the same time stretches his right hand toward the statue'). As M. P. Charlesworth remarks, 'the obvious protasis to the *ita* clause is some such phrase as e.g. "ut eius mortem ulciscar"' (*CAH* 10.7, n. 4) ('as I hope to avenge his death'). Among the other, older Augustan poets, Horace—with less obvious irony than Ovid—adopts this view of Octavian, and in *Odes* 1.2.44 portrays the princeps as 'Caesar's avenger' ('ultor Caesaris').

[45] See David Quint's illuminating discussion of the double perspective contained in *Annales* 1.9–10 (Quint 1993, 80–1).

that spelled the rout of Theban pride before his intervention. In all this (as noted at the beginning of this chapter) he merely retraces the process by which the wolf, her nurseling fratricide Romulus, and his victim Remus[46] become the icons of Roman identity and dignity.[47]

But how exactly does he work his magic? In essence, by an act of will imposed linguistically upon the slippery links between epistemology and (putative) ontology. The last two chapters, on Narcissus and Echo, unfolded the complicated relations between knowing and being both from a Kantian and a Hegelian perspective— yet from neither vantage could we reach a discrete, organic, transparent identity under which nymph or boy could shelter (as Woman or Man, self or other, even animate or inanimate). Both Narcissus and Echo kept dispersing into heterogeneous collections of contradictory properties further divided among disparate sites. Cold/passionate, shadow/image, bone/stone, voice/sound revolved unlocatably around, within, and between their two bodies and their

---

[46] David Konstan notes (*per litteras*) that Pentheus' iconic serpent also recapitulates the *Aeneid*'s staging of a crucial, aboriginal, and internally contradictory element of *Romanitas*—the Latins. Against Latinus' claim that his people enjoy Golden Age innocence—they need no laws to restrain themselves (*Aen.* 7.201–4)—arises the violence and passion they display in their war on the Trojans (cf. O'Hara 2007, 96– 8). And as Pentheus' snake and its offspring the Spartoi are native to Boeotia and crucial to forming Thebes, the Latins are native to Italy and crucial to forming Rome. In fact, Aeneas' enraged attack on Turnus reads as his becoming Turnus: native fury becomes the model for Vergil's invader hero. Moreover, killing Turnus reflects on earth what Jove has engineered in the heavens—the Trojans' reconciliation with Juno. Now her worthy subjects, they act out the very *ira* she has represented throughout the poem. Ovid reproduces and distorts both aspects of Aeneas' gesture when he has Pentheus explicitly invoke the brutal snake as his own model of Theban quintessence, and then treat Acoetes brutally. Pentheus not only emulates the worst aspects of the serpent, he also proves himself a fitting reflection of his divine adversary and cousin Bacchus' savagery.

[47] It may be alleged against this reading that Pentheus' oration does not, in fact, work at all: none of his subjects is persuaded to abandon the worship of Bacchus, and even those closest to him—his grandfather Cadmus, his uncle Athamas, his familiars—all try to dissuade him from his opposition to Bacchus (3.564–5). But as noted above, whether the Thebans and the other Cadmeioi's deference to Bacchus is a matter of free choice is unclear. Whether or not Pentheus' subjects are compelled to ignore him and worship Bacchus, my argument does not depend upon the persuasiveness of the king's speech. Rather, it turns upon the way Pentheus' oration mirrors the rhetoric of Roman national identity and patriotism, albeit in absurdly exaggerated fashion, as dramatized (and ironized) in the *Aeneid*, for example.

(visual and vocal) reflections—and all these properties were additionally scattered between the worlds of the quick and the dead. But the two Boeotians simply illustrated in particularly eye-catching fashion the problem of identity posed by any entity. Žižek frames this dilemma succinctly: if we decompose an object into its ingredients, we can find no specific feature that makes of it a unique, self-identical thing, no 'X factor' to bind together its multitude of properties into a discrete whole. With regard to its properties and ingredients, a thing is 'wholly outside itself', scattered among its external conditions. Every positive feature of the thing is already present in the circumstances that are not yet this thing. So how do we extract identity from this congeries of properties and conditions?

Both Kant and Hegel ponder how cognition produces identity; their solutions differ slightly in perspective, but correspond in mechanism. Lacan's *point de capiton* crucially depends on the two philosophers' point of convergence: for both, the supplementary operation that overcomes this conceptual deadlock and produces from a bundle of features a unique, self-identical thing is a purely symbolic, tautological gesture. In Kant's analytic of pure reason, the mathematical synthesis (concerned with quantity and quality) gathers together all the object's phenomenal properties. Only then can the dynamical synthesis (whose domain is relations of causality and dependence) organize these properties into an intelligible whole, a discrete entity. It does so by referring the manifold of appearances to a purely putative unity, to the transcendental object. The latter is an object posited as existing in itself *beyond the mere thought of it*, and believed to be in some way based upon the noumenal thing-in-itself. By definition, then, the transcendental object is not a possible object of experience, it is an algebraic X that is thinkable, but unknowable. Similarly, Hegel's 'return of the thing to itself' describes a twofold, simultaneous process: (1) the positing of external conditions as the conditions and exponents of the thing and (2) the presupposition of the existence of a ground to hold together this multitude of conditions. Each philosopher traces a circular process whereby the gathering together of phenomena *itself* produces as retrospective effect an objectal surplus. This surplus is the mysterious X that is both the ground of their appearance, and the essence that glues together the scattered properties of the thing into the thing. The unsettling conclusion is that, in order to define a thing, we must include the name of the object within its definition.[48]

And that is exactly how Pentheus gets lucky, managing to pull a chimerical 'Thebanness' out of the disparate and unpromising properties of the monster snake: blood-lust, truculence, and territoriality. He simply posits Thebanness as their ground, their unifying X factor—an essence that, because he refers it to the city's prehistory, appears anchored in the immutable. The quilting point (S1) is exactly that act of positing, of naming as itself an act of definition, in which the signifier falls into the signified.[49] Moreover, in a heroic act of circular reasoning, Pentheus essentially says, 'All these properties make the snake Theban; its Thebanness produces all these properties; ergo, qua markers of its *Thebanitas*, these properties are admirable and exemplary.' If we had cherished any nostalgic hope that a substantive, logical basis might exist in which to ground 'Thebanness', 'Romanness', 'Man', 'Woman', and the rest of the charged identities we have surveyed in previous chapters, Pentheus' sleight of hand will have dashed them quite. The king's sophistic harangue lays bare the arbitrary, performative gesture that constitutes identity both individual and collective.[50]

But Pentheus' legerdemain with the quilting point, however breathtaking, bears on more than Theban history, more even than the conceptual basis for identity. It draws into its conceptual sphere the regulation of the human community. Pentheus' speech sheds light on the dangerously plastic borderline between the Vergilian princes and leaders against whom Anderson quite naturally measures him. It illuminates the line between an Aeneas and a Mezentius—which is to say, between just and unjust rule—and discloses the

---

[48] Žižek 1993, 148–53.

[49] Žižek 1993, 148.

[50] Certainly the snake is quintessentially associated with the foundation of Thebes, and to that extent Pentheus' choice of patriotic symbol may seem less than arbitrary. But the virginal cow who led Cadmus to the site of the future city was also crucial to the city's foundation, and Pentheus passes over her without a word. Why choose the creature upon whose *destruction* hangs the future city's fate as the emblem of that city, rather than the numinous creature who peacefully guided her founder? Seemingly because Pentheus needs an icon of martiality to inspire opposition to Bacchus—but that very fit between expedience and Pentheus' revision of the snake points up the arbitrary nature of his choice.

different dimensions of the law that measures both. In Pentheus'
speech, the serpent's slaughter of Cadmus' men becomes the paradigm for what is *dulce et decorum*: emulating his territoriality
preserves what Pentheus calls the 'honour of the fatherland' ('pat-
rium . . . decus', 3.548). Feral violence furnishes the paradigm for law
and the model for Pentheus' iron enforcement of proper Thebanness.
For example, once Pentheus' men have captured Bacchus' defenceless
follower Acoetes, the king does not hesitate to 'protect' Thebes by
threatening his captive with torture and death. Before he has
even heard what Acoetes has to say in his own defence, Pentheus
offers him torture with iron and fire (3.692–8). These deadly punishments offer to be fully as gruesome as those Cadmus' men suffered
when the serpent butchered and suffocated and poisoned them
(3.48–9). I mentioned above how Pentheus' transvaluation of the
Theban past exalts the murderous dragon as the paragon of the
Theban citizen, and as the embodiment of the masculinist, martial
values he believes constitute ideal Thebanness. But Pentheus himself
adopts the serpent's sanguinary habits in his brutish summary judgement of Acoetes: he thereby also miraculously converts crime
into law, by converting murder into capital punishment.[51]

Pentheus' speech and his draconianism point to law's origin in
crime: law constitutes the ultimate crime insofar as its foundation is a
form of radical violence. The law demands our obedience regardless
of our subjective appreciation of its rationality, morality, or utility.[52]
Certainly, the idea of law as radical violence paradigmatically controls Ovid's Theban narrative, as we have often seen in analysing
other stories from the cycle. For the 'crime' of killing the monstrous
serpent, thereby defending himself and avenging his men, some

[51] That Pentheus construes Acoetes' adherence to Bacchus' worship as a crime is
indicated by the facts that (*a*) Ovid describes him as barely able to put off the
moment when he can extract a *poena* ('penalty') from Acoetes (3.578); *poena* can
mean 'recompense', but since Acoetes has not taken any physical object from
Pentheus, his 'compensation' has to be for crossing the king's will, *ipso facto* a
crime in the eyes of the tyrant; (*b*) Pentheus wants Acoetes' torture and death to be
an example for others (3.579–80)—the quintessential Roman rationale for capital
punishment (as Anderson 1997 points out, 396), which in turn construes Acoetes'
following Bacchus as a capital crime.
[52] Cf. Žižek 1991*a*, 34.

unspecified divine power changes Cadmus and his wife Harmonia into snakes (4.563–603, discussed in greater detail below). For accidentally having stumbled upon her bath, Diana transforms Actaeon into a stag to be killed by his own hounds (3.138–252; Chapter 2). For harbouring his motherless infant nephew, Bacchus, Juno drives Athamas to murder his younger son, while his wife hurls herself and his elder son into the sea (4.420–542; Chapter 3). In the Theban cycle, acts of self-defence, accident, or pity all regularly earn the same punishment: complete degradation, most often into animal form, usually followed by death. Ovid himself offers the reader a sceptical view of such precisianism when he exonerates Actaeon from blame: the Theban prince's story reveals a misdeed owed to chance, not to criminal intention ('fortunae crimen in illo | non scelus inuenies', 3.141–2). Here Ovid lays down a principle—evaluation of intent— that if applied categorically, vindicates nearly all the suffering Cadmeioi. He even evokes compassion for the less unwitting: just before Pentheus is torn apart by his own, the king tries to move his aunt Autonoë's pity by invoking her son Actaeon's near-identical fate (3.719–20). Conjuring up the explicitly exculpated Actaeon implies that even if Pentheus were guilty, yet like Actaeon he was punished far beyond his due.

Given that the gods exact the punishments I have mentioned, we might conclude they demonstrate nothing more than the generally petty and vengeful nature of Ovid's divinities.[53] But that would ignore the fact that the gods' inflexible defence of their own prerogatives conforms precisely to the chief principle of juridical thought: law is an absolute, and must be obeyed without question. Ancient philosophers and moralists regularly offer evidence of this. For example, in the fourth century, Plato has Socrates articulate this principle in the *Crito*; roughly three centuries later, it echoes again in Cicero's *De Officiis*; in the next generation, it finds expression in Livy's *Ab Urbe Condita*. Socrates refuses the chance to escape from his

---

[53] As Brooks Otis does: he includes the Theban cycle within a chapter entitled 'The Avenging Gods' (Otis 1970, 128–65). In the *Metamorphoses* stories the chapter analyses, Otis states that 'the problem of theodicy is seen, largely, from the human side'; Ovid's gods are 'types of puritanical severity, unbridled jealousy, or merciless power' (Otis 1970, 128, 165).

prison and to evade the punishment Athens has pronounced upon him. He defends his obedience to the laws that have condemned him to death, but not on the grounds that they are correct, that they realize some insight into Socrates' dangerous and pernicious character, some rational reason why Socrates should be eliminated. He alleges merely that the laws are necessary: the state would collapse without unswerving adherence to them (*Cri.* 50a–b). In essence, Socrates says we must obey the law on the basis of a tautology: we obey not because the law is true—not because it embodies principles of goodness or wisdom or beneficence or fairness—but solely because it is the law. Cicero similarly praises Regulus for honouring his oath to return to Carthage to submit to torture and death, even though the oath was given to an enemy and under duress. He commends Regulus' self-destructive choice because it protects the sacredness of oath-taking, which Cicero regards as fundamental to law (*Off.* 3.102–11). Livy offers Lucretia as another unswerving paragon. Praised as surpassing her peers in womanly virtue,[54] after being raped by Sextus Tarquinius Lucretia exacts from herself the punishment the law would demand of adulterous women. Lack of consent offers no amelioration of the facts in her eyes. Such arbitrary violence visited upon innocent persons makes the law that Plato, Cicero, and Livy revere substantively if not formally indistinguishable from crime in its mindless cruelty.[55]

---

[54] A surprise visit from the Roman princes to their wives reveals all but Lucretia engaged in dissipation; she alone is found working chastely at woolmaking. 'Mulieb-ris certaminis laus penes Lucretiam fuit' (Livy 1.57.9) ('The victory in their contest of wives belonged to Lucretia').

[55] One might allege against reading Socrates, Cicero, and Livy as aligning law implicitly with crime that juridical constraint is only criminal from the perspective of its effect on individuals, as opposed to the larger group. However, to say so does not reduce the brutality of the law. When Socrates rejects the possibility of escaping his condemnation by going into exile, he does not refute the injustice or cruelty of his sentence, nor deny its sequelae—that his children will grow up without a father, that his friends will be both bereft and contemned for having failed to save him (*Cri.* 45c5–46a8). Rather, he defends his decision to stay and be executed via a two-pronged argument. First, he agreed to abide by Athens' juridical precepts in deed if not in word by the mere fact of having lived all his life in Athens; accordingly, he must now accept the consequences (51c6–53a7). Second, outside the community ruled by legislation, no life exists worth living for any human being (53c2–54a1). This

The authoritarian gesture that conceptually founds the law accomplishes what Pentheus' speech regarding the monster snake had earlier effected: a chiastic exchange of properties between putative antipodes. Just as the snake's odious qualities are transformed into patriotic beatitudes, so the absolute criminal gesture that subtends the law excludes all other, specific crimes. The implied imperative, 'obey without regard for justice!' exchanges these particular crimes against the universal crime that pertains to law itself and makes them into its supposed opposition.[56]

Illuminated by this perspective on juridical thought, Pentheus' savage and arbitrary behaviour toward those who oppose his will can be seen to embody, not an aberration from the law, as Anderson declares ('he abuses the true values of Vergil's poem'),[57] but rather its purest embodiment, law that reveals its origins in crime. Poor unlovely Pentheus becomes thereby Roman epic's one

---

social-contract model makes no brief for the law's beneficence even for the group; it only points to worse terrors howling round the anarchic city's borders.

Cicero evidences greater discomfort than Socrates when facing the logical extrapolation of the law's absolute status. For example, he praises Manlius Torquatus Imperiosus as 'one of the greatest of the great' ('magnus uir in primis', *Off.* 3.112), yet concludes his portrait on a more qualified note. We know from other sources that Manlius executed his son while campaigning against the Latins, because he had disobeyed his father's orders not to attack the foe—this despite the youth's triumph over an enemy commander in a bravely fought single combat (cf. Livy 8.6.1–8.7.22, Sall. *Cat.* 52.30–1, August. *De Civ. D.* 1.23). Even a strict constructionist such as Cicero cannot quite stomach so stringent an application of the law; he concludes that Manlius was 'cruelly severe to his son' ('acerbe seuerus in filium', *Off.* 3.112).

Far more than either Cicero or Socrates, Livy dramatizes the inherent cruelty of the law by spelling out the consequences of strict interpretation. For example, while Rome's Twelve Tables of laws are being written and the decemvirs rule, the ten governors are praised as most just when they soften the law, but cursed as 'ten Tarquins' once they begin to interpret it strictly. The quintessential example of such self-serving literalism allows the arch-villain among the decemvirs, Appius Claudius, to gain power over the freeborn Verginia while her father is abroad on military duty. Diabolically, he does so not by abrogating the law, but by following it to the letter. He takes advantage of the fact that Verginia herself has no legal status whereby she may plead her case; the decision goes by default to the plaintiff, a creature of Appius'. See Janan 2001, 150–1, for a fuller discussion of the scepticism towards the law sketched in the Appius–Verginia tale.

[56] On the conceptual equivalence of law and crime, see Žižek 1991a, 29–31, 37–8, 40–1.

[57] Anderson 1997, 392.

'honest politician': his behaviour transparently reflects the savage and secret commerce between seeming opposites on which the very idea of the polity, of the lawfully ordered human community, ineluctably rests.[58]

THE WIFE OF GOD

The Theban king is inspired to such savagery by contemplation of his antithesis, the god Bacchus and his worship. The austerely masculine, Theban adult despot rails against the perfumed effeminacy of the Asiatic boy-god. Bacchus (in Pentheus' eyes) offends against Thebes' protocols of manly belligerence (3.553–6), and he offends the gods: Bacchus commits sacrilege by pretending to a divinity he does not in fact possess (3.557–8). Pentheus broadly represents himself and Bacchus as law ranged against licence, masculinity against femininity. Yet when Bacchus' devotee Acoetes narrates his conversion to Bacchus' worship, he reveals the conceptual ground on which Pentheus and Bacchus meet and uncannily mirror one another (3.582–691). Both god and king again enable the wondrous transformation of one conceptual element in the discursive field into its contrary.

Ovid draws upon several sources for Acoetes' story: Euripides' *Bacchae* for the encounter between enraged king and devotee, the *Homeric Hymn to Dionysus* for the conversion tale. Yet it is from Pacuvius' lost Latin *Pentheus* that Ovid draws the name for his convert (recorded in Servius Auctus on *Aen.* 4.469). Curiously, only

---

[58] Konstan has shown how Cicero's speeches against Catiline, when contextualized by other accounts of the so-called Catilinarian conspiracy, reveal the same vertigo in seemingly opposed terms (Konstan 1993). As hard as Cicero tries to distinguish himself and his political side from Catiline, the basic oppositions with which he works—public good/individual wilfulness, *boni/improbi*, insider/outsider—simply will not remain stable in the slippery realm of the Symbolic. For example, Cicero repeatedly urges Catiline to relieve Rome of her fears on his behalf by leaving the city. Though Cicero thus strives to make Catiline the ultimate outsider—his exit will confirm his wilful opposition to Rome's good—Sallust records that Catiline's response portrayed Cicero as the opportunistic *arriviste*. Calling his opponent a 'naturalized immigrant', Catiline depicts for the Senate a jumped-up Volscian nobody calumniating a native, patrician Roman for his own private ends (*Cat.* 31).

the name. H. J. Rose has cogently argued that Horace, *Epistles* 1.16.73–8 reflects Pacuvius' transformation of Euripides' votary. Behind the threats of Horace's Pentheus to confiscate the devotee's property, Rose sees Euripides' impoverished, itinerant foreign priest become Pacuvius' native, settled property-owner. Not a hint of that change makes its way into the *Metamorphoses*.[59] Odder still is the sense of what Ovid does borrow: *akoitēs* means 'husband, bed-fellow'—ironically so for Acoetes, who never speaks of a wife or even a lover. Before his religious conversion, as a poor, itinerant helmsman, he depicts only fellow sailors as companions. Post-conversion, his consuming relation is to Bacchus, for whom he shows a quasi-spousal devotion. Having joined the cult of Bacchus on Naxos and ever since been a regular adherent (*Met.* 3.691), he has followed the god all the way round the southern Aegean from Chios by way of Naxos to Thebes. Yet his own conversion-tale roots this hyperdulia in a terror and loss of control that shows Acoetes more the wife than the husband of God. Though described as 'fearless' ('metu uacuus', 3.582) before the seething and formidable Pentheus, Acoetes describes a pre-conversion apprehensiveness verging on paranoia—a fearfulness the ancients quintessentially associated with women.[60] He and his crew bound for Delos are forced one day to land on Chios; when Acoetes sends the others to find water, they lead back to the ship a pretty but inebriated young boy they plan to kidnap. Acoetes assumes this little boy to be a god, though he gives us no specific reason why he should think so. He claims that the boy's appearance and gait do not seem compatible with mortality ('nil ibi quod credi posset mortale uidebam', 3.610), but does not specify what exactly about Bacchus implies more than a drunken pre-pubescent (*Met.* 3.607–14). No other member of the crew notices any suspicious sign. Acoetes argues vigorously against the sailors' plans for abduction,

---

[59] It is always possible, though improbable, that another Republican dramatist also used the name 'Acoetes' in a play about the confrontation between Pentheus and Bacchus; we know that Accius wrote a tragedy on the theme. However, my point would remain valid: Ovid bases his version upon Euripides' *Bacchae* and the *Homeric Hymn to Dionysus*, both of which make the devotee nameless. Whether Ovid borrowed the name from Pacuvius or from someone else, his addition to the ancient Greek sources that he otherwise follows so closely cries out for an explanation.

[60] Cf. e.g. Xenophon, *Oeconomicus* 7.25.

but they repulse him with near-murderous force. Lycabas wordlessly punches Acoetes in the throat, nearly knocking him into the sea, while the rest of the sailors approve the deed and deride their helmsman's tears (*Met.* 3.623–9, 656–7). When the crew insist that Acoetes steer away from Naxos (the boy's requested destination), he refuses to have any part in guiding the ship; another sailor takes the helm (3.644–9). In the midst of these proceedings, Acoetes says that he had 'long been weeping' ('iamdudum flebam', 3.656), a failure of self-control also supposed characteristic of women.[61] He continues to sink more deeply into panic while watching Bacchus play cat and mouse with the sailors ('inludens', 3.650). Pretending ignorance of the sailors' plan to kidnap him, the god feigns tearful helplessness when he 'discovers' their intentions. Eventually Bacchus terrifies the sailors by causing tigers, panthers, and lynxes to appear on the ship. The men leap overboard, maddened either with fear or by the god, and are changed into dolphins.

Acoetes' feminizing emotionalism starkly contrasts with the brawny, aggressive bluffness of his fellow sailors. But Acoetes' intuition of Bacchus' divinity is also feminine in the Lacanian sense, precisely because he cannot cite an evidentiary basis for his belief. He makes a claim to knowledge unable to account for its own truth-value by the rules of reason. However, the 'rules of reason' are only a subset of the laws of Symbolic substitution recognized by a given community. They no more than the barred Symbolic can produce discrete, flawless 'knowledge' with which to represent the world wholly and accurately—an S2 truly and completely complementary to S1. For example, the insights that accrue to mysticism, prophecy, divine possession all fall outside the rules of reason, yet can hardly be dismissed as insignificant. Not by accident are all these forms of knowledge historically associated with the feminine; they exemplify the grounds on which ~~The~~ Woman views sceptically the institutions and rules that constitute the Symbolic, and that lead Her to reject its universalist claims. So when Acoetes claims to know what reason says he cannot know—when he simply divines the divine—his assertion firmly aligns him with the feminine.

---

[61] Cf. Richlin 2001.

But Acoetes does not remain in the feminine, either in his comportment or his thought. What he witnesses on the ship transforms him from a timid soul to a calm believer who can confront a raging king without fear. From that epiphany onwards, Acoetes' dauntless, dry-eyed calm characterizes him as Stoically masculine. Prior to the signs and wonders Bacchus performs on the ship, the violence his fellow sailors offer Acoetes reduces him to no more than passive resistance (e.g. refusing to steer). Afterwards, Bacchus' command to be fearless has preternatural effect: even Pentheus' threats of death and torture leave Acoetes undisturbed (3.579–82, 694–5). Though supernatural forces eventually free Acoetes from Pentheus' bonds, his recitation before the king indicates no prescience of rescue that might calm the captive. Nowhere in the *Metamorphoses* does Bacchus promise his adherents protection.

A divinely catalysed, radical change in perspective is familiar to classical readers from various initiation tales (of which we can see some reflection—albeit second-order and artistically elaborated—in such examples as the *Odyssey*'s 'Telemacheia', the *Homeric Hymn to Demeter*, and Catullus 63).[62] However, Ovid here puts this mechanism to specific ideological usage by unfolding the logic that makes the convert Acoetes' bravery possible. The same logic allowed Pentheus to use Thebes' noxious original serpent as the rallying cry for Theban identity; both conversions depend on the operation of the quilting point. Acoetes' tale reveals that the god in whom he reposes his faith as the worthiest object of worship bound Acoetes to himself precisely by demonstrating his divine monstrosity. Bacchus does not simply punish his would-be persecutors, he toys with them by feigning helplessness at the very moment he plans to terrify and madden them, then degrade them into beasts. Beside Bacchus, all other monsters pale into nothingness.

---

[62] In the first four books of the *Odyssey* (often called the 'Telemacheia'), the goddess Athena arranges and oversees the experiences that sweep Telemachus over the line between self-conscious boyhood and commanding maturity; the *Homeric Hymn to Demeter* has the disguised goddess reveal herself to Metaneira, converting the mortal's fears that the 'stranger' was trying to kill her baby son into devotion to the goddess's mysteries (*HHDem.* 242–300); Catullus 63 narrates the Greek boy Attis' spurning of his former privileged and urbane life, flight from home, and self-castration under the goddess Cybele's influence.

Acoetes' tale shows Bacchus undergoing a transformation similar to that of the monstrous serpent: the 'jovial sower of the grape' ('genialis consitor uuae', 4.14) splits between himself and his shadow-self, the terrifying monster who is Bacchus' dark underside. In the moment of apprehending most completely Bacchus' divine nature ('God is...'), Bacchus-as-feline-sadist cancels Acoetes' earthly misery by showing him that behind the multitude of earthly horrors gleems the infinitely more frightening horror of divine wrath ('...God'). In revealing his full powers, becoming most purely himself, Bacchus excludes all his particular properties that promise ease to human cares, and becomes the negation of his nepenthean self, becomes the god of destructive fury—which Acoetes finds strangely comforting. Now earthly terrors have transubstantiated into so many manifestations of divine anger.[63] Even a seemingly spontaneous demonstration of evil—the sailors' plans to profit from kidnapping a child—assumes its place in the divine order as a pretext for manifesting the god's wrath. Suddenly, 'it all makes sense': the *facta bruta* of existence have meaning and conform (reassuringly) to an order, an order anchored by Bacchus as quilting point.[64]

---

[63] Cf. Žižek 1991*a*, 17.

[64] Acoetes' conversion revisits the fundamental question raised by one of the most puzzling moments of the *Aeneid*: how is it that what calms Aeneas in the midst of Troy's destruction and confirms his faith in divine providence is the revelation of pure evil? Aeneas tells Dido of his stumbling upon Helen hiding in the temple of Vesta as he rushes in despair through crumbling Troy. He contemplates killing Helen as the putative cause of his city's demise. But Venus stops him by revealing to her son's sight who is really destroying Troy: the gods themselves, busy hacking away at the city's walls. Having witnessed this, Aeneas spares Helen (*Aen.* 2.567–636). There is a lapse in the text here, marked by half-lines (*Aen.* 2.614, 623), perhaps revealing that Vergil himself could not quite smoothly negotiate sense from the hideous vision of divinity bent on human destruction. Yet bizarrely, his hero can: after Venus' apocalypse of devils, Aeneas serenely declares that he reached his home safely 'with a god leading me' ('ducente deo', *Aen.* 2.632). Unlike Acoetes, he cannot retain this calm faith: he no sooner reaches home and finds his father Anchises refusing to flee Troy than a frenzy to take up arms again and die fighting seizes him, despite Creusa's pleas to the contrary. It takes another divine intervention—the unconsuming fire that sprouts on Ascanius' hair—to galvanize the family's exit from the city, a sign that Anchises, not Aeneas, reads as promising heaven's direction for their exile (*Aen.* 2.655–704).

That transformation 'makes a man out of Acoetes' in more ways than one: the ordering principle at work here is epistemologically masculine. The wrath of God quilts all the heterogeneous phenomena of the world in relation to one exceptional point. Bacchus becomes for Acoetes S1, the One signifier for whom all other signifiers represent the subject. In relation to Bacchus, Acoetes can make sense not only of the world, but of his place within its newly discovered divine order of terror. Bacchus thus converts the heterogeneous phenomena of the world into (the chain of) knowledge, into what passes for S2, the signifier whose perfect complementarity and binarity to S1 is primordially foreclosed. When Acoetes puts on this androgynous god, he conjures the glittering mirage of Man and Woman arrayed as perfect epistemological dyad and perfect calm.

GOD-SLEIGHT

Though not tightly connected by plot to the Pentheus episode, Cadmus' encounters with godhead frame Ovid's Theban cycle both formally (they begin and end the cycle) and conceptually. Their content sets the chief terms for Thebes' history: intimate conflict and divine vengeance (Chapters 1 and 2). Cadmus' experiences resonate particularly with his grandson Pentheus' vicissitudes, which centre the cycle and are its longest subsection. Cadmus' relations with the divine paradoxically combine the logic of Pentheus' story with that of Acoetes'. He reaps punishment such as rewarded Pentheus' militant atheism, but receives it for an act of faith comparable to Acoetes' conversion. As mentioned in Chapter 2, a mysterious voice admonishes Cadmus for 'staring' at the monstrous serpent he has killed, warning him that he will eventually be a serpent, too. Years later, reviewing the misfortunes of his city and family, Cadmus comes to regard his sorrows as divinely caused, punishment for his having killed the snake (4.563–73). Cadmus exclaims, 'quem si cura deum tam certa uindicat ira, I ipse, precor, serpens in longam porrigar aluum' ('if it is the gods' concern to avenge this with their inexorable wrath, may I myself be stretched out at length upon my belly as a snake!' 4.574–5). He immediately is so transformed, as is his wife Harmonia.

The process of transformation clearly inflicts grief upon the couple. Cadmus weeps and tries to speak to his wife, while Harmonia beats her breast and hysterically admonishes her husband to doff this new shape; she then asks the gods to transform her, too. Yet Ovid both progressively calms and sexualizes the process of transformation. Cadmus-snake caresses his wife's lips with his newly divided tongue, slides between her breasts 'as if he knew them' and embraces her (4.595–7). As her horrified attendants look on, she placidly fondles the new snake's smooth neck. Suddenly she becomes a snake and the two serpents coil about each other in a way that Aristotle described as characteristic of snakes mating (*HA* 5.4, 540^{a}33–540^{b}5). The two serpents then glide to a lair in the nearby glade.

In representing the two new serpents' transformation as erotically charged and capped by lovemaking, Ovid recalls the copulating snakes whose eye-catching image marked Thebes' most cynical perspective on relations between Man and Woman. Tiresias abuses a pair of mating serpents at either end of his career as a woman; his transgender experience supposedly ratifies his asymmetrical allocation of sexual pleasure between men and women (Chapter 4). Yet what the snakes allow Tiresias to 'know' signally fails to bring either peace or sexual harmony to the monarchs of Heaven. Why then does snakehood confer upon Cadmus and Harmonia a loving, passionate, complete concord that escapes both gods and humans? How did they apparently achieve the sexual relation that 'does not exist'?

The raw material for this halcyon outcome is certainly unpromising. For the reader, the transformation retrospectively darkens the already grim view adumbrated in Acoetes' tale, of divinity as the malign *primum mobile* of existence (a malevolence of which the poor sailor appears serenely unaware). Cadmus' 'conversion experience' robs him of his human status just as surely as Pentheus' belligerent incredulity robbed the younger king of the same (at least in the Bacchants' maddened eyes). Moreover (as Stephen Wheeler notes), Cadmus' theodicy is entirely erroneous. Thebes' catastrophes have nothing to do with the slain snake; they result from other causes— quarrels between Juno and Jupiter, Diana's prickly modesty, and

Bacchus' savagery against unbelievers.[65] Yet the fact that Cadmus' prayer brings about his and his wife's metamorphoses speciously confirms his assumption that the various human miseries visited upon Thebes and the Cadmeioi avenge the snake's death. The unexpected boon? Now the overall order of things appears intelligible: the metamorphoses 'prove' Thebes to be the victim, not of random malevolence, but of comprehensible (if savage) retribution. In that respect, Cadmus' disastrous prayer functionally and structurally mirrors Acoetes' conversion tale and Pentheus' exhortation to the ecstatic Thebans: each takes disparate, terrifying phenomena and quilts them into a comprehensible and ameliorating narrative.

Yet the price of that calming fallacy is high: unlike his grandson or Bacchus' devotee, Cadmus' narrative expels him from the human sphere of existence and agency. Cadmus' self-indicting wager with the gods evidences the third turn of the quilting mechanism: in the logic of his prayer and its answer, the quilting point takes the form of the scapegoat, the single explanation for evil that can and must be banished, unlike the avenging god or numinous serpent. Like the alchemy that converts Bacchus' savagery into a world-order apparent only to the faithful, and the serpent's violence into the originary lineaments of ideal Thebanness, Cadmus' transformation converts the heterogeneous data of cruelty and violence at Thebes into a sensible narrative. Now firm orientation replaces bafflement. The scapegoat becomes the poisonous figure who has brought evil upon the land, and (like Bacchus, like the snake) thus constitutes the supplementary fear that banishes fear.[66] To be sure, only in Cadmus' eyes does his sacrifice balance the books for Thebes as a whole. Yet his self-designation as scapegoat brings post-transformation peace to himself and to his wife; they are described as 'peaceful' because they 'remember what they were before' ('quidque prius fuerint *placidi* meminere dracones', 4.603).[67] By making himself the retrospective

---

[65] Juno avenges herself on Semele, her family, their progeny and familiars (3.256–312, 4.420–562); Diana destroys Actaeon (3.138–252); Bacchus retaliates against any who challenge his godhead (3.511–731). See Wheeler 2000, 96–7.

[66] Cf. Žižek 1991*a*, 16–18.

[67] When used of animals, *placidus* means 'tame, quiet, friendly'; but Cadmus and Harmonia retain their human memory and remain both gentle and fearless with people. This vestigial humanity implies that, when applied to them, the word also

object of fear, even on false premisses, Cadmus has banished his own and Harmonia's fear.

Cadmus' metamorphosis curiously recapitulates and extends the principles behind the iron law sketched in his nephew Pentheus' tyranny. The axiom that law requires obedience without regard for our subjective appreciation of its justice, and is therefore a special instance of crime, is most purely realized where punishment accrues to the blameless. Cadmus is just such an innocent victim, all the more a martyr in that he believes himself guilty and derives comfort therefrom. But what also deserves our attention is the homology between the dilemmas that Cadmus and his nephew confront. Ultimately, both kings deny that 'there is no sexual relation'. Pentheus furnishes the more obvious instance: his objurgations against Bacchus' worship single out the male citizens and decry their emasculation, implying that the proper relation between the sexes is distinct and complementary, not confused and mutually destabilizing. When he offers the monstrous serpent's example to help restore this relation, the king evidences his belief that Man and Woman can exist as two parts of a harmonious, organic whole. Merely contingent, historical circumstances have prevented this at Thebes (namely, the incursion of a degenerate divine pretender), not a structural impediment; male Thebans' copying the snake's 'virile citizenship' will solve the problem. *Mutatis mutandis*, Cadmus' offer to the gods to take all Thebes' guilt upon himself rests on denying that 'there is no political relation'. Cadmus implies that his city could have cohered as an organic, harmonous Whole, were it not for the purely adventitious, his killing of the monstrous serpent. Both kings' gestures demonstrate the workings of ideology par excellence: they explain away evidence of a structural impediment to the world working 'as it should' by attributing failure to unfortunate concrete circumstances.[68]

Little wonder, then, that the transformed, amorous Cadmus and Harmonia iconically rehabilitate those other snakes, whom Tiresias rudely disturbs in their sexual relation. The transsexual knowledge

---

connotes what it regularly does when used of human beings: 'free from stress, quiet, peaceful' (*OLD* s.v. *placidus* 2a, 4c).

[68] Cf. Žižek 1996, 31.

Tiresias gains by striking the mating snakes offers no basis on which Man and Woman could form a whole; he most un-Solomonically 'divides the baby', installing a fundamental asymmetry between the two sexes. No surprise that his refereeing drives Jupiter and Juno farther apart. But where Tiresias reifies antagonism, Cadmus offers to vindicate it. The king's self-sacrifice proposes to redeem the political disharmony that has divided citizen from citizen, brother from brother, god from mortal and god from god at Thebes. All these instances of petty jealousy, rivalry, inequality that the 'organically harmonious polity' can never fully expunge, and that evidence the impossibility of the political relation, revolve around the same unassimilable remainder: foreclosed and guilty knowledge of the polity's origins (*every* polity's origins) in a founding act of violence. The underside of the law, whose austere compulsion governs and unites the community, is sadism and cruelty (Chapters 1 and 2). Knowledge excluded from the Symbolic symptomatically produces not only ~~The~~ Woman, but also ~~The~~ City, as two loci of scepticism directed toward the specious totalities of The Perfect Couple and Utopia respectively. But when Cadmus' offer of himself reconfigures discord into redeemable happenstance, his naïve gesture of healing appropriately changes himself and Harmonia into snakes who *do* form an organic, harmonious whole, however erroneous the assumptions behind the king's sacrificial wager. The couple's post-transformation happiness is perhaps a small reward for Cadmus' 'raising the stakes' on Pentheus' ideological gesture by offering himself, rather than a captive devotee, as surety for his vision of the coherent city.

But does that not make Cadmus an Oedipus *avant la lettre*? When I discussed Oedipus-as-scapegoat in Chapter 4, I argued that Ovid had specifically excluded Cadmus' great-great grandson from the Theban cycle, because the poet did not want to introduce the alluring idea that negation could be embodied and cleanly rejected. Nor does he here. However Cadmus' transformation may impress himself, the Theban founder's assumption of the scapegoat role will not support such an idea, because we (the readers) know no causal connection exists between killing Mars' serpent and Thebes' disasters. That pure irrelation is even more profoundly disturbing than Oedipus' blundering into transgression. For us, Cadmus' and Harmonia's transfigurations, however calming to the king and queen themselves, evidence a universe inhabited by a nameless divinity far more mal-evolent than any we have yet seen in the Theban cycle. This *numen* doubly wrongs humans by letting them believe their animal trans-formations were caused by their own guilt. Moreover, Ovid's refusal to specify what divine power changes the couple into snakes robs the transformation of any intelligible motive, making the act appear pure malice.[69] The petty infighting of the gods in and around Thebes suddenly is dwarfed by this maleficent anonymity. Thebes is even more poisonously haunted than we had thought.

The last we hear of the Cadmeioi is the 'great consolation' Bacchus' expanding worship offers his grandparents Cadmus and Harmonia for their changed shape: he has defeated now-worshipful India, and his temples are thronged in Greece (4.604–6). One wonders why the former king and queen of Thebes would rejoice in yet another territory besieged and forcibly subdued by divinity as their city has been. But then, it is hardly less wondrous that Vergil's king should rejoice in the violent deeds of *his* offspring: lifting Vulcan's shield anchored by the she-wolf and her feral nurselings, Aeneas unwit-tingly rejoices in a Roman future charged with various versions of the

---

[69]   At the beginning of Book 3, Ovid had called the serpent 'Mars' snake' ('Martius anguis', 3.32), elliptically evoking the tradition that makes the snake sacred to the war-god and its death a source of anger to him (attested by, e.g., a scholion to the Iliad, *ΣA Il.* 2.494 = 4F51, and Euripides' *Phoenissae*, 931–5). Nonetheless, he nowhere specifies that the divine voice that predicts Cadmus' transformation after he has slain the snake belongs to Mars. Moreover, mythic tradition offers no evidence of a causal connection between the serpent's death and Cadmus' transformation. Our evidence is admittedly imperfect: of the extant sources that precede Ovid, Euripides' *Bacchae* has Bacchus cryptically refer to Cadmus' and Harmonia's changing into snakes as 'what the oracle of Zeus says' ('chrēsmos hōs legei Dios', *Bacch.* 1333), whereas Ares appears as the saviour who will eventually convey them to the Fields of the Blessed (1338–9). A long lacuna precedes this prediction; it is just possible that the missing lines contained a reference to Ares' wrath. Apollodorus offers no ex-planation as to why Cadmus and Harmonia change into snakes, but has Zeus convey them to the Elysian Fields (Apollod. *Bibl.* 3.5.4); Hyginus states that Ares destroyed Cadmus' children out of anger at his snake's death, and may imply—given that he mentions Cadmus' and Harmonia's transformation into snakes—that they also owe their transformations to this cause (Hyg. *Fab.* 6). However, he does not say so explicitly. It must be noted that as Apollodorus certainly, and Hyginus probably, postdate Ovid by nearly two centuries, both mythographers' evidence regarding what versions the Roman poet may have known is open to question.

brothers' originating fratricide (*Aen.* 8.729–31).[70] As Ovid's Thebes demonstrates, that is the alchemy of ideology: it converts what contradicts its claims into evidence that appears to support them.[71] Ultimately, Ovid scrutinizes Thebes' history of internecine strife, juridical cruelty, and religious terrorism not for its own sake, but as the mirror of Rome, illuminating Rome's patriotism as the darkest of conspiracies. Like the Thebans, Romans can come to self-recognition as the subjects of their own savage history only by seeing the snake in the glass.

[70] Aside from the Battle of Actium, a civil conflict presented with the trappings of a foreign war (*Aen.* 8.675–728), Vulcan's Shield portrays the kind of internal conflicts that will rend the Roman republic in such vignettes as the punishment of the traitor Mettus (8.642–5) and the infernal sufferings of the conspirator Catiline (8.668–70). See Quint 1993, 21–31, for a full explication of the polarities recorded on the Shield, and their implications for Rome's cohesiveness.

[71] As Slavoj Žižek has observed: 'An ideology is really "holding us" only when we do not feel any opposition between it and reality—that is, when the ideology succeeds in determining the mode of our everyday experience of reality itself . . . an ideology really succeeds when even the facts that at first sight contradict it start to function as arguments in its favor' (Zizek 1989, 49).

7

Ovid and the Epic Tradition

The Post-Augustans

Thebes of the 7 gates in
to whose maw
generation up
on generation
all potent heroes come
who tread the earth

and at whose out
skirts shrivel the de
tumescent un
entombed fore
fathers of the epi
goni

    in
penetrable city
spread your gates
we two come in to
lay us down with Laius
I your casta
you my swollen son in
cestuous and zestful re
enact
the play of Thebes

           Ann Deagon[1]

---

[1] 'Sphinx Ludens' (Deagon 1974).

As I have traced the psychoanalytic patterns of Thebes' doom, my aim has been to deepen understanding of just how Ovid's Theban cycle responds to Vergil's meditation on the ideal city, and to the relations between citizens and the sexes therein. Ovid's response gives body to what the *Aeneid* already shadows forth: the intractable paradoxes on which epic dreams of a harmonious, organically-united polity are so uneasily founded. But the intertextual conversation among Latin epics did not stop with the *Metamorphoses*. The methodology unfolded in this book also illumines how Ovid crucially and fundamentally shaped his epic successors' civic visions. In this concluding chapter, I can only suggest the parameters of generic revision by following a single topos from Ovid to Silius Italicus. The intrafamilial civil war regularly dramatized by Vergil's successors moulds their epic cities around political desperation and gendered conflict— exactly the despair Ovid's multiform Father of Enjoyment visited upon His excluded sons and exploited daughters.

My assessment of the *Metamorphoses*' influence runs counter to the general scholarly opinion that singles out the poem as an anomaly to be explained, an anomaly measured against the paradigm the *Aeneid* definitively established.[2] The tradition of critical evaluation that sees the *Aeneid* as the archetypal Latin epic stretches all the way back to Vergil's own time.[3] Vergil punctuates ancient and modern discussions of the other epicists' works with a regularity and frequency true of no other Latin poet,[4] with the *Aeneid* seen as a

---

[2] Some welcome recent revaluations of Ovid's effect on subsequent Latin epic: all the articles contained Tissol–Wheeler 2002; Wilson 2004.

[3] As Alison Keith records, Vergil's poetry enjoyed primacy in the pedagogical tradition of Rome. Even in Vergil's own lifetime, Caecilius Epirota was teaching Vergil's poetry to his students (Suet. *Gram.* 16.3). Aulus Gellius, Servius, Macrobius, Tiberius Claudius Donatus, and Quintilian all contribute to this tradition that sees Vergil in general, and the *Aeneid* in particular, as a repository of Roman cultural and moral values, especially of *virtus*. In this respect, the *Aeneid* performed the same function for Rome that Homer's *Iliad* and *Odyssey* did for Greece (Keith 2000, 8–35).

[4] A search under the subject entry 'Epic poetry, Latin—history and criticism' in the online database WorldCat (which lists over 40 million titles held at libraries around the world) reveals that the vast majority of entries focus solely on Vergil's *Aeneid*. But among the relatively few titles published within the last two decades that discuss all the extant Latin epicists, the greatest number of book-index entries are still to Vergil. He not only earns chapters and essays devoted solely to the *Aeneid*, his epic crops up as the most frequent comparandum for the other Latin epicists. To list only

particular lodestone for the four principal Silver Latin epics: Lucan's *Bellum Civile*, Statius' *Thebaid*, Valerius Flaccus' *Argonautica*, and Silius Italicus' *Punica*.[5] The ostensible reasons for sequestering Ovid from this generic schema of succession are ready to hand. As noted in Chapter 1, Ovid does break with epic's traditional subject matter, largely bypassing heroism and warfare organized around the defence or conquest of The Fabled City. He transfers his narrative focus outside city walls to pastoral landscapes instinct with the darker sides of eroticism, fantasy, and illusion. In style, tone, and topoi the *Metamorphoses* diverges from the *Aeneid*'s more obvious heirs.

This Vergilocentric genealogy that makes the *Metamorphoses* a black swan expresses some truth at the expense of the whole. Like Ennius' *Annales* and Naevius' *Bellum Punicum*, poems of the Roman republic now extant only in fragments, the *Aeneid* did give shape and meaning to the mythohistory of Rome. Vergil moulded the beginnings of the *urbs aeterna* into a providential narrative whose logical telos was Augustan Rome, bequeathing to later epic intense engagement with the nature and limitations of the polity. But Ovid shared

a representative sampling, this is true of Boyle 1993; Hardie 1993; Quint 1993; Von Albrecht 1999; Keith 2000; Perutelli 2000; Ganiban 2007. Even Martin Helzle, whose interest is in Silver Latin epic, and whose Foreword declares his extreme disinclination to say anything about Vergil in the wake of the 'Sintflut der Publikation' on the Augustan poet, feels obliged to devote at least a couple of substantial chapters to the *Aeneid* (Helzle 1996). Neither Donald McGuire (McGuire 1997) nor François Ripoll (Ripoll 1998) index their books, so one cannot mechanically measure their assessments of the relation between Vergil and his epic successors. However, McGuire mentions Vergil every few pages, Ovid only rarely. Ripoll remarks explicitly in his introduction that 'l'inspiration virgilienne dans les épopées flaviennes est un des éléments sur lesquels la critique a, à juste titre, mis le mieux l'accent. La valeur fondatrice de l'*Enéide* pour la littérature épique ultérieure est telle que toute étude des épopées flaviennes, quelle que soit son angle d'approche, relève dans une large mesure de l'esthétique de la réception: il s'agit de déterminer ce que les successeurs du poète de Mantoue ont reçu de l'œuvre maîtresse de ce dernier, et en quoi ils ont pu s'en écarter' ('Vergil's influence in Flavian epic is one of the elements upon which criticism has rightly placed emphasis. The founding power of the *Aeneid* for later epic literature is such that the whole study of Flavian epic, whatever the approach, in large measure is the concern of the aesthetics of reception: it involves determining what the successors of the poet of Mantua received from his masterwork, and from what they were able to separate themselves', Ripoll 1998, 11–12).

[5] See e.g. Mozely 1963–4; Gossage 1969; Horsfall 1995, 273–92; Putnam 1995, 209–45; Ripoll 1998, 11–15.

that engagement, as the preceding chapters show. Even more to the point, what the post-Augustan epicists read in Vergil they read in part through the lens Ovid had provided them; his Thebes particularizes just how the providential city comes to grief.

Specifically, the Theban cycle teases apart for separate analysis what Vergil had synthesized, and whose failures the *Aeneid* ultimately appears to redeem: the political and the sexual non-relation. As Alison Keith has brilliantly shown, despite epic's own declaration that 'war is the province of men'—a claim that would exclude women from its stage—Vergil regularly aligns the contention between Trojans and their enemies, past, present, and future, with contention between the sexes. Aeneas blames the adulterous Helen for the Trojans' war with the Greeks, while his own equally irregular 'marriage' to Dido sows future hostilities between their nations. In Italy, Aeneas' betrothal to Lavinia is the *casus belli* that sets both Italian nations and Latin king and queen at odds. However, the end of the poem dazzlingly eclipses all that, when Turnus' capitulation explicitly yields Lavinia to Aeneas ('tua est Lauinia coniunx', *Aen.* 12.937). The political effect of this conceded dynastic marriage Jupiter implied when he prophesied the Roman future, and Anchises spelled out in his expanded Underworld vision (*Aen.* 1.266–71, 6.760–6). Aeneas' marriage to Lavinia ends the Trojan–Latin war and creates the détente under which Alban kings rule the now-unified peoples for the next three centuries.[6]

The *Metamorphoses* reflects deep scepticism upon the *Aeneid*'s conjugal solution both to troubled relations between the sexes and between citizens. Despair of sexual union promising social healing

---

[6] Keith's analysis of Aeneas' marriage to Lavinia as the ground of an idealized polity is particularly pithy (Keith 2000, 49–50), but other scholars have addressed the subject. See also Gillis 1983, 85–115, 123; Mitchell-Boyask 1991, 222–7; Oliensis 1997, 307–10. It is also true that thorny questions hover about this dynastic marriage. As mentioned in Ch. 5, Vergil offers equivocal testimony to, e.g., which of Aeneas' sons will found the royal bloodline: will it be his purely Trojan son, Ascanius, or the son more symbolic of a harmonious Trojan–Latin alliance, Silvius the son from Latin Lavinia? Neither is the poet clear on whether the glimpses of a glorious future for Aeneas and the Rome he and his marriage are supposed to make possible are to be trusted. James O'Hara discusses these and other ambiguities regarding what happens at the end (and after the end) of the *Aeneid* (O'Hara 1990, 145–7; 2007, 88–90—both with bibliographies helpful as guides to previous debate on Aeneas' marriage and its implications).

particularly stands out in the most striking anomaly of Ovid's Theban cycle. As noted, the tale of Echo and Narcissus involves two non-
Thebans without any obvious connection to the city or its concerns;
they interrupt the onslaught of Thebes' disasters to act out the failures of the sexual relation *tout simple*. Organizing the siege of Thebes
and its citizens by wrath and violence around two aliens destroyed by
love, Ovid teases out of that stark juxtaposition what is less visible
within Vergil's seamless web: the strict homology between the political and the sexual non-relation. Cities ultimately cannot cohere for
the same reasons the sexes cannot form a fully complementary unity:
these putative and ardently desired 'wholes' rest upon unacknowledged exclusions. The ideal egalitarian citizenry and its citizen, the
ideal Man and His coefficient Woman, must all occlude sadism,
greed, desire—in short, everything ideologically unconformable to
the Symbolic law that constitutes these abstractions as conceptual
totalities. Ultimately they must (impossibly) exclude the human
subject's fundamental division and the alienation it introduces to
the social.

Ovid's epic successors attend closely to his analysis of conflict
between citizens and the sexes. Mapping the one antagonism upon
the other, they dramatize the implications of Ovid's insight that
political and sexual strife are not contingently, historically allied,
but logically and fundamentally parallel. Post-Vergilian epic represents as irredeemable the way sexuality shapes The Doomed City's
dire outcome. After the *Aeneid*, no marriage holds hope for a unified
commonweal; sexual union is at best unhelpful, at worst exacerbating, to conflict. Cadmus' loving marriage to Harmonia cannot save
Ovid's Thebes, nor even spare the royal couple grief until, as *placidi
dracones* (4.603), both cease to be *zoa politika*. As Jove's beloved
consort, Semele nonetheless draws Juno's wrath upon Thebes. The
wives and consorts of later epic—Lucan's Julia, Statius' Argia, Valerius'
Medea, Silius' Dido, to name only the most obvious—all become
even more extravagant Furies to stimulate war (as Keith has shown,
and as I shall detail below).[7] They do so in narrative circumstances
that make Ovid's influence even more unmistakably evident. These

---

[7] Keith 2000, 65–100.

post-Augustan elaborations of the strife the sexual relation parallels all share one detail with Ovid's Thebes that none do with Vergil's *Aeneid*: the wedding of true civil war to intrafamilial conflict.

The war between the native Italian tribes and the Trojans staged in the *Aeneid* proleptically figures civil war, inasmuch as the two peoples will eventually be united into one citizenry. The conflict also divides a marriage and a family, since (as noted) Queen Amata and King Latinus split over the question of translating to Aeneas their daughter, and eventually their kingdom. But the moment when one nation, one family, even one dynastic intermarriage emerges from the warring principals never arrives in the *Aeneid*. Strictly speaking, its war is neither civil nor familial. Even where Vergil looks ahead to a history of Rome we know to be stained with internal civic and sexual division, he regularly expunges or minimizes any references to it. King Amulius seizing his brother Numitor's throne, immuring his niece Ilia in Vestal virginity, her rape at Mars' hands and murder at her uncle's—all these disappear from Vergil's account. Jupiter simply describes her as 'pregnant by Mars', giving birth to Romulus and Remus (*Aen.* 1.273–4). Aeneas' divine Shield depicts Ilia's twins suckled by a she-wolf (*Aen.* 8.630–4), and Romulus alone as king over the Romans ('Romulidis', *Aen.* 8.638), but the fratricide that winnowed two into one never surfaces anywhere in the poem. Neither does the event bridging the Sabine women's rape and Romulus' reconciliation with their King Tatius: the kindred bloodshed the women must wager their own lives to stop (*Aen.* 8.635–41; cf. Livy 1.10.1–13.5). More contemporary Roman history is similarly whitewashed: the Shield's portrayal of the Battle of Actium turns a civil struggle between two Caesarian factions for control over Rome into war between Rome and Egypt. Once internationalized, sexual conflict can emerge as the clash between Augustus' all-male, unified forces and Cleopatra's effeminate, disorganized troops (*Aen.* 8.688, 707–13).[8] Rome's civil-familial strife surfaces only once in the poem, and that fleetingly. When Anchises surveys the heroic Roman souls waiting to be born, he singles out the discarnate Julius Caesar and Pompey, in-laws and political allies until the death of Julia—Caesar's

---

[8] Quint 1993, 23, 28–9.

daughter and Pompey's wife—helped sever both bonds. Anchises describes how the two men will war against each other, but in a conditional sentence (the bloody wars will happen only if his two hostile descendants 'attain the light of life') and exhorts both to abandon their conflict. In the elder Trojan's anticipatory perspective, the Roman past—a past we know to be fixed by kin-strife and key female deaths (or the risk thereof)—becomes a future that might still be averted (*Aen.* 6.826–35).

Scholars have argued—not without reason—that the *Aeneid's* omissions merely solicit the reader to supply what is wanting: we are to remember the history forgotten by the Shield, by Anchises' catalogue of Roman heroes, and by all the poem's other tendentiously partial accounts of Rome's history.[9] But if that is true, then Ovid is one of the readers most diligently faithful to Vergil's solicitation, and he instructs his successors by example. Ovid's Theban cycle foregrounds the problems hinted at by the silences of Vergil's poem. Unlike the struggle for control of Latium—the necessary prelude to founding Rome—Ovid's Thebes arises *ab origine* not just from real civil war, but from fratricide, capped by inauspicious marriage (Cadmus' to Harmonia, the war-god's daughter). As we have seen, Thebes' autochthonous citizens are brothers who arise from the monstrous serpent's teeth and commence killing each other almost with their first breath. This motif of consanguine civil war eventually joins gendered antagonism. Both unfurl into the struggle to control Thebes between two native sons and scions of the house of Cadmus, as Bacchus the effeminate god successfully opposes his militantly mannish cousin King Pentheus. The cousins' enmity also pits the king against his own Bacchus-worshipping, epicene people, culminating in Pentheus' death at the hands of maddened viragos, his mother and aunt. Juno's inability to compose her differences with her brother and husband Jupiter spills over into Semele's death, and into

---

[9] The bibliography on optimistic vs. pessimistic interpretations of the *Aeneid* is too vast to list exhaustively here. However, recent accounts that specifically focus on how to interpret the poem's projections of history in Anchises' Underworld exegesis, the Shield, and elsewhere are: Feeney 1986; Zetzel 1989, 1996, and 1997; Gurval 1995, 209–48; O'Hara 1990, 173–5, and 2007, 77–103; Reed 2007, 148–72. Zetzel 1997 and O'Hara 2007 in particular contain bibliographies that can usefully guide the reader to past debate on how to interpret these anticipations of Roman history in the *Aeneid*.

King Athamas' hideous murder of his child Learchus. Athamas' deed not only polarizes the house of Cadmus, but also its citizen attendants, and that along gender lines. In the wake of the insanity that divides king from queen, the Theban women-courtiers abandon Athamas and race after the maddened Ino, ready to die with her. Though none can have been born in Sidon, Ovid calls them 'Sidoniae comites'. The atavistic toponym makes Thebes seem to flow back toward its own contentious cause. With these ladies-in-waiting, the city once again suffers a royal family and a state divided between father and son, female and male. Three generations earlier, when Agenor chose his daughter over his son, just such division drew Cadmus' Thebes out of his father's Sidon (*Met.* 4.543–62).

The post-Augustan epics revisit again and again exactly that Ovidian juxtaposition of civil, familial, and sexual strife. Lucan and Statius offer the most obvious examples. Lucan chose as subject matter the conflict between Caesar and Pompey, writing of a 'war more than civil' ('bella... plus quam ciuilia', *BC* 1.1) because of the two principals' kinship. The poem repeatedly underlines Caesar's and Pompey's relation through Julia, as when she returns to Pompey in a dream. A vindictive ghost, Julia means to reclaim him from his second wife. She tells him that he cannot sever his marriage ties to her, he will always be Caesar's son-in-law. Civil war will make Pompey all hers, presumably by sending him to the Underworld to join her. Yet Julia's ghastly possessiveness ironically galvanizes Pompey into even greater fervour to oppose his former father-in-law (*BC* 3.31–7).[10] Statius goes one better than Lucan in emulating Ovid by revisiting Thebes itself and drawing his kin-war from a slightly later point in Theban history.[11] Although focused on the fraternal conflict between Eteocles and Polyneices, the *Thebaid* mines

---

[10] Keith 2000, 87–8.

[11] John Henderson notes that by choosing to focus on Thebes' most famous fratricidal conflict, Statius extrapolates Vergil to his logical conclusions (a move I would characterize as Ovidian). Where the *Aeneid* ends abruptly with the death of Turnus, Statius forces his readers to wade through the aftermath of Eteocles and Polyneices' decisive duel (*Thebaid* 11.497–573). The remainder of *Thebaid* 11 and all of *Thebaid* 12 focus on continued violence over memorializing the fallen and disgraced Thebes' subjugation at the hands of Theseus, closing grimly with scenes of universal mourning for the dead (Henderson 1998, 225–30).

intensively the myth's other possibilities for rending city and family. Oedipus precipitates the conflict between his two sons by praying for their destruction, prompted by their disrespect. That he petitions Ovid's fury Tisiphone evokes her role in inspiring Athamas' murderous madness against wife and children. Oedipus pleads that Tisiphone should heed his prayer because he slept with his mother and incestuously produced 'sons for you' ('natosque tibi', *Theb.* 1.70). He thus draws a straight line of causality between perverted sexual relations and the familial bonds Tisiphone will sunder between Eteocles and Polyneices, a breach that eventually embroils all of Thebes in conflict. Tisiphone inspires the *ius malignum*, the disastrous plan for alternating rule between the brothers (*Theb.* 1.56–87, 125–41); a vindictive Jupiter then disturbs the equilibrium of their biarchy. First the god sends the shade of their grandfather Laius to awaken in Eteocles paranoia and lust for permanent rule (*Theb.* 2.94–133), then ensures that marriage to Argive princess Argia will draw Polyneices into war (1.243–5). Like Lucan's Julia, Argia becomes a female instrument of her husband's kin-strife, as she persuades her father King Adrastus to supply Polyneices with Argive troops (*Theb.* 3.678–721).[12]

Even the two epics whose principal storyline seems far removed from civil war or kin-strife, the *Punica* and the *Argonautica*, go to great lengths to insert both into their narratives, and to align both with sexual contention. Valerius makes the tension between King Pelias and his brother Aeson the reason why Pelias imposes the almost-certainly fatal quest for the Golden Fleece upon Aeson's son, Jason. The *Argonautica*'s apparently unfinished state leaves open to question whether the completed poem would have shown that civil–familial hostility erupting into open warfare. But Valerius foreshadowed—twice—how the consanguine enmity motivating the epic might have come to a head.[13] The first rehearsal maps familial discord along gender lines on a mass scale: spurred by rumours that their men are bringing home war-brides, Lemnos' wives and daugh-

---

[12] Keith 2000, 97.

[13] On the possible relation of the books dealing with Lemnos and Colchis to the *Argonautica*'s missing ending, see Venini 1971, 611; Hershkowitz 1998*b*, 226 and n. 125; Keith 2000, 93–5.

ters turn on their husbands and fathers. Though the Argonauts only arrive after the slaughter, the island's recent bloody history becomes a pregnant silence, as Jason's blissfully ignorant men form liaisons with the Lemnian women (*Argonautica* 2.142–241, 311–73). Nothing untoward befalls the *Argo*'s crew on Lemnos, but (as Keith has discerned) the Lemnian conflict patterns the later civil strife in which the Argonauts do take part, when Colchian King Aeëtes and his brother Perses divide over what should be done with the golden fleece. Long sea journeys to hostile ground precede both slaughters, the Lemnians sailing to Thrace and the Argonauts to Colchis. The Lemnian men bring home from their conquest cattle and women, just as the Argonauts despoil Colchis of the golden fleece and Medea. Jason's dalliance with Hypsipyle anticipates his marriage to Medea.[14] And though the Lemnian myth was ready to hand as already part of Jason's mythology, Valerius goes out of his way to inscribe civil war and kin-strife a second time into the Argonauts' history. No other account has antagonism in the Colchian royal house erupt into full-scale civil war or involve the Argonauts.[15] This second instance of civil strife refines the first. Lemnos' sordid past could be effectively buried, but events on Colchis affect world-history: Jason's abduction of Medea will eventually involve the whole Mediterranean world in cataclysm. She is the Fury ('Erinys') whose theft echoes in history (*Arg.* 8.395–6). The multiple rapes the Persians name as first causes of bad blood between East and West (Hdt. 1.1–4) Valerius distils into her single abduction. The clash of empires now can be traced to the complex hostilities within one family, one people, and one marriage—the house of Aeëtes, the Colchians, and Jason and Medea respectively. The epic seeds of kin-strife and traffic in women that elsewhere grow into civil conflict Valerius ultimately expands into world war.

Silius has a similarly comprehensive vision, but comes closer to Lucan than to Valerius in drawing his imperial vendetta from Roman history rather than Greek myth. The Second Punic War would seem to have little in common with the Theban cycle. Neither civil nor familial conflicts caused the war with Carthage, and as matters of

---

[14] Keith 2000, 93–4.
[15] Fucecchi 1996, 106–13; Hershkowitz 1998*b*, 224.

historical record, its events offered less scope for wholesale plot innovation than Statius' or Valerius' mythological tales. Moreover, the action revolves around men on the battlefield; Silius largely excludes from his narrative the domestic passages, both erotic and violent, that could have drawn his Carthage and Rome closer to Thebes' intimate evils. The rare exceptions refuse to align Carthaginian with Theban ills in any obvious way. For example, when Hannibal's son is marked for sacrifice to Baal, the general's wife Imilce pleads passionately for the boy's life; Hannibal distinguishes himself from Theban Laius by not sacrificing the child burdened by doom (*Pun.* 4.763–829). Nonetheless, Silius' colloquy with the Theban cycle in all its aspects—including how he overlays a war between men of different nations with consanguine and gendered civil conflict—is singular among the Silver Latin epicists for its implications; for that reason, I have accorded the *Punica* more detailed consideration. Ovid's accursed city becomes Silius' thematic bridge between Rome and Carthage, the span over which Rome walks to become her own worst enemy. As such, Ovid's Thebes figures even more thoughtfully, if less conspicuously, in the *Punica* than in the *Thebaid*. For Statius, Thebes figures what is wrong with his contemporary Rome;[16] for Silius, Thebes summarizes how Rome got there. Silius traces Rome's troubles, not to the end of the Punic Wars, when her moralists would have it that she eliminated the self-disciplinary force of fear along with her enemy Carthage.[17] As Donald McGuire persuasively argues, Silius finds his city's most troubled history rooted in Rome confronting Carthage across the battlefield and discovering the lure of the other as unguessed mirror of the self. The *Punica*'s punctual allusions to Thebes make the Greek city preside over all these fraught transactions between Carthage and Rome. As in the *Metamorphoses*, it is Thebes' civic division joined to skewed family romance that summarize the deadlocks haunting political and sexual selfhood. In epitomizing what Carthage was and is, and what Rome shall be, Thebes symbolically effects a transfer of properties between the two civilizations.

---

[16] Cf. e.g. Dominik 1994, Hardie 1993, 2–3, 8, 44–8.
[17] Sallust, *Cat.* 10; Juvenal 6.290–1; Plutarch, *Cat. Mai.* 54.3.

Silius punctuated his epic with many scenes wherein war with Carthage caused citizens and families, husbands and wives, to turn murderously upon one another Theban-fashion, and sowed the structural seeds for later Roman tyranny and brutality.[18] I shall let the most dramatic instance of such hostilities speak for the rest. Silius strategically placed twin brothers fighting to the death for their father's throne in the penultimate book of the *Punica*. This combat of matched and mirroring foes anticipates and displaces Scipio and Hannibal's never-realized confrontation. The *Punica*'s oddly anti-climactic last book constantly expects, but forever defers, a single-combat between commanders. Yet to make clear how Silius uses the twins' fight and its narrative context to crystallize the civic and sexual relationship between Carthage, Thebes, and Rome, I must first sketch how the persistent presence of Thebes as alter-Rome more broadly organizes his epic.

Silius makes much of Sidon as Carthage's mother-city, through which he triangulates a relationship of equivalence between Carthage and Thebes as Sidon's two daughter-cities. His Carthaginians are the 'gens Cadmea',[19] as though Cadmus were the African nation's direct ancestor. This defies extant mythical tradition: Cadmus only becomes visible when he abandons Sidon forever, leaving behind no progeny whose descendants might colonize Carthage. But this fictional blood-kinship metaphorically captures a deeper affinity between the two cities: their shared status within the Roman Imaginary as Rome's other selves. Ellen O'Gorman has brilliantly established that Carthage 'must be destroyed' because it is too close to Rome in space and ambition, matching Rome in naval and agricultural science, military preparedness, the youth and strength of its citizenry; it threatens to displace Rome as premier Mediterranean power. Cato famously displayed before the Senate three ripe figs of enormous size, remarking that the land that had borne them (Carthage) was only three days' sail from Rome; he concluded from this that 'Carthage should not exist'(Plutarch, *Cato Maior* 54.1–2). Aside from

---

[18] For example, the mass suicide of the besieged Saguntines, which predictably includes vignettes of family members killing each other (2.617–49); an Italian youth who kills himself after he mistakenly kills his father (*Pun.* 9.66–177). McGuire analyses the theme of suicide in the *Punica* with great subtlety and perspicacity (McGuire 1997, 205–29).

[19] e.g. *Pun.* 1.6; cf. 'Cadmeae stirpis', 1.106.

illustrating the African city's threatening proximity and fecundity, a fruit the Romans associated with the female breast and with procreation smears Carthage with libidinous excess. How can Cato's gesture not also stain the Rome so closely mirrored by Africa's voluptuous prodigy?[20]

Silius' encroaching Carthage plays upon these kinds of anxieties, but he makes the city wormwood by modelling its reflections upon Rome after Ovid's Thebes. The *Punica* draws specifically upon Ovid's theme of the enemy-other discovered to inhabit the intimate interior of self. What the Carthaginians are already germinates within the Romans as the result of their own imperial ambitions, McGuire has shown. Silius' notoriously brutal Carthaginians ('saevis gens laeta', *Pun.* 1.170) are generally overawed by their impetuous, charismatic leader Hannibal; hence their ill-advised embroilment with the Romans. Yet Hannibal is also in thrall—to a woman, his now-deified ancestress Dido. His shield depicts her abandonment by Aeneas; he has formally dedicated himself to her revenge on the Trojan's descendants (*Pun.* 2.406–28; cf. *Pun.* 1.114–19). Identification with Dido stains Hannibal with the same feminine excess Cato's figs attributed to Carthage generally. But savagery, dependence, and effeminacy soon find similar expression among the Romans. At first, barbarities such as beheading and displaying the severed heads are seen as the appalling province of non-Romans—the Carthaginians, their allies, and even the Romans' Spanish clients. Yet as the epic progresses, the Romans themselves adopt these practices.[21]

---

[20] O'Gorman 2004.

[21] As a sample of instances of 'barbarian' cruelties, consider the following: Theron, from the Roman client-city of Saguntum, beheads the Carthaginian ally Asbyte, and has her head mounted on a pike for display before the Punic army (*Pun.* 2.201–5). The Punic ally Vosegus cuts off the head of Latin Quirinius at the battle of Ticinus (*Pun.* 4.213–15), while the Garamantian spearmen strive to behead Scipio and give his head to Hannibal. Though unsuccessful, Silius implies that such a gory trophy would be particularly acceptable to the Carthaginian general (*Pun.* 4.445–7). However, the Romans are soon happy to emulate such battlefield habits: already in book 5, at the Battle of Trasimene, the Massylian Bagasus beheads Libo, but Libo's comrade-in-arms Flaminius in turn beheads Bagasus: 'iuuit punire feroci | uictorem exemplo et monstratum reddere letum' ('it was satisfying to retaliate against the victor according to his own savage example, and to return in kind the death he had demonstrated', 5.418–19). By book 15, the Roman general Claudius Nero not only beheads Hasdrubal, but displays the head before Hannibal's camp, vaunting obscenely (*Pun.* 15.805–6, 813–17). Cf. McGuire 1997, 80.

Rome also starts to rely upon its own charismatic leaders (such as Scipio) rather than collective counsel. The poem's final tableau shows the outcome of this policy: Scipio triumphing. Yet his triumphal garb of gold and costly purple (the Punic colour) exhibits a womanish splendour. Silius underlines the point by comparing Scipio to Thebes' most problematic divine son, the epicene Bacchus. Here the god of refined cruelty trails the same riot of sensual prodigality Cato had foisted upon Carthage: sweet fragrances, vine leaves, exotic tigers (*Pun.* 17.645–8). Silius foregrounds the idolizing military strategy that won the Punic Wars and led to Scipio's triumph, but also sowed the seeds for the Republic's final decades of civil wars sprung from competition among Rome's Great Men.[22] That corrupting, bloody rivalry for power and wealth (both often flowing into sensuously feminizing display)[23] in turn made the principate grimly inevitable: *res publica delenda est.*

Against that thematic background of Thebes overlaid upon Carthage overlaid upon Rome, Silius sets an eye-catching instance of strife rending family and polity. At Scipio's funeral games for his father and uncle, Spanish brothers engage in mortal combat for their father's throne (*Pun.* 16.527–48). Livy had recorded at these games a duel between cousins to rule over the city of Ibes. Both having refused Scipio's offer of non-lethal arbitration, the elder cousin easily bested the younger in combat (28.21). The younger cousin's death already makes the duel anomalous raw material for Silius. The epic funeral games of the *Iliad, Aeneid,* and *Thebaid* leave all participants alive; only Silius' antagonists kill. Moreover, Silius makes the rival cousins into brothers who, like Eteocles and Polyneices, murder each other for power. He doubly evokes the mutual fratricide that begins Thebes' end with a dramatic detail borrowed from Statius: like the *Thebaid*'s cremation of Oedipus' sons, the flames of the Spanish twins' common funeral pyre separate into two branches. Yet in dramatizing fratricide between twins, Silius reaches behind Statius to Ovid: his duellists are not just brothers, but brothers from the same birth. They thus

---

[22] McGuire 1997, 141–2.

[23] For example, Plutarch's *Life of Antony* represents Augustus' last rival for supremacy as the victim equally of Antony's own ambition, his appetites, and his conspicuous expenditure. Ending his life as the thrall of a woman, Cleopatra, fittingly caps an existence sapped of virile discipline by visible excess: Plutarch compares him to e.g. Heracles stripped of his masculinity and liberty by Queen Omphale (Plut. *Ant.*, *Synkrisis* 3.3).

evoke Ovid's Spartoi making energetic war upon their coeval siblings. Above Statius' and Ovid's *frères ennemis* in turn floats the image of those other twins and brothers, Romulus and Remus, contending for supreme power over incipient Rome. Silius' description of the fight develops all these overlapping thematic allusions into an intricate web of ideas that shows the shadow of the Abject City—Thebes and Cadmean Carthage—falling darkly upon Rome:

> spectacula digna
> Martigena uulgo suetique laboris imago.
> hos inter gemini (quid iam non regibus ausum?
> aut quod iam regni restat scelus?) impia circo
> innumero fratres, cauea damnante furorem,
> pro sceptro armatis inierunt proelia dextris.
> is genti mos dirus erat.

(*Punica* 16.531–7)

These are sights worthy of the sons of Mars and a representation of their accustomed toil/suffering. Among these were twin brothers who, armed, joined battle for their father's sceptre (for what have kings not already dared? Or what wickedness for the sake of a throne now remains in abeyance?). Round them a vast circle gathered, condemning their madness as impiety.

The twins' duel to inherit their father's crown is 'the accursed custom of their tribe' ('genti mos dirus', 537), yet it numbers among several spectacles 'worthy of the offspring of Mars and a reflection of their accustomed toil/suffering' (531–2). *Martigena uulgo suetique laboris imago* at first glance refers to the Romans watching these funeral contests; as a people at war, combat is their 'accustomed toil'. But when Silius introduces the duel between the brothers, *Martigena* evokes the mutual fratricides bookending the history of Mars' other city, Thebes—the city's genesis with the Spartoi, born from Mars' sacred snake, and its *éboulement* with Eteocles and Polyneices, both descended from Mars' daughter Harmonia. The Spanish duel thus also reflects suffering familiar to the Thebans, whose history is deep-dyed in kindred blood.

The brother-combatants and their Roman observers together reproduce *in nuce* all three sides of Silius' mirroring triptych: Carthage, Thebes, and Rome, an elaboration of Ovid's diptych, Thebes–Rome. The watching Romans deplore the Spanish combat as 'impia proelia', but neither halt it nor turn away from the sight. Moreover, since Scipio does not intervene (as he tried to do in Livy's account), his inaction tacitly condones this spectacle. The spectators' ghoulish fascination with the fratricide they deplore as impious, but from which they cannot turn away, reveals them as Carthaginians under the skin, infected with the same feral bloodlust. The Romans betray their status as another *gens Cadmea*. By amalgamating the double fratricide that effectively ended Thebes (between Polyneices and Eteocles) and the twin-murder that began Rome (between Remus and Romulus), Silius' Spaniards stage an imagined 'return to the origins' from which Rome does *not* arise, but rather perishes because of the murderous instincts of the city's would-be leaders. The duel is an anti-*Aeneid* miniaturized and madly accelerated to be even more peremptorily terminal than Ovid's.

Curiously, Silius winds his narrative path to this all-male arena of pessimism by recapitulating some of the *Aeneid*'s potentially hopeful images of marriage, love, distinction, and ultimate redemption. Scipio's inspiration for holding the funeral games is his recent success against Carthage, success confirmed by two strategic alliances with foreign kings awed by Rome's prowess. Silius narrates both alliances by refashioning moments from the *Aeneid*'s erotic history into a cynical commentary on Vergil's hopes for the sexual relation. First, unearthly fire visits Hannibal's ally Masinissa, wreathing but not burning his hair, just as unconsuming flames crowned Lavinia's hair and clothing (*Aen.* 7.71–7).[24] The Numidian's mother

---

[24] There is no shortage of intertexts for this instance of unburned burning hair: Vergil's Ascanius also finds his hair enflamed but not burning just before his family leaves Troy (*Aen.* 2.681–4). It is even true (as one of my anonymous readers reminds me) that Livy's Servius Tullius has unconsuming flames wreath *his* head in childhood; Queen Tanaquil interprets this portent as indicating they should foster this child carefully, because he will be 'a light and a bulwark' to her royal family's doubtful fortunes, eventually bringing glory to that family and to Rome (Livy 1.39.1–4). However, Silius aligns Masinissa's miraculous flames more closely with those portending Lavinia's marital alliance to Rome by having the Numidian's prophetic mother foretell that he will be fortunate as Rome's ally (*Pun.* 16.129–31). She does not predict her son will emulate Ascanius by emigrating to Italy, or Servius by living with a people foreign to him (the uncompromising latinity of Servius' name marks him as an interruption in the line of Etruscan kings; cf. Ogilvie 1965, 156). Neither does she foresee Masinissa becoming a Roman, or ruling over Romans, as both Ascanius and Servius Tullius do.

announces that the omen portends his good fortune as Rome's ally; since he already chafes at Carthage failing to honour his prowess, his mother's words galvanize him to offer fealty to Scipio (*Pun.* 16.115–69). Masinissa's enduring fidelity contrasts strongly with Scipio's second alliance, to Syphax. The Masaesylian king's reception of Scipio recalls another erotic moment from the *Aeneid*, when King Evander welcomes Aeneas to Arcadia. Responding to Aeneas' plea for alliance, Evander notes his physical likeness to his father, who once visited Arcadia. Evander recalls the presents Anchises gave him, among them a quiver and arrows—and most importantly, his own 'youthful ardour' ('iuuenali . . . amore', *Aen.* 8.163) for the Trojan, the memory of which implicitly smooths the Trojans' path to federation (*Aen.* 8.152–74).[25] Syphax also makes much of Scipio's good looks ('pulcherrime', *Pun.* 16.191) and the Roman's likeness to his father, and tells of feeling 'a kind of wondrous love' ('quodam miro . . . amore', *Pun.* 16.197) upon meeting Scipio's father and uncle at Gades. The Roman generals gave Syphax presents, like Anchises, including instruments of archery—bows (*Pun.* 16. 191–203). Although Syphax promises allegiance to Rome, marriage to Carthaginian Hasdrubal's daughter later subverts his loyalty and ruins him (*Pun.* 16.258–61, 17.67–148). These two military pacts' linked but contrasting echoes of Vergil show Silius adopting Ovid's unsparing perspective on the *Aeneid*. The *Punica* rejects Vergil's politically redemptive sexual unions in their own terms, including the marriage to Lavinia and Evander's nostalgia for his boyhood love, both so crucial to Vergil's beleaguered Trojans. Silius' imagery of unconsuming fire recalls the *Aeneid*'s founding and victorious alliance of (proto) Roman with royal other, but transmutes marriage into a pact between men—a lasting alliance, but contracted out of self-

---

[25] Michael Putnam and Charles Lloyd (among others) have both noted the homoerotic terms in which Evander represents his own meeting with Anchises, and elucidated their significance for books 7–12 of the *Aeneid*. Putnam considers Evander's boyhood crush on Anchises part of the answer to the mystery of why Vergil invokes Erato—the Muse of erotic poetry, not epic—for the poem's emphatically militarized second half (Putnam 1985). Lloyd develops this idea even further, noting that the verses describing Evander's meeting with Anchises use the language of marriage (*coniungere, duco*) and represent for Aeneas a 'golden age' characterized by peaceful and happy male-to-male connections (Lloyd 1999, 10, 19).

regard and cemented by mutual advantage rather than devotion or even *pietas*. On the other hand, the emotional bond between men instanced in Evander's boyhood love becomes in Syphax's case no bond at all, only a form of words; marriage to the wrong woman cankers his pact with Rome and turns his loyalties. Syphax's uxoriousness shows the marital bond thwarting political unity rather than cementing it. The *Punica's* interlocking episodes of national and familial alliances forged, corrupted, and betrayed offer the counsel of despair: calculating Masinissa, treacherous Syphax, and the duelling, internecine twins dramatize the non-existence of a true sexual or political relation.

In Silius' reading of Roman history, Rome does not survive the Punic Wars. The Carthaginian conflicts disclose the seeds of everything that eventually erupts in Rome's civil wars and their aftermath, such as the rise of Caesarism, cruelty, ruthless dominion, and the corruption of every private and public bond.[26] Thebes and its history of familial–civil destruction provides the third term wherein Carthage and Rome find their mutual mirror and analogue. But the Romans, not the Carthaginians, carry the abortive burden of Thebes forward into history.

SUICIDE KINGS

Post-Augustan epic's civil–familial conflicts revisit the border between family and polity whose crossing *Totem and Taboo* dramatically stages. Yet within each epic, the transit between the hierarchy of the family and the democracy of the polity appears at an impasse, as though Freud's band of brothers were neither able to keep empty the central space the primal Father had occupied, nor find a basis on which to live with His women. Instead, like the Spartoi, epic's siblings all fall to killing one another in their rivalry to replace Him. Caesar and Pompey, Eteocles and Polyneices, Pelias and Aeson, Perses and Aeëtes, and the Spanish twins all enact the murderous implosion of

---

[26] Cf. McGuire 1997, 78–85.

society as a family romance. They thus retrace in reverse the Romans' own mythohistory of the *res publica*'s genesis from the Tarquins' dynastic tyranny. That narrative posits the more visible half of the primal Father-figure in Tarquin, the last of the Roman kings. Both Livy and Dionysius record Tarquin's enslavement of the Romans; he puts them to work at servile tasks unworthy of their dignity and identity as a martial nation (DH 4.81; Livy 1.59.9). He also contrives to eliminate all political opposition (e.g. by false criminal indictment and execution, DH 4.42; Livy 1.51). But it is his son Sextus Tarquinius' rape of the *matrona* Lucretia that precipitates the downfall of the king and his family (DH 4.64–85; Livy 1.57–60). King Tarquin's oppression makes law an extension of his will, wielding by guile or force absolute control over his male citizens' bodies and lives; his son Sextus claims the same control over a freeborn *matrona* (and by extension, all women without exception, even if freeborn or married). The tyrannical king and the libidinous prince share out between them the characteristics of the primal Father who exploits the men and women of His clan.

Though this mix of despotism and sex is hardly unusual among ancient accounts of a tyrant's downfall, its dénouement is.[27] The typical story simply places a successor on the throne, rather than recording radical regime-change. But furor over Lucretia's rape inspires the Romans both to exile the Tarquinii, and to replace their monarchy entirely with the consulship. Rather than a single ruler for life, Rome chooses two consuls elected for one year's tenure (DH 5.1; Livy 2.1.7–8). Circumscribing the power of the central authority thus prevents anyone from again attaining autocracy. The way the Romans fundamentally rethink sovereignty parallels the logic behind the political transformation in *Totem and Taboo*. Egalitarian relations must follow the tyrannical Father-figure's expulsion in order to avert internecine struggle to take his place. By definition, the republic revolves around preserving untenanted the space Tarquin held as

---

[27] Most ancient accounts of a tyrant's overthrow entail his death, not just his exile. Aristotle devotes a long section of the *Politics* to a list of tyrannicides (1311[a]23–[b]37), as does Plutarch in his *Moralia* (768e–f). See Holt 1998, 232, for these and other ancient anecdotes of tyrannicide.

supreme power in Rome. That void anchors the notional equality of all citizens in their collective renunciation of enjoyment.

In shaping the consulship, the Romans reject not just a particular tyrant, but his conceptualization of tyranny. As I have argued elsewhere, Tarquin differs from all his predecessors in the way he conceives the basis of his authority.[28] Tarquin is the first of the Roman kings to claim his throne as a hereditary right, and the first to aspire to pass it on as such. He opposed the previous king, Servius Tullius, on the grounds of genealogy: Tarquin's father was King Tarquinius Priscus, a heritage that supposedly trumped Servius' servile status (DH 4. 32, 37, 38, 80; Livy 1.48.2). Tarquin's sons also think dynastically, confidently expecting that one of them will inherit the throne (DH 4.69; Livy 1.56.10–11). To the Tarquins, kingship is properly determined by nature rather than election.

By implication, Tarquin and his family consider themselves peculiarly suited by nature to be kings, making elected kingship obsolete. The power of previous Roman kings accrued only to their offices and could in theory be held by any citizen who received the nod from the electorate;[29] Tarquin sees his power as emanating naturally from, coterminous with, himself. His reification of power in his own unique person matches the conceptualization of the primal Father's authority. Tarquin acts and speaks as though he were essentially, biologically, different from his subjects, a difference that extends to his bloodline.

Tarquin's megalomania eventually gives way to what establishes the republic, the abstraction and diffusion of power within the citizenry. But Dionysius' and Livy's accounts of Tarquin's *pur sang* monarchy reflect their contemporary historical context more than the distant past. They were written in the first decades of Augustus Caesar's reign, when a version of Tarquin's thinking suffused the ideology of the principate and offered justification for Augustus' *de facto* assumption of monarchical powers. The princeps adopted and

---

[28] Janan 2001, 48–9.

[29] Livy dutifully reports the popular legend that glosses over Romulus' mysterious final disappearance: he was a god, and was taken up bodily into the sky (Livy 1.16). However, even if Romulus himself believed in his own divinity (of which there is not a shred of evidence in Livy), he evinces no ambition on that or any other grounds to name his successor, much less found a dynasty.

expanded Julius Caesar's emphasis on the Iulii's supposed descent from the goddess Venus, while at the same time declaring his adoptive father Caesar a god and himself *divi filius*. Although Augustus himself was worshipped as a god only in the Greek provinces, he lays the foundation for imperial cult that eventually sees the Caesars addressed as living deities within Rome itself. Such representations clearly point to exceptionalism. By nature, because of Augustus' close ties to divinity and his implied divine status, he differs from other Romans; these differences singularly fit him to rule over his fellow citizens. Only such a nonpareil as he can restore peace and unity to Rome. Only he can take the internal violence that in the late Republic characterized the competition of the powerful for dominance, and thrust it outside the polity, channelled into imperial conquest. Only he can control the corrupting force of sexuality by regulating marriage, criminalizing adultery, and rewarding fecundity. The *Aeneid*'s depiction of the Battle of Actium as manly Rome opposing the degenerate and licentious East dramatically captures this official party line; it silently reconfigures internal strife between citizen and citizen, men and women, into external conquest of the alien and sexually irregular.

In the years after Augustus' institution of the principate, the emperors' claims to power implicitly based on unique natural capacity only grew in scope, duplicating and expanding upon Tarquin's ideology of imperial speciality. Caligula wanted an entire temple dedicated to himself, and deified his sister Julia, the first Roman woman to be granted divine status (Suet. *Calig.* 24.2, Dio Cassius 59.11.1–5). Vespasian declared to the Senate, 'Either my sons succeed me, or nobody!' (Suet. *Vesp.* 25)—an assertion of regal status that Augustus had avoided. Vespasian's son Domitian insisted upon being called 'Lord and god' (Dio Cassius 67.13.3–4). Moreover, Tarquin *fils* no less than Tarquin *père* finds his imperial successors. The son's implied claim to sexual exceptionalism is reflected in the emperors' nauseating appetites—their enjoyment—as symptoms of the perverse polity. Caligula rapes and prostitutes his subjects (Suet. *Calig.* 24, 36, 41); Nero is avaricious, a violent rapist and sexual mutilator (Juv. *Sat.* 10.15–18, 306–9), Claudius a bloodthirsty glutton (Suet. *Claud.* 33; Seneca *Apoc.* 5, 10, 14), Domitian an incestuous and insatiable adulterer (Juv. *Sat.* 2.29–33, Suet. *Dom.* 22). Even the narratives of the short-lived and relatively unimportant emperors between Nero and Vespasian prominently feature their squalid cravings: Galba's greed for money, food, and adult men; Otho's ambitious self-prostitution to Nero; Vitellius' sexual artistry and gourmandizing (Suet. *Galba* 12, 22; *Otho* 2; *Vitellius* 3, 13; Tac. *Historiae* 2.31, 62). This perspective shared between the moralizers and the later epicists traces the Real Father, his tyranny and licentiousness, within the Vergilian account of benevolent rulership, as what is unconformable to it.

In this historical context, Latin epic's episodes of civil–familial strife detailed above revisit Tarquin's thinking and spell out its consequences for the polity as a whole. These intrafamilial struggles contradict the premiss of Caesarism, that the rule of a man whose peerless gifts are bred in the bone will restore peace and unity to Rome. Instead, the post-Augustan epicists depict the dynasts who fill in the central space of their polities as catalysts of bloody family rivalries that widen to include whole citizenries, rivalries crisscrossed with depraved sexual trafficking.[30] Not by accident: if the emperor's authority rests upon his natural singularity, then he assumes the place, not of the Symbolic Father—the stern but impartial figure who guarantees the law's 'neutral' status, whose very abstraction allows every citizen to identify with him (Chapter 2)—but of the Real Father, the one with exclusive access to enjoyment. Only the death of this murderously envied Father promises anyone else entrée to that enjoyment. The very ideology that supports the Caesars' claim to rule invites violent contention of that claim. Little wonder, then, that later Latin epic's diverse versions of Thebes afford the Spartoi no logical limit to killing one another.

THE END OF HISTORY

As the previous chapters show, the *Aeneid* and the Theban cycle concur in making family the generative nucleus of the polity. But

---

[30] Even the Spanish twins, in attracting the Romans' fascination and Scipio's non-intervention, have already involved Rome vicariously in their *impia proelia.*

they differ markedly in the models of political authority and social cohesion anchored by Aeneas and his descendants the Iulii on the one hand, and Agenor and his descendants the Cadmeioi on the other. Vergil and Ovid's foundation stories coalesce around psychoanalysis's two contrasting but interdependent figures of paternity: Oedipus and the primal Father.

The *Aeneid* recreates the Roman empire in the image of the Oedipal family. Once Aeneas has successfully led the Trojan exiles to Italy, heterogamy confirms his predominance.[31] His marriage as a Trojan to a native Italian princess founds a stable political structure modelled on the hierarchical family anchored by the Father's supreme authority. This marriage of state even establishes a brief dynasty, since first his son Ascanius, then his son Silvius, will become kings in their father's wake (*Aen.* 1.267–71, 6.763–6).[32] But more to the point, the marriage figures a system of equivalence and exchange. In place of Troy and Creusa, Aeneas unites himself to Italy and to Lavinia; in place of the Trojan language and customs, his immigrant subjects take on Latin language and identity (*Aen.* 12.835–7). The promise is of a polity where a system of mediation brokers unity and identity, and everyone's desire finds its place. Self-abnegation approximates Aeneas to the Symbolic Father, measuring his fitness to anchor this new polity. The Trojan contrasts starkly with the heroic individuality of his epic predecessors, such as the wilful and passionate Achilles and Odysseus. Vergil largely sequesters Aeneas from the egocentric fervency that inspired his dead peers and that laid waste their communities (such as Achilles' angry refusal to help the Greeks defeat Troy, and Odysseus' pitiless slaughter of the suitors, the flower of Ithaka's youth).[33] Aeneas' *kenosis* is crucial to his status as the

---

[31] The germ of the following paragraphs evolved out of a conversation with Paul Allen Miller.

[32] Even if we do not know which of them will ultimately father the bloodline of Alban kings (O'Hara 1990, 145–7).

[33] Aeneas' belated access of perfervid wrath erodes his statesmanlike status: he kills young Lausus, obscenely overmatched in battle (*Aen.* 10.810–32), then Turnus as the Rutulian prince begs for mercy (*Aen.* 12.930–52). These acts most put into question Rome's viability, insofar as they exemplify the triumph of *furor* over the detachment necessary to the polity's governance and coherence. But even as he kills Turnus, Aeneas distances himself from the action by declaring himself only the instrument of another (dead) agent: 'Pallas te hoc uulnere, Pallas | immolat et poenam scelerato ex

proto-Romans' political centre: he is the vessel of the Roman future, and to that collective future all individual aspiration, will, independent agency must be sacrificed—in short, every component of the epic heroic personality.[34] Aeneas must embody the neutral void in which all can find space for their desires.[35]

Ignorance and blindness are the special gifts of Aeneas' leadership, enabling him to be a Symbolic Father, untouched by the passions that historically split Rome. When he gazes upon the great conspectus of Roman history unfolded in the Underworld, his father denoting the souls of future men of mark, his only reaction is to marvel ('Sic pater Anchises, atque haec *mirantibus* addit', *Aen.* 6.854). In this Parade of Heroes, the competitive rivalries for power that bedevilled the history closest to Vergil's own time are all but invisible to Aeneas, who cannot know the future. The Gracchi and the Scipiones stand amicably side by side, as though no hostility would ever erupt between their families (*Aen.* 6.842–3); Marius and Sulla appear not at all; 'the proud soul of the avenger Brutus' ('animamque superbam | ultoris Bruti', 6.817–18) turns out to be the ancient nemesis of Tarquin, while his modern namesake and the rest of Julius Caesar's assassins simply disappear from sight. As noted, even Caesar and Pompey are treated as though a timely word from Anchises could prevent their hostilities. Even after Anchises explains that the final unborn soul, Augustus' designated heir Marcellus, will die young and cheat Rome of abundant hopes, the old man can 'fire [Aeneas'] heart with love of the glory to come' ('incenditque animum famae venientis amore', 6.889). By the time Aeneas reaches Italy and commences hostilities with the Italians, the poem explicitly marks his blindness. The shield that arms him for the coming war carries images of Rome's future that function as did the Underworld's heroic pageant. Having contemplated these images and hefted them upon his shoulder, Aeneas is described as '*ignarus rerum* imagine gaudet' ('*knowing nothing of these events*, he rejoices in the pictures of them', *Aen.* 8.730–1). His joy, like his Underworld patriotism,

---

sanguine sumit', *Aen.* 12.948–9 ('Pallas sacrifices you with this wound and exacts satisfaction from your guilty blood'). Cf. Quint 1993, 95.

[34] Quint 1993, 83–96.
[35] Žižek 1992, 156.

depends on what the Shield's highly selective tableaux conceal. Drawing only from Rome's very early and very late history, these vignettes omit such events as the Social Wars and the chronic civil conflict begun with the Gracchi's tumultuous second-century tribunates. As we have seen, Remus and Ilia disappear bloodlessly inviolate, Romans and Sabines magically reconcile without risk to their womenfolk, and routed Egyptians cover over the slaughter of fellow Romans.

These two ekphrases constitute Aeneas' most extensive contemplations of Roman history; in both, the *Aeneid* proffers suppression and sublimation as the answers to Rome's discord. These lacunose panoramas of the future figure amnesia and the re-orientation of desire as correlative to the paternal brokering of desire; only thus can every citizen-subject's longings become the glue unifying a harmonious polity. Both conspectuses coalesce around the climactic figure of Augustus Caesar, the *pater patriae* whose rewriting of the egalitarian republic into a hierarchical family he heads we surveyed in Chapter 1. Augustus is the Father who confers upon his subjects their Symbolic mandate, their identity as Romans, to the extent that they identify themselves and their future with him as the one leader of the nation. The space that Augustus occupies within this schema is cleared by the emptiness of his predecessor Aeneas, the legacy of his short-lived Italian kingship nothing more than the central structural void into which all later emperors may step. Rome's prehistory thus prefigures the Name of the Father as the core of caesarism: Aeneas' self-effacement grounds the system of metonymic substitution that will ideally prevail among his distant Julian descendants. Caesar (a proper noun and specific identity) will become the caesars (common noun and an institutional identity),[36] a place to be filled by worthy successors 'of the blood', so that the empire can survive the death of one man. The order and harmony figured in Aeneas' visions of Rome turn on Augustus as the 'end of history', in both senses of 'end'. The emperor is both the final term in the series, and the purpose of that series, the

---

[36] Žižek traces a similar pattern of proper noun establishing the conceptual groundwork for the common noun in the assassination of Julius Caesar, insofar as it opens a path for Augustus Caesar's establishment of the principate (Žižek 1989, 60–1).

telos that converts the successive terms from mere arbitrary juxtaposition to a causally linked chain of events. From this absolute standpoint—the emperor as the ground of Roman history—a rational and purposive pattern obtains over the chronicle of otherwise random, violent waste. All problematic details of the past are subsumed in a narrative that makes Augustus the selfless instrument of history's law, his only desire the establishment of Rome as harmonious polity and imperial superpower. Augustus' will cannot be impugned, since it merely expresses the world order as divinely ordained. In Lacanian terms, the emperor materializes the will of the Other.

And yet this very triumphalist logic contradicts the essence of the Symbolic Father, the principle of mobility and exchange able to accommodate individual desires. The end of history can compass only one will, one desire: the emperor's. To the degree that Augustus quilts the events of Rome's past into a causal nexus that always-already tended toward himself and his regime as the divinely ordained outcome, all Rome's subjects, past and present, assume their place in the chain as merely necessary moments of the process. No one and nothing on earth is free in this schema—except the Will that finds expression in Augustus as its instrument; only that Will is freely causative.[37] We can see emerge here the lineaments of the masculine/dynamical perspective, in which the whole is only possible in virtue of a single exception, an element excluded from the laws that govern the whole. From this perspective, Augustus takes shape as the tyrannical Real Father, who makes not only agency impossible for all his citizen-sons, but even desire, and thus subjectivity. What can a cog in a machine desire? What free, meaningful act can it accomplish?

These are the pathological remainders within Vergil's narrative of Rome's genesis that speak most loudly to Ovid and his epic successors. Ovid and the post-Augustan epicists construct a feminine perspective that complements Vergil's mythohistory by elucidating what is dysfunctional in Rome's family romance. How the rule of a

---

[37] John Henderson argues that Lucan represents Julius Caesar as the aborted precursor of his adopted son's symbolic identification of the Roman state with his own person and interests (Henderson 1998, 195–211). His citation and canny translation of this line from Lucan underlines the point (211): 'toto iam liber in orbe solus Caesar erit' (2.280, 'Caesar, sole free agent in the whole world: the future tense').

benevolent patriarch organized, unified, and stabilized Rome into a whole has fallen short as a narrative. Ovid and the post-Augustans repeatedly stage the inability of the monarchist apology to form a totality without remainder, completely to marshall historical or even mythical phenomena within the framework of its justifying logic. They thus highlight its 'enjoyment', both in the common and the Lacanian senses, as 'pleasure' and as 'the point where ideological claims fall into contradiction with themselves'. The later epics focus on the suspicion that the Father takes sadistic pleasure in the cruelty and arbitrariness of his governance. We have already seen how the rage of Ovid's Agenor and the lust of his Jupiter together cause Cadmus' exile, a juncture of cruelty and carnality that reverberates in Thebes' bloody history. Ovid's successors make even more explicit the Father's obscene bloodlust. Lucan's Caesar indulges his lust for Cleopatra while still drenched in the blood of Pharsalia (*BC* 10.72–6). Valerius' Aeëtes perfervidly equates Jason's request for the golden fleece with the rape of all Colchis' women; he wants the fleece to preserve for his future viewing pleasure the slaughtered Argonauts' gore (*Arg.* 7.48–50, 551–2). Incest and rape taint Statius' two most vengeful fathers, Oedipus and Jupiter, both seeking to inspire butchery at Thebes, the site of their own crimes (*Theb.* 1.144–51). Even Silius' noble Scipio is stained by the Spanish twins' appetite for fraternal blood, indulged under the auspices of his funeral games ('multoque cruore | *exsatiata*... corda', *Pun.* 16.540–1), and by the epicene luxury of his triumphal garb. The twins' mutual fratricide is the penchant of kings (*Pun.* 16.533–4)—an allusion that cashes in on Silius' elaborate, punning associations of Scipio with the *sceptrum*, sign of kingly rule. The poet thus indirectly blemishes Scipio with the bloodlust of tyrants, including the bloody rites the despotic boy-god once imposed upon the East.[38]

Ovid made possible Silver epic's response to Vergil by creating the first cognate narrative to the *Aeneid* from the bizarre refractions of his Theban cycle. The *Metamorphoses*' very anomaly constructed the perspective from which the Silver Latinists saw Vergil. The poem's strangely fantastical surface reflects what is already inherently perverse in the Master-narrative of Roman (mytho)history that the *Aeneid* formulated so persuasively. Pursued to its limit, the chimerical landscape and monstrous transformations of Ovid's Thebes—like the *Metamorphoses* as a whole—at a certain point enter into an alien topology. The stable distinction between 'reality' and 'fantasy' disappears—between the authorizing narrative of the existing political order, claimed as truth, and its disavowed nightmare double, disclosed in the truth's internal contradictions. Like a Möbius strip, whose duplicity is less graspable the more one progresses along its surface, Ovid's epic constantly destabilizes the difference between being and seeming.[39]

This is where the intervention of psychoanalysis is crucial: the fundamental logic that organizes the conversation between the *Aeneid*'s and the Theban cycle's competing visions of the Fabled City's beginning is that of psychoanalysis, as exemplified by *Totem and Taboo*. Freud's myth of political origins, like the analysis of a symptom, aims not to recover an actual, historical event, but to give narrative form to the structure of trauma—and by so doing, to change our understanding of what invisibly wounds the human community. Similarly, the Theban cycle's prodigious tales forgo recuperating the past in favour of rewriting it, as an act of intervention. Their skew mirroring of the story Rome tells itself works to shift the Symbolic structure of that narrative. By reflecting on the story that has brought Rome to where it is now, Ovid incites his audience to look awry upon the story's blindspots, its anamorphoses, so as to bring them into focus. His epic successors are the proof that he succeeded.

---

[39] My thoughts on fantasy and reality are deeply indebted to Charles Shepherdson's discussion of history and the Real (Shepherdson 1998).

Bibliography

ABRAMS, MARSHA LYNNE. 1993. 'Coping with Loss in the Human Sciences: A Reading at the Intersection of Psychoanalysis and Hermeneutics.' *Diacritics* 23: 66–82.

ADELMAN, HOWARD. 1998. 'Of Human Bondage: Labor, Bondage and Freedom in the Phenomenology.' In *The Phenomenology of Spirit Reader*, ed. Jon Stewart, 155–71. Albany, N.Y.

AGAMBEN, GIORGIO. 1977. *Stanze: la parola e il fantasma nella cultura occidentale*. Turin.

ALEGRÍA, CLARIBEL. 1993. *Variaciones en clave de mí*. Madrid.

ALTHUSSER, LOUIS. 1971. 'Ideology and Ideological State Apparatuses.' In *Lenin and Philosophy, and Other Essays*. Trans. Ben Brewster, 127–86. New York.

——1976. 'Idéologie et appareils idéologiques d'État.' In *Positions: 1964–1975*, 81–137. Paris.

ANDERSON, W. S. 1972. *Ovid's Metamorphoses: Books 6–10*. Norman, Okla.

——1989. 'Lycaon: Ovid's Deceptive Paradigm in *Metamorphoses* I.' *ICS* 14: 91–101.

——1993. 'Form Changed: Ovid's *Metamorphoses*.' In Boyle 1993, 108–24.

——1997. *Ovid's Metamorphoses: Books 1–5*. Norman, Okla.

BAKHTIN, MIKHAIL. 1981. *The Dialogic Imagination: Four Essays*. Trans. Caryl Emerson and Michael Holquist. Austin, Tex.

——1986. *Speech Genres and Other Late Essays*. Trans. Vern W. McGee; ed. Caryl Emerson and Michael Holquist. Austin, Tex.

——and VOLOSINOV, V. N. 1986. *Marxism and the Philosophy of Language*. Trans. Ladislav Matejka and I. R. Titunik. Cambridge, Mass.

BARCHIESI, ALESSANDRO. 1984. *La traccia del modello: effetti omerici nella narrazione Virgiliana*. Pisa.

——1999. 'Venus' Masterplot: Ovid and the Homeric Hymns.' In *Ovidian Transformations*, ed. Philip Hardie, Alessandro Barchiesi, and Stephen Hinds, 112–26. Cambridge.

——2001. *Speaking Volumes: Narrative and Intertext in Ovid and Other Latin Poets*. London.

——and ROSATI, GIANPIERO, eds. 2007. *Ovidio: Metamorfosi, Volume II (Libri III–IV)*. [Milan].

BARKAN, LEONARD. 1986. *The Gods Made Flesh: Metamorphosis and the Pursuit of Paganism.* New Haven.

BARTSCH, SHADI. 2006. *The Mirror of the Self: Sexuality, Self-Knowledge and the Gaze in the Early Roman Empire.* Chicago.

BEISER, FREDERICK, ed. 1993. *The Cambridge Companion to Hegel.* Cambridge.

BERNSDORFF, HANS. 2007. 'P.Oxy. 4711 and the Poetry of Parthenius.' *JHS* 127: 1–18.

BING, PETER. 1988. *The Well-Read Muse: Present and Past in Callimachus and the Hellenistic Poets.* Göttingen.

BLACKELL, MARK. 2001. 'Democracy and Ambivalence: Totem and Taboo Revisited.' *JPCS* 6: 46–57.

BLOOM, GINA. 2001. 'Localizing Disembodied Voice in Sandys' "Narcissus and Echo".' In *Ovid and the Renaissance Body,* ed. Goran V. Stanivukovic, 129–54. Toronto.

BLOOMER, W. MARTIN. 2007. 'Roman Declamation: The Elder Seneca and Quintilian.' In *A Companion to Roman Rhetoric,* ed. William Dominik and Jon Hall, 297–306. Oxford.

BÖMER, FRANZ. 1969–86. *P. Ovidius Naso: Metamorphosen.* 7 vols. Heidelberg.

BORCH-JACOBSEN, MIKKEL. 1991. *Lacan: The Absolute Master.* Trans. Douglas Brick. Stanford, Calif.

BORGHINI, ALBERTO. 1978. 'L'inganno della sintassi: il mito ovidiano di Narciso (met. 3. 339–510).' *MD* 1: 177–92.

BOUVRIE, SYNNØVE des. 1997. 'Euripides' *Bakkhai* and Maenadism.' *C&M* 48: 75–114. Repr. in *Aspects of Women in Antiquity: Proceedings of the First Nordic Symposium on Women's Lives in Antiquity, Göteborg, 12–15 June 1997,* ed. Lena Larsson Lovén and Agneta Strömberg, 58–68. Jonsered, Sweden, 1998.

BOWIE, MALCOLM. 1991. *Lacan.* Cambridge, Mass.

BOYLE, A. J. 1993. *Roman Epic.* London.

BREMMER, JAN NICOLAAS. 1999. 'Transvestite Dionysos: On the Ritual Background of the Effeminate Dionysos of Euripides' *Bacchae.*' In *Rites of Passage in Ancient Greece: Literature, Religion, Society,* ed. Mark W. Padilla, 183–200. Lewisburg, Pa.

BRENKMAN, JOHN. 1976. 'Narcissus in the Text.' *Georgia Review* 30: 293–327.

BROWN, WENDY. 1999. 'Resisting Left Melancholia.' *Boundary 2* 26: 19–27.

BRUHL, ADRIEN. 1953. *Liber pater: origine et expansion du culte dionysiaque à Rome et dans le monde romain.* Paris.

BUCHHEIT, VINZENZ. 1963. *Vergil über die Sendung Roms: Untersuchungen zum Bellum Poenicum und zur Aeneis.* Heidelberg.

BURKE, P. F. 1976. 'Virgil's Amata.' *Vergilius* 22: 24–9.

BURNELL, PETER. 1987. 'The Death of Turnus and Roman Morality.' *G&R* 34: 186–200.

BUTLER, JUDITH. 1997. *The Psychic Life of Power: Theories in Subjection.* Stanford, Calif.

CANCIK, HUBERT. 1967. 'Spiegel der Erkentniss (Zu Ovid, *Met.* III 339–510).' *AU* 10: 42–53.

CHILTON, C. W. 1955. 'The Roman Law of Treason under the Early Principate.' *JRS* 45: 73–81.

CIORAN, EMIL. 1997. *Cahiers: 1957–1972.* Paris.

CLAUSEN, WENDELL. 1964. 'Callimachus and Latin poetry.' *GRBS* 5: 181–96.

COFFA, ALBERTO, and WESSELS, LINDA. 1993. *The Semantic Tradition from Kant to Carnap: To the Vienna Station.* Cambridge.

CONNOLLY, JOY. 2009. 'The Strange Art of the Sententious Declaimer.' In *Paradox and the Marvellous in Augustan Literature and Culture,* ed. Philip Hardie, 330–49. Oxford.

CONTE, GIAN BIAGIO. 1986. *The Rhetoric of Imitation: Genre and Poetic Memory in Virgil and Other Poets.* Ithaca, N.Y.

——1994a. *Latin Literature: A History.* Trans. Joseph B. Solodow. Baltimore.

——1994b. *Genres and Readers: Lucretius, Love Elegy, Pliny's Encyclopedia.* Trans. Glenn W. Most. Baltimore.

——1996. *The Hidden Author: An Interpretation of Petronius' Satyricon.* Trans. Elaine Fantham. Berkeley.

——and BARCHIESI, ALESSANDRO (= Conte–Barchiesi 1989). 1989. 'Imitazione e arte allusiva. Modi e funzioni dell'intertestualità.' In *Lo spazio letterario di Roma antica,* ed. Guglielmo Cavallo, Paolo Fedeli, Andrea Giardina. 5 vols. 1: 81–114. Rome.

COPJEC, JOAN. 1994. *Read My Desire: Lacan against the Historicists.* Cambridge, Mass.

CURRAN, LEO. 1978. 'Rape and Rape Victims in the *Metamorphoses.*' *Arethusa* 11: 213–41.

CUTOLO, PAOLO. 1995. *Politica, poetica, poesia nel II libro dei Tristia.* Catania.

DALY, L. J. 1983. 'The Report of Varro Murena's Death (Dio 54.3.5): Its Mistranslation and his Assassination.' *Klio* 65: 245–61.

——1984. 'Augustus and the Murder of Varro Murena (Cos. 23 B.C.): His Implications and its Implications.' *Klio* 66: 157–69.

DARWIN, CHARLES. 1986–9. *The Works of Charles Darwin.* ed. Paul H. Barrett and R. B. Freeman. 29 vols. London.

DEAGON, ANN. 1974. *Carbon 14.* Amherst, Mass.

DEFERRARI, ROY J., BARRY, M. INVIOLATA, and MCGUIRE, MARTIN R. P. 1939. *A Concordance of Ovid.* Washington, D.C.

DENCH, EMMA. 2005. *Romulus' Asylum: Roman Identities from the Age of Alexander to the Age of Hadrian.* Oxford.

DERRIDA, JACQUES. 1987. *The Post Card: From Socrates to Freud and Beyond.* Chicago.

DISALVO, MARILYN. 1980. 'The Myth of Narcissus.' *Semiotica* 30: 15–25.

DOMINIK, WILLIAM J. 1993. 'From Greece to Rome: Ennius' *Annales.*' In Boyle 1993, 37–58.

——1994. *The Mythic Voice of Statius: Power and Politics in the Thebaid.* Leiden.

DÖRRIE, HEINRICH. 1967. 'Echo und Narcissus.' *AU* 1: 54–75.

DOUGHERTY, CAROL. 1993. *The Poetics of Colonization: From City to Text in Archaic Greece.* New York.

DOYLE, ARTHUR CONAN. 1892. *The Adventures of Sherlock Holmes.* New York.

DUE, O. S. 1974. *Changing Forms: Studies in the Metamorphoses of Ovid.* Copenhagen.

ECO, UMBERTO. 1979. *The Role of the Reader: Explorations in the Semiotics of Texts.* Bloomington, Ind.

EDMUNDS, LOWELL. 2001. *Intertextuality and the Reading of Roman Poetry.* Baltimore.

ELIOT, T. S. 1971. *The Wasteland: A Facsimile and Transcript of the Original Drafts, Including the Annotations of Ezra Pound.* Ed. Valerie Eliot. New York.

ELSNER, JAS. 2000. 'Caught in the Ocular: Roman Ways of Visualising Narcissus.' In *Echoes of Narcissus,* ed. Lieve Spaas, 89–110. New York.

FABRE-SERRIS, JACQUELINE. 1995. *Mythe et poésie dans les Métamorphoses d'Ovide.* Paris.

FANTHAM, ELAINE. 2004. *Ovid's Metamorphoses.* Oxford.

FEENEY, DENIS. 1986. 'History and Revelation in Vergil's Underworld.' *PCPhS* 32: 1–24.

——1991. *The Gods in Epic: Poets and Critics of the Classical Tradition.* Oxford.

FELDHERR, ANDREW. 1997. 'Metamorphosis and Sacrifice in Ovid's Theban Narrative.' *MD* 38: 25–55.

FORDYCE, C. J. 1977. *Aeneidos Libri VII–VIII.* Oxford.

FORTER, GREG. 2001. 'Melancholy Modernism: Gender and the Politics of Mourning in *The Sun Also Rises.' Hemingway Review* 21: 22–37.

——2003. 'Against Melancholia.' *differences* 14: 134–70.

FOWLER, DON. 1997. 'On the Shoulders of Giants: Intertextuality and Classical Studies.' *MD* 39: 13–34.

FRANK, PHILIPP. 1949. *Modern Science and its Philosophy*. Cambridge, Mass.

FRÄNKEL, HERMANN. 1945. *Ovid: A Poet between Two Worlds*. Berkeley.

FREUD, SIGMUND. 1953–74. *The Standard Edition of the Complete Psychological Works of Sigmund Freud*. 24 vols. Ed. and trans. James Strachey, Anna Freud, Alix Strachey, and Alan Tyson. London. (= '*SE*').

FRIEDMAN, MICHAEL. 2000. *A Parting of the Ways: Carnap, Cassirer, and Heidegger*. Chicago.

FRIEDRICH, WOLF-HARTMUT. 1953. 'Der Kosmos Ovids.' In *Festschrift für Franz Dornseiff zum 65. Geburtstag*, ed. Horst Kusch, 94–110. Leipzig.

FUCECCHI, MARCO. 1996. 'Il restauro dei modelli antichi: tradizione epica e tecnica manieristica in Valerio Flacco.' *MD* 36: 101–65.

GANIBAN, RANDALL TOTH. 2007. *Statius and Virgil: The Thebaid and the Reinterpretation of the Aeneid*. Cambridge.

GANTZ, TIMOTHY. 1993. *Early Greek Myth: A Guide to Literary and Artistic Sources*. Baltimore.

GARDNER, JANE. 1986. *Women in Roman Law and Society*. Bloomington, Ind.

GILDENHARD, INGO, and ZISSOS, ANDREW. 2000. 'Ovid's Narcissus (*Met.* 3.339–510): Echoes of Oedipus.' *AJP* 121: 129–47.

GILLIS, DANIEL. 1983. *Eros and Death in the Aeneid*. Rome.

GIRARD, RENÉ. 1961. *mensonge romantique et vérité romanesque*. Paris.

—— 1963. *Dostoievski: du double à l'unité*. Paris.

—— 1968. 'Symétrie et dissymétrie dans le mythe d'Oedipe.' *Critique* 249: 266–81.

—— 1970. 'Dionysus et la genèsis du sacré.' *Poetique* 3: 99–135.

—— 1972. *La Violence et le sacré*. Paris.

—— 1977. *Violence and the Sacred*. Baltimore.

GLENN, EDGAR M. 1986. *The Metamorphoses: Ovid's Roman Games*. Lanham, Md.

GOSSAGE, A. J. 1969. 'Virgil and the Flavian Epic.' In *Virgil*, ed. D. R. Dudley, 67–93. London.

GOUD, THOMAS E. 1995. 'Who Speaks the Final Lines? Catullus 62: Structure and Ritual.' *Phoenix* 49: 23–32.

GREEN, PETER. 1994. *Ovid: The Poems of Exile*. London.

GREENBERG, CAREN. 1980. 'Reading Reading: Echo's Abduction of Language.' In *Women and Language in Literature and Society*, ed. Sally McConnell-Ginet, Ruth Borker, and Nelly Furman, 301–9. New York.

GRENE, DAVID, and LATTIMORE, RICHMOND, eds. (= Grene–Lattimore 1968). 1968. *Euripides*. 5 vols. Chicago.

GURVAL, ROBERT. 1995. *Actium and Augustus: The Politics and Emotions of Civil War*. Ann Arbor.

HABINEK, THOMAS. 1998. *The Politics of Latin Literature: Writing, Identity, and Empire in Ancient Rome*. Princeton.

HARDIE, PHILIP. 1988. 'Lucretius and the Delusions of Narcissus.' *MD* 20/21: 71–89.

——1990. 'Ovid's Theban History: The First "anti-*Aeneid*"?' *CQ* 40: 224–35.

——1993. *The Epic Successors of Virgil*. Cambridge.

——ed. 1994. *Virgil: Aeneid, Book IX*. Cambridge.

——2002*a*. 'The Historian in Ovid: The Roman History of *Metamorphoses* 14–15.' In *Clio and the Poets: Augustan Poetry and the Traditions of Ancient Historiography*, ed. D. S. Levene and D. P. Nelis, 191–209. Leiden.

——2002*b*. *Ovid's Poetics of Illusion*. Cambridge.

——ed. 2002*c*. *The Cambridge Companion to Ovid*. Cambridge.

HAUPT, MORITZ, and EHWALD, RUDOLF, eds. (= Haupt–Ehwald 1915). 1915. *Metamorphosen I: Buch i–vii*. Zurich. Republished in 1966.

HEATH, JOHN. 1991. 'Diana's Understanding of Ovid's *Metamorphoses*.' *CJ* 86: 233–43.

HEGEL, G. W. F. 1969. *The Science of Logic*. Trans. A. V. Miller. Atlantic Highlands, N.J.

——1977. *The Phenomenology of Spirit*. Trans. A. V. Miller. Originally published as *Phänomenologie des Geistes* (Oxford, 1807).

——1999–2000. *Werke*. Ed. Eva Moldenhauer, Karl Markus Michel, and Helmut Reinicke. 4th edn. 20 vols. Frankfurt am Main.

HEIDBRINK, LUDGER. 1994. *Melancholie und Moderne: zur Kritik der historischen Verzweiflung*. Munich.

HELZLE, MARTIN. 1996. *Der Stil ist der Mensch: Redner und Reden im römischen Epos*. Stuttgart.

HENDERSON, A. A. R. 1981. *Ovid: Metamorphoses III*. 2nd edn. London.

HENDERSON, JOHN. 1998. *Fighting for Rome: Poets and Caesars, History and Civil War*. Cambridge.

HENRY, W. B. 2005. '4711. Elegy (*Metamorphoses?*).' *The Oxyrhynchus Papyri* 69: 46–53.

HERSHKOWITZ, DEBRA. 1998*a*. *The Madness of Epic: Reading Insanity from Homer to Statius*. Oxford.

——1998*b*. *Valerius Flaccus' Argonautica: Abbreviated Voyages in Silver Latin Epic*. Oxford.

HINDS, STEPHEN. 1987. *The Metamorphosis of Persephone: Ovid and the Self-Conscious Muse*. New York.

——1995. 'Reflexive Annotation in Poetic Allusion.' *Hermathena* 158: 41–51.

——1997. 'Allusion and the Limits of Interpretability.' *MD* 39: 113–22.

HINDS, STEPHEN. 1998. *Allusion and Intertext.* Cambridge.

——2002. 'Landscape with Figures: Aesthetics of Place in the *Metamorphoses* and its Literary Tradition.' In Hardie 2002*c*, 122–49.

——and FOWLER DON, eds. 1997. *Memoria, arte allusiva, intertestualità | Memory, Allusion, Intertextuality. MD* 39: 1–225.

HOLT, PHILIP. 1998. 'Sex, Tyranny, and Hippias' Incest Dream (Herodotos 6.107).' *GRBS* 39: 221–41.

HOPE, A. D. 1992. *Selected Poems.* Pymble, NSW, Australia.

HORSFALL, NICHOLAS. 1995. *A Companion to the Study of Virgil.* New York.

HYLTON, PETER. 1993. 'Hegel and Analytic Philosophy.' In *The Cambridge Companion to Hegel,* ed. Frederick C. Beiser, 445–85. Cambridge.

JACOBY, FELIX. 1923. *Die Fragmente der griechische Historiker.* Berlin.

JAMES, A. W. 1975. 'Dionysus and the Tyrrhenian Pirates.' *Antichthon* 9: 17–34.

JAMES, PAULA. 1986. 'Crises of Identity in Ovid's *Metamorphoses.' BICS* 33: 17–25.

——1991–3. 'Pentheus Anguigena: Sins of the Father.' *BICS* 38: 81–93.

JAMESON, FREDRIC. 1981. *The Political Unconscious.* Ithaca, N.Y.

JANAN, MICAELA. 1994. *When the Lamp is Shattered: Desire and Narrative in Catullus.* Carbondale, Ill.

——2001. *The Politics of Desire: Propertius IV.* Berkeley.

JAUSS, HANS ROBERT. 1974. 'Levels of Identification of Hero and Audience.' Trans. Benjamin Bennett and Helga Bennett. *New Literary History* 5: 283–317.

JONES, C. P. 1966. 'Towards a Chronology of Plutarch's Works.' *JRS* 56: 61–74.

KAMPEN, NATALIE. 1991. 'Reliefs of the Basilica Aemilia: A Redating.' *Klio* 78: 448–58.

KANT, IMMANUEL. 1902–. *Gesammelte Schriften. Hrsg. von der Koeniglich-Preussischen Akademie der Wissenschaften zu Berlin.* 28 vols. to date. Berlin.

KASTER, ROBERT A. 2001. 'Controlling Reason: Declamation in Rhetorical Education at Rome.' In *Education in Greek and Roman Antiquity,* ed. Yun Lee Too, 317–37. Leiden.

KEITH, ALISON. 2000. *Engendering Rome.* Cambridge.

——2002. 'Sources and Genres in Ovid's *Metamorphoses* 1–5.' In *Brill's Companion to Ovid,* ed. Barbara Weiden Boyd, 235–69. Leiden.

KELLY, GEORGE ARMSTRONG. 1998. 'Notes on Hegel's "Lordship and Bondage".' In *The Phenomenology of Spirit Reader,* ed. Jon Stewart, 172–91. Albany, N.Y.

KENNEDY, DUNCAN. 1993. *The Arts of Love: Five Studies in the Discourse of Roman Love Elegy.* Cambridge.

KNOESPEL, KENNETH. 1985. *Narcissus and the Invention of Personal History.* New York.

KNOX, BERNARD. 1954. 'Why is Oedipus Called *Tyrannos?*' *CJ* 50: 97–102.

KONSTAN, DAVID. 1993. 'Rhetoric and the Crisis of Legitimacy in Cicero's Catilinarian Orations.' In *Rethinking the History of Rhetoric: Multidisciplinary Essays on the Rhetorical Tradition,* ed. Takis Poulakos, 11–30. Boulder, Colo.

—— 1996. 'De Deméter a Ceres: construcciones de la diosa en Homero, Calímaco y Ovidio.' *Synthesis* 3: 67–90.

—— 1999. 'What We Must Believe in Greek Tragedy.' *Ramus* 28: 75–87.

—— 2006a. *The Emotions of the Ancient Greeks: Studies in Aristotle and Classical Literature.* Toronto.

—— 2006b. 'War and Reconciliation in Greek Literature.' In *War and Peace in the Ancient World,* ed. Kurt A. Raaflaub, 191–205. Oxford.

KRISTEVA, JULIA. 1969. *Semeiotike: recherches pour une sémanalyse.* Paris.

—— 1983. *Histoires d'amour.* Paris.

—— 1987. *Soleil noir: dépression et mélancolie.* Paris.

LACAN, JACQUES. 1957. 'Le Séminaire de la lettre volée.' *La Psychanalyse* 2: 1–44.

—— 1966. *Écrits.* Paris.

—— 1973. *Le Séminaire de Jacques Lacan, livre XI: les quatres concepts fondamentaux de la psychanalyse, 1964.* Paris.

—— 1975. *Le Séminaire de Jacques Lacan, livre XX: Encore, 1972–1973.* Paris.

—— 1976. 'Le Sinthome et le père.' *Ornicar?* 6: 3–20.

—— 1977. *Écrits: A Selection.* Trans. Alan Sheridan. New York.

—— 1981a. *Le Séminaire III: Les psychoses, 1955–1956.* Paris.

—— 1981b. *The Four Fundamental Concepts of Psychoanalysis.* Trans. Alan Sheridan. New York.

—— 1986. *Le Séminaire de Jacques Lacan, livre VII: l'ethique de la psychanalyse, 1959–1960.* Texte établi par Jacques-Alain Miller. Paris.

—— 1991. *Le Séminaire de Jacques Lacan, livre 17: l'envers de la psychanalyse, 1969–1970.* Paris.

—— 1992. *The Seminar of Jacques Lacan, Book VII: The Ethics of Psychoanalysis, 1959–1960.* Trans. Dennis Porter. New York.

—— 1993. *The Seminar of Jacques Lacan. Book III: The Psychoses, 1955–1956.* Trans. Russell Grigg. New York.

—— 1998. *The Seminar of Jacques Lacan, Book XX: Encore, 1972–1973.* Trans. Bruce Fink. New York.

LACAN, JACQUES. 2006a. *Écrits: The First Complete Edition in English.* Trans. Bruce Fink. New York.

——2006b. *Le Séminaire de Jacques Lacan, livre XVIII: d'un discours qui ne serait pas du semblant 1971.* Paris.

LACEY, W. K. 1986. 'Patria Potestas.' In *The Family in Ancient Rome: New Perspectives.* ed. Beryl Rawson, 121–44. Ithaca.

LAFAYE, GEORGES. 1904. *Les Métamorphoses d'Ovide et leurs modèles grecs.* Paris.

——1928. *Ovide: Les Metamorphoses.* Paris.

LAMACCHIA, ROSA. 1969. 'Precisazioni su alcuni aspetti dell'epica Ovidiana.' *Atene e Roma* 14: 1–20.

LEE, A. G. 1953. *P. Ovidi Nasonis Metamorphoseon: Liber I.* Cambridge.

LLOYD, CHARLES. 1999. 'The Evander–Anchises Connection: Fathers, Sons, and Homoerotic Desire in Virgil's *Aeneid.*' *Vergilius* 45: 3–21.

LOEWENSTEIN, JOSEPH. 1984. *Responsive Readings: Versions of Echo in Pastoral, Epic, and the Jonsonian Masque.* New Haven.

LÖWITH, KARL. 1964. *From Hegel to Nietzsche: The Revolution in Nineteenth-Century Thought.* Trans. David E. Green. New York.

LUPPE, WOLFGANG. 2006a. 'Die Verwandlungssage der Asterie im P. Oxy. 4711.' *Prometheus* 32: 55–6.

——2006b. 'Die Narkissos-Sage in P.Oxy. LXIX 4711.' *APF* 52: 1–3.

LYNE, R. O. A. M. 1983. 'Vergil and the Politics of War.' *CQ* 33: 188–203.

——1994. 'Vergil's *Aeneid*: Subversion by Intertextuality.' *G&R* 41: 187–204.

McCARTY, WILLARD. 1989. 'The Shape of the Mirror: Metaphorical Catoptrics in Classical Literature.' *Arethusa* 22: 161–95.

McGUIRE, DONALD. 1997. *Acts of Silence.* Hildesheim.

MAGNELLI, ENRICO. 2006. 'On the New Fragments of Greek Poetry from Oxyrhynchus.' *ZPE* 158: 9–12.

MARIOTTI, SCEVOLA. 1955. *Il Bellum Poenicum e l'arte de Nevio: saggio con edizione dei frammenti del Bellum Poenicum.* Rome.

MARTINDALE, CHARLES. 1993. *Redeeming the Text: Latin Literature and the Hermeneutics of Reception.* Cambridge.

MASSENZIO, MARCELLO. 1992. 'Narciso/narcisismo.' *Aufidus* 17: 7–19.

MILES, GARY. 1995. *Livy: Reconstructing Early Rome.* Ithaca, N.Y.

MILLER, JACQUES-ALAIN. 1975. 'Théorie de Lalangue (Rudiment).' *Ornicar?* 1: 16–34.

——1994. 'Extimité.' *Lacanian Theory of Discourse: Subject, Structure, and Society,* ed. Mark Bracher, Marshal Alcorn, jr., Ronald J. Cortell, and Françoise Massardier-Kenney, 74–87. New York.

MILLER, PAUL ALLEN. 1998. 'Catullan Consciousness, the "Care of the Self," and the Force of the Negative in History.' In *Rethinking Sexuality: Foucault and Classical Antiquity*, ed. David Larmour, Paul Allen Miller, and Charles Platter, 171–203. Princeton.

——2003. 'Saving the Subject, Saving the Text: Lowell Edmunds and the State of the Art.' *IJCT* 9: 412–23.

——2004. *Subjecting Verses: Latin Love Elegy and the Emergence of the Real.* Princeton.

MILNOR, KRISTINA. 2005. *Gender, Domesticity, and the Age of Augustus: Inventing Private Life.* Oxford.

MILOWICKI, EDWARD J. 1996. 'Reflections on a Symbolic Heritage: Ovid's Narcissus.' *SyllClass* 7: 155–66.

MITCHELL-BOYASK, ROBIN N. 1991. 'The Violence of Virginity in the *Aeneid.*' *Arethusa* 24: 219–38.

——1996. '*Sine fine*: Vergil's Masterplot.' *AJP* 117: 289–307.

MOZELY, J. H. 1963–4. 'Virgil and the Silver Latin Epic.' *PVS* 3: 12–26.

NAGLE, BETTY ROSE. 1984. '*Amor, Ira*, and Sexual Identity in Ovid's *Metamorphoses.*' *CA* 3: 236–55.

NELSON, MAX. 2000. 'Narcissus: Myth and Magic.' *CJ* 95: 363–90.

NG, DAVID, and KAZANJIAN, DAVID, eds. 2003. *Loss: The Politics of Mourning.* Berkeley.

NICAISE, SERGE. 1991. '"Je meurs de soif auprès de la fontaine": Narcisse, Écho et la problématique du double chez Ovide.' *LEC* 59: 67–72.

NICOLL, W. S. M. 2001. 'The Death of Turnus.' *CQ* (NS) 51: 190–200.

NORTH, J. A. 1979. 'Religious Toleration in Republican Rome.' *PCPhS* 25: 85–103.

NOUVET, CLAIRE. 1991. 'An Impossible Response: The Disaster of Narcissus.' *YFS* 79: 103–34.

NUSSBAUM, MARTHA. 2001. *The Fragility of Goodness: Luck and Ethics in Greek Tragedy and Philosophy.* 2nd edn. Cambridge.

O'BRYHIM, SHAWN. 1990. 'Ovid's Version of Callisto's Punishment.' *Hermes* 118: 75–80.

OGILVIE, R. M. 1965. *A Commentary on Livy: Books 1–5.* Oxford.

O'GORMAN, Ellen. 2004. 'Cato the Elder and the Destruction of Carthage.' *Helios* 31: 99–125.

O'HARA, JAMES J. 1990. *Death and the Optimistic Prophecy in Vergil's Aeneid.* Princeton.

——1996. *True Names: Vergil and the Alexandrian Tradition of Etymological Wordplay.* Ann Arbor.

——2007. *Inconsistency in Roman Epic.* Cambridge.

OLIENSIS, ELLEN. 1997. 'Sons and Lovers: Sexuality and Gender in Virgil's Poetry.' In *The Cambridge Companion to Virgil*, ed. Charles Martindale, 294–311. Cambridge.

OTIS, BROOKS. 1963. *Vergil: A Study in Civilized Poetry*. Oxford.

——1970. *Ovid as an Epic Poet*. 2nd edn. Cambridge.

PARRY, HUGH. 1964. 'Ovid's *Metamorphoses*: Violence in a Pastoral Landscape.' *TAPA* 95: 268–82.

PASQUALI, GIORGIO. 1968. 'Arte allusiva.' In *Pagine stravaganti* 2: 275–82 (Florence). 1st pub. *L'Italia che scrive: rassegna per il mondo che legge* 25 (1942) 185–7.

PELLIZER, EZIO. 1985. 'L'eco, lo specchio e la reciprocità amorosa: una lettura del tema di Narciso.' In *Mondo classico: percorsi possibili*, Claude Calame *et al.*, 139–53. Ravenna.

PERADOTTO, JOHN. 1992. 'Disauthorizing Prophecy: The Ideological Mapping of the *Oedipus Tyrannus*.' *TAPA* 122: 1–15.

PERUTELLI, ALESSANDRO. 2000. *La poesia epica latina: dalle origini all'età dei Flavi*. Rome.

PLUTARCH. 1932. *Plutarch: The Lives of the Noble Grecians and Romans, Translated by John Dryden and Revised by Arthur Hugh Clough*. New York, The Modern Library.

PURCELL, NICHOLAS. 1996. 'Rome and the Management of Water.' In *Human Landscapes in Classical Antiquity*, ed. Graham Shipley and J. B. Salmon, 180–212. London.

PUTNAM, MICHAEL C. J. 1985. 'Possessiveness, Sexuality and Heroism in the *Aeneid*.' *Vergilius* 31: 1–21.

——1995. *Virgil's Aeneid: Interpretation and Influence*. Chapel Hill, N.C.

——2001. 'Vergil's *Aeneid*: The Final Lines.' In Spence 2001, 86–104.

QUINN, KENNETH. 1968. *Virgil's Aeneid: A Critical Description*. London.

QUINT, DAVID. 1993. *Epic and Empire: Politics and Generic Form from Vergil to Milton*. Princeton.

RABEL, ROBERT J. 1981. 'Virgil, Tops, and the Stoic View of Fate.' *CJ* 77: 27–31.

RAVAL, SHILPA. 2003. 'Stealing the Language: Echo in *Metamorphoses* 3.' In *Being There Together: Essays in Honor of Michael C. J. Putnam*, ed. Philip Thibodeau and Harry Haskell, 204–21. Afton, Minn.

REDDING, PAUL. 1996. *Hegel's Hermeneutics*. Ithaca, N.Y.

REED, J. D. 2006. 'New Verses on Adonis.' *ZPE* 158: 76–82.

——2007. *Virgil's Gaze: Nation and Poetry in the Aeneid*. Princeton.

REID, COLIN WAY. 1986. *Open Secret*. Gerrards Cross, England.

RIBBECK, OTTO. 1898. *Scaenicae Romanorum Poesis Fragmenta*. 3rd edn. 2 vols. Leipzig.

RICHLIN, AMY. 2001. 'Emotional Work: Lamenting the Roman Dead.' *Essays in Honor of Gordon Williams: Twenty-Five Years at Yale*, ed. Elizabeth Tylawsky and Charles Weiss, 229–48. New Haven.

RIPOLL, FRANÇOIS. 1998. *La Morale héroïque dans les épopées latines d'époque flavienne: tradition et innovation.* Paris.

ROSATI, GIANPIERO. 1983. *Narciso e Pigmalione: illusione e spettacolo nelle Metamorfosi di Ovidio.* Florence.

ROSE, JACQUELINE. 1986. *Sexuality in the Field of Vision.* London.

ROWELL, HENRY T. 1947. 'The Original Form of Naevius' *Bellum Punicum.' AJP* 68: 21–46.

RUBINO, CARL. 1972. Review of *La Violence et le sacré*, by R. Girard. *MLN* 87: 986–98.

RUDD, NIALL. 1986. 'Echo and Narcissus: Notes on a Seminar on Ovid, *Met.* 3.339–510.' *EMC* 30: 43–8.

RYKWERT, JOSEPH. 1976. *The Idea of a Town: The Anthropology of Urban Form in Rome, Italy and the Ancient World.* Princeton.

SALECL, RENATA, ed. 2000. *Sexuation.* Durham, N.C.

SALZMAN-MITCHELL, Patricia. 2005. *A Web of Fantasies: Gaze, Image and Gender in Ovid's Metamorphoses.* Columbus, Ohio.

SANTNER, ERIC L. 1990. *Stranded Objects: Mourning, Memory, and Film in Postwar Germany.* Ithaca, N.Y.

SAUSSURE, FERDINAND de. 1959. *Course in General Linguistics.* Trans. W. Baskin; ed. C. Bally, A. Sechehaye, A. Reidlinger. London. Trans. of *Cours de linguistique générale* (Paris, 1913).

SEGAL, CHARLES. 1969. *Landscape in Ovid's Metamorphoses.* Wiesbaden.

——1997. *Dionysiac Poetics and Euripides' Bacchae.* 2nd edn. Princeton.

SEVERY, BETH. 2003. *Augustus and the Family at the Birth of the Roman Empire.* London.

SHEPHERDSON, CHARLES. 1998. 'History and the Real.' In *Rhetoric in an Antifoundational World: Language, Culture and Pedagogy*, ed. Michael Bernard-Donals and Richard R. Glejzer, 292–317. New Haven.

——2000. *Vital Signs: Nature, Culture, Psychoanalysis.* New York.

SKUTSCH, OTTO. 1985. *The Annals of Quintus Ennius.* Oxford.

SIMON, ERIKA. 1990. *Die Götter der Römer.* Munich.

SMITH, RIGGS ALDEN. 2005. *The Primacy of Vision in Virgil's Aeneid.* Austin, Tex.

SPENCE, SARAH. 1999. 'The Polyvalence of Pallas in the *Aeneid.' Arethusa* 32: 149–63.

——2001. *Poets and Critics Read Vergil.* New Haven.

SPENCER, RICHARD. 1997. *Contrast as Narrative Technique in Ovid's Metamorphoses.* Lewiston, N.Y.

STAHL, HANS-PETER. 1990. 'The Death of Turnus: Augustan Vergil and the Political Rival.' In *Between Republic and Empire: Interpretations of Augustus and his Principate*, ed. Kurt A. Raaflaub and Mark Toher, 174–211. Berkeley.

STRZELECKI, WLADYSLAW. 1935. *De Naeviano Belli Punici carmine: quaestiones selectae.* Cracow.

SUSSMAN, HENRY. 1982. *The Hegelian Aftermath: Readings in Hegel, Kierkegaard, Freud, Proust, and James.* Baltimore.

SYED, YASMIN. 2005. *Vergil's Aeneid and the Roman Self: Subject and Nation in Literary Discourse.* Ann Arbor.

TARRANT, R. J., ed. 2004. *P. Ovidi Nasonis Metamorphoses.* Oxford.

TISSOL, GARTH, and WHEELER, STEPHEN, eds. 2002. *The Reception of Ovid in Antiquity. Arethusa* (special edn.) 35: 2002.

VENINI, PAOLA. 1971. 'Sulla struttura delle *Argonautiche* di Valerio Flacco.' *RIL* 105: 597–620.

VERENE, DONALD PHILIP. 1969. 'Kant, Hegel, and Cassirer: The Origins of the Philosophy of Symbolic Forms.' *Journal of the History of Ideas* 30: 33–46.

VEYNE, PAUL. 1978. 'La Famille et l'amour sous le haut-empire romain.' *Annales (ESC)* 33: 35–63.

VIDEAU-DELIBE, ANNE. 1991. *Les Tristes d'Ovide et l'élégie romaine: une poétique de la rupture.* Paris.

VON ALBRECHT, MICHAEL. 1999. *Roman Epic.* Leiden.

WARREN, ROSANNA. 2001. 'The End of the *Aeneid.*' In Spence 2001, 105–17.

WEBB, EUGENE. 1993. *The Self Between: From Freud to the New Psychology of France.* Seattle.

WHEELER, STEPHEN. 1999. *A Discourse of Wonders: Audience and Performance in Ovid's Metamorphoses.* Philadelphia.

——2000. *Narrative Dynamics in Ovid's Metamorphoses.* Tübingen.

WHITE, ALAN. 1983. *Absolute Knowledge: Hegel and the Problem of Metaphysics.* Athens, Ohio.

WIGODSKY, MICHAEL. 1972. *Vergil and Early Latin Poetry.* Wiesbaden.

WILSON, MARCUS. 2004. 'Ovidian Silius.' *Arethusa* 37: 225–49.

WOOD, ALLEN W. 2005. *Kant.* Oxford.

WYKE, MARIA. 1992. 'Augustan Cleopatras: Female Power and Poetic Authority.' In *Roman Poetry and Propaganda in the Age of Augustus*, ed. Anton Powell, 98–140. London.

ZANKER, GRAHAM. 1987. *Realism in Alexandrian Poetry: A Literature and its Audience.* London.

ZANKER, PAUL. 1966. 'Iste ego sum: Der naive und der bewusste Narziss.' *BJ* 166: 152–70.

———2000. 'The City as Symbol: Rome and the Creation of an Urban Image.' In *Romanization and the City: Creations, Transformations, and Failures,* ed. Elizabeth Fentress, 25–41. Portsmouth, R.I.

ZEITLIN, FROMA. 1986. 'Thebes: Theater of Self and Society in Athenian Drama.' In *Greek Tragedy and Political Theory,* ed. J. P. Euben, 101–41. Berkeley.

ZETZEL, JAMES. 1989. 'Romane Memento: Justice and Judgment in *Aeneid* 6.' *TAPA* 119: 263–84.

———1996. 'Natural Law and Poetic Justice: A Carneadean Debate in Cicero and Virgil.' *CP* 91: 297–319.

———1997. 'Rome and its Traditions.' In *The Cambridge Companion to Virgil,* ed. Charles Martindale, 188–203. Cambridge.

———2007. 'The Influence of Cicero on Ennius.' In *Ennius Perennis: The Annals and Beyond,* ed. William Fitzgerald and Emily Gowers, 1–16. Oxford.

ŽIŽEK, SLAVOJ. 1989. *The Sublime Object of Ideology.* London.

———1991*a*. *For They Know Not What They Do: Enjoyment as a Political Factor.* London.

———1991*b*. *Looking Awry: An Introduction to Jacques Lacan through Popular Culture.* Cambridge, Mass.

———1992. *Enjoy Your Symptom! Jacques Lacan in Hollywood and Out.* New York.

———1993. *Tarrying with the Negative: Kant, Hegel and the Critique of Ideology.* Durham, N.C.

———1996. '"There Is No Sexual Relationship": Wagner as a Lacanian.' *New German Critique* 69: 7–35.

———2000*a*. 'Melancholy and the Act.' *Critical Inquiry* 26: 657–68.

———2000*b*. 'The Thing from Inner Space.' In Salecl 2000, 216–59.

———2001. *Did Somebody Say Totalitarianism? Five Interventions in the (Mis) use of a Notion.* London.

Permissions

The author would like to express her gratitude for permission to reproduce the following copyright material:

Claribel Alegría: 'Hécate', from *Variaciones en clave de mí* by Claribel Alegría. Libertarias/Prodhufi 1993. ©1993 by Claribel Alegría.

Emil Cioran, excerpt from *Cahiers (1957–1972)*. ©1997 by Éditions Gallimard.

Ann Deagon: 'Sphinx Ludens', from *Carbon 14* by Ann Deagon. Copyright ©1974 by University of Massachusetts Press and published by the University of Massachusetts Press.

T. S. Eliot: 'The Death of Saint Narcissus', from *The Wasteland: A Facsimile and Transcript of the Original Drafts, Including the Annotations of Ezra Pound* (HarcourtBraceJovanovich 1971). ©1971 by Valerie Eliot. Reprinted by permission of Faber & Faber Ltd.

A. D. Hope: excerpt from 'Jupiter on Juno', *Selected Poems* (HarperCollinsAustralia, 1992). ©1992 by A. D. Hope. Reprinted by permission of Curtis Brown (Aust.).

Colin Way Reid: 'Go Loudly, Pentheus', from *Open Secret* (Colin Smythe Ltd., 1986). ©1986 by the estate of Colin Way Reid.

Earlier and rather different versions of Chapters 2 and 6 appear in the articles listed below. I am thankful for permission to reproduce that material here.

'"In Nomine Patris": Ovid's Theban Law.' *The Sites of Rome: Time, Space, Memory*, ed. David H. J. Larmour and Diana Spencer, Oxford University Press, 2007, 102–37. By permission of Oxford University Press.

'The Snake Sheds its Skin: Pentheus (Re)Imagines Thebes', *Classical Philology* 99 (2004) 130–46. ©2004 by The University of Chicago. All rights reserved.

General Index

Acoetes 44, 186, 187 n. 4, 188 n. 7, 205
n. 46, 208, 212–17, 218, 219
and the quilting point, 212–17
Aeneas 5, 6, 8, 12, 54, 72, 86, 91, 112,
168, 174, 175, 177–9, 188–9, 194,
195, 207, 222, 227, 229, 236, 240,
246–8
Agenor 23–6, 27, 29, 32, 57 n. 11,
59–62, 65, 67–9, 71–3, 74, 75, 76,
78, 82, 83, 84, 86, 87, 104, 124,
178–9, 231, 246, 250
and *pietas* 59–62, 65, 67–9, 75, 76,
86, 124, 178–9
anamorphosis 100–2, 110, 112, 135,
251
defined 100–101
Anderson, W. S. 55 n. 5, 56 n. 7, 56 n. 9,
61 n. 20, 62, 63 n. 23, 109 n. 41, 115
n. 3, 115 n. 4, 116 n. 5, 137 n. 32,
187 n. 6, 187 n. 7, 188, 193, 195–6,
198, 207, 208 n. 51, 211
Apollonius Rhodius, *Argonautica* 4
Aristophanes 16 n. 48, 49, 115 n. 2, 150
n. 50
Athamas 91, 93, 99, 107, 111, 186 n. 2,
205 n. 47, 209, 231, 232
Augustus, Emperor (C. Octavius) 3,
17, 27–9, 51, 61–2, 65, 66–8,
85–6, 88, 102, 176 n. 24, 204, 229,
237, 243–4, 248–9
and Cleopatra, Queen (Cleopatra
VII Philopator) 102, 229
and Jupiter 61–2, 65–8, 86
and the family 27–9, 88, 248–9
as refounder of Rome 3
as the Father 22 n. 60, 27, 29, 65–6,
85–6, 243–4, 248–9

Bacchus 7 n. 15, 25 n. 65, 35, 36, 44, 45
n. 107, 51, 57, 63, 74 n. 38, 82
n. 54, 90, 91, 93 n. 18, 94, 159, 160
n. 7, 183, 186, 187, 189, 190, 191

n. 15, 192, 193 n. 20, 194,
198, 200 n. 35, 202, 205
n. 46, 207 n. 50, 208, 209,
212–17, 219, 220, 222,
230, 237
and the Italian Bacchanalia,
suppression of (186 BCE)
191–2
as quilting point 212–17
in the *Aeneid* 189
in Euripides' *Bacchae* 190, 192 n. 19,
212, 213 n. 59
in the *Homeric Hymn to Dionysus*
190, 212, 213 n. 59
Bakhtin, Mikhail 11 n. 29, 13–14
Barchiesi, Alessandro 10, 12 n. 33, 12
n. 37, 123 n. 20, 149 n. 48, 173
n. 18, 192 n. 18
Bartsch, Shadi 41 n. 102
Bömer, Franz 45 n.107, 60–1, 65
n. 27, 79 n. 45, 81–2, 92 n. 16,
109 n. 41, 121 n. 13, 187,
195 n. 22
Bonaparte, Marie 18, 19, 20 n. 55

Cadmus 6, 16, 24–6, 34, 52, 54–8,
59, 60, 62, 63 n. 24, 65, 67, 69,
72–8, 80, 82, 91, 145–6, 158,
160, 178–9, 183, 186, 188,
193, 195, 202, 203, 205 n. 47,
207 n. 50, 208, 209,
217–22, 228, 230, 231,
235, 250
and the empty law 74–7
as ignorant Father 72–3
as scapegoat 217–22
Catullus 10 n. 27, 133–5, 141, 151
n. 51, 215
Chrysippus (son of Pelops, abducted
by Laius) 165–6
Cicero (M. Tullius Cicero) 27, 70–1,
209–10

Index of Ovidian and Vergilian Poetry

Note: this index lists passages discussed or translated but does not include untranslated parenthetical citations to Ovid or Vergil. References to the works of other classical authors may be found under their names in the General Index.